THE NEW YORK-NEWARK AIR FREIGHT SYSTEM

by

Arthur J. Stevenson

THE UNIVERSITY OF CHICAGO
DEPARTMENT OF GEOGRAPHY
RESEARCH PAPER NOS. 199–200
(Double number)

1982

Library of Congress Cataloging in Publication Data

Stevenson, Arthur J., 1941–
    The New York-Newark air freight system.
    (Research paper/The University of Chicago, Department of Geography; no. 199/200)
    Bibliography: p. 407.
    Includes index.
    1. Aeronautics, Commercial—New York (N.Y.)—Freight. 2. Aeronautics, Commercial—New Jersey—Newark—Freight. 3. Aeronautics, Commercial—United States—Freight. I. Title. II. Series: Research paper (University of Chicago. Dept. of Geography); no. 199/200.
H31.C514 no. 199/200   910s   82-16011
[HE9788.5.U5]   [387.7′44′097471]
ISBN 0-89065-106-X (pbk.)

H
31
·C 514
v. 199 - 200
1982

Research Papers are available from:

The University of Chicago
Department of Geography
5828 S. University Avenue
Chicago, Illinois 60637
Price: $8.00; $6.00 series subscription

Price of double number 199/200: $16.00

CONTENTS

PART I

THE REGULATORY FRAMEWORK FOR AIR FREIGHT
TRANSPORTATION IN THE UNITED STATES

PART II

AIR FREIGHT OPERATIONS AND SERVICES
IN NEW YORK-NEWARK

iii

LIST OF FIGURES

LIST OF TABLES

PREFACE

In this study an attempt is made to examine the major legal,
administrative, and physical linkages constituting the New York-
Newark air freight system. Consisting of airlines, indirect carriers, over-the-road truckers, local cartage operators, and the
regulatory machinery which binds them together, air freight systems
of varying complexity exist throughout the United States, each one
focusing on a different airport city. Since the regulatory elements
and major functional associations are common to all these systems,
this investigation, though confined to the New York-Newark situation,
helps to clarify the mechanics of air freight systems generally. It
is hoped this book will be of interest not only to those concerned
with the economic life of the New York metropolitan area, but also
to those wishing to take a closer look at an important transportation subsystem operating in every major city of the United States.

When in a 1945 survey over 1,100 members of the American business community were asked for their views on the shipment of goods
by air, a majority of the respondents confessed to having little or
no knowledge of air freight service. Less than 25 years later, however, it was possible to hear transportation industry spokesmen say
that scheduled airlines in the United States would soon attach more
importance to freight than to passengers. Such predictions have
clearly been premature, and, though the freight revenues of these
carriers account for a not inconsequential ten percent of their
total operating revenues, no evidence can be found today to support
the view that freight will, in the foreseeable future, displace passengers as the airlines' chief revenue source. The nation's air
freight service is nevertheless showing vigorous growth, expanding,
for example, from 2.4 billion ton-miles in 1967 to 5.4 billion ton-
miles in 1977 and, what is perhaps of greater significance, is increasingly accepted by the shipping public as as integral part of
the total distribution complex and no longer considered solely in
terms of emergency situations.

Less than one percent by weight of total U.S. intercity
freight is conveyed by air, a statistic that tempts one to dismiss
air freight transportation as a field of study. To do so, of course,
is to disregard the dependence of numerous specialized industries on
air service and to overlook the significance of air transportation

ix

as a link in the nation's intermodal transportation network. In the
area of international trade, where, as in the domestic field, the
air freight industry can point to impressive gains, weight considerations are equally deceptive. Thus, while only a fraction of one
percent of U.S. foreign trade tonnage moves by air, the figure seen
in terms of dollar value is about 12 percent (1977). In the case
of a more restricted situation, the New York City Customs District,
the corresponding dollar value leaps to 35 percent.

This investigation takes as its starting point the twin questions: what is the New York-Newark air freight system and how does
it function? Before we pursue these questions, however, it might be
mentioned that the air freight industry remains a relatively neglected research field. The reason for this is not hard to find:
statistics bearing on a wide range of interesting and potentially
useful topics (e.g., origin-destination patterns, commodity descrip-
tions, airline-forwarder relationships, etc.) are not readily available, making it difficult to construct a satisfactory picture of
many aspects of the industry. The present study seeks to fill at
least some of the gaps and, in that sense, to contribute to a fuller
understanding of the nation's transportation geography.

A system may be defined as "a complex of interacting elements."[1]
Putting it another way, it can be viewed as "a set of objects together with relationships between the objects and between their attributes."[2] Conceptualization of a system focuses not so much on the
objects or elements forming that system as on the nature of the relationships between the constituent elements. A system's structure
may be thought to consist of a network of functional linkages in
which changes introduced into one part of the system lead in general
to changes in other parts. Clarification of the interactions between its components brings about a greater understanding of the
structure and function of the system as a whole.

Figure 1 illustrates two distinct conceptions of systems. In
order to facilitate the analysis of a problem, system 1 has been
partitioned into system A (which is itself made up of systems a, b,
and c) and system B (consisting of systems d and e). The critical
interaction is considered to be taking place directly between A and
B, which constitute the basic elements of system 1. A and B are

---

[1]L. von Bertalanffy, "An Outline of General System Theory," British Journal
for the Philosophy of Science 1, no. 2 (1950):143.

[2]A. D. Hall and R. E. Fagen, "Definition of System," General Systems, 1
(1956):18.   Also see H. M. Blalock and Ann B. Blalock, "Toward a Clarification
of System Analysis in the Social Sciences," Philosophy of Science 26, no. 2
(1959):84-92.

"black boxes," that is, interdependent entities whose internal structure is examined only to the extent that it helps to explain the working of system 1. In the second case (system 2) the relevant interactions are considered to be taking place directly between a, b, c, d, and e, which now form the basic elements of system 2. A and B are here regarded as subsystems, with no attempt being made to delineate the direct interaction between the two. Figure 1 also indicates that a system may be but a member of a hierarchy of systems. In view of the fact that even the simplest component of a system can be modeled in such detail as to form a complicated subsystem, such a hierarchy is never absolute. The objectives of a particular study, its scope, the analyst's subjectivity, convenience, etc., will govern the level at which an examination of interrelated units takes place.

System 1

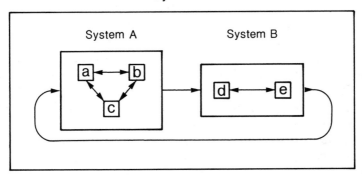

System 2

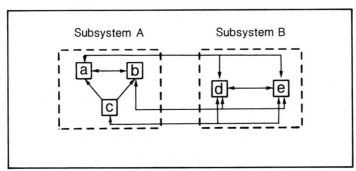

Fig. 1.   Contrasting viewpoints of systems (after Blalock and Blalock, loc. cit.)

The New York-Newark air freight system is here defined as consisting of two subsystems: (1) a regulatory subsystem and (2) a physical subsystem. The approach is that shown in figure 1, system 2 (the latter is more suggestive of the dynamics of the air freight industry than is system 1). The principal elements of the regulatory subsystem are: the Congress, the Civil Aeronautics Board, the Interstate Commerce Commission, the White House, the courts, and the Port Authority of New York and New Jersey. The physical subsystem, on the other hand, is made up of: the three New York-Newark airports, the airlines (various classes), the truckers (long-haul and short-haul), and the forwarders.

This book is divided into two parts. Part I (chapters I-III) introduces the reader to the Federal regulators and defines the regulatory parameters not only for the New York-Newark air freight system's freight services but for U.S. air freight transportation as a whole. In part II (chapters IV-VIII) the focus is narrowed to the New York-Newark area, and here the emphasis is on the air freight-related activities and services found in that area.

Chapters I and II concentrate on the efforts of the Civil Aeronautics Board and the Interstate Commerce Commission (during the period 1938-1977) to meet the system's objectives as defined by the Congress. These chapters examine the two agencies' use of their regulatory powers and show how the carriers, through the provision of various freight services, petitions to the agencies, and appeals to the courts, responded to these powers. Recent (1977-1978) Congressional actions against various system dysfunctions are discussed in chapter III, which also looks at the effects of these actions on the carriers and the shipping public. Chapter IV outlines the early aviation rivalry between Newark and New York City and notes the attempts of the regional airport manager, the Port Authority of New York and New Jersey, to unify some of the region's airport operations. Chapter V defines the Port Authority's freedom of action vis-à-vis the Federal Government. Chapter VI is concerned with several facets of integration and competition within the system and the freight services they have produced. Spatial aspects of the system are analyzed in chapters VII and VIII.

Air freight has been examined from several perspectives. For instance, Orion, in his study covering the period 1945-1965, discusses competitive developments between U.S. trunklines and all-cargo carriers with particular reference to operating costs and rate structures.[1] He concludes that, in view of the cost advantages

---

[1]Henry Orion, "Domestic Air Cargo, 1945-1965: A Study of Competition in a Regulated Industry" (doctoral dissertation, Columbia University, 1967).

enjoyed by the combination airlines, certificated all-cargo carriers
have survived only as a result of certain public policy decisions,
which he sees as having been unjustified and counterproductive. The
question of competition between airlines has also been taken up by
Snoek, who reviews the subject at the international level and broadens it to encompass a consideration of various factors, e.g., technological advances, with which the air freight industry must contend
if it is to woo a greater number of shippers away from surface transportation.[1]

A much discussed and controversial issue has been that of air
cargo[2] economics. Questions which have long been raised and still
await final resolution include: (1) what is the "true" cost of air
cargo service and (2) how should that cost be reflected in a new
and, for the shipper, attractive rate structure? The issue is complicated not only because of the many variables (e.g., aircraft
utilization, stage length, load factor, cargo density, etc.) having
an impact on costs,[3] but also because of the difference in pricing
philosophies adopted by the various airlines. Generally speaking,
the combination (passenger-cargo) airlines, when their commitment
to all-cargo service has been relatively minor or nonexistent, have
favored byproduct costing. On the other hand, as their investment
in all-cargo equipment has grown, these carriers have tended increasingly to use a joint product formula to arrive at their cargo costs.
The all-cargo operators have made use of the fully allocated cost
approach.

The applicability (in the long run) of the term "joint product"
to freight carried in combination aircraft has been rejected by
Miller on the ground that changes in aircraft configuration can produce predetermined shifts in an aircraft's relative passenger and
freight capacities.[4] Prior to the enactment of Public Law 95-163
(November, 1977) the Civil Aeronautics Board was frequently criticized for setting combination aircraft freight rates at average

---

[1]Gerd Snoek, Wettbewerbs- und Wachstumsprobleme im internationalen Luftfrachtverkehr, Forschungsberichte des Instituts für Weltwirtschaft an der Universität Kiel, no. 79, 1967.

[2]The term "cargo" includes freight, mail, and priority (express) traffic.
In this study the emphasis is placed entirely on freight.

[3]Costing procedures are discussed in Domestic Air Freight Rate Investigation, Order 77-8-62. Also see IATA Financial and Economic Studies Subcommittee,
Economics of Air Cargo Carriage and Service (Montreal: International Air Transport Association, October, 1969).

[4]James C. Miller, "The Optimal Pricing of Freight in Combination Aircraft,"
Journal of Transport Economics and Policy 7, no. 3 (1973):258-268.

freighter cost levels. Miller has defended this particular Board practice, arguing that where a combination airline also offers all-cargo service, its imputed belly freight costs may be considered to be the cost of the next available (i.e., all-cargo) service. The Board's former difficulties in establishing new costing procedures and the attendant problem of imparting a "new look" to air freight rate structures[1] were compounded by the absence of various fiscal and traffic statistics. Nonavailability of these data, it has been suggested on many occasions,[2] seriously impaired the agency's capacity to effectively analyze the financial affairs of the carriers and hampered the regulatory process. The Civil Aeronautics Board has conceded that it lacked data in a number of critical areas[3] and, prior to deregulation, was considering the imposition of additional reporting requirements to remedy the matter.

Numerous models have been developed for the purpose of measuring air freight demand. Such models are of importance to those engaged in transportation planning and regulation and are applied to a wide range of problems, such as the multitude of investment decisions with which the aviation industry must constantly grapple. Although the number of variables applicable in any given situation is governed by such factors as data availability, the scope of the study, etc., demand studies invariably allow for price and income considerations. For example, Schad, in his investigation of demand for air freight service in the United States bases the price variable on average air freight rates for the years 1946 to 1968; the income variable is the Gross National Product.[4] The study points to a strong elasticity of demand with respect to price over the entire 22-year period and attributes the pronounced elasticity increase

---

[1]Cost studies dealing with specific commodities or commodity groups include: Electronic Equipment--A Brief Total Cost of Distribution Analysis. Marietta: Lockheed-Georgia Co., Commerical Operations Analysis Department, Advanced Studies Division, ER-10517, June, 1969; California Lettuce--A Brief Total Cost of Distribution Analysis. Marietta: Lockheed-Georgia Co., Commercial Operations Analysis Department, Advanced Studies Division, ER-10518, June, 1969; David J. Clarke and Edward W. Tyrchniewicz, Air Shipment of Perishable Fruits and Vegetables into Canada: Potentials and Problems, Center for Transportation Studies, University of Manitoba, Research Report no. 13, July, 1973.

[2]See, for instance, Francis E. Corry, "An Analysis of the Domestic Air Freight Rate and Cost Structures" (master's thesis, Northwestern University, 1973), p. 40.

[3]"Breaking the Data Dam," Cargo Airlift 60, no. 3 (1972):10; Docket 22859, Order 77-8-62, p. 73.

[4]Thomas W. Schad, "An Econometric Study of the Demand for Air Freight in the Domestic United States" (doctoral dissertation, Wayne State University, 1970).

during the second half of the period to the introduction of jet air-craft. A 40-fold increase is forecast in the volume of domestic air freight carried during 1969-1980, and, in view of the market's price elastic nature, Schad cautions that freight rates must be revised downward if the carriers are to meet effectively the challenge posed by excess capacity. That these findings cannot be applied equally to all regions of the world has been demonstrated by Sletmo, whose work indicates that the aggregate international demand for air freight is price inelastic. He too states that demand within the United States is price elastic and believes that the difference between this and the international situation is due to the greater availability of trucks as an alternate transportation mode in the United States.[1] These and similar studies clash with the findings of an administrative law judge, who, in the course of the Air Freight Forwarders' Charters Investigation, concluded that because of the many variables involved, no "absolute statement that air freight is or is not price elastic is possible."[2]

The lack of appropriate statistical information has made it difficult to examine flow patterns of airborne commodities. One contribution along these lines is that of Maurer, who has described the air traffic in horticultural products for a number of West European countries.[3] He has also produced a useful review of basic principles in the field of unitization, which, for the purposes of this brief literature sketch, may be regarded as representative of one facet of the substantial volume of published material pertaining to the technological and engineering aspects of the air freight industry.[4]

---

[1]Gunnar K. Sletmo, Demand for Air Cargo: An Econometric Approach (Bergen: Norwegian School of Economics and Business Administration, 1972). For an analysis of various air cargo industry forecasts, see Steve A. Demakopoulos, "Methods and Efficacy of Long-Range Industry Forecasts: A Case Study of the Domestic Air Cargo Industry" (doctoral dissertation, New York University, 1970).

[2]Docket 23287, initial decision, July 29, 1975, p. 62.

[3]R. Maurer, Role of Air Transport in International Shipments of Flowers in Europe (Paris: Institut du Transport Aérien, 1967).

[4]R. Maurer, Pallets and Containers in Air Transport (Paris: Institut du Transport Aérien, 1970). Also see: Frank E. Wood, Air Cargo Container Study (Reynolds Metals Co., 1968); P. F. Calkins, The Density Story (Marietta: Lockheed-Georgia Co., 1968); "Emcon's Electronic Bead on Consignments Gives Shippers Instant Whereabouts," Skytrader 9 (July, 1970):9-12; "747F Will Test Air Cargo Market Potential," Aviation Week and Space Technology 95, no. 22 (1971):25-26; Ingward Bey, Simulationstechnische Analyse der Luftfrachtabfertigung, Schriftenreihe des Instituts für Verkehrswesen der Universität Karlsruhe, no. 7, 1972; Manalytics, Inc., Cargo Flows and Facility Requirements at the New Montreal International Airport (San Francisco: Manalytics, Inc., 1973); "Intermodal Questions

Throughout the writing of this book I have enjoyed the gener-
ous assistance of a large number of people. First and foremost I
wish to thank for their helpful suggestions and encouragement Brian
J. L. Berry of Harvard University, Harold M. Mayer of the University
of Wisconsin-Milwaukee, and Chauncy D. Harris of the University of
Chicago. Numerous individuals shared with me their specialized
knowledge of the air freight industry and gave me access to unpub-
lished material, for which I am most grateful. In particular I
would like to mention John W. Barnum, former Deputy Secretary, U.S.
Department of Transportation; Senator Howard W. Cannon, Chairman,
Senate Subcommittee on Aviation; B. Errol Corea, Economist, Aviation
Economics Division, The Port Authority of New York and New Jersey;
Harold J. McCarthy, Area Director, Air Cargo, Inc., New York City;
George H. Mundell, Executive Director, Air Freight Motor Carriers
Conference; and Virginia Sweetland, Boeing Computer Services, Inc.
My cordial thanks go also to the many airline, forwarder, and truck-
ing officials with whom I was able to discuss various facets of the
New York-Newark air freight system and who kindly provided statisti-
cal information about their companies. I must also record my debt
to Gertrude Lewis and Dorothy Ramm, whose unfailing efficiency great-
ly aided my work at the Transportation Center Library, Northwestern
University.

Widely Discussed at International Air Freight Forum," Traffic World 160, no. 2
(1974):35-39; "Automation of Cargo Flow Data Sought," Aviation Week and Space
Technology 102, no. 2 (1975):34-35; "Air Freighter Options for the '80s," Traffic
World 170, no. 12 (1977):66-68; "Containerization: Present and Future," Traffic
World 170, no. 12 (1977):26-28; "What's New in Cargo Equipment," Air Transport
World 14, no. 7 (1977):37-43.

PART I

THE REGULATORY FRAMEWORK FOR AIR FREIGHT

TRANSPORTATION IN THE UNITED STATES

CHAPTER I

THE CIVIL AERONAUTICS BOARD AS A REGULATOR OF

AIRLINE BEHAVIOR

In 1938 the Civil Aeronautics Act, later amended as the
Federal Aviation Act, became law and during the next four decades
provided the statutory basis for the public regulation of U.S. air
carriers. This chapter shows how the Civil Aeronautics Board (CAB),
the agency established to administer these acts, has sought to
effectuate the intent of Congress during the years 1938-1977 and
how its actions have shaped the development of U.S. air freight
transportation in this period. The chapter also examines Congress'
direct intervention in the regulatory process and clarifies the
role of the White House with respect to the Board's international
route and rate decisions. The competitive struggle among the several carrier classes is discussed and reference is made to various
court rulings bearing on the Board's regulatory responsibilities.

Economic Regulation of U.S. Air
Transportation: 1938-1977

Publication of an air freight tariff by American Airlines in
the latter part of 1944 marked the beginning of regularly scheduled
air freight service in the United States. Prior to this, packages
were accepted only by the Railway Express Agency (later known as
REA Express), which released them to the airlines under its own
tariff as "air express."

The new tariff listed door-to-door conveyance of freight at an
average price of 44 cents per ton-mile (the corresponding figure for
air express was 70 cents), a discount being granted in instances
where shippers and consignees were responsible for pickup and delivery service. The rate structure was built about a four-tier commodity classification (based essentially on bulkiness and value) with
certain items moving at specific commodity rates.[1]

American Airlines' initiative soon prompted similar action on
the part of other trunklines (long-haul carriers). Thus, during
July, 1945 a separate freight tariff was issued by Transcontinental

---

[1]"American Airlines Freight Tariff," Traffic World 74, no. 12 (1944):699-
700.

and Western Air (Trans World Airlines) with Braniff Airways following suit several months later. By January, 1947 all certificated air carriers had made public their first freight tariff.

Several of the later tariffs differed somewhat from that issued by American Airlines.[1] Transcontinental and Western Air, for example, did not duplicate the door-to-door concept but, rather, gave separate quotations for air and ground services, a practice which quickly spread through the entire industry. Later tariffs were simplified, weight breaks were introduced to encourage larger shipments,[2] and, in order that long-haul traffic might be stimulated, certain of the carriers adjusted rates according to a tapering principle whereby rates decreased with an increase in distance.

The former legal structure within which the nation's certificated air carriers operated was established through the Civil Aeronautics Act of 1938.[3] The Act created a new regulatory agency, the Civil Aeronautics Authority, and granted for specific routes permament certificates of public convenience and necessity[4] to carriers having rendered continuous service during the period May 14 to August 22, 1938 over those routes.[5] Carriers were prohibited from changing

---

[1]Harold W. Torgerson, "History of Air Freight Tariffs," _Journal of Air Law and Commerce_ 15, no. 1 (1948):47-63.

[2]Under the weight breaks formula, a graduated rate scale was applied to different weight groups.

[3]Amended in 1958 as the Federal Aviation Act (Act of August 23, 1958, Pub. L. no. 85-726, 72 Stat. 731). With the exception of various elements of safety regulation, the new law left virtually intact the functions of the Civil Aeronautics Board as defined in 1938 (with subsequent modifications), so that, from a practical standpoint, the Civil Aeronautics Act of 1938 remained the legal instrument through which Federal economic control was exercised over the nation's interstate air carriers.

[4]Section 401(a) of the Federal Aviation Act states that "no air carrier shall engage in any air transportation unless there is in force a certificate issued by the Board authorizing such air carrier to engage in such transportation." 72 Stat. 754, 49 U.S.C. 1371. The Act also stipulated (section 401[j]) that no air carrier was to "abandon any route, or part thereof, for which a certificate has been issued by the Board, unless, upon the application of such air carrier, after notice and hearing, the Board shall find such abandonment to be in the public interest." 72 Stat. 756, 49 U.S.C. 1371. Section 401(j) was amended in 1978 by 92 Stat. 1720. (See Appendix.)

[5]The 1938 "grandfather" rights, as they are known, applied only to the trunklines. In 1944 the CAB announced that it would establish a new carrier class (local service or "feeder" airlines) for the purpose of providing air service between small communities and to link these to the larger airport cities. It was believed that the new carrier group, using aircraft specifically designed for short-haul, low-density routes, could serve the small points more effectively than the trunks, whose major interest lay in the development of long-haul, large-volume traffic markets. _Investigation of Local, Feeder, and Pickup Air Service_, 6 CAB 1 (1944). In order to ensure adequate service quality, the new certificates (which

their rates and fares, restructuring their route network, and acquiring control of other carriers without the express approval of
the Civil Aeronautics Authority. In addition, the agency was

---

were issued on an experimental basis but were made permanent through legislative
action in 1952) contained several restrictions, the most important of which was
that carriers had to stop at each intermediate point named in their certificates
irrespective of a point's traffic potential. These restrictions, which were also
intended to prevent a diversion of traffic from the trunks to the local service
carriers, were soon seen to be stunting the growth of the latter, and, in order
to strengthen these operators and reduce the Federal subsidies on which they were
largely dependent, the CAB undertook various remedial measures. These have
included:

1. The extension of the local service route network. This has sometimes led to
   the suspension (by the CAB) of competing trunk service, since the markets in
   question were unable to support service by more than one airline. The courts
   have recognized small community air service as being in the public interest
   and protesting trunklines were told: "when conflicts between private and
   public interests occur, the private interests of the certificate holder should
   yield to the broader interests of the public embodied in the concept of the
   public convenience and necessity." United Air Lines, Inc. v. Civil Aeronautics
   Board, 198 F. 2d 100, 107 (7th Cir. 1952)

2. Authority for the local service carriers to terminate flights in selected
   markets

3. A reduction of the number of flights eligible for subsidy payments

4. Certificate amendments which have enabled the trunk airlines to transfer
   certain routes to the local service specialists and have eased the latter's
   entry into larger and more profitable markets

5. Approval for commuter carriers to replace local service airlines in certain
   markets. Allegheny Airlines, for instance, has concluded such replacement
   agreements with three commuter operators for several of its New York-Newark
   routes. The markets in question are:

Market	Commuter	Replacement Service Inaugurated
Catskills/Sullivan Co., N.Y.		
--New York	Ransome	1978
Lancaster, Pa.--Newark	Suburban	1973
Philadelphia--Newark	Ransome	1975
Philadelphia--New York	Ransome	1977
Reading, Pa.--Newark	Suburban	1973
Trenton, N.J.--New York	Ransome	1975
Wilkes-Barre/Scranton, Pa.		
--Newark	Pocono	1968
Williamsport, Pa.--Newark	Pocono	1974

6. The granting of Federal subsidies to noncertificated commuter operators, who,
   with their small aircraft (see below, p. 23, note 4), are frequently able to
   serve small-volume markets more efficiently than can the local service carriers. In 1975, however, a Federal appeals court ruled that the Board could
   not authorize subsidies for noncertificated airlines (Air Line Pilots Association v. Civil Aeronautics Board, 515 F. 2d 1010 [D.C. Cir. 1975]), following
   which the agency asked the Congress for appropriate action so that, in the
   future, subsidized commuter airlines could be substituted for local service
   carriers in markets below a given traffic density (U.S., Congress, House,
   Committee on Public Works and Transportation, Aviation Regulatory Reform,
   Hearings before the Subcommittee on Aviation, House of Representatives, on
   H.R. 8813, 95th Cong., 1st sess., [1977], part 1, pp. 187-188). In 1978 subsidy support for commuter carriers was authorized by the Congress.

empowered to control entry of new carriers into the air transportation industry, restrict competition over a given route, and impose a "fair return" ceiling on profits. Under a reorganization scheme of 1940--designed, in the words of President Roosevelt, to integrate air transportation regulation "more closely into the Federal family"[1]--the Civil Aeronautics Authority was reconstituted as the Civil Aeronautics Board.

The two principal tools with which the Board has been able to effectuate economic regulation of the air freight industry have been (1) its authority to suspend and reject air carrier rates and tariff rules and (2) its control over the number of air carriers operating in any given market. Although the agency was given broad discretionary authority in these and other areas, its regulatory powers were not unlimited in scope. In the domestic sphere its actions were to be scrutinized by the courts; decisions dealing with international air transportation were made subject to Presidential approval. Its position has been aptly summarized by the Supreme Court as follows: "the Board is entirely a creature of Congress and the . . . question is not what the Board thinks it should do but what Congress has said it can do."[2] Congress stipulated that the Board's actions should be in accordance with "the public convenience and necessity" and laid down for the agency's guidance a policy declaration (section 102 of the Federal Aviation Act; section 2 of the Civil Aeronautics Act), under which the following objectives were considered to be in the public interest:

a. The encouragement and development of an air-transportation system properly adapted to the present and future needs of the foreign and domestic commerce of the United States, of the Postal Service, and of the national defense

b. The regulation of air transportation in such manner as to recognize and preserve the inherent advantages of, assure the highest degree of safety in, and foster sound economic conditions in, such transportation, and to improve the relations between, and coordinate transportation by air carriers

c. The promotion of adequate, economical, and efficient service by air carriers at reasonable charges, without unjust discriminations, undue preferences or advantages, or unfair or destructive competitive practices

d. Competition to the extent necessary to assure the sound development of an air-transportation system properly adapted to the needs of the foreign and domestic commerce of the United States, of the Postal Service, and of the national defense

---

[1] Congressional Record 86 (Appendix), part 15 (1940): 2688.

[2] Civil Aeronautics Board v. Delta Air Lines, Inc., 367 U.S. 316, 322 (1961).

e. The promotion of safety in air commerce

f. The promotion, encouragement, and development of civil aeronautics[1].

Caves, whose much-cited <u>Air Transport and Its Regulators</u> remains an invaluable guide to the Board's early regulatory powers, has termed this policy declaration "rather unusual."[2] The reason for this is that these goals are potentially contradictory and that the absence of an appropriate Congressional directive left the CAB free to set its own priorities and to decide on the relevance of the Act's various policy objectives in any given situation. As Caves has said:

> policies designed to maximize or optimize the achievement of one of these goals may not achieve the same result for some or all of the others. What if present needs and future needs call for different policies? What if a maximal contribution to the national defense does not square with optimal service of the needs of foreign and domestic commerce? What if 'sound economic conditions' require substantial price discrimination? Apparently this statement of policy requires an impossibility of the Board, on the one hand, and leaves it with considerable freedom of action, on the other. Taken literally, it requires an impossibility by suggesting the simultaneous maximization of things that probably cannot be simultaneously maximized. Taken more realistically, it identifies a number of desirable goals and leaves it up to the Board to choose which ones it will pursue.[3]

The period immediately following the close of World War II seemed, in the view of many observers, especially propitious for the launching and rapid development of the air freight industry. Impressed by the scope of the military's air freight operations[4] and noting rising incomes and a growing demand for a wide variety of consumer goods, numerous individuals, trade organizations, and governmental agencies were persuaded that a period of vigorous air

---

[1]72 Stat. 740, 49 U.S.C. 1302. Legislation passed in 1977 (Public Law 95-163) and 1978 (Public Law 95-504) has drastically amended section 102. The amendments are discussed in chapter III. (See Appendix.)

[2]Richard E. Caves, <u>Air Transport and Its Regulators</u> (Cambridge, Mass.: Harvard University Press, 1962), p. 126.

[3]Ibid., p. 127. Also see: Hugh S. Norton, <u>Modern Transportation Economics</u> (2nd ed.; Columbus: Charles E. Merrill, 1971), p. 289; Dudley F. Pegrum, <u>Transportation: Economics and Public Policy</u> (3rd ed.; Homewood: Richard D. Irwin, Inc., 1973), p. 357; Steven C. Dupré, "A Thinking Person's Guide to Entry/Exit Deregulation in the Airline Industry," <u>Transportation Law Journal</u> 9, no. 2 (1977):278.
    The CAB's authority under the Act has been described as "so comprehensive and pervasive as almost to amount to governmental operation." G. E. Hale and Rosemary D. Hale, "Competition or Control IV: Air Carriers," <u>University of Pennsylvania Law Review</u> 109, no. 3 (1961):358. Another writer believed the power which Congress conferred on the Board was so sweeping as to make the agency an "anomaly" in the nation's political system. Harold A. Jones, "The Anomaly of the Civil Aeronautics Board in American Government," <u>Journal of Air Law and Commerce</u> 20, no. 2 (1953): 140-157. The Board has never accepted this interpretation of its authority and has stressed repeatedly that the Act imposed a number of restrictions on its activities. A Special Staff panel has similarly noted that in several areas (e.g., national defense, postal service) the Act left the agency little freedom of action. Civil Aeronautics Board, <u>Report of the CAB Special Staff on Regulatory Reform</u> (Washington, D.C.: Civil Aeronautics Board, 1975), p. 39.

[4]During the years 1942-1945 the armed forces transported about 40 times the amount of freight carried by the entire domestic air fleet for the period 1926-1945.

freight expansion was imminent. Cessation of hostilities, furthermore, made available surplus military cargo equipment, encouraging
many entrepreneurs[1] to establish their own airlines. Although precise figures regarding new entrants are unavailable, a number of
sources indicate that the rush to form airline companies quickly
assumed sweeping dimensions.[2] Most of these ventures, however, were
characterized by an absence of long-term planning, frequently lacked
managerial expertise, and, with only slender financial resources,
were unable to sustain initial economic reverses. Beset by difficulties and unable to realize "quick" profits, a majority of these
enterprises inevitably failed.

Although the new entrants offered various kinds of services,[3]
they shared one critical attribute: they were all functioning under
the nonscheduled operation exemption of the CAB.[4] As such, they
enjoyed unrestricted entry into the market but (unlike the certificated operators) were barred from offering scheduled services.[5]
Free to set their own rates and to negotiate specific agreements
with individual shippers, many carriers established uneconomical
rates in an effort to broaden their share of the market. Their
aforementioned problems and the response of the certificated common
carriers set the stage for subsequent developments.

In July of 1945 one of the largest of the new freight specialists, the Flying Tiger Line, issued a tariff showing rates below
those then charged by American Airlines. Retaliating, the latter
set up its Contract Air Freight Division,[6] via which it offered a

---

[1]A large number of these were returning servicemen who possessed the
technical skills required in the running of an airline.

[2]According to one estimate, about 3,000 nonscheduled air carriers attempted
to penetrate the market during this period. Of these, less than ten percent were
interested solely in freight. Civil Aeronautics Administration, Statistical Handbook of Civil Aviation (Washington, D.C.: U.S. Government Printing Office, 1949),
p. 38. A cautionary comment regarding the integrity of these figures is given in
"American Air Cargo Development," Air Affairs 2, no. 1 (1947):93.

[3]Contract/charter work involving: (1) freight only, (2) passengers only,
(3) a combination of the two.

[4]The exemption from the Civil Aeronautics Act's economic regulatory provi-
sions is discussed in chapter V of Lucile Keyes, Federal Control of Entry Into Air
Transportation (Cambridge, Mass.: Harvard University Press, 1951). Also see Neal
Pilson, "The Exemption Provision of the Civil Aeronautics Act: The Problems Inher-
ent in the Exercise of 'Pure' Administrative Power," Journal of Air Law and
Commerce 29, no. 4 (1963):255-298.

[5]In contrast to the scheduled airlines, which had authority to serve only
those cities shown in their certificates, these carriers could provide service to
any point in the nation.

[6]"Freight Division Will Operate Independent of American Airlines," American
Aviation 10, no. 2 (1946):24.

reduced basic rate of 11 cents per ton-mile over transcontinental
routes, which in turn forced the other certificated carriers to
lower their rates. The unprofitability of the new rates compelled
American Airlines to dissolve its contract operations in early 1947,
at which point the nonscheduled airlines announced a general rate
increase. The continuation of the rate war between the scheduled
and nonscheduled operators led in August of 1947 to the abandonment
by the former of their individual general commodity tariffs and the
adoption of a consolidated tariff. Known as the Johnson Tariff,[1] it
reduced rates by about 25 per cent, contained a modified tapering
principle, and eliminated weight breaks for shipments in the 100 to
16,000 pound range. This induced the noncertificated all-cargo
carriers, which had now won the CAB's approval to engage in scheduled operations, to reduce their own rates once again while retaining the weight breaks pattern.[2] The instability of the entire rate
structure was further accentuated when, during the latter part of
the year, the scheduled carriers initiated a new series of rate
reductions. Some of these were suspended by the Board, which, now
under considerable pressure to intervene, undertook an examination
(called the Air Freight Rate Investigation) of the overall rate
structure which was to culminate in the issuance of a minimum rate
order in April, 1948.

We have already noted that one of the Board's most important
regulatory tools was its veto power over the rates charged by the
certificated airlines. This power sprung in part from section 404(b)
of the Federal Aviation Act which states that

> no [domestic] air carrier or foreign air carrier shall make, give, or cause
> any undue or unreasonable preference or advantage to any particular person,
> port, locality, or description of traffic in air transportation in any
> respect whatsoever or subject any particular person, port, locality, or
> description of traffic in air transportation to any unjust discrimination
> or any undue or unreasonable prejudice or disadvantage in any respect what-
> soever.[3]

(Unjust discrimination results "if different fares [or rates] are
charged for like and contemporaneous services for like traffic under

---

[1]Participating carriers were free to deviate from various provisions of the
Johnson Tariff, which was made up of three components: (1) a pickup and delivery
tariff, (2) a rate tariff, (3) a rules tariff. The consolidated pickup and
delivery tariff provided the framework for the reestablishment of Air Cargo, Inc.
(see below, p. 61).

[2]"Industry's Lowest Freight Rates Offered by Slick Airways Tariff,"
Aviation Week and Space Technology 47, no. 2 (1947):52. Slick Airways, for
example, offered reduced rates at the 100, 1,000, 3,000, and 10,000 pound levels.

[3]72 Stat. 760, 49 U.S.C. 1375.

substantially similar circumstances and conditions."[1] On the other hand, undue preference or prejudice "concerns the charging of like fares [or rates] for different but related services."[2]) In enforcing the Act's antidiscrimination provisions, the agency, upon concluding that a carrier's "rate, fare, or charge . . . or any classification, rule, regulation, or practice affecting such rate, fare, or charge, . . . is or will be unjust or unreasonable, or unjustly discriminatory, or unduly preferential, or unduly prejudicial, . . . shall determine and prescribe the lawful rate, fare, or charge (or the . . . maximum/minimum thereof) thereafter to be demanded, . . . or the lawful classification, rule, regulation, or practice thereafter to be made effective."[3] The lawful rates and practices prescribed by the Board were to be in harmony with the basic public interest objectives of the Act.[4] In addition, Congress established various other factors which the agency, in devising a rate formula, was to take into consideration. These included:

1. The effect of such rates upon the movement of traffic;

2. The need in the public interest of adequate and efficient transportation of persons and property by air carriers at the lowest cost consistent with the furnishing of such service;

3. Such standards respecting the character and quality of service to be rendered by air carriers as may be prescribed by or pursuant to law;

4. The inherent advantages of transportation by aircraft; and

5. The need of each air carrier for revenue sufficient to enable such air carrier, under honest, economical, and efficient management, to provide adequate and efficient air carrier service.[5]

As was shown above, the initial postwar period witnessed the entry of a large number of nonscheduled carriers into the market. Although legally prohibited from doing so, many of these were offering de facto scheduled service, and, while the CAB initially took little action against such practices, it was alive to the problems engendered by uncontrolled competition, having as early as 1944

---

[1]Multicharter Cargo Rates Investigation, 47 CAB 626, 628 (1967). See also Transcontinental Bus System, Inc., v. Civil Aeronautics Board, 383 F. 2d 466, 484-485 (5th Cir. 1967).

[2]Multicharter Cargo Rates Investigation, p. 627.

[3]Federal Aviation Act, section 1002(d). 72 Stat. 789, 49 U.S.C. 1482. In 1978 section 1002(d) was amended by 92 Stat. 1741.

[4]See above, pp. 6-7. The Board also had the power to prevent new tariffs from going into effect, since it was able to suspend these pending a review of their lawfulness. A detailed examination of the agency's suspension and rejection powers is found in Delta Air Lines, Inc. v. Civil Aeronautics Board, 543 F. 2d 247 (D.C. Cir. 1976).

[5]Federal Aviation Act, section 1002(e). 72 Stat. 789, 49 U.S.C. 1482. In 1978 section 1002(e) was amended by 92 Stat. 1742. (See Appendix.)

instituted a review of the situation.[1] The Board's involvement was
taken one step further when, in March of 1946, the applications of
the major all-cargo carriers for permanent certification were consolidated into a proceeding known as the Air Freight Case. Once it
became clear that the case would not be quickly decided, the applicants, many of whom were struggling for survival, petitioned the
agency for swifter action. This came on May 5, 1947 in the form of
Section 292.5 of the Board's Economic Regulations, under which the
applicants won authorization to undertake scheduled operations as
common carriers pending termination of the Air Freight Case. With
this ruling the competitive position of these noncertificated
operators was somewhat strengthened, and, against the background of
an intensifying rate war,[2] the CAB in early 1948 made known its
findings in the Air Freight Rate Investigation.

Noncompensatory rates, the Board concluded, were contributing
to an unhealthy air freight industry, which appeared unable to provide the public with "economical, . . . adequate, and efficient"
transportation.[3] Such rates failed to meet the statutory standard
of justness and reasonableness and were ordered canceled. A continuing deterioration of the industry's "unsound competitive condition"
would, it was further concluded, lead to the destruction of the
freight specialists. Central to this evaluation was the imposition
of a minimum rate level below which new charges were not permitted
to fall. Minimum rates, set for any one shipment at 16 cents per
ton-mile for the first 1,000 ton-miles and 13 cents per ton-mile
thereafter,[4] applied equally to the all-cargo carriers and to the

---

[1] Investigation of Nonscheduled Air Services, 6 CAB 1049 (1946).

[2] The passenger-cargo carriers were able to charge rates lower than those of
the all-cargo airlines, since they calculated their costs according to the addi-
tive cost (also out-of-pocket cost) theory while the latter used the fully
allocated cost approach. In practical terms the combination carriers, unlike
their competitors, were able to subsidize the carriage of freight with revenues
derived from mail and passenger operations.

[3] "The rates now in effect and proposed are not sufficient to meet the need
of each air carrier for revenues sufficient to enable such air carrier under
honest, economical, and efficient management to provide safe, adequate, and
efficient air carrier service." Air Freight Rate Investigation, 9 CAB 340, 355
(1948).

[4] Computation of these figures was based on the cost data of the all-cargo
carriers for the third quarter of 1947. The Board's methodology was assailed by
the certificated airlines on the grounds that: (1) calculation of freight rates
according to the fully allocated cost concept would hinder the industry's growth,
(2) combination carrier costs were not at an uneconomical level, and (3) the CAB
had overlooked "value of service considerations." Ibid., p. 358. The Board
responded by noting that, at this early stage in the air freight industry's development, the all-cargo carriers' costs, "constituting as they do the only pure
freight costs available, are the most usable guide to the determination of the
reasonableness of the rates under investigation." Ibid., p. 348.

combination (passenger-cargo) airlines and would, it was hoped, "curb the injurious consequences of a rate competition."[1] They could be disregarded only after the interested party had received the Board's permission to do so. No attempt was made by the agency to specify particular rate structures, the carriers retaining the freedom to raise these "above the rate floor to permit the sound development and promotion" of freight service.[2] The minimum rate order was not extended to air freight forwarders (indirect air carriers).[3]

Also considered was the question of weight breaks.[4] The Johnson Tariff dispensed with these for the weight ranges encompassing the major proportion of freight traffic, a factor which had led forwarder interests to petition the Board for its suspension. Volume-related rates, the agency concluded, were economically justified and individual carriers were left free to decide whether or not they would be abolished.

After nearly three years of litigation the CAB reached a decision in the Air Freight Case on July 29, 1949. Of the fourteen all-cargo operators who had requested certificates of public convenience and necessity only four were successful.[5] However, due to the developmental nature of the service, certification was restricted to a five-year trial period at the end of which the situation was to be reviewed. Route authorization differed from customary practice in that, rather than connecting specified urban centers, the new network linked areas (e.g., the northeastern United States, the Portland-Seattle region, southern and central California).[6] This, it was believed, made for greater operational flexibility than could

---

[1] Ibid., p. 351.

[2] Ibid., p. 352.

[3] "Restricting the incentive and ability of the forwarder to develop new sources of traffic," the Board said, "would inevitably operate to the detriment of the direct air carriers." Air Freight Rate Case, Minimum Rates for Air Freight Forwarders, 26 CAB 339, 342 (1958).

[4] Generally speaking, the noncertificated carriers favored weight breaks while their certificated competitors did not.

[5] Airnews, Flying Tiger Line, Slick Airways, and U.S. Airlines. The remaining applications were dismissed for a number of reasons, such as failure to provide the CAB the requested operational data and lack of funds to properly finance the proposed services.

[6] Air Freight Case, 10 CAB 572 (1949). Operating certificates at this time covered only inter-area traffic. Limited intra-area service, making possible more efficient aircraft utilization, was authorized in 1959. Intra-Area Cargo Case, 28 CAB 200 (1959).

otherwise be achieved. The areas selected (each had within it
specified terminal and intermediate points; a number of the latter
were to receive service only on the basis of demand) were those most
likely to support the air freight industry, that is, those having
the greatest potential as generators and/or consumers of air freight.

Issuance of the certificates rested on a number of factors,
the most important being the Board's conviction that the national air
freight potential could only be fully developed through the participation of the all-cargo carriers. Their certificates did not include express and mail awards and the companies would thus "live and
prosper only through their ability to develop an economic [freight]
business."[1] Unable to carry passengers and mail (mail services of
the combination carriers were subsidized by the Federal Government),
the carriers were expected to provide a "yardstick" with which the
Board might measure the cost level and efficiency of the combination
airlines' freight operations. In addition, the agency was not un-
sympathetic to the argument advanced by the applicants that it was
they who had been largely responsible for the expansion of freight
markets and that this growth had not been accomplished at the expense of the all-purpose carriers. The latter, it should be noted,
had long rejected such an interpretation. It was their contention
that they had suffered a diversion of traffic (to the new entrants),
could meet adequately the future demands of the air freight industry
(demand projections had been grossly inflated by the all-cargo
carriers it was alleged), and that, as such, the entry of new all-
cargo carriers was unjustified and should not be countenanced.

The Board recognized that all-cargo service had not been
profitable and had failed to live up to initial traffic estimates
but attributed this in large measure to the fact that the applicants,
awaiting the outcome of the Air Freight Case, had been working in an
atmosphere of uncertainty and had thus been denied a "full opportunity to prove their case."[2] It reminded its critics that it was
mandated by Congress not only to regulate but also to promote air
transportation and that furtherance of the public interest dictated
its (the Board's) "encouragement and development of a national system of air transportation which will be adequate to the needs of
commerce, the postal service, and the national defense."[3] Certification of all-cargo operations was considered to be in harmony with

---

[1] Air Freight Case, p. 589.

[2] Ibid., p. 580.

[3] Air Freight Case, p. 588. Also see above, p. 6.

these Congressional objectives. The agency also pointed out that its action took into account the changing requirements of the air freight industry and that, once their services received an official stamp of approval, the new entrants could more readily pioneer technical and marketing innovations from which the entire industry stood to benefit.

The Board's decision was not unanimous, for two of its members Lee and Jones, dissociated themselves from the majority position on the ground that the public convenience and necessity did not call for the certification of additional carriers. The majority had, in Jones' view, been insufficiently critical in their examination of the various facets of the case,[1] basing their judgement entirely on expectations for the future. Their actions ran counter to the Board's proper role, characterized by Jones (in cases of this type) as being judicial, not legislative, in nature. It was also noted that the applicants' parlous fiscal state would compel them, in time to request governmental subsidies, that additional certifications would deprive the combination airlines of badly needed revenues, and that certification by area did not carry with it any public utility obligation.

One of the most vexing problems facing the airlines has been the question of directional imbalance. More freight traffic, for example, has traditionally moved from East to West than from West to East,[2] which has meant that a carrier operating between, say, New York and California has had to absorb revenue losses on the flight to New York due to underutilization of space on the eastbound part of the trip. The severity of the backhaul problem caused several carriers to restrict their flight schedules, and the CAB, granting a petition for modification of the newly established minimum rates, agreed to the introduction of below-minimum directional rates. Its rate order of 1950 provided, temporarily, for backhaul minima;[3] two years later these were extended indefinitely.[4] Minimum rates for eastbound and northbound traffic remained unchanged for distances up to 650 and 550 miles, respectively. For greater distances rates were progressively reduced, falling to 60 per cent once the eastbound and northbound distances traveled exceeded 1,300 and 1,100

---

[1] Such as, for example, existing and anticipated freight volumes.

[2] To cite but one case, Slick Airways' westbound load factor (for September, 1948) was 81 percent , the eastbound load factor 60 percent.

[3] Air Freight Rate Investigation--Directional Rates, 11 CAB 228 (1950).

[4] Air Freight Rate Investigation--Directional Rates, 16 CAB 254 (1952).

miles, respectively. A number of items,[1] including apparel and cut flowers, remained unaffected by the new rate order, as volume shipments of these commodities were such as to preclude the need for promotional rates.

The outbreak of the Korean War and the overall state of the nation's economy combined to bring a short-lived period of prosperity to the Flying Tiger Line and Slick Airways, the two principal all-cargo carriers. These now introduced the Douglas DC-6 aircraft, but the advantages gained vis-à-vis the combination carriers through the use of faster and more economical planes were quickly negated when the latter inaugurated their own reequipment program. In 1953, economic losses, exacerbated by an ill-fated Flying Tiger Line-Slick Airways merger attempt, spurred Slick Airways to seek an increase in the minimum rate. In presenting its case the company stressed that operating costs had risen substantially since the inception of minimum rates in 1948. The Board's favorable response[2] to what it termed an "emergency situation" was criticized by American Airlines, one of the largest of the combination carriers, which, pointing to the profitability of its own freight services at existing rate levels, alleged that higher minimum rates were injurious to its expanding freight operations.

In 1955 the CAB took up the question of the renewal of temporary certificates issued the all-cargo operators in 1949. The proceeding was divided into two parts. The first, in which North-South routes were considered, was concluded at the end of the year and resulted in the certification of Airlift International[3] and AAXICO[4] for a five-year period. Certification was not extended to U.S. Airlines, which, due to insolvency and other reasons, was judged to be "not fit, willing, or able" to undertake freight service.[5] The CAB refrained from granting permanent authorizations at this time, saying that "there are many obstacles still to be hurdled before air freight carriers can assume their proper role in our certificated

---

[1]The full list is found in Air Freight Rate Investigation--Directional Rates (1950), p. 237.

[2]Air Freight Rate Case, 18 CAB 22 (1953). The new minimum rates were set at: below the first 1,000 ton-miles, 20 cents per ton-mile, above that figure 16.25 cents per ton-mile.

[3]At the time its corporate name was Riddle Airlines.

[4]American Air Export and Import Co.

[5]Fitness, willingness, and ability were examined in terms of a company's: (1) organizational structure, (2) financial resources, and (3) operational plans.

air transportation system."[1]   It answered the charges of the combination carrier intervenors (these maintained that their own freight
services were adequate and that traffic volume did not justify the
Board's action) by noting that the air freight potential of the
Southeast, especially Florida, could best be exploited by all-cargo
specialists, since the combination carriers, "whose primary interests are in providing passenger service, cannot be expected to
exercise the ingenuity and effort that an independent company would
use in developing the air freight business through an all-cargo
service."[2]   Although the combination airlines denied a lack of
interest in freight operations, it remained a fact that freight contributed a mere two per cent of their total operating revenues.
Only one carrier, Delta Air Lines, employed all-cargo equipment over
North-South routes, and even here the aircraft used was the small
C-47. Freight carried over North-South routes between 1947 and 1954
had grown about 600 per cent (ton-miles), and a number of intervenor
(these included the Secretary of Agriculture, the Port Authority of
New York and New Jersey, and many civic interest groups) feared that
further expansion (without the all-cargo operators) was threatened,
since increasingly greater shipments called for the introduction of
larger all-cargo aircraft. (A further consideration working against
the combination airlines was that the time of year [winter] during
which passengers made a maximum demand on aircraft space coincided
with the period of heaviest North-South freight traffic.) The
Department of Defense, another intervenor in the case, also urged
long-term Board support for the all-cargo operators. Certificated
all-cargo carriers had transported 21 million pounds of freight for
the Department during 1953 (as opposed to 9 million pounds carried
by scheduled combination airlines) and were expected to carry substantially greater quantities within the next few years. The importance of all-cargo equipment was enhanced by the fact that it could,
during a national emergency, be readily converted to military uses.

     The second phase of the certification renewal proceeding dealt
with East-West routes and was terminated in March of 1956. Here
again the Board felt that all-cargo services promoted the nation's
commercial and military interests and should be continued. The two
carriers in question, Slick Airways and the Flying Tiger Line, had
rendered "useful and necessary service;" however, their inability to

---

     [1]The major "obstacle" was the companies' unsound financial condition.
North-South Air Freight Renewal Case, 22 CAB 253, 257 (1955).

     [2]Ibid., p. 301.

operate profitably on a sustained basis militated against permanent certification and led to renewals for another five-year experimental period.[1] The combination airlines' argument that renewed certification subjected them to further business losses and thus was incompatible with the public interest was unpersuasive; no acceptable supporting evidence was offered by the complainants, who in any event received the overwhelming proportion of their total revenues from passenger services.

The 1955-1956 all-cargo certificates included, for the first time, authority to carry mail and express (express traffic consisted of goods delivered to the airlines by REA Express). Mail grants had been withheld in the Air Freight Case since it would have been counterproductive to channel mail revenues away from the combination airlines at a time when mail rates, subsidized by the Federal Government, were intended to strengthen and promote scheduled passenger transportation. Similarly, the nature of the limited express market had made it illogical to divert that traffic from the subsidized airlines to the experimental carriers.[2] Now, however, the air freight industry was on a surer economic footing, the role of mail subsidies had decreased, and the restriction placed on express shipments was increasingly an anachronism.

The Board's about-face in the matter of mail service reflected a crucial change in the position taken by the Postmaster General. Whereas in the 1940s the postal authorities had demonstrated little interest in an extension of mail rights to nonscheduled operators, they now declared that all-cargo carrier mail authority on an "as and when needed" (and non-subsidized) basis would be extremely helpful to the Postal Service. Improved mail service, a policy goal of the Federal Aviation Act, was, of course, of interest to the CAB, which shared the Postmaster General's assessment that all-cargo carrier mail rights provided him with greater routing flexibility and permitted more expeditious handling of mail during peak periods and strikes.[3] The objections of the combination airlines were

---

[1]Air Freight Certificate Renewal Case, 23 CAB 186 (1956).

[2]This contrasts sharply with the argument used about freight. Here the CAB believed that the equipment and operations of the all-cargo carriers would appeal largely to that segment of the shipping public not using combination carrier service.

[3]Section 405(a) of the Federal Aviation Act states: "the Postmaster General is authorized to make such rules and regulations, not inconsistent with the provisions of this Act, or any order, rule, or regulation made by the Board thereunder, as may be necessary for the safe and expeditious carriage of mail by aircraft." Section 405(b) empowers the Postmaster General to "designate any . . . schedule for the transportation of mail between the points between which the air

rejected. American Airlines, Trans World Airlines, and United
Airlines, for example, derived less than three percent of their
total operating revenues from mail operations and could hardly claim
that the all-cargo carriers' limited mail services would deprive
them of a significant portion of their income. The Board's decision,
which was appealed, received judicial affirmation in 1957.[1]

In order to make air freight service more competitive with
surface transportation and to help the airlines towards greater utilization of their total freight capacity, the CAB in April of 1956
confirmed an earlier tentative decision approving the introduction
of "deferred" freight operations. A central feature of this service,
which was offered on a space-available basis only, was its lower
rates,[2] and, so as not to attract freight moving at regular rates to
the less expensive service, shipments under the "deferred" plan were
held back at the destination airport for a period of about two days.[3]
Critics of this arrangement contended that the new rates were noncompensatory and unlawful,[4] that "deferred" service would grow at
the expense of regular freight service, and that the backhaul problem would be aggravated. The Board considered these charges to be
groundless and in a subsequent review of the matter authorized the
continuation of "deferred" freight operations.[5]

---

carrier is authorized by its certificate to transport mail, . . . [and to] require the air carrier to establish additional schedules for the transportation of
mail between such points." 72 Stat. 760, 49 U.S.C. 1375.

[1]Delta Air Lines, Inc. v. Civil Aeronautics Board, 247 F. 2d 327 (5th Cir.
1957). Under section 406(a) of the Federal Aviation Act the CAB may "fix and
determine from time to time, after notice and hearing, the fair and reasonable
rates of compensation for the transportation of mail by air-craft, the facilities
used and useful therefore, and the services connected therewith . . . by each
holder of a certificate authorizing the transportation of mail by aircraft."
72 Stat. 763, 49 U.S.C. 1376. A separate treatment of mail service lies beyond
the scope of this chapter. For a fuller discussion of this topic, see Gilbert L.
Gifford, "The Evolution of Air Mail Rate Making," Journal of Air Law and Commerce
22, no. 3 (1955):298-342. Mail rates form the subject of two recent Board en-
quiries: Domestic Service Mail Rate Investigation of Priority and Nonpriority
Mail, Docket 23080 (newly introduced containerized mail service is included in
the proceeding) and Transatlantic, Transpacific, and Latin American Mail Rates
Case, Docket 26487.

[2]The minimum rates for this service were: (1) for westbound and southbound
traffic 65 percent of the minimum charged for regular air freight service,
(2) on backhaul routes 55 percent of the minimum charged for regular freight
service.

[3]The mandatory delay was a minimum of two days for shipments carried less
than 2,100 miles and three days in the case of traffic carried for distances of
more than 2,100 miles.

[4]Deferred Air Freight Case, 23 CAB 651 (1956).

[5]Deferred Air Freight Renewal Case, 27 CAB 627 (1958).

Minimum rates, prescribed for domestic air freight since 1948, were rescinded in 1961. Three major developments prompted the Board to take this step. The first of these was the significant change in the competitive climate between all-cargo and passenger-cargo lines which had taken place in the intervening period. In 1948 the combination carriers were able to offer low added-cost rates with which noncertificated operators could not compete over a prolonged time span. Now, however, several of the combination carriers had themselves made substantial investments in all-cargo equipment, and there was greater similarity in some of the cost accounting procedures used by the two airline groups. Also, it had become evident that the overall rate structure was now more stable than it had been during the industry's earlier phase, and the CAB determined that abolition of the minimum rate floor would not jeopardize this equilibrium (a view, incidentally, not shared by a number of intervenors who viewed the measure as a prelude to a renewed rate war). Technological changes, too, played a role in the agency's decision. These changes included new aircraft and ground-handling techniques which, it was reasoned, would ultimately lead to lower costs for consumers. The Civil Aeronautics Board's action in no sense implied that it had relinquished control over future rate trends. Rather, the Board had given the carriers greater latitude in rate-making decisions, which, however, remained subject to its own powers of suspension and investigation. In this connection the carriers were cautioned that future uneconomical rates remained unacceptable and that an "incipient return to the domestic rate practices which originally necessitated the issuance of minimum rate orders"[1] would not be tolerated.

With the granting of new certificates of public convenience and necessity to the Flying Tiger Line and Slick Airways in 1962, permanent certification was finally achieved by the all-cargo operators. Airlift International was authorized to continue service for another five-year trial period and AAXICO, inoperative due to fiscal problems, was denied certification. The CAB's advocacy of permanent certification rested in part on the expectation that this would bolster the financial position of the all-cargo carriers. Their hoped-for profits had failed to materialize and, indeed, their continued existance had frequently been dependent on nonscheduled operations such as specialized charter work for the Department of

---

[1]Minimum Rates Applicable to Air Freight, 34 CAB 263, 267 (1961).

Defense.[1] The loss by Slick Airways of a military contract had
forced suspension (in 1958) of its common carrier service,[2] which it
was able to resume, in part, only four years later. AAXICO, too,
had received permission in 1959 to suspend common carriage operations.[3]

Although the Board acknowledged that the all-cargo carriers
presented a sombre financial picture, it held that the long-term
needs of the nation's commerce and defense took precedence over considerations of the "immediate present." In order to ease the financial pressures on the carriers, however, demand points,[4] having
failed to promote traffic growth, were not included in the new
certificates. Also eliminated were a number of duplicating points
named in the earlier certificates of both the Flying Tiger Line and
Slick Airways. In authorizing two airlines to engage in East-West
service the CAB overruled its examiner, who had recommended that
certification be restricted to one carrier (the Flying Tiger Line)
because the East-West route would not support two all-cargo operators competing not only with each other but also with several all-
purpose airlines. Its decision, the Board again stressed, was
predicated on the need for a long-term view. It felt, as it had in
the past, that the freight potential of the East-West market was
substantial and that it could be developed more effectively with the
aid of the all-cargo airlines.[5] The agency believed that the air
freight industry would witness its "long-delayed . . . breakthrough
in the foreseeable future,"[6] basing its optimism on the ability of
the two carriers (which had now acquired the CL-44D) to institute a
rate structure more competitive with surface transportation. In

---

[1]Various issues bearing on military charters are examined in U.S., Congress,
House, Committee on Armed Services, Military Airlift, Hearings before the Subcommittee on Military Airlift, House of Representatives, 91st Cong., 2d sess.,
(1970). Also see Stanley H. Brewer and James E. Rosenzweig, Military Airlift and
Its Relationship to the Commercial Air Cargo Industry (Seattle: Graduate School
of Business Administration, University of Washington, 1967).

[2]"Slick Quits Air Freight Service; Rentzel Blames CAB, Pentagon," American
Aviation 21, no. 21 (1958):14.

[3]AAXICO, Suspension of Service, 29 CAB 1329 (1959).

[4]See above, p. 13.

[5]The combination carriers contended (as on other occasions) that the all-
cargo experiment had been a failure and that combination carrier service would
suffice to meet the requirements of the shipping public.

[6]Domestic Cargo-Mail Service Case, 36 CAB 344, 360 (1962).

this context it was noted that recent improvements in the inventory-ing, handling, warehousing, and promotion of air freight were rein-forcing the competitiveness of the airlines vis-à-vis surface carriers and would lead to a more significant penetration of surface freight markets. American Airlines' demand that it, like the all-cargo carriers, be granted intra-area authority was rejected. "We think it clear," observed the Board, "that special considerations apply to the all-cargo carriers, which are engaged in the develop-ment of a relatively young industry without the supporting benefits of passenger traffic."[1] A request by the all-cargo carriers for subsidy eligibility was denied.[2] Such a plea, it will be recalled, had been predicted in the minority opinion of the Air Freight Case and must have caused the CAB considerable embarrassment, since it had long maintained that their ability to function without govern-mental support constituted one of the chief virtues of the all-cargo operators. Now, however, subsidies were sought as a cushion against "temporary economic setbacks" and as an aid in the raising of capi-tal. The Board refused to accept that subsidies should be approved "as a kind of protective insurance against depression or competi-tion"[3] and rejected the suggestion that subsidy payments to local service carriers represented a precedent to be followed here.

Permanent certification, the CAB felt, had been "earned" by the all-cargo carriers and marked the "coming of age" of the domes-tic air freight industry. It is difficult to see how the agency can have been entirely sincere, for not only had the all-cargo operators been enmeshed in a series of financial difficulties throughout the greater part of the experimental period, they had clearly failed to bring about the "breakthrough" in the freight field which the CAB had long anticipated and upon which it had based in large measure a number of freight-related decisions.[4] Rather, the record indicates that, having long ago committed itself to a policy of support for the all-cargo airlines, the Board was simply unwilling to abandon them, especially now that changing shipper attitudes appeared to be

---

[1]Ibid., p. 377.

[2]"Flying Tiger Line Enters Subsidy Fray," Air Cargo 2, no. 6 (1958):26.

[3]Domestic Cargo-Mail Service Case, op. cit., p. 355.

[4]Although the air freight industry has continued to grow steadily, the unrealistic expectations of the past have given way to cooler judgement. Thus, one industry observer recently said: "there is little hope of a major cargo breakthrough." For a discussion of various problems plaguing the industry, see John C. Cook, "Air Freight Breakthrough Lags Behind Predictions," Air Transport World 14, no. 3 (1977):32-35.

moving the air freight industry to the threshold of its greatest period of growth to date.

Before approving new operating authority for a given air carrier, the Board must be satisfied that the proposed service is in the public interest. It is important to recognize that, while the traditional Section 102 public convenience and necessity standard applied to all certificated air carriers irrespective of the group to which they belonged (e.g., trunk lines, local service carriers, all-cargo carriers, supplemental carriers, etc.), the criteria upon which it was based differed markedly for the various carrier groups involved. The permanent operating certificates issued the trunk lines in 1938 covered, in the words of Congress, "mail and all other classes of traffic." Thus, while the trunks' interest focused primarily on passengers, freight rights automatically became an integral part of their operating authority. The combination airlines, in other words, were not required to demonstrate that the communities named in their certificates were in need of all-cargo flights. Similarly, the 1938 "grandfather" rights did not rest upon a prior showing of economic need by the carriers concerned. In the case of the all-cargo operators, on the other hand, certification was granted in the belief that this would contribute significantly to the development of the air freight industry. These specialized carriers, of course, were almost entirely dependent on freight revenues, and, accordingly, their route requests were viewed from the standpoint of a city's (or area's) need for and ability to support the all-cargo services in question. Other public/national interest considerations which have had a bearing on all-cargo route applications are: (1) the use of these services as a "yardstick" with which the efficiency of the combination carriers' freight operations might be measured, (2) national defense requirements, (3) the role of additional awards in strengthening the self-sufficiency of all-cargo carriers, and (4) the benefits (e.g., lower freight rates) which might result from additional all-cargo flights. The creation of a new carrier class did not imply inadequacy or incompetence on the part of existing airlines. Rather, the Board believed that every carrier class offered the shipper "unique advantages" and made a specific contribution to the overall effectiveness of the nation's air transportation system. As already noted, the services of each carrier class had to be in harmony with Federal policy objectives. However, in pursuing these objectives the agency was under no obligation to accord identical treatment to the various classes in question. Indeed, its perception of their functional and historical differences has led to differential treatment not only in terms of

the initial certification criteria but also with regard to the permissible scope of the carriers' subsequent activities.[1]

The Air Freight Case had dealt only with the major all-cargo
carriers and had thus left unanswered the regulatory questions posed
by the large number of other airlines involved in nonscheduled
("irregular") passenger and freight operations. The exemption of
nonscheduled carriers from the economic regulatory provisions of the
Civil Aeronautics Act had been affirmed in 1946[2] but was modified a
year later to the extent that certain of these provisions now came
into force, especially with respect to the larger carriers. Further
regulatory adjustments meant that by 1949 the large operators enjoyed relief only from sections 401(a), 404(a), and 405(e) of the
Act's Title IV provisions.[3]

The disorder, one might almost say chaos, which had characterized the earlier years of the nonscheduled air carrier industry was
still clearly in evidence at this point. Numerous new requests for
letters of registration were being lodged with the CAB, letter-
holders complained that newly introduced regulations were too
restrictive, and the prohibition against scheduled operations was
widely disregarded. In addition, the economic and technological
environment in which the nonscheduled carriers functioned was undergoing rapid change, underlining the need for a fresh evaluation of
their role within the overall structure of the national air transportation industry.

The first stage of the ensuing Large Irregular Air Carrier
Investigation, in which the CAB concluded that the large nonscheduled carriers--they were now designated "supplemental" air carriers--
were a "significant" part of U.S. air transportation and provided
"useful and necessary" service not rendered by the certificated airlines, was completed in 1955.[4] Their contribution to the nation's

---

[1]According to section 416(a) of the Federal Aviation Act, "the Board may
from time to time establish such just and reasonable classifications or groups of
air carriers . . . as the nature of the services performed by such air carriers
shall require; and such just and reasonable rules and regulations, . . . to be
observed by each such class or group, as the Board finds necessary in the public
interest." 72 Stat. 771, 49 U.S.C. 1386.

[2]Investigation of Nonscheduled Air Services.

[3]Section 401(a) is shown on p. 4, note 4. The two other exemptions dealt
with certain "adequate service" provisions and foreign postal arrangements. Full
compliance with these provisions of the Act, the Board declared, would place an
"undue burden" on the carriers.

[4]Smaller carriers (the distinction rested on aircraft capacity) were not
included in the investigation and continued their activities under an exemption
(section 416) from economic regulation.
    At the beginning of 1978 these companies, known as air taxis, numbered

military posture was deemed especially valuable[1] and the Board
proposed a strengthening of their financial base as a means of
assuring their continuing ability to help meet national defense
commitments. The permissible scope of the carriers' operating
authority was now expanded, enabling them to offer:

> (a) unlimited charter operations on a planeload basis for the carriage
> of passengers and property in domestic, overseas, and territorial
> (except intra-Alaska) operations, and . . . (b) individually ticketed
> or individually way-billed operations . . . not to exceed 10 trips per
> month in the same direction between any single pair of [U.S.] points.[2]

The first stage of the supplemental carrier proceeding had
concentrated essentially on public interest considerations and on
the delineation of the services that were to be permitted. The
second stage, completed in 1959, focused on the qualifications of
individual applicants and on the manner in which supplemental
authorization was to be effectuated. The outcome was that operating
rights were approved temporarily for twenty-three carriers, the
authorization being by certification rather than exemption. Certification, it was argued, by lending "stability, dignity, and protection" to supplemental air services, tended to reinforce the air
transportation industry generally and hence came closer to realizing

---

about 4,100. They are not required to hold Board-approved certificates provided
they utilize "small" aircraft, i.e., aircraft having a maximum passenger capacity of 56 seats or a maximum payload capacity of 18,000 pounds. (Prior to 1978
these limits were, respectively, 30 seats and 7,500 pounds.) They have also been
exempt from the Federal Aviation Act's passenger and freight tariff filing requirements. The Board recognizes a special group of air taxis, which it calls
commuter air carriers. (At the beginning of 1978, 250 of these were registered
with the agency.) A commuter air carrier is one which (1) performs at least five
round trips per week between two or more points and publishes flight schedules
which specify the times, days of the week, and places between which such flights
are performed, or (2) transports mail by air pursuant to contract with the
United States Postal Service. Regulation ER-929, section 298.2.
      The CAB's recent denial of Federal Express' request to use the DC-9-15 was
in harmony with a Congressional admonition that the certification exemption
should apply only in "limited and unusual circumstances" (House Report no. 1950,
87th Cong., 2d sess., [1962], p. 13). The Board's narrow construction of the
section 416 exemption has been upheld by the courts (Utah Agencies v. Civil
Aeronautics Board, 504 F. 2d 1232 [10th Cir. 1974]; Air Line Pilots Association v.
Civil Aeronautics Board, 458 F. 2d 846 [D.C. Cir. 1972]).

[1]During the Soviet blockade of Berlin, for instance, supplementals accounted
for roughly 60 percent of the cargo flown to the beleaguered city in civilian
aircraft; in 1950 they provided about half of the commercial airlift used in
support of the Korean War effort. The supplemental carriers no longer depend on
military charters to the extent they once did. Thus, in 1963 military operations
contributed 79 percent of their total operating revenues; by the end of 1977 the
figure had fallen to 22 percent .

[2]Large Irregular Air Carrier Investigation, 22 CAB 838, 853-854 (1955).

the objectives of the Federal Aviation Act.[1]

The legality of the Board's 1959 order was immediately challenged by the scheduled airlines. These held that the agency was
without authority to certificate supplemental air carriers since,
under the Federal Aviation Act, certificates had to show all applicable terminal and intermediate points and were not to restrict a
carrier's schedules. In other words, the agency, by not specifying
the points to be served (transportation had been authorized simply
"between any single pair of points"[2]) and by imposing a ten-trip
frequency limitation, was deemed to be in violation of the Act.[3] In
1960 the order was found legally deficient in several ways (United
Air Lines, Inc. v. Civil Aeronautics Board),[4] whereupon the Board,
seeking clarification of its statutory authority to regulate supplemental carriers, referred the issue to the Congress. There, stop-
gap legislation designed to permit more careful consideration of the
problem (and confirming the status quo ante) was adopted on July 14,
1960.[5] Two years later Congress passed an amendment to the Federal
Aviation Act investing the CAB with the power to issue to qualified
supplemental carrier applicants certificates of public convenience

---

[1]Large Irregular Air Carrier Investigation, 28 CAB 224, 228 (1959).

[2]The Board believed supplemental operations would be more flexible and
effective, and the public interest better served, if certificates did not name
individual city pairs. Legislation adopted in 1962 retained this distinction
between supplemental and route carrier certificates.

[3]According to the Board, the section 401(e) provisions did not apply to
newly authorized, special-purpose operations.

[4]278 F 2d 446 (D.C. Cir. 1960); vacated sub nom., All American Airways,
Inc., v. United Air Lines, Inc., 364 U.S. 297 (1960). The court ruled that the
order was contrary to section 401(e) of the Act and that, given the uncertain
financial position of several supplementals, the Board had shown laxity in applying its "fitness" criteria.
     Section 401(e)(1) provides: "each certificate issued under this section
shall specify the terminal points and intermediate points, if any, between which
the air carrier is authorized to engage in air transportation and the service to
be rendered; and there shall be attached to the exercise of the privileges
granted by the certificate, or amendment thereto, such reasonable terms, conditions, and limitations as the public interest may require." 72 Stat. 755, as
amended by 76 Stat. 143, 49 U.S.C. 1371.
     Section 401(e)(4) provided: "no term, condition, or limitation of a
certificate shall restrict the right of an air carrier to add to or change schedules, equipment, accommodations, and facilities for performing the authorized
transportation and service as the development of the business and the demands of
the public shall require; except that the Board may impose such terms, conditions,
or limitations in a certificate for supplemental air transportation when required
by subsection (d)(3) of this section." 72 Stat. 755, as amended by 76 Stat. 144,
49 U.S.C. 1371. (The underlined part was added to the Act in 1962. It was
deleted [92 Stat. 1719] in 1978.)

[5]Act of July 14, 1960, Pub. L. no. 86-661, 74 Stat. 527.

and necessity (Public Law 87-528).[1] The first permanent domestic
certificates, ten in number, were awarded in March of 1966.[2]

Public Law 87-528, which now provided the legal basis for
supplemental air transportation, had three basic objectives. These
were: the elimination of

> irresponsible supplementals, especially those violating safety
> regulations; . . . [the stabilization of] the operating authority
> of the supplementals under certificates, including authority to
> authorize 'charter trips' on a broad enough basis so that through
> performance of civilian and military charter operations the
> supplementals might remain viable economic organizations capable of
> meeting supplemental transportation needs and able to comply fully
> with safety requirements; . . . [the maintenance of] the regulatory
> scheme of the Federal Aviation Act and the protection of the
> certificated carriers . . . by eliminating unregulated individually
> ticketed point-to-point competition from the supplementals.[3]

The legislators, then, were primarily concerned with: (1) safety,
(2) the stabilization of supplemental service, and (3) the elimination of unlawful practices. The last point led to the loss of ten-
trip per month individually ticketed or waybilled authority, which
a number of carriers, through various pooling arrangements, had used
to circumvent restrictions on their operating rights.

Congress' failure to enact a statutory definition of "charter
trips" gave the Board considerable flexibility with respect to
supplemental air operations.[4] The agency used this flexibility to
approve various services, which, while retaining the distinction
between regularly scheduled transportation and charter flights,
increasingly broadened the legal parameters within which supplemental carriers were able to function. The supplementals' right to

---

[1]Act of July 10, 1962, Pub. L. no. 87-528, 76 Stat. 143.

[2]Order E-23350. Temporary international certificates were issued later
in the year (Supplemental Air Service Proceeding, 45 CAB 231[1966]) and were
renewed in 1977 (Supplemental Renewal Proceeding, Order 77-1-98).

[3]American Airlines, Inc. v. Civil Aeronautics Board, 365 F. 2d 939, 944-
945 (D.C. Cir. 1966).

[4]"Supplemental air transportation," according to section 101(36) of the
Federal Aviation Act, meant "charter trips, including inclusive tour charter trips
in air transportation, other than the transportation of mail by aircraft, rendered
pursuant to a certificate of public convenience and necessity issued pursuant to
section 401(d)(3) of this Act to supplement the scheduled service authorized by
certificates of public convenience and necessity issued pursuant to sections
401(d)(1) and (2) of this Act." 82 Stat. 867, 49 U.S.C. 1301. In 1978 section
101(36) was replaced by section 101(15).

[5]Although these services were developed primarily for the traveling public
they had certain implications for shippers. See below, p. 141.

27

offer these services, which included split charters, travel group
charters, foreign originating travel group charters, and one-stop-
inclusive tour charters (enforced foreign area specialization was
also reduced[1]), was disputed by the scheduled air carriers but was
upheld by the courts. Thus, in American Airlines, Inc. v. Civil
Aeronautics Board the court affirmed the legality of certain split
charters and declared that

> the term charter trips [does not] ha[ve] a fixed meaning. . . . We
> conclude Congress intended, although not without limits, that the
> Board should be free to evolve a definition in relation to such
> variable factors as changing needs and changing aircraft.[2]

The scheduled airlines have repeatedly attributed a number of
their economic difficulties to the inroads made by charter operators
and have frequently urged the Board to order a reduction of their
service levels. The agency, however, while recognizing that supplemental flights "should not be allowed to jeopardize the soundness
and dependability of needed elements of scheduled service," believed
the two carrier groups had "equal rights to compete for the bulk
traffic market."[3] Claims that supplemental service had appreciably
hurt scheduled carriers were rejected by the Board, which instead
stressed the beneficial aspects of competition. (This position, too,
won judicial approval, the court arguing that "our national and consumer interest [demands] 'a market structure conducive to maximum
feasible competition' [between the two carrier groups]."[4]) The
scheduled carriers' charge that the supplementals' services were at
variance with the National Environmental Policy Act of 1969 and the
Energy Policy and Conservation Act of 1975 was similarly rejected
as "totally without merit."[5]

Differing interpretations of section 401(d) of the Federal
Aviation Act have been another source of friction between the scheduled airlines and the Civil Aeronautics Board. The former have
argued on various occasions that, in the absence of proof that the
supplementals' services were required by the public interest, these
services could not be authorized. The Board, on the other hand,

---

[1]Dockets 25908 and 23944, Order 77-1-98 (adopted January 6, 1977).

[2]348 F. 2d 349, 354 (D.C. Cir. 1965). See also: Saturn Airways, Inc. v.
Civil Aeronautics Board, 483 F. 2d 1284 (D.C. Cir. 1973); Pan American World
Airways, Inc. v. Civil Aeronautics Board, 517 F. 2d 734 (2d Cir. 1975); Trans
World Airlines, Inc. v. Civil Aeronautics Board, 545 F. 2d 771 (2d Cir. 1976).

[3]Order 77-1-98, p. 28.

[4]National Air Carrier Association v. Civil Aeronautics Board, 442 F. 2d
862, 872 (D.C. Cir. 1971).

[5]Order 77-1-98.

believed the nature of charter service was such that proof of need did not necessarily have to be judged by the standards applied to scheduled operations. Here the agency has had the backing of the Federal Aviation Act. Unequal treatment of the two carrier groups has been inherent in the language of the Act, which stated (section 401[d][1]) that permanent scheduled authority "shall" be approved upon a finding that "such transportation is required by the public convenience and necessity," whereas supplemental certificates (section 401[d][3]) "may" be issued "as may be required by the public convenience and necessity."[1] (Emphasis added.)

Section 401(d) has been at the center of another controversy. In 1975 World Airways, a supplemental carrier, requested scheduled transportation rights between Newark, New Jersey, and Baltimore, Maryland, on the one hand, and Ontario and Oakland, California, on the other. The company did not wish to surrender its supplemental status and maintained that, though section 401(d)(3) barred the acquisition of supplemental certificates by scheduled operators, it contained no proscription against the holding of route authority by supplemental airlines. After due consideration, the CAB, while allowing that "a literal reading of section 401(d)(3) supports World's position," concluded that it lacked the power to authorize dual certification and dismissed the application.[2] Three principal

---

[1]Section 401(d) stipulated:

"(1) The Board shall issue a certificate authorizing the whole or any part of the transportation covered by the application, if it finds that the applicant is fit, willing, and able to perform such transportation properly, and to conform to the provisions of this Act and the rules, regulations, and requirements of the Board hereunder, and that such transportation is required by the public convenience and necessity; otherwise such application shall be denied.

(2) In the case of an application for a certificate to engage in temporary air transportation, the Board may issue a certificate authorizing the whole or any part thereof for such limited periods as may be required by the public convenience and necessity, if it finds that the applicant is fit, willing, and able properly to perform such transportation and to conform to the provisions of this Act and the rules, regulations, and requirements of the Board hereunder.

(3) In the case of an application for a certificate to engage in supplemental air transportation, the Board may issue a certificate, to any applicant not holding a certificate under paragraph (1) or (2) of this subsection, authorizing the whole or any part thereof, and for such periods, as may be required by the public convenience and necessity, if it finds that the applicant is fit, willing, and able properly to perform the transportation covered by the application and to conform to the provisions of this Act and the rules, regulations, and requirements of the Board hereunder. Any certificate issued pursuant to this paragraph shall contain such limitations as the Board shall find necessary to assure that the service rendered pursuant thereto will be limited to supplemental air transportation as defined in this Act." (Section 401[d][3] became part of the Act in 1962.) 72 Stat. 755, as amended by 76 Stat. 143, 49 U.S.C. 1371. In 1978 section 401(d) was amended by 92 Stat. 1712. (See Appendix.)

[2]Application of World Airways for a Certificate of Public Convenience and Necessity, Order 76-1-88.

arguments were used to buttress this decision. The first of these
was that Congress intended scheduled and supplemental carriers to
function as two separate and independent groups and had expressed
this intent in several amendments to the Federal Aviation Act, especially in those which were adopted contemporaneously with section
401(d)(3). In this connection sections 401(e)(6),[1] 401(n),[2] and
406(b)[3] were considered particularly significant, the point being
that if a carrier could receive both scheduled and charter certificates,

> the wholly anomalous result would be that the carrier would at one and
> the same time be (a) granted and denied section 401(e)(6) authority;
> (b) subject to and not subject to section 401(n) requirements; and
> (c) eligible and not eligible for subsidy.[4]

The Board has also contended that its actions prior to passage
of Public Law 87-528 ruled out dual certification and that these
actions were taken into account by the authors of the 1962 legislation. An example of one such action is found in the first phase of
the Large Irregular Air Carrier Investigation, above, in which the
supplementals were informed that their certification exemptions
would be terminated in the event that they received certificates of
public convenience and necessity. Earlier agency decisions, according to the Board, merit "significant weight" and played a major role
in its examination of World Airways' application. The agency has
also attempted to justify its World Airways ruling in terms of the
legislative history of Public Law 87-528. Legislation permitting
services of the type proposed by the applicant had actually been
adopted by the Senate but was replaced by a House bill which greatly
restricted the conditions under which supplemental operators might
offer individually ticketed or waybilled services.[5] The Senate's
bill would have substantially weakened the distinction between

---

[1]Section 401(e)(6) stated that: "any air carrier, other than a supplemental
air carrier, may perform charter trips (including inclusive tour charter trips) or
any other special service, without regard to the points named in its certificate,
or the type of service provided therein, under regulations prescribed by the
Board." (The underlined part was added in 1962.) 72 Stat. 755, as amended by 76
Stat. 144, 82 Stat. 867, 49 U.S.C. 1371. In 1978 "supplemental air carrier" was
changed to "charter air carrier" (92 Stat. 1719).

[2]76 Stat. 144, 49 U.S.C. 1371. Section 401(n) sets forth various supplemental carrier requirements dealing with fitness, insurance, and minimum service.
In 1978 section 401(n) was amended by 92 Stat. 1721.

[3]72 Stat. 763, as amended by 76 Stat. 145, 80 Stat. 942, 49 U.S.C. 1376.
The section withheld Federal subsidies from the supplemental operators.

[4]Order 76-1-88, p. 5.

[5]Federal Aviation Act, section 417. 76 Stat. 145, 49 U.S.C. 1387.

supplemental and scheduled carriers, and its defeat, in the Board's view, showed that Congress did not wish to see a carrier simultaneously holding both types of authority.

The Board's decision was recently reversed by a U.S. appeals court (December, 1976). This action--which in a sense anticipates the enhanced freedom the supplementals will enjoy as a result of Public Law 95-163[1]--did not mean that supplemental operators could now automatically claim route certification. What the court was saying was that, since under section 401(d)(3) and other relevant parts of the Act supplemental airlines were not specifically precluded from holding scheduled transportation rights, the Board was obligated to examine "on its merits" any supplemental's application for such rights. The court's ruling in effect indicates that the Board: (1) was confused as to the meaning of section 401(d) and the applicability of sections 401(e)(6), 401(n), and 406(b); (2) misinterpreted the role of its early policy in shaping the 1962 legislation; and (3) did not understand the legislative history of Public Law 87-528. Specifically, the court "fail[ed] to see" why World's performance of scheduled route service would lead to a "wholly anomalous result" with respect to sections 401(e)(6), 401(n), and 406(b), since

> it would not be unreasonable for Congress to deny benefits and impose requirements on supplemental air carriers operating scheduled routes, while granting benefits and waiving requirements for carriers holding only scheduled authority, if Congress felt such a distinction were required to ensure that supplemental air carriers would fully carry out their responsibilities.[2]

"The Board's pre-1962 interpretation of the Act," continued the court, provided no

> persuasive support for its reading of the 1962 amendments. It seems reasonable to suppose that a policy formulated at the time the Board was attempting to justify an exemption of supplemental carriers from the provisions of the Act would not survive the establishment of a clear statutory basis for awarding supplemental certificates. Certainly Congress did not think the prior Board policy was incorporated as such in the 1962 amendments: the express prohibition in section 401(d)(3) against acquisition of supplemental authority by a regular carrier would not have been necessary had Congress thought the Board's policy against dual certification was being carried forward by the legislation. We note, moreover, that until the instant litigation the Board had not formally determined the effect of the 1962 amendments upon its prior policy.[3]

---

[1]See below, p. 152.

[2]World Airways, Inc. v. Civil Aeronautics Board, 547 F. 2d 695, 701 (D.C. Cir. 1976).

[3]Ibid., p. 699.

The court also held that earlier Congressional actions (3, above) demonstrated concern, not for the establishment of "two mutually exclusive classes of air carriers"[1] but for the "delimit[ation of] the rights which attach to supplemental certification."[2] As the relevant documents reveal,[3] the House Committee on Interstate and Foreign Commerce rejected the Senate's bill because it contained features which were contrary to the Federal Aviation Act and which had been invalidated in United Air Lines v. Civil Aeronautics Board, (1960), above. Understandably, the Board's World Airways decision is silent on this point. The Board's "illegal" issuance (1959) of "so-called" supplemental certificates, noted the House Commerce Committee, "violated" the Act's "regulatory philosophy," particularly with respect to sections 401(d)(1), 401(d)(2),[4] and 401(e).[5] The House amendment also defined "supplemental air carrier" (formerly section 101[35]) and "supplemental air transportation" (formerly section 101[36]),[6] and limited the terms under which supplementals could engage in regular service between two points (section 417). The Committee rejected the "restrictionist philosophy" implied in the Board's ten-trip rule and reminded the agency "that a carrier's ability to provide good public service should not be hampered by artificial limits on the number of regular schedules for ticketed [and waybilled] traffic it can operate over its routes."[7]

The American Air Export and Import Co. (AAXICO) had, as we have seen, suspended common carrier service in 1959. The carrier's attempt to have its certificate renewed in the Domestic Cargo-Mail Service Case had failed and its activities were now restricted to contractual work performed for the Department of Defense. A departmental policy change, however, threw into jeopardy the continued existence of the company, for under the new ruling carriers deriving less than thirty percent of their revenues from commercial sources were declared ineligible for future military contracts. Under these circumstances AAXICO had little choice but to merge with another

---

[1]Ibid., p. 703.

[2]Ibid., p. 702.

[3]Senate Report no. 688, 87th Cong., 1st sess., (1961); House Report no. 1177, 87th Cong., 1st sess., (1961); House Report no. 1950, 87 Cong., 2d sess., (1962).

[4]See above, p. 28, note 1.

[5]See above, p. 25, note 4.

[6]See above, p. 26, note 4.

[7]House Report no. 1177, 87 Cong., 1st sess., (1961), p. 12.

carrier and this it did in 1965.[1] The other party was Saturn Airways (a Florida-based company specializing in transatlantic charter service), which welcomed the merger since it provided the necessary capital for the purchase of jet aircraft. In authorizing the merger under section 408 of the Federal Aviation Act the CAB noted that the operations of the two carriers complemented one another and that the newly formed company presented no monopolistic threat to other airlines.[2]

The examiner's apprehension regarding excess freight capacity on the transcontinental East-West route[3] was borne out when the 1965 Slick Airways requested that it be allowed to suspend common carrier service. Operating losses from this service had reached an alarming $10,000 per day, endangering all areas of the corporation's business activities including those of a nonaeronautical nature.[4] In its appeal to the Board the carrier urged that a comprehensive examination of all air freight services be undertaken immediately. It requested that all-cargo operators be authorized to carry passengers and called on the agency to reintroduce the minimum rate floor, realign all-cargo routes "to equalize competitive advantages," and investigate the combination airlines' freight costs.[5] Suspension of its scheduled services would, according to Slick Airways' president, "give Slick a period of relief pending development and introduction of the regulatory measures necessary to correct the present unequal

---

[1]Saturn-AAXICO Merger Case, 43 CAB 150 (1965).

[2]Section 408 provided, inter alia, that it was unlawful without the Board's consent "for two or more air carriers, or for any air carrier and any other common carrier . . . to consolidate or merge their properties, or any part thereof, into one person for the ownership, management, or operation of the properties theretofore in separate ownerships." 72 Stat. 767, 49 U.S.C. 1378 (in 1978 section 408 was amended by 92 Stat. 1726). Similarly, interlocking directorates (section 409) and intercarrier agreements regarding equipment, rates, safety, schedules, etc. (section 412), had to have the Board's approval before they could come into force. Favorable Board action in the aforementioned areas automatically conferred antitrust immunity on the parties in question, shielding them from the antitrust standards normally applied to U.S. industry as a whole. (The Board, for instance, examining a pooling arrangement, was free to conclude that emphasis should be placed on section 102 public interest factors other than competition, enabling it, in effect, to approve the arrangement despite its potentially anticompetitive character.) Recently enacted deregulation legislation (chapter III) has essentially stripped the agency of its traditional antitrust authority.

[3]See above, p. 20.

[4]"Slick, Losing $10,000 Daily, Asks that CAB Expedite Service Discontinuance Plea," Traffic World 123, no. 7 (1965):62.

[5]These, it was alleged, were being subsidized by passenger services.

competitive situation with the combination passenger carriers."[1]
The carrier did not name a date on which its operations were to be
resumed and, indeed, indicated that a resumption would not be feasible unless the economics of its common carrier service were funda-
mentally transformed. In alluding to this point the Board observed
that "operating rights are granted not as mere contingencies awaiting favorable circumstances, but for the present use."[2] It authorized a 90-day suspension and cautioned that a request for an
extension would have to be supported by specific details pertaining
to the resumption of scheduled operations. The corporation, of
course, retained the freedom to adopt another course of action,
namely the total abandonment (with Board approval) of common carrier
service.

The CAB declined to accede to Slick Airways' request for a
broadly-based freight investigation. In this, needless to say, it
had the enthusiastic support of the combination airlines. These
had taken no position on the suspension itself but asserted that
there existed no need for the type of proceeding suggested and that
the company's problems were attributable to its "lack of skill and
foresight" and in no way reflected "wider regulatory neglect or
industry injustice."[3]

In 1968 the CAB authorized the acquisition by Airlift International of Slick Airways' common carrier certificate. The latter
had been unable to reinstitute scheduled service, having been
compelled towards the end of the initial 90-day suspension period
to seek a further suspension period in order to "regain its strength
and fully plan its future."[4] To this the agency had agreed and,
following the two carriers' joint approach in regard to the certificate's transfer, ordered the suspension continued[5] pending final
disposition of the case.

The first phase in the dismantling of Slick's air transport
business consisted of the sale of aircraft to Airlift International
for use in Military Airlift Command operations. The sale of this
equipment was not directly linked to the question of the certificate's transfer (for which evidentiary hearings were required) and

---

[1]"Slick Airways Asks Over-All Investigation of Profitless Growth Pattern
in Air Cargo," Traffic World 123, no. 5 (1965):62.

[2]Slick Corporation, Suspension of Service, 43 CAB 742, 743 (1965).

[3]Ibid.

[4]"Slick Airways Would Extend Suspension of Services," Traffic World 124,
no. 10 (1965):68.

[5]Order E-24234.

aroused little concern on the part of the other airlines.[1] In order
to expedite matters (time was of the essence since Airlift International needed Slick's equipment in order to assume the latter's
military contract obligations at the beginning of the new fiscal
year), the CAB exempted the carriers from the section 408 provisions[2]
of the Federal Aviation Act, enforcement of which, by placing an
"undue burden" on the applicants, was considered not to be in the
public interest.

Favored by the examiner,[3] Airlift International's ownership of
the certificate was strongly opposed by American Airlines, Braniff
Airways, the Flying Tiger Line, and Trans World Airlines, which, in
briefs to the Board, petitioned for review of the matter. The intervenors' basic argument was that no need had been demonstrated for
additional freight service over the "dormant" route and that existing services (especially since the introduction of all-cargo jet
aircraft) were sufficient to satisfy projected market demands. The
Board, however, having granted the petitions for discretionary review, remained firm in its support of the examiner's findings. It
dismissed the objections of the petitioners, pointing out that,
though it was true that freight capacity stood at an all-time peak,
it was equally true that the amount of freight carried was now
greater than ever before. The agency, in any case, took a long-term
view of the situation. It considered the certificates's demise
undesirable and believed that through its transfer a stronger Airlift International[4] could help--using the now familiar argument--"to
develop and realize the potentially vast air freight market."[5]

What the intervenors were saying was that only through a showing of public convenience and necessity could transfer of the certificate be contemplated. In its rebuttal the CAB noted that the
initial grant of the certificate had met the public interest criteria and that such a test was not required a second time. It ruled

---

[1]The exception was National Airlines, which objected to the transaction
since it felt this would influence the outcome of the related route transfer case.

[2]See above, p. 32, note 2.

[3]"Transfer of Slick Airways' Cargo Route to Airlift Is Approved by CAB
Examiner," Traffic World 132, no. 7 (1967):154-155.

[4]Airlift International's financial predicament was another factor behind
the Board's decision. Airlift's original North-South route consisted of relatively short hauls, which had been termed a "financially marginal operation." Integration of this route with Slick's East-West network would, it was hoped, lead to
more efficient and profitable service.

[5]Airlift-Slick Route Transfer, Order E-26810, pp. 6-7.

that transfer of an operator's certificate was subject only to the parameters imposed by sections 401(h)[1] and 408 of the Federal Aviation Act and stated that the intervenors had failed to show that the transfer was adverse to the public interest. The Flying Tiger Line's fear of losing considerable traffic to an enlarged Airlift International was regarded as unrealistic.

It was not until 1973 that Airlift International's domestic certificates were renewed on a permanent basis. Despite hopes that its expanded operating authority would lead to greater profitability, the carrier had continued to be financially troubled after acquiring Slick's certificate and, indeed, had found it necessary on several occasions to halt service temporarily at various cities. These difficulties, the Board felt, would be overcome. It believed that permanent certification had been "earned" (an expression employed earlier in connection with the award of permanent certificates to the Flying Tiger Line and Slick Airways) and that the company's new status would facilitate corporate planning and ease problems bearing on future financing.[2] At the same time, Airlift International's route network was consolidated, thereby eliminating a number of mandatory stops at segment junction points. This was done to reduce unprofitable services and enhance operational flexibility. Points for which service had been temporarily suspended were included in the renewed certificates. An exception was St. Thomas in the Virgin Islands, which, as a terminal point, was to become the subject of a further investigation to determine when profitable operations might be resumed there.

Revocation of the minimum rate order in 1961 precipitated another rate war between the combination and all-cargo carriers. Numerous new tariffs were filed, many of which were suspended by the Board. In addition, most of the "deferred" rates were canceled as a result of new rate reductions now coming into force. With the continuing downward trend in rates the position of the all-cargo operators steadily deteriorated and towards the end of 1963 they requested the Board's aid,[3] citing the overcapacity created by their

---

[1] Section 401(h) stipulates that "no certificate may be transferred unless such transfer is approved by the Board as being consistent with the public interest." 72 Stat 756, 49 U.S.C. 1371.

[2] Airlift International, Inc.--Renewal and Amendment of Certificates, Order 73-3-59, p. 5. For reasons with which the reader will now be familiar, the Board's action was sharply criticized by several combination carriers.

[3] "All-Cargo Air Carriers Ask CAB To Ease Competition from Trunks," Aviation Week and Space Technology 79, no. 12 (1963):51.

trunkline competitors[1] and the ability of these to offset losses from freight operations with revenues from their principal source of income, passenger service.[2]

The Board's solution, which came in 1964 in the form of "blocked" space service, did nothing to arrest the problems of the petitioners and served only to provoke a further confrontation between the two carrier groups. Basically, "blocked" space service, which only the all-cargo operators could sell, allowed a specified volume of aircraft space to be reserved or "blocked" at wholesale rates for periods of not less than sixty days.[3] In denying the combination airlines the right to offer the service the Board hoped that (1) the financial position of the all-cargo carriers would be improved and (2) large-volume shipments would be more readily diverted from surface to air transportation through the formal designation of all-cargo carriers as bulk freight specialists.

Virtually all interest groups, including ultimately those for whom it was designed, were critical of the "blocked" space arrangement. For example, the Air Freight Forwarders Association objected on the ground that it failed to differentiate between its members and the combination carriers,[4] and a number of chambers of commerce were fearful that shippers in cities without all-cargo service would not be able to compete with those to whom that service was available. The strongest opposition, however, came from the combination airlines, which denounced the Board's action as "arbitrary and unreasonable" and called into question its legality (it was contended that the Board had not given opponents of its policy time to make written submissions and that it lacked the statutory authority to

---

[1]The combination airlines were putting all-cargo jet aircraft into service at about this time. For example, see "American Cargo Jet Starts Daily Flights," Aviation Week and Space Technology 80, no. 2 (1964):36. Another innovation during this period was the "quick-change" jet, which, in a matter of hours, could be converted from a passenger to an all-cargo configuration.

[2]Referring to the difficulties of the all-cargo carriers in a speech at the Fourth Annual Eastern Regional Air Cargo Seminar, CAB Chairman Alan S. Boyd said, "I am seriously concerned about a situation in which carriers with superior credit, gained largely from the relatively lucrative passenger business, use that credit access to purchase equipment for all-cargo use which can, if need be at little expense, be turned into passenger service to offset losses incurred in cargo services. This is a vicious circle. It is not my idea of fair competition. It quite obviously makes it impossible for the all-cargo carriers to compete in these circumstances." "Where Do We Go from Here?" Air Transportation 44, no. 3 (1964): 40.

[3]During the time span involved the service had to be used on a regular basis.

[4]"AFFA on Blocked Space," Air Transportation 45, no. 4 (1964): 39-41.

approve the new service without first holding adjudicatory hearings).[1]
Claiming that the "blocked" rate order made it impossible for them
to compete on equal terms with the all-cargo operators, American
Airlines, Trans World Airlines, and United Airlines filed petitions
for review with the U.S. Court of Appeals for the District of
Columbia Circuit. The court, however, sustained the Board's order,
having found that the plaintiffs had not been deprived of their
procedural rights[2] and that their business losses, where attributable to the Board's action, were minimal.[3] An appeal to the Supreme
Court to overturn this decision was unsuccessful.[4]

In protesting their inability to offer "blocked" rates the
combination airlines had accused the CAB of doing violence to (in
their view) one of the fundamental principles governing the exercise
of its powers. The principle at issue was that the Board, charged
with the promotion of air transportation as a whole, could not show
any bias towards a particular carrier class. The agency, of course,
had seen nothing arbitrary or improper in the new rates or in the
manner in which they had been adopted and responded by noting that
decisions frequently had to be made which, while seemingly favoring
one class of carrier, ultimately were of benefit to the entire
industry.[5] Unequal treatment of the two carrier groups was considered to be in harmony with actions previously taken and reflected
the Board's mandate as defined by Act of Congress.[6]

---

[1]The CAB was empowered "after notice and hearings [to] alter, amend,
modify, or suspend" an operator's certificate. Federal Aviation Act, section
401(g). 72 Stat. 756, 49 U.S.C. 1371.

[2]The applicability of section 416(a) of the Federal Aviation Act ruled
out the need for an adjudicatory proceeding. See above, p. 23, note 1.

[3]American Airlines, Inc. v. Civil Aeronautics Board, 359 F. 2d 624 (D.C.
Cir. 1966). While upholding the ban on combination carrier participation in
"blocked" space service, the court noted at page 633: "to avoid any possible mis-
apprehension, our affirmance of the Board's action is without prejudice to the
right of the combination carriers to reopen the question of their exclusion upon
a showing that the Board's assumptions could not reasonably continue to be maintained in the light of actual experience, that their overall cargo business was
significantly impaired, or that the air freight market had sufficiently expanded
so that the promotion of the air cargo industry through blocked space reduced
rates would not be imperiled by their participation."

[4]American Airlines, Inc. v. Civil Aeronautics Board, 385 U.S. 843 (1966).

[5]Greater specialization, the CAB seemed to feel, was in the interests of
the industry as a whole. Restricting bulk shipments to the all-cargo carriers
would make the combination airlines small-volume specialists, "and the ultimate
result may be increased revenues for both combination and all-cargo carriers."
Blocked Space Service, 41 CAB 774, 775 (1964).

[6]See above, p. 23, note 1.

Slick Airways had been the first carrier to file a "blocked"
space tariff. Similar tariffs, described by the combination airlines as purely "defensive" in nature, were then submitted by
American Airlines, Trans World Airlines, and United Airlines but
were rejected since they ran counter to Board policy. A later
filing by Continental Airlines, also characterized as "defensive,"
was similarly rejected even though the carrier was able to document
that this would lead to monthly losses of at least $15,000.[1] The
issuance of further "blocked" space tariffs by the all-cargo operators proved to be a continuing source of friction not only between
the two classes of carriers but among the all-cargo operators themselves. To give but one example, a Flying Tiger Line tariff which
was to come into effect in December of 1964 was assailed by Slick
Airways as well as by several trunklines, all of them pressing the
CAB for its repeal. Slick took the position that the tariff, by not
excluding small-shipment service (shipments under 200 pounds), was
not in accord with the program's objectives.[2] The other critics
asserted that the tariff was not legal since they were barred from
making a similar filing, that its rate levels were "unjustly discriminatory," and that if it were upheld they would be deprived of
a substantial volume of business.[3]

Viewed in terms of its objectives, the "blocked" space experiment was essentially a failure. It had not produced a more vigorous all-cargo carrier class and, in a broader sense, had clearly
been unable to appreciably strengthen air transportation as a whole.
The CAB conceded this in 1967 and, noting that there were now fewer
all-cargo carriers in operation, suggested that it would be in the
industry's interests if combination airlines, too, offered "blocked"
space service.[4] At this point, however, only one "blocked" space
tariff was still in effect and, when this too was withdrawn, the

---

[1]"Blocked-Space Rates Denied Despite Likelihood that CAL Will Lose Shipper's Traffic," Traffic World 125, no. 4 (1966):80.

[2]"All-Cargo Airlines Feuding Over Small Shipment Role in 'Blocked-Space'
Service," Traffic World 120, no. 7 (1964):64.

[3]"Suspension of FTL Tariff on 'Blocked-Space' Sought by United, American,
TWA," Traffic World 120, no. 8 (1964):77.

[4]"It now appears," said the CAB, "that the policy of confining blocked-
space service exclusively to the all-cargo carriers may be impeding rather than
promoting the blocked-space experiment as initially contemplated. "CAB Acts To
Ease Rules on Blocked-Space Service and Off-Route Charters," Traffic World 132,
no. 5 (1967):20. The Flying Tiger Line's conclusion in 1965 that the service
had "proved of little value" had been viewed by the Board as "premature." Domestic
Minimum Air Freight Rates, 43 CAB 800, 803 (1965).

Board's investigation of such tariffs, initiated more than four years earlier, was terminated.[1]

Although the CAB had rejected a request in 1965 for the restoration of the minimum rate floor in domestic air transportation,[2] it had under advisement at the time a case which involved minimum rates in a more restricted context. The proceeding in question,[3] in which tariffs between New York, Newark, Washington, Baltimore, and Philadelphia, on the one hand, and points in Puerto Rico, on the other, were examined, had arisen because of destructive competition in those markets. The initial phase of the investigation had been conducted by a CAB examiner, and, following his recommendations, which included imposition of minimum general commodity rates, a number of carriers (these included Airlift International, Eastern Air Lines, Pan American World Airways, and Trans Caribbean Airways) petitioned the Board for a review of the findings.[4] The agency agreed to the proposed review but its conclusions turned out to be basically those of the examiner for it too supported the use of minimum rates as a means of ending the rate war over northeastern U.S.-Puerto Rico routes. However, whereas the examiner, in calculating the minimum rates, had relied solely on cost figures pertaining to Airlift International, the CAB, producing its own set of data, also took into consideration costs incurred by Airlift's competitors.[5] The examiners approach, which was a duplication of the methodology applied in the Air Freight Rate Investigation, above, was found to be too narrow and generally inapplicable to the changed circumstances. Airlift International was the only carrier utilizing piston aircraft on the New York-San Juan route (the others were combination airlines using turbojets), so that undue emphasis on its relatively uneconomical equipment would have resulted in inordinately high rate levels. These would have had a negative impact on the market's traffic volume and would have clashed with the Board's duty to relate rate levels to "the lowest cost consistent with the furnishing of [the]

---

[1] Blocked Space Air Freight Tariffs, Order 68-12-118. The service had been used primarily by forwarders. From the shipping public's standpoint, its major drawback was that space requirements had to be determined ahead of time.

[2] The request originated with the Flying Tiger Line. The basis for its rejection was that the Board did not believe that a general rate war was then in progress.

[3] New York-San Juan Cargo Rates Investigation, Order E-23431.

[4] "Review Planned for Rulings in New York-San Juan Case, Traffic World 123, no. 2 (1965):59-60.

[5] The Board's figures were based on a load factor of 70 percent and included a 7 percent return on investment.

service" in question.[1] The agency was anxious to set aside the minimum rate order as quickly as possible and considered a seven-month
period sufficiently long for the market to stabilize. The carriers,
on the other hand, believed that such a period would be too short
and at their behest it was extended indefinitely.[2]

In the latter part of 1977 Congress revised the Board's traditional regulatory functions with respect to all-cargo service (chapter III). Prior to this, its mandate (as well as the underlying
section 102 policy objectives) had been the same for combination
(i.e., passenger-cargo) and all-cargo service, and it may be wondered whether the Board had the authority to differentiate between
the restrictions it placed on an airline's combination and all-cargo
flights in any given market. The matter arose formally in connection with the Detroit-California Nonstop Service Investigation,[3] in
which three combination carriers, American Airlines, Trans World
Airlines, and United Airlines sought certificate amendments permitting nonstop turnabout service between Detroit, on the one hand, and
Los Angeles and San Francisco-Oakland, on the other. For reasons
which need not detain us, the amendments which applied to combination aircraft were approved. The carriers, however, were claiming
the additional right to operate all-cargo aircraft over the same
routes and under the same conditions, citing section 401(e)(4) of
the Federal Aviation Act to support their contention that the CAB
was powerless to prevent management from changing equipment if this
was dictated by market conditions. Section 401(e)(4) states that

> no term, condition, or limitation of a certificate shall restrict the
> right of an air carrier to add to or change schedules, equipment, . . .
> and facilities for performing the authorized transportation and service
> as the development of the business and the demands of the public shall
> require[4]

and, while the Board had no quarrel with the wording of the Act, it
stipulated that resolution of the matter would have to await a determination of whether all-cargo service was warranted[5] and whether
it was "a qualitatively different type of service" than that which

---

[1]See above, p. 10.

[2]New York-San Juan Cargo Rates Investigation, 44 CAB 599 (1966).

[3]43 CAB 557 (1966).

[4]See above, p. 25, note 4.

[5]The Flying Tiger Line and American Airlines were already providing all-
cargo service, so the reference here was actually to additional all-cargo flights.

the carriers were providing with their combination aircraft.[1]

The examiner's investigation of the Detroit-California air freight market led him to conclude that the requested all-cargo non-stop service was consistent with the public interest and should be authorized.[2] The market's existing level of business activity (Detroit, Los Angeles, and San Francisco were among the nation's ten leading generators of air freight) and growth potential were thought to be sufficiently strong to support the type of service under consideration. Furthermore, the routes concerned did not constitute the major freight market of any of the applicants, and it did not appear likely that they would become the focus for another bitter rate war. The diversionary impact of the new service on the Flying Tiger Line was termed "nonexistent or minimal."[3] The examiner expressed considerable dissatisfaction with the superficial manner in which the Flying Tiger Line had computed financial losses attributable to additional all-cargo flights and reminded the company that it could best meet new competition by improving its existing services.

The examiner also found that no significant qualitative differences existed between the freight services a company provided with its combination equipment, as opposed to all-cargo aircraft, and that, accordingly, the Board could not maintain restrictive distinctions (in a given market) between these two services. Asked to comment on the relative merits of combination and all-cargo services, REA Express, the airlines' single largest customer, saw no product differentiation but nonetheless supported the lifting of restrictions on all-cargo operations in order to enlarge its own flexibility. This position was generally reflected in the remarks of other users

---

[1]Detroit-California Nonstop Service Investigation, p. 561.
Unrestricted all-cargo authorizations were opposed by the CAB's Bureau of Economic Regulation, which claimed that a precedent existed under which the agency could, in fact, specify the type of aircraft to be used. This opinion was based on the Los Angeles Airways Renewal Case, in which an applicant was permitted to continue an airport-feeder service in the Los Angeles area with the proviso that only helicopters be employed. The Bureau erred in believing that this was a valid precedent, for the helicopter, the only type of aircraft capable of performing the service being authorized, was specified only inasmuch as it formed part of the CAB's definition of that service. Los Angeles Airways Renewal Case, 27 CAB 36, 39-40 (1958).

[2]The Board's acceptance of the examiner's conclusion that the public convenience and necessity justified additional all-cargo service eliminated the need for a formal statement on his other findings. Reopened Detroit-California Nonstop Service Investigation, 47 CAB 201 (1967).

[3]Reopened Detroit-California Nonstop Service Investigation, (initial decision of the examiner), Order E-25462, p. 37.

of freight service. Those showing a marked preference for all-cargo equipment cited size/weight considerations[1] and the ability to make greater use of containerization.

The Board's continuing concern for the competitive position of the all-cargo operators manifested itself in several investigations conducted during the late 1960s. In one of these[2] this concern focused on Seaboard World Airlines, an all-cargo international carrier operating between the northeastern United States (Baltimore, Boston, Philadelphia, and New York[3]) and a number of countries in Western Europe. Although 45 percent of the total traffic moving over the North Atlantic (1966) in U.S. all-cargo aircraft was carried by Seaboard, more than 60 percent of the carrier's revenues originated through charter work for the Department of Defense. Such a high degree of dependence on fluctuating military requirements was considered undesirable, especially in view of other difficulties facing the company. These included substantial competition from U.S. and foreign airlines on the North Atlantic route and the ability of its competitors to provide services linking interior U.S. cities with Western Europe. Seaboard's financial base, it was reasoned, would be stabilized if the carrier were authorized to originate/terminate transatlantic flights in cities other than the four shown above, and one of the Board's examiners was instructed to determine whether an amended certificate should name Atlanta, Chicago, Cleveland, Dallas, Detroit, Los Angeles, Minneapolis, San Francisco, and Washington D.C. as additional domestic coterminal points.[4]

---

[1]Shipments which by virtue of their size or weight could not be carried in combination aircraft accounted for well under ten percent of the traffic in the Detroit-California market. Similarly, shipments (such as certain corrosive or radioactive materials) having other properties which precluded their conveyance in passenger aircraft accounted for only a fraction of one per cent of the traffic

[2]Domestic Coterminal Points--Europe All-Cargo Service Investigation, Order E-25122. The issue here was whether new all-cargo service between various cities in the United States and Western Europe was in the public interest.

[3]New York served as the exit point for traffic originating in the other cities.

[4]Only those cities producing more than 1.5 percent of total domestic freight and express originations were eligible for inclusion in the proceeding. Seattle and Oakland were added to the list of possible coterminal points at a later date. The applications of other municipalities wishing to be part of the investigation were rejected, since their low freight generating capacity would only have resulted in an unnecessary prolongation of the case.
Petitions for reconsideration and modification filed by several other airlines were denied. Pan American World Airways, for example, which sought unsuccessfully to introduce service on some of Seaboard's new routes, stated that section 401(e)(4) of the Federal Aviation Act (see above, p. 40) did not invest the Board with authority to exclude combination aircraft from the freight operations

Seaboard's modified operating certificate, approved in 1969,
contained the following additional coterminal points: Chicago,
Cleveland, Detroit, Los Angeles, San Francisco-Oakland, and Washington, D.C.-Baltimore. The cities omitted accounted for less than
four percent of transatlantic traffic, a figure considered too low
to justify regularly scheduled all-cargo service. Authorization to
serve these relatively minor air freight centers would not have been
in the interests of Seaboard, as it would have forced that carrier
to divert some of its financial resources and organizational efforts
from more lucrative routes. Cleveland, if measured solely in terms
of its freight generating capacity, should also have been omitted,
but here an exception was made on the ground that the city's location permitted easy integration into the carrier's route network.

Citing a need to decrease its dependence on military charter
service and hoping to make its operations more profitable, Seaboard
World Airlines had requested authorization to carry freight domestically, that is, between its U.S. coterminal points. The examiner
refused to support this request since the scope of the company's
existing scheduled operations indicated that it was able to survive
in the event of the loss of its charter work. The Board, however,
overruled the examiner and, with the exception of New York, granted
Seaboard interstate "filler" rights, provided such domestic operations were restricted to flights originating or terminating in
Europe. It was hoped that "filler" rights would make the company
more competitive with other carriers and that the denial of domestic
authority at New York would encourage it to accelerate the development of services and facilities at other gateway cities.[1]

The Flying Tiger Line's 1967 application for an expansion of
its domestic route network led to the institution of another proceeding involving only all-cargo service. Wishing to add twelve
cities[2] to its route authority, the applicant, at this time the only
transcontinental all-cargo operator, felt that a number of recent

___

under review. Refusing to be drawn into a discussion of section 401(e)(4), the
Board replied that it possessed the power to define pretrial restrictions pertaining to any proceeding and that the parties in question were required to conform to the restrictions adopted.

[1] Domestic Coterminal Points--Europe All-Cargo Investigation, Order 69-4-140.

[2] Atlanta, Baltimore, Charlotte, Indianapolis, Minneapolis, Nashville,
Norfolk, Oklahoma City, St. Louis, St. Paul, Syracuse, and Washington, D.C.
Application of the Flying Tiger Line, Inc., Order E-25910. A number of other
communities seeking all-cargo service subsequently received the Board's permission to participate in the proceeding.

developments justified such a proceeding. These developments included: (1) the rapid growth in freight volume during the early
1960s; (2) a three-fold increase in the number of points included
in Defense Department contracts, as opposed to a mere 50 percent
rise in the number of airport cities receiving all-cargo service;
(3) the difference in freight rates between markets with and without all-cargo service (rates in the latter were approximately 40
percent higher); and (4) the improving financial position of the
all-cargo carriers. At the same time, the Board was called upon to
act with all possible speed so as to enable the applicant to meet
the challenge arising from anticipated favorable agency decisions
in pending combination carrier proceedings.

In view of the fact that many years had passed since the conclusion of the last comprehensive all-cargo investigation, the Board
agreed to open a new enquiry but stated that this would be limited
in scope and would not, for example, include an assessment of competition on the Flying Tiger Line's existing routes. At issue were
to be only the markets for which the Flying Tiger Line had requested
new operating rights as well as those other cities which had asked
to be included in the case.

A number of trunklines took exception to the Flying Tiger
Line's application, pointing out, inter alia, that no need had been
shown to exist for its proposed services. These intervenors were at
this time themselves pressing for new route authority in other proceedings (covering both combination and all-cargo flights) and,
since some of the cities involved also appeared in Flying Tiger's
application, they urged their deletion from that application so as
to be spared the costs of duplicating their route requests. The
Board concurred that prosecution of the same route requests in parallel cases was needlessly wasteful but chose instead to remove all-
cargo services from the other proceedings, consolidating them with
the Flying Tiger Line's application to form a single all-cargo investigation.

The final decision in the case was made known in November of
1971 and denied the Flying Tiger Line its hoped-for route expansion
with the exception of Syracuse, which became an intermediate point
on its network. Basically, the action was taken in the light of the
decreasing growth rate now characterizing the air freight industry.
Large losses were again being sustained by freight services, and,
though the Board continued to express confidence in the future of
the all-cargo operators, it conceded that no major upturn could be
expected "within the immediate future."[1] The investigation had

---

[1] The Flying Tiger Line, Inc. Additional Points Case, Order 71-11-33, p. 1

revealed that those points which the Flying Tiger Line wished to add
to its network were already receiving ample freight service from the
combination airlines and that an all-cargo operator could not, under
prevailing conditions, engage in profitable operations there. Thus,
the argument which had frequently been used in the past, namely that
all-cargo operators would be strengthened through an enlargement of
their route network, was no longer applicable. Similarly, the civic
parties which had asked to be included in the investigation learned
that their requests for all-cargo service had been rejected. In all
cases the freight potential at these cities was such that their integration into the all-cargo route network appeared not to be justified. The Board's attitude towards the combination airlines[1] seeking more extensive all-cargo rights was more positive. These
requests were approved, and, while this may appear to contradict what
has been said above, it has to be remembered that the combination
carriers' overwhelming dependence on passenger revenues made it easy
for the agency to show some indifference towards the profitability
of their additional all-cargo services.

The aforementioned cases have dealt primarily with the domestic situation. In order to arrive at a more complete understanding
of the CAB's role in the field of freight traffic regulation, however, we shall now turn our attention to two proceedings illustrating differing facets of that role with respect to international
transportation. The first of these, the Transpacific Route Investigation, is of particular interest here because it demonstrates how
the Board's international decisions, which, unlike their domestic
counterparts must receive the approval of the President before they
may be effectuated,[2] have been subject to the vicissitudes of the
political process. The investigation,[3] one of the largest ever to
come before the Board, involved the application of eighteen airlines
to provide service between twenty-five U.S. metropolitan areas and

---

[1]American Airlines, Eastern Air Lines, Northwest Airlines, United Airlines,
and Western Air Lines.

[2]Section 801(a) of the Federal Aviation Act provided, in part, that "the
issuance, denial, transfer, amendment, cancellation, suspension, or revocation of,
and the terms, conditions, and limitations contained in, any certificate authorizing an air carrier to engage in overseas or foreign air transportation, or air
transportation between places in the same Territory or possession, . . . shall be
subject to the approval of the President." 72 Stat. 782, as amended by 86 Stat.
96, 49 U.S.C. 1461. In 1978 section 801(a) was amended by 92 Stat. 1740. (See
Appendix.)

[3]The investigation was divided into a domestic and an international phase.
Only the latter is considered here.

points in the Pacific and the Far East.[1] The applicants included
ten of the eleven domestic trunk carriers as well as the three
scheduled all-cargo operators, Airlift International, the Flying
Tiger Line, and Seaboard World Airlines. Inclusion in the proceeding of the all-cargo operators was ensured through the Defense
Department's strong interest in additional transpacific freight
capacity.

Predictably, the combination airlines argued that, since
Pacific aviation had been pioneered by them and since the capacity
they provided sufficed to meet the needs of U.S.-Far East commerce,
the participation of the all-cargo carriers in the proceeding
was unwarranted. The all-cargo carriers' reply to this was that:
(1) the Pacific market's growth rate (a nine-fold increase in
freight tonnage was projected for the period 1965-1970), one of the
highest in the world, indicated that all-cargo route authorizations
were justified; (2) the combination airlines had been negligent in
developing the freight market, as their principal interest lay in
passengers; all-cargo operators would provide much-needed competition; (3) passenger equipment was unsuitable for a substantial proportion of the traffic; and (4) all-cargo carriers would introduce
lower rates.

Willingness to offer sharp rate reductions was viewed by the
all-cargo operators as one of their most powerful weapons in the
struggle against the combination airlines. In exhibits submitted
to the Board it was shown that rates in the North Atlantic market
were on average about 50 percent below transpacific rates, a difference that was attributed largely to the existence of a transatlantic all-cargo carrier. An assurance of Pacific rate reductions
of as much as 55 percent was forthcoming from the president of the
Flying Tiger Line (in the event of his company winning acceptance of
its route proposal) which, he stated, would be put "into effect, one
way or another, and irrespective of the attitudes of the other carriers."[2]

The all-cargo operators, it should be noted, were pointing the
rate weapon not only towards the combination airlines but also at
each other. Airlift International announced that it would undercut

---

[1]Pan American World Airways and Northwest Airlines were the only U.S.
carriers offering scheduled transpacific service (i.e., service to points beyond
Hawaii) at this time.

[2]"3 All-Cargo Carriers Aim at Major Market in Pacific Case," Aviation Week
and Space Technology 86, no. 24 (1967):59. The speaker failed to point out that
the company, acting unilaterally, was not in a position to put new rates into
effect (see below, pp. 54-55).

Flying Tiger's reduction by five percent and, in an effort to further differentiate its proposed service from those of the other all-cargo applicants, made reference to various "blocked" space rates it would put into effect. Airlift was at this time engaged in negotiations regarding acquisition of Slick Airways' transcontinental (East-West) certificate and considered the Pacific route a logical extension of this (anticipated) operating authority. Hoping thereby to lend weight to its application, it told the CAB that integration of an international route with its domestic network would make it more competitive with the Flying Tiger Line. That company, on the other hand, based its application in part on the practical experience it had gained in Asia and the Pacific as a contract carrier.[1] Its existing base facilities in the region would enable it (unlike its competitors) to avoid major base-related expenditures and permit it to place greater emphasis on the development of other aspects of its operations. Seaboard World Airlines, the third all-cargo operator, found the rate proposals of the Flying Tiger Line and Airlift International "unrealistic" and was unable to match them but claimed to be more qualified than the other two on account of being an international common carrier. Seaboard alone, it was asserted, had the necessary background for the successful establishment of scheduled transpacific service.

Although the all-cargo operators had briefly entertained the hope that Board action would result in certification for more than one of them, only the Flying Tiger Line's application was successful. Traffic forecasts ruled out service by more than one all-cargo airline, which in any case would be facing strong competition from the combination carriers. The countries included in Flying Tiger's certificate were: Japan,[2] South Korea, Taiwan, Hong Kong, The Philippines, South Viet-Nam, and Thailand. The new all-cargo route to Asia was via Alaska; authority to fly between the U.S. mainland and Hawaii, Guam, and points beyond was withheld, as this route would then have been burdened by an overabundance of freight capacity.[3]

Essentially, some of the contentions of the all-cargo operators were affirmed by the examiner and accepted by the Board. The

---

[1]This included extensive work for the Department of Defense. For instance, during the 1952 fiscal year the carrier transported about 20,000 personnel and eight million pounds of freight as part of the Korean War effort. Transpacific Route Case, 32 CAB 928,1107 (1961).

[2]Japan accounted for over sixty percent of U.S.-Far East air freight tonnage. Okinawa, then not constitutionally part of Japan, was named separately.

[3]Transpacific Route Investigation, Order 68-12-105, p. 29.

examiner considered the market's freight potential to be "vast" and believed an all-cargo carrier could aid in its continuing development. (In this context all-cargo service was seen to be contributing to a favorable U.S. balance of payments.) Preference for the Flying Tiger Line rested in part on its financial fitness, its relatively strong domestic operations, and the choice of countries it proposed to serve. It is difficult to assess the precise role played by military considerations; that it was considerable cannot be in doubt. The United States during this period was deeply involved in the Viet-Nam War, and, while the Department of Defense wa not officially sponsoring a particular company, it had a well-defin interest in the growth of a carrier with which it had enjoyed a lon and close working relationship. In any event, the examiner recognized the Department's need for "expanded and strengthened commercial airlift capability, particularly cargo capability"[1] and took note of the Flying Tiger Line's "superior claim on the basis of historical participation and interest in commercial cargo development in the Pacific."[2]

The Pacific freight rights of the combination airlines were treated as an integral part of their passenger applications. Two of these carriers (Northwest Airlines and Pan American) already hel transpacific authority and were thus concerned with its enlargement while attempting to exclude new entrants from the market. Potentia entrants, on the other hand, drew the Board's attention to the need for additional flights, pointing to alleged shortcomings in the ser vice supplied by the incumbents. Eastern Air Lines charged Pan American with failure to develop its South Pacific route and was critical of its equipment; American Airlines asserted that with a load factor of about seventy percent[3] on its Central Pacific route Pan American was clearly in need of the "spur of U.S. flag competition." Little is to be gained from a recapitulation of all the arguments and counterarguments; suffice it to say here that the Board approved transpacific certification for three new carriers (America Airlines, Continental Airlines, and Trans World Airlines),[4] expande

---

[1]"Transpacific Routes and the Transpacific Shipper," Air Transportation 5 no. 5 (1968):22. The link between all-cargo service and the nation's defense posture was stressed in a subsequent transportation report approved by the White House. "International Air Transportation Policy," Weekly Compilation of Presidential Documents 6, no. 26 (1970):805.

[2]"Flying Tiger Is Logical Choice To Operate Pacific All-Cargo Runs, Says CAB Examiner," Traffic World 134, no. 3 (1968):76.

[3]Pan American's load factor on the transatlantic route, where competition was intense, was 55 percent.

[4]Braniff Airways was given route authority linking Hawaii with the mainla

the rights of the two incumbent carriers,[1] and transmitted its findings, together with the Flying Tiger Line decision, to the President
for ratification.

In his reply to the Board, President Johnson admitted to "serious reservations" regarding the advisability of authorizing scheduled Pacific service for an all-cargo carrier, approving the Board's
recommendation only in view of the fact that the Flying Tiger Line's
operations would not be subsidized by the government and were to be
reviewed after an experimental five-year period. With respect to
the combination airlines generally the President said: "the addition
of new carriers and the extension of service is consistent with our
longstanding policy of encouraging competition to the maximum extent
possible. This will insure that the full benefits of modern technology accrue to both passengers and shippers."[2] Only in the case
of American Airlines was the President unable to support the CAB's
recommendation. Service to Japan by a third U.S. combination airline was considered to be inconsistent with the national interest,
and the carrier's proposed services were accordingly disapproved for
points West of Hawaii. In commenting on this decision the President
made reference to "foreign policy considerations," and, although no
elaboration was offered, it is not difficult to imagine what these
might have been, especially if one looks back to a parallel situation in 1961 in which President Eisenhower rejected a CAB proposal
calling for an additional U.S. airline to provide service to Japan.
His action, President Eisenhower had assured the Board, was based
entirely on "considerations of foreign policy, a responsibility that

---

U.S. and Mexico.
    Briefly, the new transpacific routes were: (1) American Airlines: Central
Pacific route--several cities (including New York) within the continental United
States linked to Hawaii and Japan; (2) Continental Airlines: South Pacific route--
several cities on the U.S. mainland linked to Hawaii, American Samoa, Fiji, New
Zealand, and Australia. This route also had an American Samoa-Guam-Okinawa seg-
ment; (3) Trans World Airlines: Central Pacific route--Los Angeles linked to
Hawaii, Guam, Okinawa, Taiwan, and Hong Kong.

[1]These were: (1) Pan American World Airways: North Pacific route--Seattle
and Portland linked with Fairbanks and Japan. Also, New York linked with Fairbanks, San Francisco, and Los Angeles. (Pan American's existing certificate
provided for services between the latter two cities and the Far East); (2) Northwest Airlines: Central Pacific Route--links between various cities on the U.S.
mainland (including New York) and Hawaii, Okinawa, and Japan. (The carrier was
already providing service between Anchorage, Seattle and Japan.) Service was also
authorized between Anchorage and several other U.S. cities in the Northeast
(including New York) and the Midwest.

[2]A copy of the President's letter, dated December 17, 1968, is attached to
Order 68-12-105.

is mine and which the Board, of course, does not share."[1] He had
then gone on to point out that the Board's proposal would have led
to a significant increase in U.S.-flag carrier capacity between the
United States and Japan and that such an increase would be of "considerable concern to other nations engaged in international commercial aviation."[2] Both presidents presumably had in mind the adverse
impact enlarged U.S. carrier capacity could be expected to have on
Japan Air Lines, Japan's national flag carrier, and sought to avoid
making this an issue between the two nations' governments.

Charges of "cronyism" greeted President Johnson's actions in
the Transpacific Route Investigation. The most lucrative route
awards, it was alleged, had been won by companies having in their
employ persons formerly connected with the Johnson Administration.
Demands for a review of the case were made on the Senate floor on
January 23, 1969, and in a letter released to the public the following day President Johnson's successor rescinded the earlier presidential actions and ordered the CAB to refrain from all further
involvement in the international phase of the case pending his re-
evaluation of the route awards.[3] He had taken this step, President
Nixon explained during a subsequent news conference, at the request
of the chairman of the Senate Foreign Relations Committee and the
chairman of the House Foreign Affairs Committee. The fact that
pleas for reconsideration of the case had originated with legislators of both parties, he emphasized, was indicative of his nonparti-
san approach to the matter. The international and domestic route
awards were to become effective on February 17 and March 5, respectively, and the CAB, in its reply to the President, proposed to stay
the date applying to the international routes. This was deemed unacceptable and in a second letter to the Board (February 11) Mr.
Nixon declared that a stay order would not be approved. Instead the
Board was directed to submit to the President an order vacating its
entire international route ruling (which it did on February 14) and
was told that it had no further responsibility in the matter. Cus-
tomarily, a president, upon rejecting a CAB order will invite the
agency to come forth with alternate proposals; when new proposals

---

[1]Transpacific Route Case, p. 976.

[2]Ibid.

[3]"Nixon Rescinds Transpacific Airline Routes Awarded by Johnson: Move Likely Will Affect Domestic Runs," Wall Street Journal, January 27, 1969, p. 3. Uncertainty regarding the President's final decision delayed implementation of the
domestic route awards forming part of the case.

are initiated by the White House, the Board usually has been given an opportunity to present its views on the matter. In this instance, however, Mr. Nixon was determined to take action without the supporting role of the agency and did not intend to "receive communications from any source on the subject of the transpacific case other than the Secretary of State, the Secretary of Defense, or his other foreign affairs and national security advisors."[1]

President Nixon's decisions in the Transpacific Route Investigation, reached in the light of "considerations of foreign relations and national security,"[2] were set forth in a letter to the CAB dated April 11 and ranged from severe in the case of one applicant to very mild in the case of others. In the latter group were the Flying Tiger Line and Trans World Airlines, both of which lost landing rights at satellite airports (San Jose, Ontario, and Long Beach), the use of which "in this case appears unwise and should not be required." In every other respect the route authority granted the two carriers by President Johnson remained unimpaired. Two other airlines, Pan American World Airways and Northwest Airlines, lost the right to provide services to the Far East via Great Circle routes originating in the Pacific Northwest and California. Continental Airlines, on the other hand, was stripped of its international route award.[3]

Although spokesmen for Continental Airlines questioned the President's right to nullify his predecessor's certificate awards, the company was unable to seek relief through the courts. This was because the Board's orders dealing with

> certificates for overseas or foreign air transportation are not mature and are therefore not susceptible of judicial review at any time before they are finalized by Presidential [action] . . . . After such [action] . . . has been [completed] . . . , the final orders embody Presidential discretion as to political matters beyond the competence of the courts to adjudicate.[4]

Nonreviewability by the courts rests on the assumption that the

---

[1]"CAB Is Likely To Withdraw International Route Awards Made in Trans-Pacific Case," Traffic World 137, no. 7 (1969):84.

[2]The President's letter forms appendix A, Order 69-4-102.

[3]The President believed that a carrier competing with Pan American on the South Pacific route should bypass the California gateway. The route was later awarded to American Airlines. See "President Nixon and CAB Finally Resolve Issues in Trans-Pacific Route Case," Traffic World 139, no. 4 (1969):70. In 1971 Continental Airlines received authorization to participate in transpacific transportation. Pacific Islands Local Service Investigation, Order 71-7-174.

[4]Chicago and Southern Air Lines, Inc. v. Waterman Steamship Corp., 333 U.S. 103, 114 (1948). See also Diggs v. Civil Aeronautics Board, 516 F. 2d 1248 (D.C. Cir. 1975); certiorari denied, 424 U.S. 910 (1976).

Board's construction of the Federal Aviation Act's regulatory provisions is compatible with Congressional intent. Where this assumption is violated, transmittal of its recommendations to the White House has little meaning, since in that case "there is nothing Presidential action can approve."[1] The President may set aside any foreign route award approved by the Board. In addition, he has ultimate control over the "denial, transfer, amendment, cancellation, suspension, or revocation" of any certificate for foreign air transportation.[2] Presidential authority "is not limited to a negative but is a positive and detailed control over the Board's decisions, unparalleled in the history of American administrative bodies."[3]

The President's veto power over all Board decisions concerning international route and rate cases has been strongly criticized by the American Bar Association (ABA), whose administration law division has urged that section 801, which forms the basis for Presidential review of the Board's recommendations, be deleted from the Federal Aviation Act. Such an action would leave untouched the President's constitutional powers but would remove from the White House a review process which has fallen prey to "manipulation and abuse."[4] The authors of section 801, of course, were concerned essentially with foreign policy and national defense considerations. However, the language of section 801(a) was not sufficiently specific on this score, enabling the Executive Branch to overrule the Board on purely domestic rather than foreign policy grounds. In actual practice, Presidential review of a Board decision involves numerous governmental departments and agencies (e.g., the Departments of Interior, Justice, and Treasury, and the Office of Management and Budget), whose representatives have frequently not participated in public proceedings before the Board and whose decisions, the ABA and other critics contend, have often been politically motivated. Thus, the Transpacific Route Investigation, above, is often cited as an example of an international route proceeding in which the outcome was determined by domestic political interests. Political analysts at the time saw a connection between Mr. Nixon's treatment of

---

[1]American Airlines, Inc. v. Civil Aeronautics Board, (1965), p. 352.

[2]See above, p. 45, note 2.

[3]Chicago and Southern Air Lines, Inc. v. Waterman Steamship Corp., p. 109.

[4]U.S., Congress, Senate, Committee on Commerce, Regulatory Reform in Air Transportation, Hearings before the Subcommittee on Aviation, Senate, on S. 2551, S. 3364, and S. 3536, 94th Cong., 2d sess., (1976), p. 808.

Continental Airlines and support by that company's president for
Senator Humphrey's presidential campaign. Similarly, it was noted
that the president of American Airlines (whose company was granted
Pacific rights by Mr. Nixon) was one of President Nixon's early
transportation advisors. An executive order issued in 1976 has
modified the review procedure without, however, diluting the President's ultimate authority over the Board's international route
decisions.[1]

Airline officials as a whole have long been in favor of a
section 801 amendment restricting Presidential actions to foreign
policy and national security considerations, and recently adopted
legislation appears to meet that objective. Under Public Law 95-
504 the White House has lost its ability to overturn Board recommendations on purely domestic grounds,[2] creating a substantially
larger area within which the carriers are able to seek judicial
redress. There have also been recent Congressional proposals calling for the complete removal of section 801 from the Federal Aviation Act. However, as the chairman of Pan American World Airways
has pointed out,

> since repeal of section 801 would not diminish the President's consti-
> tutional authority, confusion and litigation would result in the clash
> between private and national interests. Whatever the outcome of any
> specific dispute, the dispute itself could engender foreign relations
> difficulties.[3]

An altogether different type of international case was con-
cluded in 1973. It involved the charge, brought by a number of
Baltimore civic and shipping parties,[4] that the then existing trans-
atlantic air freight structure favored New York at the expense of
Baltimore and resulted in a diversion of traffic from Baltimore to
New York.[5] In requesting that the Board disapprove the tariffs in

---

[1] Executive Order 11920 (June 10, 1976).

[2] See below, p. 167.

[3] Statement of William T. Seawell, Chairman, Pan American World Airways,
remarks made before the Senate Aviation Subcommittee, March 24, 1977, mimeographed,
p. 7. Also see: Statement of Edward J. Driscoll, President, National Air Carrier
Association, remarks made before the House Aviation Subcommittee, June 8, 1976,
mimeographed, pp. 13-17; U.S., Congress, Senate, Committee on Commerce, op. cit.,
p. 1005.

[4] These included the mayor and city council, the Chamber of Commerce of
Metropolitan Baltimore, the Baltimore Customhouse Brokers and Forwarders Association, and Air Freight International, Inc. The scope of the proceeding was subsequently widened to include Washington, D.C., Boston, and Philadelphia (Order
69-4-139), and Chicago, Cleveland, and Detroit (Order 69-10-111).

[5] "Baltimore Interests Urge Airport Rate Equalization on Trans-Atlantic
Cargo," Traffic World 136, no. 10 (1968):70.

question, the complainants noted that specific commodity rates
between various European cities and Baltimore exceeded by 17 to 26
percent the rates in effect between the same European cities and
New York. Similarly, with regard to general commodity rates, the
Baltimore figures were from 12 to 14 percent higher than those for
New York. These rate differentials could not be justified in terms
of operating costs given the very minor differences in distance
between European points and New York, on the one hand, and Europe
and Baltimore, on the other.

Hoping to forestall Board action, Pan American World Airways
and Trans World Airlines stated that they had already attempted to
reduce Baltimore's rates within the framework of the International
Air Transport Association's traffic conferences and that further
efforts along these lines would be forthcoming during the Association's next Atlantic freight rate conference. Foreign airlines,
too, held that the Board's intervention was unwarranted in view of
the Association's upcoming reexamination of transatlantic rates.
The agency could not, it was contended, move against rates it had
itself approved on an earlier occasion[1] and, were it to do so, it
would be in violation of section 1102 of the Federal Aviation Act.[2]

The CAB does not set international air freight rates, these
being established on the basis of resolutions passed unanimously[3]
by the members of the International Air Transport Association
(IATA).[4] The Association's resolutions are subject to approval by
the governments concerned. Rates adopted by IATA are reviewed on
behalf of the United States by the CAB and, if found unlawful within

---

[1]Section 1102 states, in part, that performance of the Board's duties shall
be consistent "with any obligation assumed by the United States in any treaty,
convention, or agreement that may be in force between the United States and any
foreign country or foreign countries." 72 Stat. 797, 49 U.S.C. 1502.

[2]Their argument suggests the airlines were not aware of or chose to disregard the agency's authority under section 412(b). See below, p. 56, note 1.

[3]Abolition of IATA's unanimity rule has been urged by a number of industry
observers. For example, see Kurt W. Streit, "Luftfracht: IATA-Stiefkind auch in
1973?" Wehr und Wirtschaft 17, no. 1 (1973):29. The Board recently agreed to a
modification of the unanimity rule (Order 76-7-92).

[4]An extensive body of literature dealing with IATA is in existence, making
unnecessary yet another recitation of the Association's functions and problems.
The interested reader is referred to: Mahlon R. Straszheim, The International Air-
line Industry (Washington, D.C.: The Brookings Institution, 1969), ch. VII;
Richard Y. Chuang, The International Air Transport Association (Leiden: A. W.
Sijthoff, 1972); Wolfgang Specht, Die IATA: Eine Organisation des grenzüberschrei-
tenden Luftlinienverkehrs und ihre Allgemeinen Beförderungsbedingungen (Bern and
Frankfurt/M.: Lang, 1973); "The Airlines' Shaky Cartel," Wall Street Journal,
October 15, 1975, p. 24; J. W. S. Brancker, IATA and What It Does (Leiden: A. W.
Sijthoff, 1977); Peter P. C. Haanappel, Ratemaking in International Air Transport
(Deventer: Kluwer, 1978).

the meaning of the Federal Aviation Act, are rejected. The agency
has exercised its right of veto more frequently than all foreign
governments combined.[1]

In weighing the merits of the Baltimore complaint, the Board
was confronted by two related questions: were the parties correct in
asserting that they were being subjected to undue prejudice while
New York enjoyed undue preference,[2] and was IATA's rate formula in
accord with the public interest provisions of the Federal Aviation
Act? Arising from a consideration of the first question was the
problem of whether the complainants, representing seven airport
cities, were actually competing with New York and whether such competition could be shown to have produced adverse economic repercussions for the parties.

The Board's ruling that the rate structure was, in fact, unduly preferential in respect of New York and unduly prejudicial with
regard to the other gateway cities, and therefore unlawful, rested
on the following factors:[3] (1) the rate per mile for most specific
commodity rates was, as claimed, higher for the seven gateway cities
than for New York; (2) shipper testimony indicated it was not uncom-
mon for freight to be trucked to New York from other parts of the
United States in order to exploit that city's lower air freight
rates; (3) non-New York shippers were disadvantaged as a result of
Europe's common-rating system; (4) the so-called "add-ons" between
London and various other European cities were lower than "add-ons"
charged for equivalent distances between New York and other points
in the United States.

The unlawfulness of the rate structure was compounded by a
further consideration. Congestion, delays, and the high incidence
of theft at New York's airports are the perhaps inevitable concomi-
tants of the city's preeminence in the field of air transportation.[4]

---

[1]The Board's new mandate in the field of air freight regulation (discussed
in chapter III) makes it likely that the antitrust exemption covering U.S. airline
participation in IATA's cooperative measures may be revoked.

[2]See above, p. 10.

[3]Agreement Adopted by IATA Relating to North Atlantic Cargo Rates, Order
73-2-24, p. 6.

[4]Crime is a significant problem for the New York-Newark air freight industry. Congressional investigators have concluded "that it is imperative to the
continued growth and economic well-being of the States of New York and New Jersey
that every possible effective measure be taken to prevent the pilferage and theft
of air freight and the criminal infiltration of the air freight industry." U.S.,
Congress, House, Committee on the Judiciary, New Jersey-New York Airport Commission
Compact, Hearings before Subcommittee no. 3, House of Representatives, on H.J. Res.
375, et al., (1970-1972), p. 8. See also Civil Aeronautics Board, Air Freight Loss
and Damage Claims (Washington, D.C.: Civil Aeronautics Board, November 1977), p. 25.

These ills run counter to the public interest and are clearly accentuated by rate disparities which attract traffic to New York that, under more equitable conditions, would be sent to other gateways. Such a rate structure, the Board stated, was incompatible with the policy objectives of the Federal Aviation Act and had to be voided "whether or not previously approved."[1] The carriers were ordered to calculate new rates for the seven gateway cities based on the New York-Europe rate per mile multiplied by the distance between the seven gateways and points in Europe. Despite their denials, the agency concluded that various carriers not offering direct service to New York's competitors had used rate inequities to dissuade shippers from using airports other than those in New York-Newark. Commenting on this situation, the agency stated that

> the private interests of carriers in preserving their yields from
> traffic originating at or designated to points not served by them
> is clearly insufficient justification for a discriminatory rate
> structure. Where the Board has found direct service to be in the
> public interest, the rate structure should reflect the availability
> of those services. Carriers not providing direct service cannot be
> permitted to deny the shipping public the benefits accruing from
> the direct services provided by other carriers.[2]

The new North Atlantic rate structure was challenged by various civic parties on the ground that it enabled New York to retain a certain "undue preference." However, an appeals court upheld the Board's decision, noting that the Federal Aviation Act's antidiscrimination provisions were not "intended to deprive a locality of the natural advantages of its geographic location. . . . New York is closer to European cities than Baltimore and Washington, by an average distance of 190 miles, and this fact alone should support a higher overall rate differential for the latter."[3]

Domestic rate cases have demanded much of the Board's attention in the last few years. These cases, a small number of which are now discussed, are of interest here primarily for two reasons: they illustrate the Board's continuing concern for the lawfulness of the carriers' rate proposals and show the carriers' interest in using new rates as a marketing tool. Following the cancellation of its "blocked" space service, the Flying Tiger Line announced the introduction of a new rate structure, designed to enhance profitability

---

[1]"The Board shall by order disapprove any . . . contract or agreement, whether or not previously approved by it, that it finds to be adverse to the public interest, or in violation of this Act." Federal Aviation Act, section 412(b). 72 Stat. 770, 49 U.S.C. 1382. In 1978 section 412(b) was amended by 92 Stat. 1729.

[2]Agreement Adopted by IATA Relating to North Atlantic Cargo Rates, pp. 13-14

[3]Commonwealth of Virginia v. Civil Aeronautics Board, 498 F. 2d 129, 134 (4th Cir. 1974).

by reflecting more closely costs incurred at a time of rapid technological change. Two years in the developmental stage, the rate
innovations were to accompany the placing into service of a new cargo plane, the DC-8-63F, and would, it was claimed, stimulate containerization and attract large-volume shippers to air transportation.
The principal features of the new pricing structure were:

1. Density-related price reductions for single and multi-container (five or
    more) shipments

2. Restructuring of the weight breaks system to provide greater incentives to
    large-volume shippers

3. Simplification of the specific commodity rate structure and its consolidation
    into some thirty categories, each of which was further subdivided into
    density-related groups

4. Elimination of what might be termed "level-of-service" tariffs (e.g., economy
    and deferred rates). Flying Tiger's management had concluded that tariffs of
    this type were essentially nonproductive.

According to American Airlines and Trans World Airlines, density
could not be considered the sole rate determinant, the Flying Tiger
Line's specific commodity rate reductions would not be offset by a
traffic increase, and price discounts for containers could not be
supported in terms of a carrier's cost savings. The CAB, however,
was generally sympathetic towards the new tariff and dismissed the
complainants' request that it be suspended.[1]

Another interesting rate proposal[2] was one which originated
with American Airlines. It consisted of a three-level "package,"
which, the carrier informed the transportation industry, was specifically designed to attract larger numbers of shippers to air transportation. The individual elements making up the new rate experiment, it should be noted, did not represent a sharp departure from
earlier services; rather, the plan's novel feature consisted of
offering the shipper three types of service and allowing him to
choose the one which came closest to meeting his particular requirements. The three services were:

1. The existing "standard service" at the then prevailing rates

2. A so-called premium "certified service" designed for emergency shipments.
    The shipper was to receive an appropriate refund in cases where a shipment
    could not be moved via guaranteed priority service. The rate was approxi-
    mately 30 percent higher than American's general commodity rate

---

[1]Revised Air Freight Rate Structure Proposed by the Flying Tiger Line,
Order 68-10-111. The rates were to be effective for an experimental period only,
in order to permit an assessment of shipper acceptance. In subsequent appearances
before the Board the Flying Tiger Line was unable to show that multi-container
rates were economically justified and that they did not discriminate against the
single-container shipper. (Orders 69-12-111 and 70-11-137.)

[2]This applied only to general commodity rates.

3. A door-to-door "space available" service (at significantly lower rates) intended for shippers unwilling to pay the standard rate and not concerned with overnight delivery. Unlike "deferred" operations[1] this service imposed no restrictions on delivery time. It was also seen as a partial solution to another problem, namely the more efficient utilization of ground personnel. This would be accomplished in that loading would normally take place during nonpeak hours.

Despite American Airlines' conviction that its new rates would make important contributions to the air freight industry, the CAB sided with opponents of the proposal and informed the company its tariff could not be implemented.[2] The effect the carrier's limited liability might have on shippers in instances where guaranteed priority service could, after all, not be provided was a source of concern to the agency. Also, it appeared to share the view of various airline officials who felt that the new rate structure would tempt many users of "standard service" to change over to "space available" service and would thus lead to significant revenue losses for the air carriers.[3]

Although American Airlines was unable to overcome industry-wide opposition to its three-level rate experiment, it continued in its struggle to win acceptance for what had been the experiment's most contentious element, namely "space available" service. A second approach to the CAB towards the middle of 1970 was also unsuccessful, but in December of that year the agency finally agreed to the introduction of modified "space available" service over certain of the carrier's routes. Braniff Airways, in order to protect its competitive position, filed an identical tariff for its New York-Dallas route. Although the opposition of other carriers[4] to this development was as strong as ever, the CAB now suggested that the lower rates[5] would be instrumental in adding to the volume of freight moving by air and that American's modified proposal differed sufficiently from "standard" service to warrant affirmative action

---

[1]See above, p. 18.

[2]Order 70-1-149.

[3]The Board was also critical of the "space available" price discounts on the ground that these were "out of proportion to the differences in cost and value of service as compared with standard services." Ibid., p. 3.

[4]These stated that the service would be subsidized through increased passenger fares, that American Airlines was not presenting documentary evidence supporting claims of reduced costs, and that, in any case, the tariff was virtually identical to that which the Board had rejected on two earlier occasions.

[5]These were 40 percent below general commodity rates.

pending further investigation.[1]

In 1973 the Board terminated the exemption order under which REA Express had operated since 1941.[2] All the express agency's contractual agreements with the airlines were similarly ordered discontinued. Given the growth of the air freight industry, the advantages (such as speed and geographic coverage) which had once made the agency unique had evaporated, making it all but impossible to justify its retention as the exclusive ground agent for express traffic.[3] The needs of those shippers requiring expedited service, the Board declared, could best be met directly by the certificated airlines, which were told that their common carrier obligation included the provision of priority (express) service.[4] Many airline priority tariffs were now introduced, the Board suspending a large number of these pending an investigation of their lawfulness. Of particular concern was whether proposed premium charges could be justified in terms of the service to be offered and whether priority service tariff rules adequately defined the services in question.

Once the published tariff rate falls below a given point it is set aside and replaced by a minimum charge. In the past, minimum charges were arrived at in one of two ways. In 1968 these were (for general commodity shipments): (1) a flat charge of $6 and (2) a charge equal to that levied on a 50-pound shipment, the shipper being required to pay the higher of the two. The Flying Tiger Line's revised rate structure[5] included provisions for substantial minimum charge increments, which the Board refused to treat as an integral part of the carrier's overall tariff application, electing instead to make them the subject of a separate enquiry. The scope of this enquiry quickly expanded with the filing of higher minimum charges by other airlines, which, generally speaking, argued that existing minimum rates were noncompensatory and that upward revisions would have no adverse effect on small-volume shippers.[6]

---

[1]Data submitted by the two carriers revealed that there had been no appreciable defection of shippers from "standard" to "space available" service. See p. 3 of Order 71-12-78.

[2]See below, p. 82.

[3]The company had a long history of financial difficulty and collapsed in 1975.

[4]Express Service Investigation, Order 73-12-36, p. 41.

[5]See above, p. 57.

[6]Small-volume shippers, it was contended, could always turn to the lower rates offered by forwarders.

The Board's investigation of minimum charges was concluded in April of 1972. Increased minima based on a flat dollar charge were found to be not "unreasonable, or otherwise unlawful" and were permitted to remain in effect.[1] On the other hand, the pricing method based on the charge for a 50-pound shipment was thought to produce excessively high rates and was canceled. The agency refused to exempt horticultural products from its ruling[2] and informed the Flying Tiger Line that certain aspects of its tariff application had been made part of the then ongoing Domestic Air Freight Rate Investigation.

In 1977 the Board concluded the Domestic Air Freight Rate Investigation, its most comprehensive review of domestic freight rates since the Air Freight Rate Investigation of 1948. The latter enquiry, as we have seen, had led to the imposition of minimum rates which, following the stabilization of the overall rate structure, were abolished in 1961 (they were, however, reintroduced for specific markets; New York-San Juan Cargo Rates Investigation, above). During the 1960s and 1970s rate increases were generally permitted as long as rates remained below industry average costs. In addition various promotional rates (e.g., specific commodity rates, directional rates, and container rates) were encouraged provided they were able to recover noncapacity costs and some portion of the capacity cost. The carriers' operating expenses had been increasing steadily since the late 1960s. Rates, of course, were also rising, though apparently not enough to permit domestic carriers as a whole to recover their economic costs including a "fair" return on investment. Thus, the Domestic Air Freight Rate Investigation (for which new costing procedures were developed) was concerned with two principal issues: (1) the future relationship between basic domestic rates and revised industry cost levels and (2) the lawfulness of discount rates.

The Board's major conclusions, which it released in August of 1977, were as follows:

a. Domestic air freight rates of the trunk carriers, Flying Tiger and Airlift [International] should not exceed industry average costs.

b. Domestic air freight rates of the local service carriers should not exceed industry average costs by more than thirty percent.

---

[1]Minimum Charges per Shipment of Air Freight, Order 72-4-105. Petitions for reconsideration were denied. See Order 72-6-68.

[2]The Society of American Florists and Ornamental Horticulturists had requested that increased minimum charges not be made to apply to floral products.

    c. Domestic air freight rates should, except in unusual situations, exceed industry average noncapacity costs.[1]

These were the parameters within which rates were to be considered just and reasonable, and all domestic rates failing to meet this standard were ordered canceled. Such an approach was considered sufficiently broad to permit management considerable pricing flexibility and was thought to be preferable to a more rigid pricing formula recommended by one of the agency's administrative law judges. In addition, the Board affirmed its support of discount rates but cautioned the airlines that only upon a "convincing showing" would these rates be permitted to fall below industry average noncapacity costs.

    It had taken the Board seven years to complete the Domestic Air Freight Rate Investigation. Various parties argued that the many changes which were taking place during this period (e.g., the termination of freighter service by several trunklines, the collapse of REA Express, the introduction of wide-body combination aircraft, and the emergence of Federal Express as an important new freight specialist) made the investigation pointless and requested that it be halted. The Board, however, refused to accept that these and other industry changes would invalidate its findings and pressed on with its costly and time-consuming effort. Ironically, the investigation was ultimately to have little meaning, for, towards the end of 1977, newly adopted legislation (chapter III) altered the agency's terms of reference and deprived it of authority to enforce its standard of rate justness and reasonableness.

Establishment of Air Cargo, Inc.

    Air Cargo, Inc. (ACI) was formed by several scheduled air carriers in 1941 for the purpose of undertaking research into various freight-related problems on their behalf. It produced a number of fundamental market research studies (which showed, incidentally, that over three quarters of those questioned intended to use air freight service only if it included a door-to-door component[2]), examined legal issues and airline tariffs, and established the earliest industry specifications for the design and construction of cargo aircraft. The personnel shortage imposed by World War II caused the corporation to lapse into a period of dormancy which lasted until 1947, at which time it was reactivated and, under an amended charter, launched as the certificated route air carriers' ground service

---

[1] Domestic Air Freight Rate Investigation, Order 77-8-62, p. 77.

[2] "How the Air/Truck Program Grew--and Grew," Air Transportation 51, no. 4 (1967):46.

In the mid-1940s each of the airlines offering freight service made its own arrangements with respect to ground operations. Thus, individual air carriers hired local cartage contractors to provide the link between a shipper's place of business and the air terminal. In abolishing this arrangement and replacing it with a more unified approach centered on Air Cargo, Inc., the airlines were able to introduce economies of scale, a factor not overlooked by the Civil Aeronautics Board and one which it found to be consistent with section 2 of the Civil Aeronautics Act.[1]

Although the CAB gave its approbation to the airlines' joint venture, it stipulated that "any holder of a certificate of public convenience and necessity issued by the Board authorizing transportation of property by aircraft [should] be authorized to participate in Air Cargo, Inc. as a matter of right."[2] This qualification implied equality of treatment for all certificated route carriers, and its repeal was promptly sought by two corporation members, Eastern Air Lines and United Airlines, on the grounds that: (1) the Board lacked the authority to impose the aforementioned requirement, (2) the Board's stand discriminated against the founder-members since it was through their efforts alone that the corporation was established, and (3) the Board was acting in anticipation of future events, which, at this point, were unforeseeable. The CAB clearly had competence to pass on the merits of pooling arrangements among air carriers[3] and, in rejecting the contentions of the two airlines, pointedly noted that such arrangements could be approved only as long as they satisfied the Act's public interest criteria. Denial of the petition rested on the belief that the value of the newly introduced ground service would be maximized through an increase in ACI's membership, and, while the agency recognized that the agreement establishing Air Cargo, Inc. placed no limit on the number of participating air carriers, it regarded as vital inclusion of its qualifying provision so as to clarify at the outset its response to possible future exclusionary practices. Even if the Board had accepted the petition and allowed the interairline agreement to stand as proposed, it seems probable that subsequent efforts to restrict airline membership in Air Cargo, Inc. would have been challenged

---

[1] See above, pp. 6-7.

[2] CAB Agreement 1041 (adopted 1947). The agreement covered only domestic pickup and delivery service; overseas operations were approved in 1975.

[3] Federal Aviation Act, section 412. 72 Stat. 770, 49 U.S.C. 1382. See above, p. 32, note 2.

under the Sherman Antitrust Act and disallowed through court action.
The Supreme Court had, in fact, only recently concluded a case in
which one business group's attempt to curb competition by barring a
second group from membership in a cooperative association had been
found unlawful.[1] While it was not compelled to echo the Court's
ruling and remained free to exercise its own judgement, the Court's
decision clearly buttressed the CAB's position and it declared the
ruling "a sound public policy which should be applied to air carrier
agreements."[2] The discrimination charge (2, above) was dismissed,
since the right of the corporation's original members to insist that
newcomers make a fair contribution towards the developmental costs
of ground services remained unaffected. Finally, the CAB justified
the anticipatory aspect of its approval of Air Cargo, Inc. by re-
minding the petitioners that future national aviation needs were one
of its legitimate concerns[3] and as such could be used to help evaluate and modify any new service proposed by the airlines.

Under the airlines' joint approach to freight problems, responsibility for the selection of cartage contractors was delegated to
the corporation. In this connection Air Cargo, Inc. drew up a standard pickup and delivery cartage service contract--approved by the
CAB in 1948 and left substantially unaltered since that time--which
is used throughout the United States to secure for the airlines the
services of trucking concerns. The first contract between Air Cargo,
Inc. and a trucker was put into effect in Milwaukee in 1947. Today,
about 500 contractors (table 1) serving approximately 6,000 domestic
points provide pickup and delivery service under the aegis of the
corporation.

In 1961 the corporation's board of directors voted to extend
cartage contracts to the air freight forwarders (hopes of the corporation itself becoming a forwarder were dashed several years earlier by the CAB which thought this would have given ACI an unfair
advantage over other forwarders). In the same year Air Cargo, Inc.
instituted its so-called "air/truck service," an interline operation
involving long-haul motor carriers and air carriers. The initial
reluctance of many truckers to participate in this service hinged
upon the fact that, in contrast to the limited liability of the air
carriers, their liability was for the full value of a given shipment.

---

[1]*Associated Press v. United States*, 326 U.S. 1 (1945).

[2]*Agreement Establishing Air Cargo, Inc., Petitions of Eastern Air Lines, Inc., and United Air Lines, Inc., for Reconsideration*, 9 CAB 468, 470 (1948).

[3]See above, p. 6.

Following a petition from the National Motor Freight Traffic Association (supported by Air Cargo, Inc.) to the Interstate Commerce
Commission, motor carrier and air carrier liability limitations were
in 1965 brought into conformity with one another and ten years later
the air/truck program had 180 participating truckers who provided
service to roughly 5,000 domestic points. In 1977 ACI offered
associate membership to the commuter airlines, enabling this carrier
group to participate in its air/truck and pickup/delivery services.

TABLE 1

AIR CARGO, INC.: U.S. PICKUP AND DELIVERY OPERATIONS

Year	No. of Contractors	No. of Shipments	Revenues($)
1948	151	676,274	979,479
1955	234	1,168,934	2,089,084
1960	353	2,061,019	4,940,510
1965	457	4,068,717	11,631,807
1970	475	5,898,755	23,792,114
1975	475	4,505,722	31,195,433

SOURCE: Air Cargo, Inc.

Air Cargo, Inc. has authority to amend or terminate contracts
and agreements between airlines and surface operators. It is involved in marketing analysis but (with the exception of its New York
Trucking Division) does not provide actual freight services such as
packaging, documentation, etc. Routing problems must be worked out
between shipper and originating carrier. Close cooperation between
ACI and its airline owners is maintained through the establishment,
mostly in major cities, of local air freight committees, which are
composed of airline personnel who advise the corporation on a broad
spectrum of freight-related matters. The corporation has represented the airlines' interests in a number of Civil Aeronautics Board
and Interstate Commerce Commission proceedings.

Concluding Remarks

Chapter I has explored the relationship which existed between
the Civil Aeronautics Board and the airlines (direct air carriers)
during the period 1938-1977. Rather than turning immediately to the
forwarders (indirect air carriers), let us pause briefly and review
the basic regulatory constraints which have governed airline behavior during these years. In the 1930s, policymakers confronting the
then infant airline companies were convinced that the private sector

left to its own devices, would fail to produce a transportation system capable of serving properly the national and public interest. Only the guiding hand of the Federal Government, it was believed, could prevent "cutthroat" competition,[1] control mergers,[2] ensure maximum safety,[3] and provide for the nation's defense needs.[4] These and other concerns are reflected in Congress' 1938 policy statement,[5] which was to shape Washington's approach towards the airline industry for the next four decades.

That civil aviation was being viewed along the lines of a regulated utility became clear even before the Civil Aeronautics Act came into effect. Thus, in a 1935 report the Federal Aviation Commission declared that "even after air transport shall have attained a purely commercial footing, needing no direct support from the government, . . . it will still require control as a public utility and one which in some cases must take on a monopoly character."[6] This position was affirmed by the Senate Committee on Commerce (1938), which noted that the forthcoming Civil Aeronautics Act contained "the recognized and accepted principles of the regulation of public utilities, as applied to other forms of transportation."[7] The CAB has always been unhappy with the regulated utility analogy. While imperfect, it nevertheless provides a useful framework within which

---

[1]House Report no. 2254, 75th Cong., 3d sess., (1938), p. 2.

[2]Congressional Record, 83, part 6 (1938): 6728-6729.

[3]Ibid., p. 6635.

[4]Ibid., p. 6411.

[5]See above, pp. 6-7.

[6]Senate Document no. 15, 74th Cong., 1st sess., (1935), p. 52.

[7]Senate Report no. 1661, 75th Cong., 3d sess., (1938), p. 2. Public regulation of transportation and other industries has been studied extensively. For instance, see: Charles F. Phillips, The Economics of Regulation: Theory and Practice in the Transportation and Public Utility Industries (Homewood: Richard D. Irwin, Inc., 1965); Dudley F. Pegrum, Public Regulation of Business (rev. ed.; Homewood: Richard D. Irwin, Inc., 1965); Alfred E. Kahn, The Economics of Regulation (New York: John Wiley and Sons, Inc., 1970-1971). (Two volumes.) Kahn was named chairman of the CAB in mid-1977; George J. Stigler, "The Theory of Economic Regulation," Bell Journal of Economics 2, no. 1 (1971):3-21; George W. Hilton, "The Basic Behavior of Regulatory Commissions," American Economic Review 62, no. 2 (1972):47-54; George W. Douglas and James C. Miller, Economic Regulation of Domestic Air Transport: Theory and Policy (Washington, D.C.: The Brookings Institution, 1974); Arthur S. De Vany, "The Effect of Price and Entry Regulation on Airline Output, Capacity and Efficiency," Bell Journal of Economics 6, no. 1 (1975):327-345.

the agency's role may be examined. Obviously, there are differences
between air transportation and the more traditional type of public
utility (the Act's endorsement of competition is one such difference); the similarities between the two, however, are substantial
and the analogy should not be dismissed.[1]

The Board has had, as we have seen, the authority to "prescribe the lawful rate, fare or charge" where the existing rate,
etc., was deemed to be unreasonable, discriminatory, or unduly preferential. Carriers have been required to give advance notice of
rate changes and changes in any practice or procedure likely to affect rates. Rates and tariff regulations have been evaluated in
terms of various public convenience and necessity criteria and have
at times been rejected even before taking effect. In addition, the
Board has imposed what it considered a "fair" return on investment,
halted "ruinous" rate wars, and introduced maximum and minimum rate
levels. (The Air Freight Rate Investigation, above, provides an
example of the latter point.) To help the struggling all-cargo
operators, the agency initially calculated lawful rates on the basis
of this carrier group's fully allocated costs. With the development
of air freight transportation, however, this approach was abandoned
and freight rates were based on industry average costs. The agency
has also had (and continues to have) authority to act on subsidy
requests. Subsidy payments amounted to $78 million for the 12
months ended June 30, 1977 and have long been a particularly trou-
blesome and controversial issue both for the airlines and for the
Board. In 1977 these payments went largely to local service operators, whose common carrier obligation has forced them to serve a
number of marginal (i.e., less profitable) markets.

Arguments over the merits of a publicly controlled air transportation industry are as old as the industry itself. Proponents of
regulation believe the Board has: (1) stabilized the industry,
(2) checked monopolistic tendencies,[2] and (3) guaranteed the continuation of air service at small communities. Unbridled competition,
it is contended, will serve only to undermine the fiscal health of
the carriers, forcing them to discontinue operations over their

---

[1]The main features of public utility regulation have been defined as:
(1) control of entry, (2) price fixing, (3) prescription of quality and conditions
of service, and (4) imposition of an obligation to serve all applicants under reasonable conditions. Kahn, I, op. cit., p. 3.

[2]Some carriers, according to one early advocate of Federal regulation
(Representative Lyle H. Boren; 1938), "are grasping for monopolies on all profitable route territories, and their motives are sufficiently sinister to the public
interest to demand the Government's attention." Congressional Record 83, part 6
(1938):6406.

low-density routes. Concern for the carriers' economic well-being was particularly acute during the industry's early years (a period in which the largest carriers, the trunklines, were receiving subsidies), since financially troubled companies invariably made further demands on the public purse.[1] (The all-cargo airlines, as was shown above, functioned without direct governmental aid, an important factor in their certification.) On the other side of the regulation controversy, of course, is the claim that competition enhances industry responsiveness to the needs of shippers and the traveling public and that it makes for more innovation, lower prices, and greater overall efficiency. Congress, seeking a compromise between a market economy and demands for rigid regulation, authorized the Board to allow "competition to the extent necessary"[2] to meet national transportation goals and gave the agency three ways in which to limit the number of carriers operating in any given market. These were: (1) control over entry (both of new firms moving into the industry and existing firms expanding into new markets), (2) control over route abandonment, and (3) control over mergers and acquisitions. The principal form of entry control has been the certification process, which in turn has rested on the Board's construction of the Federal Aviation Act's public interest criteria.[3] The various system objectives (summarized in table 2) have not necessarily been given equal attention in any one proceeding and their relative importance has changed on the basis of new market conditions, carrier class(es) involved, etc.

In considering the evolution of the airlines' route network (whether it be the national network or that of the New York-Newark system), several points should be kept in mind: (1) route awards have been made on a case-by-case basis; (2) for the individual markets the general trend has been one of growth, both in terms of the number of operators and the number of carrier classes; (3) this

---

[1] The subsidy program for trunk carriers was terminated in the 1950s. A CAB Special Staff study notes that the agency's route policy during the subsidy period "could . . . be interpreted as a means of holding the total cost of subsidization to a reasonable level. However, the control of the cost of subsidization clearly was not the major objective of the legislative sponsors of the Act in providing for route certification. On the contrary, the continuation of an essentially similar route policy after the end of subsidization seems to have been fully justified by the legislative aim of generally reconciling new competition with protection of the incumbents." Report of the CAB Special Staff on Regulatory Reform, p. 43.

[2] See above, p. 6.

[3] Certification proceedings have frequently been time-consuming and costly. Filing and license fees (which amounted to $1.9 million during the 12-month period ended June 30, 1976) have been another (though minor) form of entry control.

growth has varied with time and has been most pronounced in markets having the greatest traffic potential; (4) to stave off bankruptcy airline mergers have been authorized provided this did not create a monopoly situation; (5) suspension of service at specified points has been permitted where this was considered essential to a carrier's financial well-being. Route transfers have also been approved. An example of the latter is the trunks' exit from numerous small markets and their replacement by local service operators. Similarly, some routes have been transferred from the local service carriers to commuter airlines.[1]

TABLE 2

THE PUBLIC INTEREST OBJECTIVES: 1938-1977

Objective	Which Means	How Measured
Basic Objectives		
Respond to national defense needs	Long-range cargo and passenger aircraft available for emergencies and war situations	Number and type of aircraft in use
Respond to Postal Service needs	Reasonable delivery time and reliable service	Service penetration, passenger and all-cargo
	Reasonable rates	Average yields. Degree of carrier competition
Respond to domestic commerce	Regularly scheduled passenger and freight service between geographic areas and co-terminals	Service penetration, passenger and all-cargo. Load factors (scheduled and all-cargo)
	Support of tourist industry	Service penetration, passenger Load factors (scheduled and all-cargo) Increase in traffic (scheduled, charter and all-cargo)
Just and reasonable fares/rates	No discrimination between classes of travelers and between freight categories No discrimination between points	Average yields Fare/rate/point discrimination

[1]See above, p. 5.

Objective	Which Means	How Measured
Basic Objectives		
	Reasonable load factors	Load factors
	No excess carrier profits	Carrier profit-ability
Respond to public demand	Meeting total demand for geographic areas and service: (a) point-to-point (b) nonstop (c) scheduled (d) charter	Service penetration, passenger and all-cargo. Load factors Increase in traffic (scheduled, charter, and all-cargo)
	At reasonable load factors	Load factors
Development of civil aeronautics	Technological progress	Number and type of aircraft in use
Safety in air transportation	No overloading of the air traffic system	Load factors
	No deterioration of aircraft maintenance and practices	Carrier profit-ability
Foster sound economic conditions	Scheduled, supplemental, and all-cargo carriers	Carrier profit-ability
	Total demand for aircraft	
Foster economy and efficiency of carriers	Lowest fares/rates consistent with service	Load factors
	No excess carrier profits	Carrier profit-ability Average yields
Supportive Objectives		
Equal opportunity for all carriers to compete	No unjust discrimination	Market share
	No undue preference or advantages	Carrier profit-ability
	No unfair or destructive competition	
Competition among carriers	More than one carrier per market	Degree of carrier competition Competitive balance

TABLE 2--Continued

Objective	Which Means	How Measured
Supportive Objectives		
Energy use	Minimization of fuel requirements	Total fuel consumed
Favorable environ-mental conditions	Promotion of new equipment development for a cleaner and less noisy system	Number and type of aircraft in use Carrier profit-ability
	Minimization of land use needs (airports)	Number and type of aircraft in use Load factors
Employment	Employment in the U.S. air transporta-tion industry	Number of U.S. citizens employed (carriers and supply/ support industries)

SOURCES: Federal Aviation Act, sections 102 (see above, pp. 6-7), 404(b) (see above, p. 9), and 1002 (see above, p. 10); 40 FR 28722, (July 8, 1975), figure 1.

Over the years several specialized carrier classes have been permitted to emerge. Board action has limited their competitive impact on one another, and, indeed, the operations of the entire group (trunklines, local service carriers, all-cargo carriers, supplementals and commuter carriers-air taxis), converge at only a relatively small number of airport cities (of which New York is one). Anticompetitive measures affecting entire classes have included: (1) a prohibition against scheduled operations by supplemental carriers; (2) an aircraft size limitation for commuters and other air taxi operators;[1] (3) a ban on regular passenger traffic in the case of the all-cargo airlines (prompting these to complain on many occasions that the combination carriers' ability to support freight operations with passenger revenues, a form of cross-subsidization, gave the latter an unfair advantage); (4) severe route restrictions for the certificated all-cargo airlines; and (5) the exclusion of the local service carriers from long-haul markets.

Chapter I, of course, has focused on Board actions pertaining primarily to the freight industry. It should be emphasized, however, that the majority of route cases to have come before the agency during the years 1938 and 1977 were concerned not with freight but with

[1]See above, p. 23, note 4.

the traveling public. The latter accounts for about ninety percent of the airlines' transportation revenues, and it is hardly surprising that the certificated combination (passenger-freight) carriers should have framed their route requests from the standpoint of the passenger market. Under the terms of their operating authority these carriers have been able to transport freight in pure freighters as well as combination aircraft. In actual practice the trunks are the only combination carriers for whom scheduled all-cargo service has been a viable option, and even here flights have been restricted to a small number of cities or, in some instances (e.g., Continental, Delta, Eastern, Western), discontinued altogether.

With the exception of Trans Caribbean Airways no new trunkline has entered the industry since the 1938 issuance of the "grandfather" certificates. This, together with the fact that existing trunks have frequently been denied entry into particular markets on the grounds that this would harm the incumbent (to say nothing of the aforementioned restraints placed on competition from other carrier classes), has laid the CAB open to the charge that it has been unduly protective of the long-haul airlines. The agency insists its regulatory policy has been free of bias but concedes that "the desirability of establishing a coordinated system gave a substantial advantage for new route authority to applicants which already held existing routes and could thus offer improved single-plane or on-line connecting service to communities beyond the particular city-pair market at issue in a given case."[1]

While open entry into the industry has traditionally been rejected by the Board, its policy on trunkline entry into new markets has been characterized by considerable flexibility. The generally bright outlook for air transportation during the 1940s caused the agency to embrace a "presumption doctrine," under which there existed a "presumption in favor of competition" in the case of high-volume traffic markets.[2] This doctrine, which implied that incumbents had to show that no additional flights were required, was soon

---

[1]U.S., Congress, Senate, Committee on Commerce, op. cit., p. 372. Also see Report of the CAB Special Staff on Regulatory Reform, p. 50.

[2]"While no convenient formula of general applicability may be available as a substitute for the Board's discretionary judgment it would seem to be a sound principle that, since competition in itself presents an incentive to improved service and technological development, there would be a strong, although not conclusive, presumption in favor of competition on any route which offered sufficient traffic to support competing services without unreasonable increase of total operating cost." Transcontinental and Western Air, Inc. et al., Additional North-South California Services, 4 CAB 373, 375 (1943). The activities of the trunklines centered on passengers rather than freight, so the reference to "sufficient traffic" is to high passenger load factors.

replaced by a more cautious approach, which placed the burden of proving inadequacy on the applicant. The mid-1950s saw a partial return of the "presumption doctrine," which, however, was abandoned once more following the introduction of jet aircraft.[1] By 1960 about ninety percent of the major routes were served by more than one carrier. Up to that point the assault on trunk monopoly markets had essentially taken two forms. One of these was the certification of additional carriers; the other was the amendment of existing multistop route certificates, placing their holders on an equal footing with carriers providing nonstop service. (Where more than one new trunkline attempted to enter a given market, the Board, seeking to balance the strength of these carriers, usually awarded the route to the more "needy" applicant.) A new dimension was added in the mid-1960s when local service operators were permitted to initiate nonstop flights over certain routes served by trunk carriers.

The liberality with which new route awards have been made has varied according to the financial position of the airlines, traffic projections, and changes in Board membership. Generally speaking, overall economic growth, optimistic traffic forecasts, and an applicant's ability to develop a market's traffic potential have heightened the Board's readiness to authorize additional competition. Critics of the agency contend that carriers, anxious to have their certificate amendments in hand during periods of economic expansion, have been forced to initiate services prematurely. The regulatory process is thus seen to contribute to the underutilization of aircraft. An associated problem focuses on the selection method itself. Some economists believe that operator rights have been awarded to a particular company, not so much on the strength of its application, but, rather, as compensation for the denial of earlier route requests. This "pacification" of the air carriers would seem to be in the interests of regulators who, upon leaving the agency, are likely to continue their careers in the airline industry.[2]

The Board's international orders must be approved by the President before they can come into force. In the case of domestic proceedings, on the other hand, the final word belongs to the courts, to which aggrieved parties may turn for review of the agency's decisions. Appellate review, however, is limited in the sense that an

---

[1] "The increased capacity and speed inherent in jets means that the amount of traffic which might have supported duplicating operations with piston aircraft will not necessarily support the same level of duplicating service with jet equipment." Southern Transcontinental Service Case, 33 CAB 701, 715 (1961).

[2] Hilton, op. cit., p. 49.

administrative agency's decisions, where based on substantial evidence, cannot be overturned on grounds other than arbitrariness or abuse of statutory authority.[1] Citing public interest considerations, the Board has sanctioned various intercarrier arrangements such as capacity limitations[2] and commission agreements, which in other branches of the economy the courts would have viewed as violations of the antitrust laws. These arrangements have served to protect the certificated route carriers and have in effect acted as partial compensation for their lack of pricing freedom. "The entire regulatory scheme set up by the Federal Aviation Act is severely anticompetitive," the U.S. Court of Appeals for the District of Columbia Circuit declared in 1975. "However, the remedy is not to seek judicial reinterpretation of statutory language that permits the Board, in an appropriate case, to override antitrust considerations but to seek from Congress amendment of the Board's statutory charter."[3] The court's sentiments were shared by the U.S. Department of Justice, which had long argued that generally accepted antitrust standards rather than the Board's public interest criteria should govern the lawfulness of intercarrier agreements.[4]

There can be little doubt that one result of economic regulation has been that the number of carriers (at least with respect to the more important city pairs) has been kept below the level expected to operate under a free entry regime. This, together with the agency's disinclination to certificate newcomers on the basis of price proposals suggests that incumbents have been shielded from potentially more efficient would-be entrants.[5] The security provided by the certification process (only "willful failure" to heed the provisions of the Federal Aviation Act has resulted in major

---

[1]Pillai v. Civil Aeronautics Board, 485 F. 2d 1018, 1023 (D.C. Cir. 1973). Also see: Federal Communications Commission v. Schreiber, 381 U.S. 279, 290-291 (1965); National Labor Relations Board v. Brown, 380 U.S. 278, 291-292 (1965); Burlington Truck Lines v. United States, 371 U.S. 156, 167-169 (1962).

[2]Multilateral capacity reduction agreements were approved (1973-1975) as a fuel conservation measure.

[3]United States v. Civil Aeronautics Board, 511 F. 2d 1315, 1322-1323 (D.C. Cir. 1975).

[4]See below, p. 137.

[5]One much-cited example of the CAB's protective attitude towards the trunks involved World Airways, a supplemental airline which in 1967 sought to offer scheduled transcontinental service at fares substantially below those charged by the incumbents. The Board's response, in the words of Senator Edward Kennedy (D. Mass.), one of the agency's harshest Congressional critics, was to permit World's request "to remain on the bureaucratic shelf for six years and, in 1973, [dismiss] the application as 'stale.'" "The Route to Lower Air Fares," Boston Globe, June 20, 1975, p. 25.

reductions of operating authority[1]) has, in the view of many critics
lowered the air transportation system's ability to perform its functions. Effective price competition has been stifled, and competition has been largely restricted to such service elements as flight
frequency. Several transportation economists have compared the relatively unregulated intrastate carriers with the interstate airlines
and have concluded that the Board's regulatory policies have produced excess capacity and high passenger fares in interstate markets.[2] Similarly, a CAB Special Staff panel has noted (1975) that
the traditional regulatory process blunted industry innovativeness
and that "regulatory protection may have encouraged the inflation of
at least some cost elements because of the resulting relative lack
of pressure on the carriers to keep prices down."[3] These findings,
which were later accepted by Congressional investigators, undermined
the Board's position and helped to fuel demands for deregulation of
the airline industry.

During virtually the entire period 1938-1977 the Board had
never seriously questioned Congress' original mandate. As the cho-
rus of protest against its authority grew, the agency was put

---

[1] Bankruptcy, of course, would also have led to a loss of service rights but
in the case of the trunklines, has been avoided through the Board's merger policy.
Commenting on this situation, President Ford's Council of Economic Advisers said:
"although exit from an industry via bankruptcy is a normal characteristic of efficient competitive markets, the bankruptcy of a regulated firm tends to be viewed
as a sign of regulatory failure. To prevent bankruptcies, regulators are thus
prone to protect firms from competition--frequently to the detriment of efficient
service. For example, since the establishment of the Civil Aeronautics Board
(CAB) in 1938, not a single trunk air carrier has gone bankrupt, although several
trunk airlines at the brink of bankruptcy have merged with stronger carriers."
Economic Report of the President (Washington, D.C.: U.S. Government Printing Office, 1975), p. 151.

[2] For instance, see: William A. Jordan, Airline Regulation in America:
Effects and Imperfections (Baltimore: The Johns Hopkins Press, 1970); Theodore E.
Keeler, "Airline Regulation and Market Performance," Bell Journal of Economics 3,
no. 2 (1972):399-424. The conclusions of these writers have been challenged by
various transportation specialists. See: U.S., Congress, Senate, Committee on
Commerce, op. cit., pp. 450-451; "The Spectre of Deregulation: To Think It Will
Work Is Nonsense!" Air Transport World 14, no. 5 (1977):33-34. In a 1976 review
of the industry's problems, the Deputy Secretary of Transportation noted that,
"the current regulatory system exacerbates the industry's financial instability.
Under this system, [the airlines] have tended to buy too many aircraft. They have
become overly capital intensive because they compete on service rather than on
price. They put relatively few seats on aircraft and get low effective load factors. Compared with the less regulated carriers, they use more aircraft per unit
of service provided. This tends to make their fixed costs high and consequently
their earnings volatile because the demand for air travel will always tend to
swing with the economy." Remarks by Deputy Secretary of Transportation John W.
Barnum, Airline Industry Seminar, Financial Analysts Federation, New York, July 2,
1976, mimeographed, p. 13.

[3] Report of the CAB Special Staff on Regulatory Reform, p. 55.

increasingly on the defensive but failed to develop a convincing response to its critics. In early 1977 it conceded that greater carrier freedom would lead to "a more efficient, lower cost system."[1] By that time, however, the initiative for regulatory reform was firmly in the hands of the Congress (chapter III) and the agency was little more than a bystander as that body moved towards the deregulation of interstate air freight and passenger transportation.

---

[1]Civil Aeronautics Board, Annual Report (Washington, D.C.: U.S. Government Printing Office, 1977), p. 72.

CHAPTER II

SURFACE MOVEMENTS TO AND FROM AIRPORTS: REGULATED

VERSUS NONREGULATED TRANSPORTATION

Having discussed the regulatory constraints imposed on air transportation, we now turn to a consideration of the legal framework governing surface movements to and from air terminals. The importance of these movements is immediately apparent if it is borne in mind that, to be acceptable to most potential air shippers, air service must include a surface component. The surface movements are discussed from the standpoint of the Civil Aeronautics Board and the Interstate Commerce Commission, the two regulatory bodies directly involved. Emphasis is placed on the position of the forwarders, from whom, as is shown in chapters VI and VIII, the airlines receive the major proportion of the freight flowing through the New York-Newark airports.

Regulation of Forwarders Prior to Air Freight

Freight forwarding has long been a contentious issue in American transportation, of which it has been a part since the era of the post rider. The initial form of forwarding consisted of the expediting of goods via some kind of "express" system. Packages carried unofficially with letters in the pouches of the post rider are the earliest example of property moved by such a system. Traffic in packages was a valued source of additional income and was solicited by some post riders with such zeal that a contemporary of Peter Mumford (the post rider from Newport to Boston) was moved to exclaim that in Newport "there are two post offices, the King's and Peter Mumford's."[1] The post rider's forwarding function was later exercised by coach drivers, who in turn gave way to railway conductors and baggage men.

With the advent of the railway there arose a number of express companies, which, working under the slogan "nothing too difficult, nothing too unusual," solicited commissions involving the forwarding

---

[1]Cited in Alvin F. Harlow, Old Waybills (New York and London: D. Appleton-Century Co., 1934), p. 3.

77

of small-volume freight.[1] Initially, the "expressman" carried his
packages on the train as might any other passenger, but, with a
growth in business, this quickly became impracticable and formal
agreements covering this traffic had to be concluded between the
railway carriers and the express companies.[2] Since agreements could
be terminated unilaterally by either party, the express companies in
effect existed by the grace of the railways.[3] These, recognizing
the profitability of forwarding, caused the collapse of a number of
independent forwarders,[4] replacing them with railway-controlled organizations.

Passage of the Interstate Commerce Act of 1887 brought the
railways under Federal control. In one of its earliest proceedings,
the Interstate Commerce Commission (ICC), the regulatory agency established under the Act, decided that independent express companies
remained unaffected by the provisions of the Act. On the other hand
the position of the railway-controlled forwarders (from a regulatory
standpoint) was in a number of instances held to be analogous to
that of the railways themselves. The Hepburn Act of 1906 terminated
the legal distinction between the two groups of express companies
and, in placing them both under the jurisdiction of the ICC, enabled
that agency to undertake an examination of the entire express industry. The Commission found that a number of accusations[6] long leveled against the industry had validity and required the companies to
effect remedial measures.

The latter part of the 19th century saw the emergence of a
second type of forwarder. He differed from the "expressman" primarily in that his revenues were derived from consolidating many small

---

[1]The establishment of the first express company is generally attributed to
W. F. Harnden, who, traveling by rail between Boston and New York in 1839, adver-
tised in Boston's newspapers that he "would purchase goods, collect drafts and
bills, take charge of small packages of goods and bundles, and see that they were
safely delivered." Alfred L. Hammel, Wm. Frederick Harnden, 1813-1845 (New York
and Montreal: The Newcomen Society of North America, 1954), p. 10.

[2]For a discussion of the early phases of the express industry see Alvin F.
Harlow, Old Waybills, and H. Wells, Sketch of the Rise, Progress, and Present
Condition of the Express System, paper presented before the American Geographical
and Statistical Society, February 4, 1864.

[3]In the Matter of Express Rates, Practices, Accounts, and Revenues, 24 ICC
380, 384 (1912).

[4]Through imposition of "unjust" rates, nonrenewal of contracts, etc.

[5]Re. Express Companies, 1 ICC 677 (1887).

[6]These included double collection of lawful charges, excessive insurance
rates, delays in the settlement of claims, discrimination between shippers, cir-
cuitous routing of shipments, and tariff complexity. In the Matter of Express
Rates, Practices, and Revenues, p. 388.

individual shipments (belonging to different owners) into larger
ones and then offering these to the railways for conveyance to terminal points, where they were segregated into their constituent
units preparatory to being transported to ultimate points of destination.[1] The forwarder, in a sense, was now purchasing transportation at wholesale rates and selling it at retail rates, a practice
made possible through the introduction (by the railway carriers) of
rate structures under which shippers were charged less for full car-
load amounts than for less-than-carload shipments. (Volume-related
rate differentials, based on a demonstrable reduction of costs, were
approved by the ICC in 1890.[2])

Seeing a diminution in their less-than-carload traffic, the
rail companies issued new tariff rules, enforcement of which would
have required the shipper of any item to also be the owner of that
item. The railways' action was, however, disallowed by the ICC
(California Commercial Association v. Wells, Fargo and Co.[3]), which
stated that "the carrier deals with the shipment that is tendered,
not with its ownership,"[4] and "the shipper is the one who tenders
the shipment to the carrier, and the law forbids discrimination
between shippers."[5] In a parallel case, Export Shipping Co. v.
Wabash R.R. Co., the Commission took a similar position,[6] which was
sustained by the Supreme Court in 1911.[7]

The introduction of the motor vehicle greatly enhanced the
effectiveness of the forwarders,[8] who were now able to rely on motor

---

[1]Pickup and delivery was conducted via horse-drawn vehicles.

[2]Thurber v. N.Y.C. and H.R.R.Co., 2 ICC 742 (1890).

[3]14 ICC 422 (1908).

[4]Ibid., p. 427.

[5]Ibid., p. 428.

[6]"A carrier may not properly look beyond the transportation to the ownership of the shipment as a basis for determining the applicability of its rates."
14 ICC 437, 440 (1908).

[7]Interstate Commerce Commission v. Delaware, L. and W. R.R., 220 U.S. 235
(1911).

[8]Competition between the forwarders and the railways had already become a
matter of concern to the ICC, which was advocating Federal control over the activities of the former. This concern was heightened by the fact that due to railway-
domination many forwarders had ceased to be "dependent wholly on their own financial resources." Also, with increasing competition for a limited volume of traffic, forwarders were engaging in a variety of unethical practices, such as nonad-
herence to published tariffs. Referring to the zeal with which a number of forwarders attempted to enlarge their share of the market, the Commission noted
disapprovingly that "even cash payments to industrial traffic managers are not

carriers to provide pickup and delivery service to off-line areas. The truckers, initially unregulated, were free to enter into various contractual relationships[1] with the forwarders and, with improved technology, quickly expanded the scope of their operations. Enactment of the Motor Carrier Act of 1935, however, imposed Federal control upon the motor carriers and led to abrogation of the forwarder motor carrier agreements. Passage of the Act precipitated the filing by a number of trucking concerns functioning also as forwarders of applications in which single certificates of convenience and necessity were sought. The Commission dismissed the applications on the ground that forwarder activities did not fall within the purview of the Motor Carrier Act. In addition, the agency declared void all existing joint forwarder-motor carrier tariffs and, when a number of carriers attempted to circumvent this ruling by offering "proportional" rates to forwarders, disapproved these also.[2] The Commission's actions vis-à-vis the motor carriers affirmed the principle (enunciated in the earlier railway-related cases) of nondiscrimination between forwarders and other shippers, which, certain amendatory legislation notwithstanding, remains in force to this day.

In 1942 part IV of the Interstate Commerce Act became law and formally brought all surface forwarders under the control of the ICC The Commission now had responsibility for the granting of surface forwarder permits[3] and was invested with authority "to establish

---

unknown." Interstate Commerce Commission, Annual Report (Washington, D.C.: U.S. Government Printing Office, 1930), pp. 81-82. Reviewing the forwarding industry some years later, the ICC saw the continuation of a number of abuses and again called for the introduction of appropriate legislation to combat the problem. Freight Forwarding Investigation, 229 ICC 201 (1938).

[1] For example, preferential rates were offered to individual forwarders. Joint forwarder-motor carrier rates were also a common feature during this period.

[2] Chicago and Wisconsin Points Proportional Rates, 10 MCC 556 (1938) and 17 MCC 573 (1939). In 1940 the Supreme Court upheld the ICC's ruling, reversing a lower court opinion which had favored the motor carriers. United States v. Chicago Heights Trucking Co., 310 U.S. 344 (1940).
In rejecting the motor carriers' claim that the Motor Carrier Act applied not only to "direct" but also to "indirect" transportation, the ICC emphasized the crucial distinction between the two services: "the applicants' operations as a carrier may for convenience be divided into those which are direct and those which are indirect. The direct operations are those in which the carriage is performed by vehicles under the immediate ownership or control of applicant and without utilization of the services of any other carrier, and are confined to motor-vehicle operations. The indirect (i.e., forwarding) operations, which are more extensive are those in which the services of other carriers, by rail, by water, or by motor vehicle, are utilized." Acme Fast Freight, Inc., Common Carrier Application, 8 M 211,215 (1938).

[3] "Any permit issued under this section shall specify the nature or general description of the property with respect to which service subject to this part may be performed, and the territory within which, and the territories from which and

reasonable requirements with respect to continuous and adequate [forwarder] service."[1] Part IV sought to curb the abuses of which the industry had been found guilty in the past[2] and prescribed penalties for noncompliance with the new regulations. Under Section 408 of the Act motor common carriers were authorized to charge forwarders assembly and distribution rates lower than those charged other shippers, subject to the proviso that carriers could demonstrate that lower rates were based on reduced costs. Regulations governing contracts between forwarders and motor common carriers were amended in 1950. At the same time the Commission also modified its stand regarding the right of motor common carriers to charge forwarders under certain conditions rates below the published line-haul service tariff rate.

Air Freight Forwarders: Regulatory Role of the Civil Aeronautics Board, 1938-1977

The Civil Aeronautics Board defines an air freight forwarder as an "indirect air carrier," by which is meant:

> any citizen of the United States, who undertakes indirectly to engage in air transportation of property only, and who (1) does not engage directly in the operation of aircraft in air transportation, and (2) does not engage in air transportation pursuant to any Board order which has been issued for the purpose of authorizing air express service under a contract with a direct air carrier.[3]

An air freight forwarder is classified by the Board as

> an indirect air carrier which: (1) engages in interstate, overseas, or foreign air transportation, and (2) which in the ordinary and usual course of its undertaking, assembles and consolidates or provides for assembling and consolidating of property or performs or provides for the performance of break-bulk and distributing operations with respect to consolidated shipments, is responsible for the transportation of property from the point of receipt to point of destination and utilizes for the whole or any part of such transportation either the services of a direct air carrier . . . or those of another air freight forwarder.[4]

---

to which, service subject to this part may be performed, under authority of such permit." Interstate Commerce Act, section 410(e), 56 Stat. 292.

[1]Interstate Commerce Act, section 403(b), 56 Stat. 285.

[2]Forwarders, for instance, were required to adhere strictly to the specifications set forth in their tariffs and were prohibited from offering "undue" advantages to particular individuals, ports, transit points, etc.; common carriers were not permitted to discriminate between forwarders; control by a forwarder of an ICC-regulated common carrier was declared illegal.

[3]14 CFR 296.1(e). A "direct air carrier," on the other hand, is defined as "an air carrier directly engaged in the operation of aircraft pursuant to (1) a certificate issued under [the Federal Aviation Act] and (2) authority conferred by any applicable regulation or order of the Board." 14 CFR 296.1(d).

[4]Ibid., section 296.1(b).

The Civil Aeronautics Board's policy vis-à-vis the air freight forwarders was first codified in 1948. Prior to this the agency had concluded two investigations which were to contribute to the formulation of that policy. The first of these (Railway Express Agency, Inc.--Certificate of Public Convenience and Necessity[1]) dealt with an application by REA Express for a permanent certificate of public convenience and necessity and resulted in an order exempting the company from Federal economic regulatory control. At the time the application was submitted (1938), REA Express had sole jurisdiction over tariffs and ground operations of all freight ("express") tendered to the scheduled airlines.[2] The company believed that a permanent certificate would stabilize and generally strengthen its position but disclaimed any interest in becoming an airline operator, that is, a direct air carrier.

While there was no disagreement between the Board and the applicant over the latter's status as an air carrier within the meaning of the Civil Aeronautics Act, the company's operations were held to be incompatible with the operational restrictions demanded of certificate holders. REA Express, unlike the scheduled airlines, was free to serve any number of markets and therefore was unable to comply with a Congressional ruling limiting an air carrier's activities to the routes specified in its certificate. Since lack of a certificate would have placed the company in violation of section 401(a) of the Act,[3] a temporary order exempting it from the Act's certification requirements was issued. (This order was subsequently modified but was not made permanent.) Still in its infancy, the Board had no precedent of its own to guide it in a case such as this and, in concluding that the Civil Aeronautics Act "does not require nor authorize the issuance of certificates for operations such as those conducted by applicant,"[4] placed considerable emphasis on several ICC proceedings (including Acme Fast Freight, Inc., Common Carrier Application, above) concerned with the distinction between direct and indirect transportation. The Board, of course, was entirely free to disregard decisions reached by the ICC. In this instance, however, it considered the essential differences between

---

[1] 2 CAB 531 (1941).

[2] A detailed description of the early phases of the air express industry is found in John H. Frederick and Arthur D. Lewis, "History of Air Express," Journal of Air Law and Commerce 12, no. 3 (1941):203-231.

[3] See below, p. 88.

[4] Railway Express Agency, Inc.--Certificate of Public Convenience and Necessity, p. 539.

direct carriers and indirect carriers, as defined by the Commission, to be supportive of its own designation of REA Express as an indirect carrier.

The second of the two investigations referred to above was undertaken on the Board's own initiative and reflected its concern over the activities of the Universal Air Freight Corporation. The corporation's work consisted essentially of consolidating into larger units packages collected from the shipping public and tendering these to REA Express for shipment via the domestic airlines. At destination airports the corporation disassembled the units and delivered the packages to the individual consignees. Such operations, claimed Universal, were not those of an air carrier and placed it beyond the jurisdiction of the Board.

The CAB rejected this interpretation, termed the corporation's activities unlawful, and ordered them terminated. "Anyone who holds himself out to the public as ready to undertake for hire or reward the transportation of goods from place to place [as Universal was doing], and so invites the patronage of the public, is a common carrier,"[1] declared the Board. The fact that Universal, unlike REA Express, did not issue its own tariff had no bearing on the legality of its operations. Rather, once the Board's investigation revealed that Universal's activities were those of an air common carrier, it followed automatically that the corporation was in violation of the Civil Aeronautics Act, since such activities (whether direct or indirect) had to have the agency's approval.

At the time the Civil Aeronautics Act became law, REA Express had exclusive "express" contracts with the scheduled airlines which the CAB initially recognized. The express agency was not disputing the Board's jurisdiction over indirect air carriers and here the Board's principal objective had been to consider the manner in which that jurisdiction might best be exercised. In the case of the Universal Air Freight Corporation, on the other hand, the Board's efforts focused on an affirmation of its statutory responsibility towards indirect air carriers. Since the corporation functioned without authority (which the CAB was willing to grant only for "compelling reasons of public interest"), its activities could not be continued and it was ordered to "cease and desist from engaging in air transportation."[2]

---

[1] *Universal Air Freight Corporation--Investigation of Forwarding Activities*, 3 CAB 698,705 (1942).

[2] Ibid., p. 710.

Termination in 1943 of REA Express' exclusive contracts with the scheduled airlines opened the way for a number of companies to enter the forwarding field. Some of these, it should be noted, were already consolidating packages into volume lots prior to 1943 but could offer them only to nonscheduled carriers as these had no exclusive arrangement with the express agency. The legality of these operations was, at this point, contingent upon the companies in question functioning as agents for particular airlines or shippers, without holding any carrier responsibility whatsoever. Also, the companies were not permitted to publish their own tariffs. In an attempt to have their legal designation changed from "agent" to "carrier," these operators, whose growth was being accelerated through the filing of airline freight tariffs, lodged applications with the CAB urging it to undertake appropriate action on their behalf. Responding, the Board consolidated the applications into a single proceeding (known as the Air Freight Forwarder Case), held hearings lasting from February to July of 1947, and released its conclusions in September of the following year.[1]

The central issue facing the Board in the Air Freight Forwarder Case was the question of the applicants' future status, and this it resolved by determining that they would henceforth function as common carriers. Their agency status abolished, they became free to solicit the custom of the shipping public, consolidate freight collected from any number of shippers, and operate under their own tariffs. In sanctioning this status change the Board was motivated by what it viewed as public interest considerations. It reasoned that the forwarders, relieved of the restriction of serving merely as agents for individual shippers and given full access to the combined commercial air fleet, could offer consignors a more flexible service than was formerly possible. It was also anticipated that competition among forwarders would help to assure the public of "reasonable" rates[2] and that the airlines would benefit from the additional freight generated through the forwarders' sales efforts.

A number of the applicants seeking air freight forwarder authority were, in a sense, in a special category because of their affiliation with surface common carriers or surface forwarders. The Board's attitude towards such applicants, discussed more fully below, revolved about one crucial question: whether such an affiliation

---

[1] These conclusions concerned domestic applications only. Since the Board's decisions in regard to overseas and foreign commerce require the approval of the President, applications for international forwarder authority were treated separately.

[2] Air Freight Forwarder Case, 9 CAB 473,493 (1948).

adversely affected the air freight forwarder industry. Where it appeared interrelationships with surface carriers would have a negative impact on the industry's development, forwarder rights were rejected. Applications insufficiently detailed with regard to the nature of interlocking relationships (thereby preventing their examination within the framework of section 409 of the Civil Aeronautics Act[1]) were denied without prejudice pending further clarification.

The Board's recognition of the applicants as common carriers was vigorously protested by the certificated airlines. It was their contention that the forwarders would impose (on the airlines) uneconomical rate spreads, a fear the agency sought to allay by stressing that it possessed "ample authority to deal with any such situation that may arise."[2] The airlines also advanced the view that the forwarders would accentuate the directional imbalance in air traffic, that individual operators, in order to secure "special considerations" from the direct carriers, would divert traffic under their control from one airline to another, and that forwarder activities would lead to an overall diversion of traffic from air to surface transportation.[3] These fears, too, were largely discounted by the Board. Although it was possible that certain forwarders might be tempted to extract financial concessions from an airline by threatening to take their business to a competing carrier, the agency's regulatory powers were considered sufficient to cope with such an eventuality. Directional traffic imbalances were attributed "primarily to the economics of production and distribution,"[4] the Board adding that the forwarders could, in fact, be expected to help solve the problem. With respect to freight diversion from air to surface transportation, the agency conceded that a precise determination of the forwarders' impact was impossible given the absence of appropriate statistical data.

At this stage, of course, the air freight industry had produced virtually no data on forwarder activities and the CAB was unable to buttress its position by pointing to the "track record" of the forwarder community. It was this absence of data which earned

---

[1] See above, p.32, note 2.

[2] Air Freight Forwarder Case, p. 494.

[3] In a separate petition to the CAB the scheduled air carriers, fearful that they would lose traffic to their nonscheduled counterparts (whose rates were not regulated), requested that the latter be barred from accepting freight from forwarders. "Scheduled Airlines See Irregular-Forwarder Air Freight Threat," Traffic World 83, no. 7 (1949):45.

[4] Air Freight Forwarder Case, p. 495.

the Board much criticism, some of it coming from within its own
ranks. For example, one of its members, Jones, asserted his colleagues had paid insufficient heed to the concerns of the airlines.
Dismissing the forwarders as "middlemen parasites," he contended
the Board had accepted "self-serving declarations by the interested
applicants . . . as proven ultimate facts."[1] Jones felt the Board's
belief in the beneficial role air freight forwarders would play was
illusory and adamantly maintained the public interest did not call
for the creation of this carrier class.

In a collateral development the CAB granted authorization to
a number of applicants to operate as indirect air carriers in overseas and foreign transportation. Although the Board recognized that
the development of interstate freight transportation--which it had
cited in support of its claims regarding the contributions domestic
air freight forwarders could be expected to make--was not directly
applicable in the case of international commerce, it justified this
action in terms similar to those adopted in the domestic portion of
the Air Freight Forwarder Case, saying:

> we conclude that the differences alleged to exist between the domestic and
> foreign phases of this proceeding are not of sufficient import to cause us
> to reach a conclusion with respect to the need for freight forwarder oper-
> ations in overseas and foreign air transportation different from that here-
> tofore arrived at in our prior opinion with respect to the need for such
> operations in domestic air transportation. On the contrary, the complex-
> ities of international transportation make that need even greater in over-
> seas and foreign air transportation than in the domestic field.[2]

The "complexities" referred to included export/import procedures and
warehousing problems at international gateways, which, the applicants
insisted, could be more effectively handled by themselves than by
the various underlying direct air carriers. Airline officials who
argued forwarders would weaken the financial position of international air carriers, were told their case was without merit. The
Board noted that the scope of Air Cargo, Inc., the ground service
organization of the scheduled airlines, was far narrower than the
service the forwarders proposed to offer, and suggested that nothing
prevented the airlines from introducing a more attractive, and hence
competitively more effective, ground service of their own.[3]

The fact that the Board's initial approval of forwarder operations, both domestically and internationally, was provisional, reflected its recognition of the experimental nature of air freight

---

[1]Ibid., p. 516.

[2]Air Freight Forwarder Case (International), 11 CAB 182, 190 (1949).

[3]Ibid., p. 194.

forwarding and indicated a more cautious attitude towards indirect
carriers than some of its earlier statements might have implied.
Indeed, the CAB felt that several years would be required to collect
and evaluate appropriate statistical data on the basis of which a
permanent forwarder policy could be constructed. In the case of
foreign commerce especially, the agency took cognizance of the constantly shifting transportation patterns, saying that a trial period
was critical and that a permanent policy would have to await greater
stabilization of the international air transportation industry.
Flexibility, the agency believed, was essential during the trial
period if the forwarders were to be given a fair opportunity to show
what they could do. To this end a general relief order was promulgated, exempting them from certain provisions of the Civil Aeronautics Act. Accordingly, applicants, pursuant to section 1(2) of the
Act (now section 101[3] of the Federal Aviation Act), were not required to demonstrate their "fitness, willingness, and ability" to
enter the forwarding field and were relieved of the requirement of
operating under certificates of public convenience and necessity.
The total number of forwarders permitted to operate at any one time
was not restricted and no limitation was placed on the number of
points between which their services might be rendered.

Charging that licensing via an exemption order constituted an
unlawful maneuver and that the imposition "on the existing air transportation system [of] a duplicating system of indirect air carriers
which will compete with the direct air carriers for freight business"[1] was subjecting the airlines to "irreparable injury and damage,"[2] fifteen certificated airlines petitioned the U.S. Circuit
Court of Appeals at Chicago to stay the CAB order. This the court
did in November, 1948, basing its decision largely on the dissenting
opinion in the Air Freight Forwarder Case, above (domestic phase).
However, upon hearing oral argument in which the CAB, restating its
earlier position, maintained that the plaintiffs had not shown that
rescinding the stay order would cause them "irreparable injury" and
in which counsel for the Air Freight Forwarders Association accused
the airlines of forming "a cartel which was alien to American business," the court vacated its order in January, 1949.[3] This was not

[1]"Court Delays CAB Exemption Order," Aviation Week 49, no. 22 (1948):36.

[2]"Air Forwarder Case to Be Heard in January by U.S. Court of Appeals,"
Traffic World 83, no. 1 (1949):42.

[3]"U.S. Court of Appeals Hears Oral Argument in Air Forwarder Case," Traffic
World 83, no. 6 (1949):52.

a formal response to the airlines but, rather, a half-way measure designed to ease the plight of the forwarders. Uncertainty over their legal status was making their position untenable, and the court evidently shared their view that lengthy proceedings constituted "a burden too onerous to be sustained." Their "burden" was not to be reimposed, for the final decision, made known in December of 1949, represented an unequivocal victory for the applicants.

The court was only tangentially interested in air freight diseconomies and related problems imputed to the forwarders; it recognized that there was little empirical evidence for or against forwarder operations and noted the essentially experimental intent behind the CAB's order. Rather, its concern centered on whether the agency in exempting the applicants from the Civil Aeronautics Act's certification requirements had, as charged by the airlines, exceeded its statutory authority. The Civil Aeronautics Act of 1938 stipulated that

> no air carrier shall engage in any air transportation unless there is in force a certificate issued by the Board authorizing such air carrier to engage in such transportation[1]

and

> the Board shall issue a certificate authorizing the whole or any part of the transportation covered by the application, if it finds that the applicant is fit, willing, and able to perform such transportation properly, . . . and that such transportation is required by the public convenience and necessity.[2]

At the same time the agency was empowered to

> relieve air carriers who are not directly engaged in the operation of aircraft in air transportation from the provisions of this Act to the extent and for such periods as may be in the public interest.[3]

Had the court found against the forwarders, it would in effect have been saying, "the test for determining whether an indirect carrier should be relieved of the obligation of proving necessity is to require proof of necessity in every case,"[4] an absurd proposition and one which would have destroyed the unique regulatory position of the forwarders. Congress had set its imprimatur on the distinction between direct and indirect air carriers and it was this

---

[1]Civil Aeronautics Act, section 401(a); in 1958 this became section 401(a) of the Federal Aviation Act. 72 Stat. 754, 49 U.S.C. 1371.

[2]Civil Aeronautics Act, section 401(d)(1); in 1958 this became section 401(d)(1) of the Federal Aviation Act. See above, p. 28, note 1.

[3]Civil Aeronautics Act, section 1(2); in 1958 this became section 101(3) of the Federal Aviation Act. 72 Stat. 737, 49 U.S.C. 1301.

[4]American Airlines, Inc. v. Civil Aeronautics Board, 178 F.2d 903,906 (7th Cir. 1949).

distinction which was now being affirmed. Said the court:

> there can be no question that the Board properly construed each of the
> sections and that there is no requirement of proof of convenience and
> necessity of the proposed operations to be read into Section 1(2) in
> order to preserve other portions of the Act and its basic objectives.[1]

Following a five-year trial period the Board reopened its
enquiry into the domestic air freight forwarder industry, making
known its findings and conclusions after an investigatory period
lasting about two-and-a-half years.[2] Now concerned with the formulation of a permanent forwarder policy, the agency focused its
attention on three principal issues, namely: (1) the renewal of
existing licenses, (2) the adjudication of new forwarder applications, and (3) the revision of its Economic Regulations (part 296)
pertaining to forwarder rules and practices. Domestic air freight
forwarder service during the trial period was judged, despite the
financial embarrassment of a number of operators, to have been generally successful in meeting the public interest, and existing authorizations were renewed for an "indefinite" period. The trial period had seen substantial shipper acceptance of forwarders, who, the
Board noted approvingly, were functioning without governmental subsidies. Moreover, it appeared the indirect carriers were developing
new air freight markets and that the increased traffic was contributing (in certain freight categories) to lower freight rates. Renewal of forwarder authorizations on an "indefinite," as opposed to
a "permanent," basis was justified as a means of avoiding legal
complications at some future point when the operational authority
in individual instances or for the industry as a whole might have
to be modified. Still unable to reconcile itself to the presence
of the forwarders, the airline industry, having failed to persuade
the Board to cancel their permits, now suggested that forwarder
operations be limited to a fixed time period.[3] This, however, was

---

[1]Ibid., p. 907.

[2]Air Freight Forwarder Investigation, 21 CAB 536 (1955).

[3]American Airlines, Trans World Airlines, and United Airlines characterized
the results of the experimental authorization as "inconclusive" and recommended
renewal for a further five-year period. The airlines insisted that "no clear
pattern of forwarder services has thus far emerged," that the promotional efforts
of the forwarders had led to diversion of traffic from one direct carrier to
another, and that shipments were being delayed due to the forwarders' desire to
maximize consolidations. In reply, the Board noted that any inconclusiveness
attaching to the forwarder experiment was confined solely to the "profit prospects"
of various individual operators and that, in fact, several patterns of forwarder
service had developed (such as lower-rate service). Traffic diversion had, according to the CAB, not been proven; furthermore, it was noted that during the
test period domestic airline revenues had risen by approximately 65 percent. The

considered unacceptable as it would have subjected the indirect carriers to a series of costly renewal proceedings and lowered their standing in the business community.

Unhindered market entry was retained as the central element of the Board's policy towards the forwarders, the number of active operators to be determined by free market forces rather than through some restrictive regulatory mechanism. The shipping public was considered the ultimate judge of forwarder service, obviating the need for public hearings at which applicants would be called upon to demonstrate a need for their work and prove that they were "fit" to engage in forwarding operations.[1] This "free entry" policy, however, applied only to independent applicants. Air freight forwarder authority for applicants who were affiliates of motor carriers or surface forwarders or were themselves surface forwarders was approved only where it was evident that the relationship with surface transportation would have no negative impact (by weakening competition, etc.) on air freight forwarding as a whole.

The CAB also decided to grant bona fide shippers associations authorization to function, for an indefinite period, as indirect carriers.[2] Similarly, it approved, albeit for a limited trial period only, entry into air freight forwarding by two surface forwarders controlled by railway interests. These latter authorizations were assailed by both independent forwarders and airline officials, who, given the rail companies' considerable capital resources, believed these would be used to depress prevailing rate levels, thus destroying the independent operators and setting up essentially monopolistic conditions in the air freight forwarder industry. Other criticisms of surface-dominated air freight forwarders were: (1) they would not make a maximum effort to promote air freight, (2) they would, under certain circumstances, attempt to divert traffic from air to the more established patterns of surface transportation, and (3) the conflict of interest between air and surface modes

---

business practice of shipping at the end of the day's output was cited as the prime reason behind certain delays, which, in any case, were considered too brief to be of concern to the shipping public.

[1] In order to enhance shipper protection the CAB raised the minimum insurance coverage which forwarders had to carry from $2,000 to $10,000 per conveyance. It conceded that ability to satisfy this minimal requirement did not constitute absolute proof of a forwarder's financial "fitness" and defended the relatively lax entry criteria (as compared with the far more stringent tests faced by those wishing to function as direct air carriers) on the grounds that forwarder operations were independent of aircraft safety and did not touch on national security.

[2] See below, p. 275.

of transportation would result in a lessening of competition within the air freight forwarder field. These points were similar to those raised earlier against authorization of air freight forwarders having surface carrier affiliations, and the Board disposed of them much as it had done in other instances. Its basic posture was that entry into the market by these applicants was not inconsistent with the public interest, as it could lead to lower rates, and that potentially adverse repercussions would be outweighed by advantages derived from the additional traffic generated by the new entrants. The threat of traffic diversion (from air to surface transportation) was not taken seriously, since it appeared unlikely that shippers willing and able to pay for air transportation would become regular users of an admittedly less expensive but substantially slower ground service. The Board held as improbable the setting up of air freight subsidiaries if the rail companies did not consider air forwarder service a viable business proposition and argued that denial rather than approval of air forwarder rights would produce a hostile attitude towards air shipments on the part of the parent companies. The existence of a large number of independent forwarders would, it was further stated, compel surface-affiliated forwarders to maintain a high level of competition and would serve to act as a brake to any ambitions they might have which could endanger the independent operators. Other decisions reached by the CAB were:

1. It was permissible for forwarders to cooperate with one another by "joint loading" their freight for movement on the same flight. Such arrangements (which enable participants to pay lower rates for the larger units thus produced) were to be open to all interested parties on a nondiscriminatory basis[1]

2. The public interest did not require restrictions on chartering of aircraft by forwarders. Restrictions, requested by American Airlines (which believed it would otherwise lose its more profitable scheduled business), were thought by the CAB to "unnecessarily hinder and impede" the development of air traffic[2]

3. An increase was ordered in various kinds of insurance coverage carried by forwarders

4. Forwarders were enjoined from entering into space allocation agreements with direct air carriers. Such agreements, noted the Board, might give certain forwarders an "undue" advantage over others and would provide all forwarders with a weapon against shippers associations (the associations were handling smaller volumes of freight). Although "first come first served" was to be the rule for the time being, the Board allowed that an expansion in airlift capacity at a future date could dictate a change in this policy

---

[1]See below, p. 261.

[2]See below, p. 264.

5. Existing forwarder reporting procedures were considered to be "in a confused state," and it was deemed advisable to revise these so as to give the Board a clearer financial and operational picture of forwarder services[1]

6. Forwarders were given the option of acting as shippers' agents in cases where the available volume of freight did not permit consolidation. While acting in an agency capacity, they were forbidden to charge commissions and had to restrict their remuneration to rates listed in their tariffs

7. A forwarder request seeking establishment of joint rates with the direct air carriers was denied, the Board emphasizing that where rates were concerned, forwarders had been and would continue to be treated as shippers, not carriers.[2]

With the termination of the forwarder investigation's international phase (1958) the CAB was able to redefine its policies towards indirect carriers holding international authority.[3] These carriers, too, were granted operating rights for an indefinite period and like their domestic counterparts were not required to undergo fitness tests. No limitations were placed on the types of commodities carried or on the number and location of points served. The supporting arguments for the various measures adopted were similar to those used in the domestic phase of the enquiry and need not be repeated here. One interesting departure from precedent, however, was in the matter of forwarders acting as agents for direct carriers. Whereas previously it had been determined that "allowing the forwarder to act as carrier's agent permits the creation of a situation where conflicts of interest are almost inevitable,"[4] the Board now authorized forwarders to assume the status of carriers' agents on the grounds that international forwarding was less developed than domestic forwarding and because, in the words of the examiner, payment of commissions was "a standard part of the international process."[5] In practical terms this meant that, when no consolidation

---

[1]Reporting requirements have been amended on several occasions. See, for example, CAB Regulation ER-945 (adopted in 1976) and EDR-350 (issued in 1978).

[2]*Air Freight Forwarder Investigation*, second supplemental opinion, 24 CAB 755 (1957).

[3]*International Air Freight Forwarder Investigation*, 27 CAB 658 (1958).

[4]Here the CAB was thinking of what it considered the forwarder's primary obligation, namely, the promotion of the shipper's interests. *Air Freight Forwarder Investigation*, supplemental opinion, 23 CAB 376,377 (1956).

[5]This was a reference to the fact that international forwarders in their capacity as registered IATA agents collect a commission on freight procured for IATA carriers. The legality of the Board's action was challenged by Trans World Airlines in a petition for reconsideration, which was dismissed by the CAB in the latter part of 1959. *International Air Freight Forwarder Investigation*, supplemental opinion, 30 CAB 13 (1959). The fixing of commission levels by agreement has recently been criticized by the Board and, in view of the industry's move towards greater competition (chapter III), seems likely to be disallowed in the near future.

could be effected, a forwarder, acting as a direct carrier's agent, was free to ship freight at the latter's regular tariff rate, collecting a commission in the process.

It should be noted that the Board's jurisdiction did not extend to inbound-U.S. traffic controlled by foreign freight forwarders. Absence of such jurisdiction was deplored by several U.S. international forwarders, who complained that foreign competitors held an advantage over Americans since only the former were able to receive commissions on consolidated shipments entering the United States (enabling them to undercut rates charged by U.S. operators). Moreover, alleged the complainants, the Board's impotence vis-à-vis foreign forwarders contributed to the existence of various illegal practices involving rebates and "kickbacks." The CAB's refusal to assume authority over certain non-U.S. forwarder operations stemmed from a fear of provoking retaliatory measures on the part of other governments and from the realization that enforcement of extraterritorial regulations was virtually impossible. In order to place U.S. forwarders on a more equal footing with their foreign competitors, however, the CAB approved abolition of adherence (by American forwarders) to filed tariffs on inbound-U.S. freight and instituted a relaxation of airline-forwarder compensation agreement rules.[1]

The forwarding industry entered a new phase in 1964, for in that year a group of motor common carriers of household goods were permitted to engage in domestic and international air freight forwarding. This was, of course, not the first time surface carriers had won approval to extend their work to air transportation. Nonetheless, it constituted a turning point in that never before had these applicants held such extensive ICC operating rights.[2] Air forwarder authorization was limited to the carriage of household goods, which the CAB defined as

(1) personal effects and property used or to be used in a dwelling when a part of the equipment or supply of such dwelling; and (2) furniture, fixtures, equipment, and the property of stores, offices, museums, institutions, hospitals, or other establishments, when a part of the stock, equipment, or supply of such stores, offices, museums, institutions, hospitals, or other establishments,[3]

and as such was somewhat more restrictive than that sought by the

---

[1]The Board's order enabled U.S. international forwarders to collect commissions from the airlines on consolidated shipments. Compensation agreements were subject to Board approval and were open to participation on equal terms by all international forwarders and airlines.

[2]One carrier, for example, held nationwide authority.

[3]Air Freight Forwarder Authority Case, 40 CAB 673, 675-676 (1964).

applicants who had hoped to see adoption of a definition (of such goods) employed earlier by the Interstate Commerce Commission.[1]

In their applications to the Board the motor carriers claimed that, if they were allowed to apply their expertise in the household goods field to air transportation, the volume of these goods carried by air would quickly rise above existing levels. The effort needed to promote the transportation of household goods, they contended, had not and would not be made by the established forwarders and airlines, since these lacked "the incentive, skilled personnel, special facilities, and equipment to develop the traffic or to operate the services."[2] The movement of household effects called for specialization of the type recognized under the Motor Carrier Act of 1935, which had established separate categories of carriers.[3] In addition to their unique skills, they noted, the facilities and equipment already at their disposal sufficed to permit entry into air freight forwarding without major capital expenditures. Their sales efforts, they assured the Board, would stimulate traffic growth and bring about a lowering of rates, which in their existing form were recognized by all parties to the case to form a major stumbling block to the volume movement of household goods.[4]

The grant of air freight forwarder authority to the motor carriers was strongly opposed by a number of established forwarders. Concerned lest numerous other surface carriers now also demand air forwarder permits, these intervenors attempted to persuade the Board that the proposed service was not needed by the shipping public and that it would not, as claimed, lead to lower rates. The intervenors held that any Board action favorable to the motor carriers subverted the interests of existing air forwarders and belittled the significance of the motor carriers' specialized skills, arguing that containerization had rendered these obsolete. Stung by the charge that they had defaulted in their responsibility to promote the movement by air of household goods, they conceded that traffic volume was low but attributed this to the absence of specific commodity rates for these goods and to the high level of air freight rates generally.[5]

---

[1] Practices of Motor Common Carriers of Household Goods, 17 MCC 467, 505 (1939).

[2] Air Freight Forwarder Authority Case, p. 682.

[3] The Act enjoined general commodity carriers from transporting household goods.

[4] Air Freight Forwarder Authority Case, p. 681.

[5] Ibid., p. 684.

The motor carriers, it was further alleged, had no interest in fostering the expansion of air traffic; air freight forwarder authority was sought only as an adjunct to their established ground operations and, indeed, would result in the diversion of traffic from air to surface modes of transportation.[1]

Joining the intervenors in their opposition to the motor carriers was the CAB's Bureau of Economic Regulation. The Bureau saw a parallel between the issues in the current case and those in Railway Express Agency, Inc.--Air Freight Forwarder Application[2] and felt that issuance of air freight forwarder authority to the motor carriers represented a new policy which should be implemented only following a series of procedural steps. To this the Board replied that the grounds on which the express agency's request for forwarder authority had been rejected did not obtain in the present proceeding.[3] The Bureau, so the Board believed, had confused the earlier treatment of REA Express with a general policy designed to exclude surface carriers as a whole from the air freight forwarder field and now had difficulty accepting what appeared to be a reversal of that policy. The Board stressed that the decisions reached in a number of earlier proceedings demonstrated its consistent attitude towards surface-oriented would-be air freight forwarders. Congressional intent, it pointed out, had been its guide in the adjudication of applications involving direct surface carriers and their affiliates; had Congress intended adoption of an exclusionary policy, it would have so directed and would have avoided the language appearing in the second proviso of section 408(b) of the Federal Aviation Act.[4]

---

[1]It was the unanimous view of the applicants that any modal diversion of traffic that might take place would be from surface to air. The most lucrative sectors of their business consisted of storage, packaging services, and local cartage (as opposed to the line-haul movement of goods); these they could best protect by offering their customers (through the addition of air transportation) a more flexible and comprehensive service.

[2]27 CAB 500 (1958). This case concerned the application by REA Express for air freight forwarder rights. The Board rejected the application on the grounds that its position as the nation's leading nongovernmental small-package carrier, its worldwide surface operations, and its exclusive relationship with the domestic rail companies gave the company an unfair competitive advantage over other forwarders. The Board also believed that the express agency would inevitably divert some air traffic to rail express because of the low rail rates offered shippers through a special export/import tariff.

[3]Air Freight Forwarder Authority Case, pp. 674-675.

[4]"If the applicant [for a merger or consolidation] is a carrier other than an air carrier, or a person controlled by a carrier other than an air carrier or affiliated therewith within the meaning of Section 5(8) of the Interstate Commerce Act, as amended, such applicant shall for the purposes of this section be considered an air carrier and the Board shall not enter such an order of approval unless

Section 408 of the Act deals with mergers between air carriers and between air carriers and other common carriers and was enacted in part to prevent surface carrier control of air transportation. The Board's discretionary powers enabled it to approve certain surface carrier-air carrier relationships, but only where it found that such relationships would promote the public interest.[1] The establishment of monopolies (and their impact on competition) has generally been considered adverse to the public interest and explains, for example, the denial of REA Express' forwarder applications. The Board, in countering the arguments of parties attempting to automatically block entry into air freight forwarding by surface-oriented applicants, has always held that the second proviso of section 408(b) did not apply in cases where direct or indirect surface carriers sought control over air freight forwarders and that it was restricted to situations in which a direct surface carrier wished to acquire control of a direct air carrier.[2]

In approving air freight forwarder authority (for an experimental five-year period) for the motor carriers, the CAB refuted the entire range of arguments presented by the intervenors. It listed the advantages to be gained from these authorizations (such as additional freight traffic, lower rates, and single-carrier responsibility) and declared itself satisfied that a need existed for the specialized service the applicants intended to provide.[3] The existing air forwarders, concluded the Board, were uninterested in the development of the proposed service--out of over ninety forwarders only two were handling household goods shipments--and as such there could be no question of the new entrants taking traffic away from established companies since the latter "have nothing to take."[4] The creation of a monoply by the applicants was ruled out because,

---

it finds that the transaction proposed will promote the public interest by enabling such carrier other than an air carrier to use aircraft to public advantage in its operation and will not restrain competition." 72 Stat. 767, 49 U.S.C. 1378. In 1978 section 408 was amended by 92 Stat. 1726.

[1]Prior to the enactment of Public Law 95-504 (chapter III) it was unlawful without the Board's approval "for any air carrier or person controlling an air carrier, any other common carrier, any person engaged in any other phase of aeronautics, or any other person to acquire control of any air carrier in any manner whatsoever: Provided, that the Board may by order exempt any such acquisition of a noncertificated air carrier from this requirement to the extent and for such periods as may be in the public interest." Federal Aviation Act, section 408(a)(5) 72 Stat. 767, as amended by 83 Stat. 103, 49 U.S.C. 1378.

[2]See below, p. 157.

[3]Air Freight Forwarder Authority Case, p. 707.

[4]Ibid., p. 716.

limited as it was to the conveyance of household goods, their operating authority would not enable them to obtain a "stranglehold" on
the air freight market.

In a more recent proceeding, Household Goods Air Freight Forwarder Investigation, a total of forty-one household goods motor
common carriers and surface forwarders of household goods received
authorization to engage in air freight forwarding for an indefinite
period. This case differed significantly from the preceding Air
Freight Forwarder Authority Case, because now no restriction was
placed on the nature of the commodities to be carried. Excess
freight space in aircraft, the willingness of the applicants to provide service to additional communities, as well as related points
noted elsewhere in this chapter, combined to form the basis for the
Board's decision. Where interlocking relationships between companies or affiliates were seen to impair competition, air forwarder
permits were withheld.[1] In this connection the Board decreed that
"any individual who is a director, officer or controlling shareholder of an authorized air freight forwarder, or its affiliates,
may not act in any capacity (i.e., either as a director, officer or
controlling shareholder) with another air freight forwarder."[2]

Although the Household Goods Air Freight Forwarder Investigation and the case preceding it were confined to surface carriers of
household effects, the two proceedings are indicative of a broader
trend in the air freight industry, namely the growing role of general commodity surface carriers as air freight forwarders. It has
never been, as we have seen, the Board's objective to bar surface-
affiliated carriers from the air forwarding business, and the agency
has emphasized on many occasions that no such restriction was called
for under the Federal Aviation Act. Nevertheless the agency has
shown greater restraint in its approach to affiliates than to independent air freight forwarder applicants and has denied applications
(submitted by surface-connected carriers) which were deemed to be
detrimental to the public interest. Unsuccessful applicants have
usually been perceived as a threat to independent forwarders in one
or more of the following ways: (1) the large financial resources of
the applicant's corporate parent might give rise to unfair competitive practices, (2) conflicts of interest between a company's air

---

[1] For example, the application of Greyhound Van Lines was rejected because
its common control relationship with Greyhound Leasing and Finance Corporation
(one of the nation's leading aircraft lessors) could have invited a situation in
which its shipments received preferential treatment from the airlines. Household
Goods Air Freight Forwarder Investigation, Orders 72-7-33 and 72-10-59.

[2] Ibid., Order 72-7-33, p. 7.

and surface activities might lead to a diversion of traffic to surface transportation, (3) surface carrier interests could establish a monopoly over the air freight forwarding business. The development of the air freight industry and the growth of the independent forwarders led to greater willingness on the part of the Board to permit surface-connected carriers to enter the air forwarder field. This the agency has justified on the grounds that the independent forwarders had become less vulnerable to competitive pressures and that additional competition was beneficial for what has become an established industry. Apart from the benefits of competition (such as lower rates and service to additional points), the Board felt that surface carriers and their affiliates aided the air freight industry in a number of ways. For instance, they tended to reinforce intermodal transportation coordination and brought to air freight forwarding: (1) nationwide communication networks, (2) electronic systems for tracing and billing, (3) experienced personnel, and (4) innovative promotional programs.

Surface-affiliated applicants have been required to indicate how they intend to "conscientiously promote" air freight, and in this context it is instructive to look closely at one such application and consider the kind of arguments the Board has found persuasive.[1] In a joint application filed in 1971, Burlington Northern (a rail carrier) and its motor carrier affiliate, BN Transport, requested that the Board allow their newly-formed corporation (Burlington Northern Air Freight) to engage in air freight forwarding and at the same time approve various control relationships under section 408(a)(5) of the Federal Aviation Act.[2] Favorable action by the Board, asserted the applicants, would not lead to a conflict of interest between the corporate affiliates because the two surface carriers had virtually no involvement with the small-shipment business. Having been found unprofitable in the past, small shipments held no interest for the surface carriers and would, whenever possible, be diverted to the new air freight forwarder.

The fact that Burlington Northern Air Freight was to have an independent sales program geared to the needs of a particular segment of the shipping public would help to ensure (according to the applicants) that its interests remained separated from those of allied companies. The new company intended to hire 34 experienced air freight executives who would be "committed solely to the

---

[1] Application of Burlington Northern Air Freight, Inc. for Domestic and International Air Freight Forwarder Authority, Order 72-3-3.

[2] See above, p. 96, note 1.

promotion of air cargo exclusive from the operations of other Burlington affiliates," as well as 30 field managers and supervisors
who, with "the hundreds of Burlington affiliate sales personnel,"
would be "encouraged" to solicit air traffic.[1] Initially services
were to be offered through 65 United States and 4 Canadian airport
cities. Since terminals and other facilities of the corporate affiliates were to be at the disposal of the new company, coordinated
air-highway movements could be expected to provide air forwarder
service to some 460 points within the Burlington system's area of
operation. (The application was approved in 1972.)

The entry of surface carriers into the air freight forwarding
industry was examined once more in the Motor Carrier--Air Freight
Forwarder Investigation. The Board's initial decision (1967) was
one of the most controversial the agency had reached since formally
authorizing forwarder activities in 1948 and confirmed the trend,
discussed above, towards greater surface carrier involvement in air
freight forwarding. Its conclusions in the case, so the Board believed, were but a logical extension of a policy long in force; its
critics, on the other hand, argued that the agency had abandoned its
limited protection of the forwarder industry and had cast the independent operators adrift in a hostile competitive environment.

At issue were the applications for forwarder rights submitted
by several long-haul motor carriers of general commodities.[2] Their
financial background and their experience in the handling and documentation of small-package freight, the carriers told the CAB, enabled them to offer the public a substantially improved forwarder
service. While not accepting all their claims (these included the
elimination of congestion at shippers' terminals, greater efficiency
due to single-company responsibility, and improved accounting procedures), the examiner nevertheless took the stand, subsequently
adopted by the Board with only minor modifications, that entry by
the truckers into the air freight forwarding business was in the
public interest and merited approval on a trial basis.[3] The growth

---

[1]Order 72-3-3, p. 5.

[2]This was the first time long-haul motor carriers (of general commodities)
were permitted to enter the air freight forwarding field. The Board defined a
long-haul motor carrier as "a motor carrier holding operating rights issued by the
Interstate Commerce Commission to haul general commodities between any pair of
points which are over 500 air miles apart, or an affiliate of such a carrier."
14 CFR 296.1(h).

[3]In accepting the examiner's findings the Board noted especially that the
motor carriers indicated they would be generating additional air traffic and that
the nature of their operations was such that intermodal transportation coordination would be strengthened. The Board's order granting the truckers air freight

of air freight transportation, to quote the examiner, was largely
dependent upon the "zeal, effort, and resources" of those concerned
with its promotion and could be expected to gain momentum through
the participation of the applicants.

The Board's decision, it need scarcely be emphasized, drew
strenuous objections from a number of forwarders and direct air carriers. Once again it was averred that the forwarder business was
already saturated, that the Board's action invited a diversion of
freight from air to surface carriers, and that the forwarding industry would come under the domination of surface interests. Another
concern, captured perfectly in the headline "If Truckers Get Forwarding Watch Out For Head Hunters" was that the newcomers would
draw skilled personnel away from the ranks of the established forwarders.[1] Although conceding that there would be some traffic diversion, the examiner believed this would be relatively insignificant and would affect only the weakest companies. The applicants,
he observed, would be competing for traffic among themselves and
would not be able to form a united front against the established
operators.

The independent forwarders, having stated from the outset that
the CAB lacked the statutory authority to permit the long-haul motor
carriers to engage in air freight forwarding, reacted to the Board's
order by lodging with the U.S. Court of Appeals a petition for judicial review. Responding affirmatively, the court vacated the
order and remanded the case to the CAB for reexamination. The Board,
the court felt, had underestimated the likelihood of a conflict of
interest (on the part of the truckers) between air and surface transportation and had thus misjudged the impact its action would have on
the air freight industry generally. Of greater concern, however,
were certain ambiguities in the Board's order, the wording of which
was considered imprecise to the point where it appeared to offer air
forwarder authority to all interested long-haul truckers, not merely
the applicants. The court was here seeking to protect the existing
forwarders, whose competitive position it saw threatened in the
event of a potentially massive invasion of air freight markets by

---

forwarder authority was opposed by its vice chairman (Murphy) on the grounds that
the truckers would be faced by a conflict of interest and that it would bring
about an "anticompetitive" situation. Murphy rejected also the claim that they
would broaden intermodal transportation coordination. Motor Carrier--Air Freight
Forwarder Investigation, Order E-25725.

[1]Editorial, Air Cargo 13, no. 7 (1969):42. The editorial ends on a com-
bative note, pointing out that, "this might be the ideal time for air freight
forwarders to make some discreet raids on trucker personnel."

long-haul truckers. The agency's order, opined the court, constituted "a commitment to grant authorization to all comers" and represented a significant departure from earlier policy. As such, it
was found

> wanting in the careful investigation, the substantial evidence and the
> rational explication that are demanded before an expert agency may law-
> fully embark on a new course apparently so fraught with danger to the
> industry Congress has confined to its regulation and seemingly so
> opposed to the general policy Congress has long decreed.[1]

The CAB's remand decision, issued in 1969, was again appealed
by the Air Freight Forwarders Association but this time was upheld
by the court.[2] The Board reiterated the major points raised in its
earlier decision; more important, however, was its elucidation of
those issues on which the court's initial opinion had been based.
Authority for the applicants to enter the air freight forwarder
field was not to be construed as an automatic entry policy applying
to all truckers; on the contrary, future applicants were to be closely examined to ensure that their operations were in the public interest. To this end, a "monitored" (rather than "free") entry procedure was introduced with respect to long-haul motor carriers,
subjecting them to various new entry criteria and reporting requirements. The Board explained again that the Federal Aviation Act did
not prohibit acquisition of an indirect air carrier by surface carrier interests and that, as a consequence, it was free to reshape
its forwarder program without having to "compile an evidentiary
record to justify each adjustment of policy."[3]

The CAB's willingness to lower its "shield of protection
enough to allow increased competition from surface interests"[4] was
demonstrated anew in 1970 with a grant of authority to two rail companies, Southern Pacific and Santa Fe, to engage in domestic and
international forwarding by air for a five-year experimental period.[5]
The scope and nature of the rail companies' surface operations were
such that they constituted no threat to the existing pattern of air
service: for example, of the nation's fifty leading air forwarder

---

[1]ABC Air Freight Co., Inc. v. Civil Aeronautics Board, 391 F.2d 295,307
(2d Cir. 1968).

[2]ABC Air Freight Co., Inc. v. Civil Aeronautics Board, 419 F.2d 154 (2d
Cir. 1969); certiorari denied, 397 U.S. 1006 (1970).

[3]Motor Carrier--Air Freight Forwarder Investigation, opinion on remand,
Order 69-4-100, p. 10.

[4]Ibid., pp. 9-10.

[5]Southern Pacific--Santa Fe Air Freight Forwarder Case, Order 70-10-100.

city-pairs, only three were being served by the Southern Pacific rail network. Also, diversion of shipments from air to surface operations was considered unlikely since neither company wished to carry less-than-carload traffic. The Air Freight Forwarders Association, which originally had planned to oppose the applicants, altered its stance upon learning of the Supreme Court's refusal to review the appellate court's 1969 long-haul motor carrier decision. The Association reasoned that, in view of the similarity between the two cases, little was to be gained through the initiation of another judicial investigation.

The forwarder licenses held by long-haul motor carrier affiliates and rail companies (both groups had been licensed on a temporary basis) were reexamined in 1974. These carriers, one of the Board's administrative law judges noted, had made a positive contribution to the air freight industry and were no longer to be held to higher licensing standards than independent forwarders. They had not, as initially feared by the court in ABC Air Freight, above, inundated the air freight market, restrained competition, or diverted freight to surface modes of transportation, and permanent operating authority was accordingly recommended.[1]

Opinion on the Board's "monitored entry" experiment was, not surprisingly, divided. Pronounced "a huge success" by CF Air Freight, Inc. (a long-haul air freight forwarder), it was dismissed as "an abject failure" by Emery (one of the so-called independent forwarders). In defense of its record CF noted that it had opened major terminals (including one in New York) within the time limit initially proposed to the Board; moreover, it had avoided concentrating on the largest markets and had set up five[2] terminals in small or nonhub cities and eight in medium air traffic hubs.[3] The conflict of interest argument, CF asserted, had no validity; its air freight operation was almost totally divorced from affiliated trucking interests, was profitable, and was winning new customers for air transportation.[4] Burlington Northern Air Freight (to cite one other surface-affiliated forwarder) informed the Board of similar accomplishments. For instance, it had, since receiving its forwarder permit in 1972, initiated a sales program at some 360 points lying

---

[1] Long-Haul Motor/Railroad Carrier Air Freight Forwarder Authority Case, Docket 26907, initial decision (served: October 22, 1975).

[2] These represented eighteen percent of its total terminals.

[3] See below, p. 197.

[4] The transcript of the oral argument (January 21, 1976) is on file in the Board's Washington offices.

outside its pickup and delivery areas and was providing forwarder service at a substantial number of medium and small air traffic hubs.[1]

Emery, in common with other independent forwarders, had hoped the initial decision would go against the surface-affiliates, either expelling them from the industry or restricting their activities to points forming part of the transportation systems of affiliated surface carriers. The long-haul forwarders, protested Emery,

> by and through their affiliates, control vast networks of surface transportation facilities. Emery and other independent forwarders depend upon a broad and unfettered availability of all direct carriers, both surface and air. When surface carriers are affiliated with competing forwarders, they are, in reality, no longer available to Emery, or, indeed, any other forwarder. This proceeding must address this and other anticompetitive factors which lie ahead for the air freight forwarding industry if the affiliated forwarders are to continue to participate in the industry.[2]

Fear of the Board's countermeasures, continued Emery, had prompted the affiliated forwarders to curtail

> their power to affect adversely the public interest and the independent air freight forwarding industry. Conversely, we may assume that they have attempted, albeit unsuccessfully, to accentuate the benefits which the Board contemplated would inure from their experimental entry. The results of the experiment, therefore, must be viewed with a wary eye particularly in attempting to predict the future performance of the affiliated forwarders in an uncontrolled and unmonitored atmosphere.[3]

Accusations leveled against the long-haul forwarders by other independent operators were that they had "pirated" the latter's key personnel, had not increased intermodal traffic, and had failed to "stimulate" air freight growth.[4]

The independent operators were unable to realize their objective, for in 1977 the Board adopted the administrative law judge's decision as its own, giving the affiliated forwarders "substantial parity" with the independents. However, whereas the judge had favored the outright abolition of the "monitored entry" policy, the Board ordered its suspension for a ten-year period. The order provides the Board with a further opportunity to review the situation and puts the interested parties on notice that the "final word" on the matter has not yet been given.[5]

---

[1]Brief to the Civil Aeronautics Board of Burlington Northern Applicants, Docket 26907, (1975).

[2]Brief of Emery Air Freight Corporation to the Civil Aeronautics Board, Docket 26907, (1975), p. 4.

[3]Ibid., pp. 4-5.

[4]Exceptions of the Nine Independent Air Freight Forwarders, Docket 26907, (1975).

[5]Long-Haul Motor/Railroad Carrier Air Freight Forwarder Authority Case, Order 77-6-126.

The Interstate Commerce Commission's Role
in Air Freight Regulation

The Interstate Commerce Commission waives certification and permit requirements in the case of "transportation of . . . property by motor vehicle when incidental to transportation by aircraft" (frequently called the section 203[b][7a] exemption).[1] Since the Interstate Commerce Act does not define which motor services are "incidental to transportation by aircraft," the Commission has had to decide in individual instances whether a motor carrier's operations constitute line-haul transportation (making the carrier subject to the ICC's regulatory requirements) or whether only local, nonregulated pickup and delivery service is involved.

In exempting from its economic regulations motor carriers engaged in pickup and delivery of air freight within a certain distance of an airport, that is, within the so-called air terminal area (also pickup and delivery zone), it has been the practice of the Commission to adopt as its own delineations of such areas once these had won the approval of the Civil Aeronautics Board. Pickup and delivery points (and thus distances) were specified in tariffs which the air carriers filed with the CAB, and the Commission reasoned that the Board's regulatory powers sufficed to preclude an "unreasonable" enlargement of such distances.

The first detailed discussion of services "incidental to air transportation" is found in Sky Freight Delivery Service, Inc. Common Carrier Application,[2] wherein the ICC ruled that the section 203(b)(7a) exemption encompassed transportation services consisting of collection, delivery, and interline transfer of freight within an airline's "reasonable terminal area." The exemption implied that ground service was considered an adjunct to an immediately prior or subsequent movement by aircraft and in effect ascribed a subordinate or secondary role to the motor carrier. Once the motor carrier's service was enlarged to the point where it became connecting-carrier line-haul service forming part of a through interline movement, it could no longer be designated an adjunct to air transportation and the exemption ceased to apply. These conclusions were affirmed in Peoples Express Co. Extension of Operation--Air Freight,[3] in which a motor carrier sought certification for operations linking points anywhere in New Jersey with airports in New York-Newark. The

---

[1] Interstate Commerce Act, section 203(b)(7a), 52 Stat. 1029.

[2] 47 MCC 229 (1947).

[3] 48 MCC 393 (1948).

Commission found that the proposed service was in the public interest and awarded the certificate, obviating the need for a delineation of the area within which the motor carrier's activities constituted services "incidental to air transportation." At the same time
it was noted, however, that a number of communities in southern New
Jersey were in any event ineligible for certification exemption
since they were so far from New York-Newark that truck movements
linking them with the airports "must be considered to be independent
of the connecting air services and not an adjunct of such air services."[1] Another category of points in Peoples Express were those
lying substantially closer to Philadelphia than to New York-Newark.
One might have expected the bulk of their air freight to be directed
at Philadelphia's air terminal instead of being trucked to New York-
Newark, and the Commission characterized motor transport in such
cases as "interterminal line-haul service in substitution for,
rather than incidental to, air transportation."[2] This proceeding is
of interest also because it foreshadows the ICC's apprehension over
a possible infringement of its authority by the Civil Aeronautics
Board. The applicant's proposed contract with the airlines and use
of their door-to-door tariffs were deemed "significant" but could
not of themselves justify relief from certification requirements.
For it to disregard the distance factor in evaluating whether a surface movement was "incidental to air transportation," said the Commission, would be to

> place in the hands of the airline the power to legalize or authorize new
> motor-carrier operations of virtually unlimited scope merely through the
> device of a contract and door-to-door rates published by the air line only.[3]

The mileage limit is set aside in cases involving substitute motor-
for-air service, provided such a substitution reflects an emergency
situation.[4] The economic needs of a motor carrier play no role in
the determination of whether or not an exemption will be approved.[5]

The Commission's interpretation of what constitutes services
"incidental to transportation by aircraft" was next tested in Kenny

---

[1]Ibid., p. 396.

[2]Ibid.

[3]Ibid., p. 397.

[4]Graff Common Carrier Application, 48 MCC 310 (1948); Motor Transportation
of Property Incidental to Transportation by Aircraft, 95 MCC 71 (1964), appendix
III. See below, p. 243.

[5]Commercial Zones and Terminal Areas, 54 MCC 21, 71 (1952).

Extension--Air Freight,[1] a case in which a motor carrier sought a
certificate of public convenience and necessity in order to undertake operations between two airports in Allegheny County, Pennsylvania, on the one hand, and points in Pennsylvania within fifty
miles of these airports, on the other. Since the proposed motor
service was restricted to traffic "having an immediately prior or
immediately subsequent movement by aircraft"[2] and since the shipments involved were to move on air express or airline bills of
lading, the ICC felt that the main features of the service satisfied
the partial exemption requirements of section 203(b)(7a) of the
Interstate Commerce Act and dismissed the application. Following
a petition for reconsideration public hearings were held in the
course of which American Trucking Associations, Inc. (ATA),[3] supported by various railway companies but opposed by Air Cargo, Inc.,
asserted that the ICC could not establish regulations for air
freight differing from those applying to other types of traffic.
American Trucking Associations, Inc. viewed the exemption under
section 203(b)(7a) as having validity only relative to work performed between an airport and points within the commercial zone of
the city served by that airport and urged adoption of a nationwide
rule embodying this principle.[4]

Although the Commission was of the opinion that a rule defining the boundaries of every major air terminal area was desirable

---

[1]49 MCC 182 (1949).

[2]Ibid., p. 185.

[3]American Trucking Associations, Inc. is the national organization of the
trucking industry.

[4]Under section 203(b)(8) of the Interstate Commerce Act local short-haul
motor carrier transportation "within a municipality or between contiguous municipalities or within a zone adjacent to and commercially a part of any such municipality or municipalities" is, under certain circumstances, exempt from economic
regulation. Air terminal areas are frequently larger than section 203(b)(8) commercial zones and ATA was protesting that the Commission appeared to be according
more favorable treatment to air carriers than to motor carriers.
    The initial boundaries of New York City's commercial zone are set forth in
New York, N.Y. Commercial Zone, 1 MCC 665 (1937) and Commercial Zones and Terminal
Areas, 53 MCC 451 (1951). A revised population-mileage rule, on which commercial
zones are based, came into effect in 1977 (Ex Parte no. MC-37 [Sub-no. 26]
Commercial Zones and Terminal Areas), and New York's commercial zone now extends
twenty miles beyond the city's corporate limits. The new formula, which enlarges
pre-1977 zones, is supported by the Port Authority of New York and New Jersey but
has been challenged by certain motor carrier interests in a lawsuit which is
pending before the U.S. Court of Appeals for the Ninth Circuit (Brief of Petitioner, American Trucking Associations, Inc., in Civil Action nos. 77-1070, 77-1774,
and 77-2083, Short Haul Survival Committee v. United States).

it regarded as "difficult and impractical" any attempt to make air terminal areas coextensive with section 203(b)(8) commercial zones. Differential treatment of air and surface traffic (with respect to certification exemption) was, in its view, justified given the difference in modus operandi involved, and, rather than endorsing ATA's proposal, it put forward its own formula regarding future exemptions. These were to apply to

> bona fide collection, delivery or transfer service of shipments which have been received from, or will be delivered to, an air carrier as part of a continuous movement under a through air bill of lading covering in addition to the line-haul movement by air the collection, delivery, or transfer service performed by motor carrier.[1]

To this was added a qualification which further narrowed the circumstances under which a motor carrier's "collection, delivery or transfer" activities would be recognized as service "incidental to air transportation." While declining to specify the boundaries of individual pickup and delivery zones, the Commission stressed that freedom from economic regulation applied only to motor carrier operations confined to "a reasonable terminal area of the air carrier." By "reasonable" was meant an airline's terminal area as defined in pickup and delivery tariffs accepted by the Civil Aeronautics Board, the underlying assumption being that the Board would not hesitate to reject terminal areas large enough to accommodate independent line-haul motor service. This approach was judged to be sufficiently rigid to differentiate between exempt and nonexempt motor carriers, while retaining the necessary flexibility to permit future terminal area changes.

The Kenny doctrine, as it has come to be known, was extended to air freight forwarders in 1961.[2] However, the exemption was restrictive in that it applied to a forwarder's collection, delivery, or transfer services only so long as these were confined to points appearing not merely in his own pickup and delivery tariff but also in that of the airline responsible for the related airport-to-airport movement. Although traffic moving under a through air freight forwarder bill of lading now qualified for the section 203(b)(7a) exemption, broader participation by air freight forwarders in intermodal carriage remained questionable. This was because the Commission also concluded that any air freight forwarder exchanging shipments with a motor common carrier operating to/from points outside

---

[1]Kenny Extension--Air Freight, 61 MCC 587, 595 (1953).

[2]Panther Cartage Co. Extension--Air Freight, 88 MCC 37 (1961).

the terminal area (i.e., with an ICC-regulated motor common carrier
operating to/from nonexempt points) was acting as a surface forwarder, thereby violating the operating authority requirements of part
IV of the Interstate Commerce Act.[1] When it became clear that the
aforementioned restrictions did little to enhance the forwarders'
intermodal capability, the ICC reversed itself, erasing the distinction between consignments moving under airline as opposed to forwarder tariffs. A revised definition, adopted in 1964, reflects
this departure from earlier Commission decisions:

> transportation of property by motor vehicle is transportation incidental
> to transportation by aircraft within the meaning of section 203(b)(7a) of
> the Interstate Commerce Act provided (1) that it is confined to the trans-
> portation of shipments in bona fide collection, delivery, or transfer ser-
> vice performed within the terminal area of the direct air carrier or air
> freight forwarder (indirect air carrier) providing the line-haul transpor-
> tation, which terminal area, if the line-haul air transportation is provided
> by a carrier subject to economic regulation under the Federal Aviation Act,
> has been described in a tariff filed with and accepted by the Civil Aero-
> nautics Board, and (2) that it is confined to the transportation of ship-
> ments which have been received from or will be delivered to a direct air
> carrier or air freight forwarder as part of a continuous movement which,
> if provided by an air carrier subject to economic regulation under the
> Federal Aviation Act, shall be provided for in tariffs filed with and
> accepted by the Civil Aeronautics Board, and shall be performed on a through
> air bill of lading covering, in addition to the line-haul movement by air,
> the collection, delivery, or transfer service performed by the motor
> carrier.[2]

It is important to note that, even if the motor transportation is
confined entirely to an air carrier's pickup and delivery zone and
forms part of a through air-motor service, the exemption does not
come into force unless the surface movement is on an air bill of
lading.[3] In other words, where the surface haul is rendered independently and the trucker's charges paid by the shipper or consignee
rather than the air carrier, the exemption does not apply. With
respect to the forwarders, the Commission also declared that an exchange of shipments between them and regulated motor common carriers
was permissible (without the former first having to apply for surface forwarder authority), provided that they disclaimed all responsibility for shipments before/after transfer from/to the certificate
carriers and that they received no compensation whatsoever for groun
services pertaining to movements outside their own terminal areas.
The limited nature of a forwarder's responsibility was to be clearly

---

[1]See above, p. 80.

[2]49 CFR 1047.40.

[3]William R. Fisher and Montford R. Fisher Common Carrier Application, 83
MCC 229 (1960).

indicated in his tariff publications, advertising material, etc.[1]

Strangely enough, the Commission's 1964 delineation of exempt transportation failed to include a definition of a "through air bill of lading," and it was only recently that the agency, reviewing the activities of a New Jersey-based motor carrier, Marotta Air Service, Inc., provided such a definition. A through air bill of lading, the Commission stated, "is the single bill of lading governing the transportation service from origin to final destination, issued by a carrier to a shipper upon the receipt of the shipper's traffic for transportation in a continuous ground-air movement."[2] Marotta's pickup/delivery service was conducted under air carriers' bills of lading, was confined to the New York-Newark air terminal area, and its charges were advanced directly by the air carriers. Critics of Marotta (such as Air Cargo, Inc.) nevertheless argued that the company did not meet the "through bill" requirement, since the airlines in question had not formally designated Marotta as their agent and assumed responsibility for its shipments only after these were in their custody. This position was explicitly rejected by the Commission, which, in not identifying the carrier issuing the bill (the definition states only that the single bill of lading must be issued by "a carrier"), has enlarged the earlier concept of a "through air bill of lading."[3] "We conclude," declared the Commission,

> that if goods are delivered into the possession of a carrier for transportation over several lines between origin and destination and that simultaneously a bill of lading governing the entire transportation service is issued by the receiving carrier under circumstances which indicate acquiescence by the connecting carrier(s) in the arrangement, then the bill falls within the purview of the 'through air bill of lading' requirement[4]

forming part of the 1964 exemption regulations.

In 1964 the Commission adopted a new series of regulations setting forth the procedure via which it intended to examine the applicability of the section 203(b)(7a) exemption to points not included in CAB-approved pickup and delivery tariffs. The necessity

---

[1] 49 CFR 1082.1.

[2] Marotta Air Service, Inc., Petition for a Declaratory Order, 129 MCC 100, 105-106 (1978).

[3] The Commission had ruled in several cases (Colorado Cartage Co., Inc. v. Murphy, 100 MCC 745 [1966]; Commodity Haulage Corp. Common Carrier Application, 106 MCC 135 [1967]) "that the bill issued by a ground carrier is not a determinative bill of lading until such time as it is executed by the airline upon taking physical possession of the goods transported."

[4] Marotta Air Service, Inc., Petition for a Declaratory Order, p. 105.

for this arose as a result of a parallel action taken by the CAB
(discussed below), which was developing rules under which it proposed to examine future requests for extensions of pickup and delivery zones to areas beyond those previously approved. The ICC had
long made CAB tariffs the major criterion for its section 203(b)(7a)
exemption. With the Board's modification of its so-called 25-mile
rule-of-thumb (upon which CAB-approved pickup and delivery tariffs
were based) the Commission faced the prospect of having to allow the
section 203(b)(7a) exemption in instances where it deemed motor carrier service not to be "incidental to air transportation." The ICC'
new regulations were designed to enable the agency to continue to
discharge fully its statutory responsibilities and showed the transportation industry that the ultimate decision on the scope of nonregulated surface movements would continue to lie with the Commissio

   The Commission's policy vis-à-vis CAB pickup and delivery zone
has come under frequent attack by various parties. For instance,
when the new regulations concerning points outside CAB-approved zone
were being considered in the early 1960s: (1) Air Cargo, Inc. suggested that the section 203(b)(7a) exemption be limited to the terminal areas of the scheduled airlines (as defined in tariffs accepte
by the Board), (2) one air freight forwarder felt the exemption
should apply to air freight shipments anywhere on the ground as long
as the related air movement was greater than the distance moved by
truck, (3) numerous air freight forwarders and uncertificated motor
carriers stated that the exemption should hold for distances of up
to 125 miles (from the air terminals), while (4) certificated motor
carriers favored a far more restricted territorial limit. The Commission has been unable to satisfy the contradictory demands made by
such a diverse collection of interest groups. Adjured by Congress
to "recognize and preserve the inherent advantages" of each transportation mode subject to the Interstate Commerce Act, the agency
felt during this period that it could not authorize large new exemptions for one group of carriers at the expense of another group and
declared that only "compelling reasons" would cause it to approve
enlargements in the case of specific air terminal areas.

   The ICC's 1964 definition of the "incidental" exemption and
the Civil Aeronautics Board's concurrent modification of its mileage
rule greatly encouraged the forwarders, who were soon applying for
pickup and delivery rights to points lying substantially beyond previously approved air terminal areas. This has brought them into
conflict with certain segments of the regulated motor carrier industry, since expanded business opportunities for the forwarders come,
in part, at the expense of the truckers. "They [the forwarders] are

taking the business away from the guys who developed it,"[1] says the
Air Freight Motor Carriers Conference, an organization representing
the interests of the ICC-regulated air freight motor carrier specialists. The Conference has consistently opposed expansion of forwarder pickup and delivery rights to areas served only by regulated
motor carriers and, in an independent but related development, has
lent its support (1977) to the legal battle against the ICC's blanket enlargement of section 203(b)(8) commercial zones.[2] The confrontation between forwarders and air freight motor carrier specialists is encountered to some degree in many parts of the United
States. It is a phenomenon to which the air freight industry in the
New York-Newark area has not been immune; quite the contrary, a
sequence of events there has cast the constituent factors into particularly bold relief and has helped to focus attention on the problem generally.

Figure 2 shows the growth of Emery Air Freight's Newark air
terminal area during the 1960s. The figure is based on Emery's
pickup and delivery tariffs and indicates the zones for 1965 and
1968, within which the company, pursuant to section 403(a) of the
Federal Aviation Act,[3] was able to provide pickup and delivery service between specified points and Newark Airport.[4] (Other forwarders, of course, have also expanded their operating territory. Emery
is used as an example here because it is the region's leading air
freight forwarder and because it was criticized more frequently than
other forwarders in the course of discussions the author held with
the major air freight motor carrier specialists.) Emery's initial
request for an enlarged pickup and delivery zone was received by the
Civil Aeronautics Board in 1965 and approved in 1967; a second request covering additional points was granted in 1968. In recognizing an extended Newark air terminal area, the CAB declared itself

---

[1]Discussion between George H. Mundell, Executive Director, Air Freight
Motor Carriers Conference, and the author, 1976.

[2]See above, p. 106, note 4.

[3]Section 403(a) of the Federal Aviation Act provides, inter alia: "every
air carrier and every foreign air carrier shall file with the Board, and print,
and keep open to public inspection, tariffs showing all rates, fares, and charges
for air transportation between points served by it, and between points served by
it and points served by any other air carrier or foreign air carrier when through
service and through rates shall have been established, and showing to the extent
required by regulations of the Board, all classifications, rules, regulations,
practices, and services in connection with such air transportation." (Emphasis
added.) 72 Stat. 758, 49 U.S.C. 1373. See below, pp. 158-159.

[4]Our discussion is restricted to the terminal area's New Jersey sector.

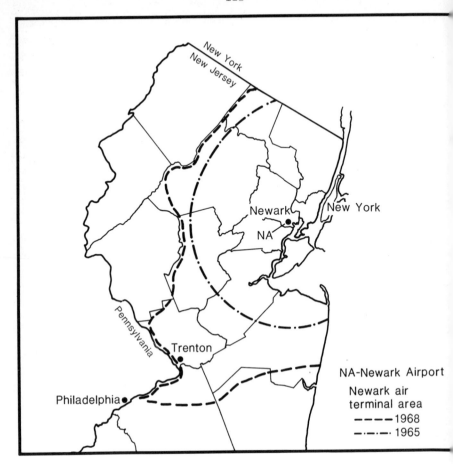

Fig. 2. Emery's Newark air terminal area: 1965-1968

satisfied that the proposed service was indeed a genuine pickup and delivery service[1] (as opposed to line-haul transportation), which would contribute to the development of the air freight potential of the area concerned. This position had the support of American Airlines, Trans World Airlines, and a number of air freight shippers and receivers, all of whom had earlier emphasized Trenton's inadequacy as a regional air center and had pointed to the need for improved truck connections between central New Jersey and Newark

---

[1]The criteria used by the Board to define such service are found on p. 119

Airport. Trenton and a number of nearby points formed part of
Emery's new pickup and delivery zone, and the sentiments of airline
officials and local shippers reflected the fact that almost all air
freight originating in the Trenton area had to be trucked to air
terminals other than Mercer County Airport.[1]

Although support for Emery's enlarged Newark Airport terminal
zone was substantial, the company's request did not go unchallenged,
a motion for dismissal of the application being filed by Harbourt
Air Freight Service, Inc. (an ICC-regulated motor carrier licensed
to carry air freight between central New Jersey-eastern Pennsylvania
and airports in New York-Newark and Philadelphia) and the Air Freight
Motor Carriers Conference. Responding to the competitive threat
inherent in Emery's action, these parties sought to persuade the
Board to cancel the proposed forwarder operations on the ground that
they violated section 403(a) of the Federal Aviation Act. Distances
between Emery's new customers and Newark Airport, so their argument
went, were so great that they precluded true pickup and delivery
services, i.e., "services in connection with . . . air transportation" at the Newark terminal, leaving as Emery's only course of
action an appeal to the Interstate Commerce Commission for certification as an over-the-road motor carrier. If the intervenors har-
bored any illusions about the CAB's concern over the question of an
ICC permit, they were soon disabused of these, for the agency refused
to be drawn into any discussion of the Commission's attitude towards
Emery. Its decisions in the matter, the CAB said, did not "reflect
any views as to whether applicant or its motor carrier agents require additional authority from the ICC or other regulatory agencies."[2] The motion to dismiss Emery's application was denied, no
proof of wrongdoing on its part having been produced, and, following
a further review of the case (upon petition), the orders approving
the service were affirmed.

Harbourt, however, was determined "as a matter of principle"[3]
to press the issue further and, in a letter of March 7, 1969, again
brought to the Board's attention what it considered to be Emery's
infractions of the Federal Aviation Act. Part of that letter is
worth quoting here, not only because of what it tells us about

---

[1]Mercer County Airport, adjacent to Trenton, offered only two northbound
and two southbound flights per day.

[2]Docket 16344, Order E-25798, p. 4.

[3]Discussion between Richard A. Harbourt, President, Harbourt Air Freight
Service, Inc., and the author, 1976.

Harbourt's interpretation of Emery's activities in this particular instance, but because its wording characterizes the way a number of motor common carriers in the New York-Newark region view the role of air freight forwarders with whom they must compete for local traffic. "It is readily apparent," Harbourt complained,

> that the service being performed by Emery is not pickup and delivery service within the Newark Airport terminal zone, but pickup and delivery service at Trenton with a subsequent or prior line-haul movement by motor in interstate commerce between Emery's terminal at Trenton and Newark Airport. Control of the pickup and delivery service is not exercised by Emery at Newark but by its personnel at the Trenton terminal. Rather than coordinating the pickup and delivery vehicles at Newark with the schedules of direct air carriers, the service is necessarily coordinated at Trenton with, and dependent on the schedule of the line-haul vehicle operating between that terminal and the Airport at Newark. Rather than their being typical pickup and delivery rates applicable to the service, the charges for the so-called pickup and delivery service at Trenton and nearby points obviously bear no relation to and patently discriminate against the pickup and delivery rates charged by Emery to shippers located at Newark and points immediately surrounding Newark Airport. . . .[Emery's] tariff does not provide for . . . a service incidental to transportation by air as required by Section 403(a) of the Federal Aviation Act, and no tariff covering . . . [Emery's] service has been filed with the Interstate Commerce Commission.[1]

What steps, Harbourt wished to know, would be taken "to bring Emery within compliance of the law." The Board's reply was brief and to the point: its investigation, it informed the carrier, had confirmed Emery's observance of the section 403(a) pickup and delivery criteria throughout the Newark air terminal zone, and, accordingly, no additional action was contemplated.

Following this rebuff, Harbourt, supported by the Air Freight Motor Carriers Conference, focused its attention (1970) on the Interstate Commerce Commission. The gravamen of its complaint to that agency was that, since Emery was providing over-the-road transportation (rather than pickup and delivery service) between its newly-approved points and Newark Airport without holding ICC authority as a motor carrier (under part II of the Interstate Commerce Act) or as a surface freight forwarder (under part IV of the Act),[2] its activities were unlawful and had to be terminated. Emery's truck service, argued Harbourt,

> is the same transportation between the same points for the same persons which Harbourt has performed and performs pursuant to certificates issued by the Commission . . . upon a determination that such transportation is subject to its regulation under Part II of the Act; [Emery] has diverted

---

[1] The letter forms Exhibit I of *Complainants' Reply to Defendant's Motion to Dismiss*, Docket MC-C-6746, (1970).

[2] See above, p. 80.

traffic and revenue important to its [Harbourt's] operation as a common carrier and has impaired its ability to meet its common carrier duty to serve all points within its certificated authority, including those points Emery chooses not to serve.[1]

In replying to this salvo Emery noted that, since its modus operandi within the expanded Newark air terminal area had been approved by the CAB, any appeal to the ICC for relief was improper and should be dismissed by the Commission. Several months later the complaint was in fact dismissed, the Commission stating in its final order that, as Emery's activities were consistent with the guidelines laid down in 1964,[2] it would continue to enjoy the section 203(b)(7a) certification exemption.

The Commission's statutory authority to decide whether motor service is "incidental to air transportation" has been disputed by the air freight forwarders, who, given the CAB's mandate to promote (as well as regulate) air transportation, have viewed the Board as more sympathetic to their aspirations and alone competent to pass on the validity of their pickup and delivery proposals. Their attempt to deny the ICC a role in air freight regulation has been frustrated by the Supreme Court, which has upheld that agency's right not to exclude particular motor services from its licensing and rate powers even after such services have been designated as pickup and delivery by the CAB.[3] The Supreme Court has also sustained CAB rulings (these having been challenged by the regulated air freight motor carrier specialists) authorizing forwarders to offer pickup and delivery service to new points lying substantially beyond the limits of existing air terminal areas.[4]

The framework for air freight forwarder-motor carrier cooperation (as formulated in 1964) has been reviewed in a test case (decided in 1968), in which several motor carriers sought to undertake transportation on behalf of air carriers (direct and indirect) outside the latter's pickup and delivery zones.[5] The applications,

---

[1]Formal Complaint for Violations of the Interstate Commerce Act, Docket MC-C-6746, (1970), p. 11.

[2]See above, p. 108.

[3]Air Dispatch, Inc. v. United States, 237 F. Supp. 450 (E.D. Pa. 1964); affirmed per curiam, 381 U.S. 412 (1965).

[4]Law Motor Freight, Inc. v. Civil Aeronautics Board, 364 F.2d 139 (1st Cir. 1966); certiorari denied, 387 U.S. 905 (1967). National Motor Freight Traffic Association, Inc. v. Civil Aeronautics Board, 374 F.2d 266 (D.C.Cir. 1966); certiorari denied, 387 U.S. 905 (1967).

[5]Savage Contract Carrier Application, 108 MCC 205 (1968).

to the extent that contract carrier authority was requested, were
denied. Permitting motor contract carriers to perform the proposed
service, observed the Commission, would result in giving an air carrier control over freight movements beyond its terminal area and
would contravene its earlier ruling authorizing connecting-line service only in cases where air and surface carrier responsibility were
clearly separated. In the contractual service proposed, residual
control over air shipments would have remained with the air carriers
irrespective of whether shipments moved on through-air or separate
bills of lading. The participation of air carriers in joint air-
motor service linking points inside with those outside the air terminal areas, it was concluded, was only permissible when the air
carrier in question held a surface forwarder permit (as provided
under part IV of the Interstate Commerce Act) and the surface segment of the through movement was undertaken by a motor common carrier.
The first such permits were granted to air freight forwarders in
1971[1] They signaled a gain for intermodal transportation coordination throughout the United States because they enabled the holders--
termed "intermodal freight forwarders" by the ICC--to offer single-
responsibility air-surface forwarder service to any locality in the
nation, regardless of its distance from an airport. Issuance of
these permits was contested by the Air Freight Motor Carriers
Conference and other parties but has been defended by the Commission
as being "consistent with the public interest and the national
transportation policy."[2]

Interagency Conflict

The Civil Aeronautics Board considers bona fide air freight
pickup and delivery by truck to be a service "in connection with
. . . air transportation." To come within the meaning of section
403(a) of the Federal Aviation Act,[3] however, pickup and delivery
operations must be confined to specified air terminal areas. Under
a Board policy of long-standing, air terminal points have been
recognized as lying either within 25 miles of an airport or within

---

[1]Emery Air Freight Corporation Freight Forwarder Application, 339 ICC 17
(1971). A permit-holder's authority was limited "to the transportation of traffic
having an immediately prior or subsequent movement by air in the [holder's own]
air forwarder service."

[2]Ibid., p. 38. Factors influencing the issuance of the permits include
the "prevailing competitive situation" and the adequacy of existing service.

[3]See above, p. 111, note 3.

25 miles of an airport city's corporate limits. Considered "reasonable" by the ICC, these distances fall within the scope of the
Interstate Commerce Act's section 203(b)(7a) exemption. In the case
of several major airport cities (e.g., Chicago, Los Angeles, New
York) the areal distribution of shippers and receivers calls for
more regulatory flexibility, and here the CAB has accepted pickup
and delivery distances of considerably greater magnitude. With respect to these special cases the ICC too has tended to disregard the
conventional mileage rule and has shown substantial willingness to
approve certification exemptions for off-line points. (The situation outlined here is as of the end of 1977. As indicated elsewhere
in this study, airline deregulation and various related developments
suggest the Board may soon play no role vis-à-vis the air terminal
areas. Given Congress' interest in the deregulation of interstate
surface transportation, the Commission also may soon cease to function as a regulator of pickup and delivery service.)

While the Interstate Commerce Commission is charged with the
regulation of commerce, the Civil Aeronautics Board has traditionally had broader functions which embraced not only regulatory but also
promotional policy considerations.[1] In this context it will be recalled that, whereas the CAB has permitted forwarders virtually free
entry into the market, usually on a nationwide or international
scale, the ICC's authorizations have normally been limited to service between specified points and then only after an applicant has
satisfied various regulatory provisions of the Interstate Commerce
Act. In its Regulation ER-407 (June 12, 1964) the Board expressly
acknowledged the dependence of "full" air freight development on
"efficient surface transportation" and further stated that the quality of surface operations could best be maintained if the direct and
indirect air carriers controlled the motor vehicles involved. In
practical terms, the air carriers were invited to assume authority
over and responsibility for certain ground movements (which might or
might not be performed by independent surface carriers). This situation posed a problem for the ICC, which could hardly view with
sympathy the enhancement of certain carriers' surface authority when
those carriers, enjoying statutory exemption, lay beyond its regulatory reach.

The confusion arising out of the Interstate Commerce Act's
lack of a definition for operations "incidental to transportation by
aircraft" is compounded by the wording of the Federal Aviation Act.

---

[1]See above, p. 6-7.

Section 403(a) of the latter sets forth air carrier tariff filing requirements but fails to elaborate on the meaning of "services in connection with . . . air transportation." A jurisdictional overlap implied in the latitude each agency has to interpret the act within its purview, has formed the core of a possible conflict of authority between the two regulatory bodies. Aware of the potential for conflict, the two agencies adopted in 1964 a framework for the handling of future pickup and delivery applications. This framework allowed for limited cooperation between the two regulators and recognized that in some instances identical treatment of an application would not be possible. With respect to these latter instances, the agencies, in effect, "agreed to disagree." Their post-1964 approach to the question of pickup and delivery service, an appeals court observed, has served a dual purpose: it has preserved "agency sovereignty" and eliminated interagency conflict.[1]

Prior to 1964 the Board, in accepting pickup and delivery tariffs filed by air carriers, applied the 25-mile rule-of-thumb on an ad hoc basis. In that year, however, the agency modified its position and the situation with regard to new service proposals became somewhat as follows. If an air carrier (direct or indirect) wished to provide pickup and delivery service within the 25-mile zone (either using its own equipment or through a local cartage agent[2]), routine approval could be expected, no special permission being required to file the appropriate tariff. Similarly, tariffs could be filed without a special showing for points lying outside the 25-mile boundary, provided these points already appeared in the pickup and delivery tariff of another air carrier. Where a carrier wished to institute pickup and delivery service to a previously unapproved point lying beyond a recognized pickup and delivery zone, Board authorization was required before that service could be considered lawful. In regulations promulgated simultaneously by the ICC that agency announced it would continue to accept the Board's actions relating to localities within the traditional 25-mile zone but would have to examine, independently of the Board, the latter's acceptance of pickup and delivery service involving new points outside the zone. Board action, the ICC stated, would be taken into consideration but could not be binding on the Commission.

---

[1] Law Motor Freight, Inc. v. Civil Aeronautics Board, p. 145.

[2] Air Cargo, Inc. contractors are the scheduled airlines' official agents in the United States. Generally speaking only these agents may provide pickup and delivery service for the airlines (under the airlines' authority) within the entire air terminal zone.

In weighing the merits of new surface tariff applications the Board has been primarily concerned with whether the services to be performed constituted "services in connection with . . . air transportation" (i.e., pickup and delivery) or whether they were more accurately described as line-haul transportation. In this connection applicants have had to: (1) indicate the distance between the airport (or municipal boundary) and the desired point(s), (2) demonstrate that the rates to be charged and the equipment to be used were characteristic of pickup and delivery operations, and (3) provide evidence that ground services were coordinated with airline schedules and oriented towards customers' air transportation requirements. These criteria differ markedly from those applied by the ICC to its "incidental to air transportation" exemption. The Commission relies on a "community homogeneity" concept under which it analyzes the area between the airport city and the proposed off-line point(s) in terms of several economic and demographic factors.[1] Given the conceptual differences involved, it comes as no surprise that instances have arisen when the two agencies disagreed as to the status of an applicant's motor service. A complaint heard frequently in the transportation industry is that this involvement of the two Federal bodies has created (for the carriers) confusion and additional expense, which could have been avoided through the adoption of a common set of regulatory criteria. This, however, is a move both the Board and the Commission have resisted. The two agencies recognize each other's authority, and each has given assurances that its regulatory actions are in no sense prejudicial to the independence of the other. Thus, the CAB, in authorizing the Flying Tiger Line to engage in truck service between Philadelphia and Newark Airport, has said:

> we are not asserting jurisdiction over the motor carrier as an air carrier nor are we determining the status of the truck operation under the Interstate Commerce Act. Whether the Philadelphia-Newark truck haul should be considered as incidental to air transportation within the meaning of the Interstate Commerce Act, and thereby exempt from economic regulation under that statute, is a matter for the Interstate Commerce Commission. We do not intend that our action here should influence what that decision should be. If the Commission should conclude under the standards normally applied by it that the truck operation is not exempt, the trucker must have or

---

[1] Nonregulated motor transportation is permissible within an area corresponding to an airport city's "homogeneous community." The following considerations have been used to define such an area: (1) The subdivisions constituting the "homogeneous community" must be contiguous. (2) A substantial proportion of the residents in the non-central sections (i.e., environs) must commute to work to the central section. (3) The population density just before the outer limits of the area must be greater than the farm-level density. <u>Motor Transportation of Property Incidental to Transportation by Aircraft</u>, 112 MCC 1, 18 (1970).

obtain the requisite ICC authority in order for Flying Tiger Line to operate in the manner it proposes.[1]

The ICC is no less emphatic on this point, and has declined to

> take issue with the criteria utilized by the Board in determining whether the points in the . . . extended terminal areas are served by motor carriers "in connection with air transportation" within the meaning of the Federal Aviation Act, for these matters are within the exclusive jurisdiction of that agency and not this Commission.[2]

The Proposed 100-Mile Pickup and Delivery Zone

The "winds of change" which swept over the air freight industry in 1977-1978 (chapter III) will continue to be felt in 1979 and beyond, for in a recent announcement (May, 1977) the ICC made known its intention to replace the traditional 25-mile "incidental" exemption with a new limit of possibly as much as 100 miles. The Commission notes that it receives many applications for motor carrier authority between air terminals and points beyond the 25-mile limit and has been petitioned to enlarge several air terminal areas. These petitions "would seem to evidence an increasing belief that the air terminal areas as currently defined ought to be expanded."[3] Enlarged air terminal areas, the agency adds, will give airlines and forwarders greater operational flexibility, thus improving the "climate for intermodalism and containerization." Under the new scheme the special definitions for particular air terminal areas are to be eliminated, thereby simplifying regulatory procedures.

As is customary in such instances, the Commission has invited interested parties to submit their views and opinions on its notice of proposed rule-making. One of these parties, of course, is the Civil Aeronautics Board, which, in a counterproposal, urged that it be given sole jurisdiction over future delineations of air terminal areas. "Only such unitary control," the Board declared,

> can properly develop air transportation of property and the services incidental to it, insure the flexible regulation necessary for the growth of a dynamic industry, and encourage the rendering of increasingly rapid and specialized high quality services demanded by a growing class of shippers.[4]

---

[1] The Flying Tiger Line, Inc., Air-Truck Service, 30 CAB 242, 245 (1959).

[2] Motor Transportation of Property Incidental to Transportation by Aircraft, (1970), p. 15.

[3] 42 FR 26668, (May 25, 1977).

[4] Civil Aeronautics Board, Comments of the Civil Aeronautics Board on the Proposal of the Interstate Commerce Commission to Modify Its Rules Governing the Motor Transportation of Property and Passengers Incidental to Transportation by Aircraft, n.d., mimeographed, p. 3.

(A somewhat similar conclusion appears to have been reached by an ICC Blue Ribbon Study Panel, which, in a 1975 report, recommended the elimination of the section 203[b][7a] exemption criteria and their replacement by a single exemption standard as defined by the Board.[1]) The Board has emphasized that if it alone were responsible for the demarcation of air terminal areas it would avoid any action which might "thwart the objectives" of the Interstate Commerce Act.

The CAB believes that the existing 25-mile pickup and delivery limit has become burdensome for shippers and air carriers and favors an enlargement of the traditional pickup and delivery zones. The monopoly position held by some ICC-regulated motor carriers frequently slows the movement of air freight; such delays, according to the Board, would be removed or at least reduced under the proposed formula, since more shippers and receivers would gain direct access to nonregulated local cartage operators whose services are more attuned to the specific needs of air shipments. The Board agrees with the Commission that their regulatory flexibility, which previously has enabled them to accept pickup and delivery points lying outside the recognized 25-mile air terminal areas, should be retained in the future.

The ICC has shown no inclination in the past to yield its prerogatives to the Civil Aeronautics Board, and there is no reason to suppose that it will do so now. Presumably recognizing this, the Board requested sufficient lead time (following adoption of a new mileage rule) to enable it to make "responsive amendments" to its own procedures and thus ensure the compatibility of the two agencies' regulations. Shortly after this request was received by the Commission, however, deregulation legislation was enacted into law, which in turn has forced the Board to reconsider its future role with respect to "services in connection with . . . air transportation." Despite the uncertainty now surrounding pickup and delivery operations, it seems safe to say that agency sovereignty and agency cooperation, the two principles at issue in Law Motor Freight, Inc. v. Civil Aeronautics Board, above, will remain intact as these operations enter a new regulatory phase. Also, there is little doubt regarding the carriers' attitude towards the 100-mile proposal. A dramatic break with the past, the proposal has polarized the air freight industry into two groups, those favoring the extension and those opposing it. The position of the interested parties and the

---

[1]Interstate Commerce Commission, Internal Staff Study Recommendations Announced in Commission's Review of Regulatory Modernization, no. 187-75, July 7, 1975, p. 6.

implications of such a rule for the New York-Newark air freight system as a whole are considered in chapter VII.

Concluding Remarks

Unlike the certificated airlines, air freight forwarders (indirect air carriers) have long been able to operate with relatively little Board control or supervision. The Board rightly recognized the forwarders as important generators of freight traffic and concluded that their partial exemption from the Federal Aviation Act's regulatory provisions served the best interests of the air freight industry. This policy was initially opposed by the airlines, which feared the forwarders might disrupt air freight transportation and gain undue control over the direct air carriers' freight activities Interestingly enough, the Board's "free entry" forwarder program ha been criticized by many forwarders themselves on the ground that an unchecked influx of new entrants could only weaken their industry. (This subject is discussed further in chapter VI.) Despite repeate predictions of disaster, however, the forwarding industry has continued to prosper, expanding rapidly both in terms of membership an in terms of the freight volume handled. The position of the forwarders, of course, differs from that of the airlines in a number o respects. Nevertheless, one cannot help but think that the pre-197 performance of the forwarders should be carefully considered by those who foresee only catastrophe (chapter III) for a deregulated air freight transportation industry.

Truck movements between a shipper's (or receiver's) place of business and the local airport are an indispensable part of air freight transportation. Congress gave two Federal agencies, the Civil Aeronautics Board and the Interstate Commerce Commission, jur isdiction in this area, empowering the former to approve certain types of trucking operations, provided these constituted "services in connection with . . . air transportation" (section 403[a] of the Federal Aviation Act), and permitting the latter to exempt from its certification requirements "transportation of . . . property by motor vehicle when incidental to transportation by aircraft" (section 203[b][7a] of the Interstate Commerce Act). The absence of statutory definitions of "services in connection with . . . air transportation" and of truck hauls "incidental" to aircraft movements left the two agencies free to use their discretion to delineate the permissible scope of nonregulated surface movements, that is, to differentiate between nonregulated local pickup and delivery service and regulated, independent line-haul surface movements.

Disagreement between the two agencies was initially avoided because the Commission applied its regulatory exemption automatically to surface movements conducted under pickup and delivery tariffs accepted by the Civil Aeronautics Board. In 1964, however, the Board amended its approach to pickup/delivery applications, prompting the ICC to similarly review its position towards airport-related surface movements. The outcome of this review was a reduced willingness on the part of the Commission to confirm the exempt status of Board-approved surface movements for points lying at distances of more than twenty-five miles from an airport (or the municipal boundary of the airport city), since nonregulated movements of such magnitude appeared in some cases to violate the Commission's regulatory responsibility.

The CAB has traditionally used (and the ICC has endorsed) the aforementioned 25-mile limit to define air terminal areas (pickup and delivery zones) within which it recognized surface movements to/from an airport as "services in connection with . . . air transportation." In the case of New York-Newark, pickup and delivery authority for points substantially beyond the 25-mile zone was approved by both agencies, resulting in one of the largest air terminal areas in the United States. Requests for enlarged pickup and delivery rights have come mainly from the air freight forwarders, who, anxious to extend their single-entity door-to-door service to as large a proportion of the market as possible, viewed the 25-mile rule as an unnecessary restriction and repeatedly pressed for its abolition.

The forwarders' expansionism, as might be expected, has generated hostility on the part of ICC-regulated truckers. The latter, fearing an invasion of their service territories by nonregulated operators, have appealed (unsuccessfully) to the ICC and the CAB to reject forwarder pickup and delivery requests for points outside the 25-mile air terminal area (we shall return to various aspects of this topic in chapters VI and VII). This involvement of the two agencies has meant, for various air freight specialists, lengthy and costly procedural steps as they (the specialists) sought protection for their competitive position and clarification of the nature of nonregulated pickup and delivery service. The overlapping, and in a sense, duplicative responsibilities of the two agencies with respect to air terminal areas have produced unnecessary confusion in the air freight industry, which could have been avoided had Congress designated one regulator (preferably the Board) as the sole arbiter of the scope of nonregulated truck movements to and from air terminals. The two agencies' right to reach air terminal

CHAPTER III

THE CIVIL AERONAUTICS BOARD DETHRONED:

DEREGULATION AND ITS IMPLICATIONS

Enactment of Public Law 95-163 has brought the Civil Aeronautics Board's long and seemingly secure role as a regulator of domestic air freight transportation to a sudden and, in the view of many, unexpected end. Dissatisfied with traditional regulatory practices and their effects on the air freight industry and bowing to widespread criticism of the Board, Congress dismantled the agency's statutory powers, essentially deregulating interstate air freight transportation. The following discussion reviews the pro- and anti-reform positions of the various parties involved, examines the new legislation, and identifies the major implications deregulation has for the New York-Newark air freight system.

The Move Towards Deregulation

So firmly entrenched have Federal transportation regulators been throughout the past forty-odd years that it is easy to overlook the initial efforts of Washington's would-be reformers during this period. As early as 1942 Congress was urged by the National Resources Planning Board to "move in the direction of relaxing regulation in order to give competitive elements in transport markets freedom to have their full force and effect."[1] In 1949 the then Secretary of Commerce questioned various aspects of national aviation policy and recommended a review of regulatory practices throughout the transportation industry.[2] Several years later (1955) a Presidential Advisory Committee on Transport Policy and Organization emphasized that "adjustment of regulatory programs and policies . . . is long overdue"[3] and called for greater efficiency in the

---

[1]National Resources Planning Board, Transportation and National Policy (Washington, D.C.: U.S. Government Printing Office, 1942), p. 236.

[2]Secretary of Commerce, Issues Involved in a Unified and Coordinated Federal Program for Transportation (Washington, D.C.: mimeographed, 1949).

[3]Presidential Advisory Committee on Transport Policy and Organization, Revision of Federal Transportation Policy (Washington, D.C.: U.S. Government Printing Office, 1955), p. 2.

transportation field through a reduction of governmental controls.
In 1960 President Eisenhower was advised by his Secretary of Commerc
that the nation's

> transportation system should be regulated by the same forces as the rest
> of the American free enterprise system: fair competition in price and
> service to the customers. Regulation in the long run should remain only
> where monopoly or the threat of destructive competition remains. This
> approach requires greater freedom for the carriers in setting their own
> rates and determining and developing their routes and services. The
> tighter regulation that was well adapted to protecting the public under
> the predominant monopoly of the railroads is no longer well suited to
> highly competitive transportation networks.[1]

A year later a Senate report on the transportation industry conclude
that "in some respects, there is too much regulation."[2] The documen
noted that the existing regulatory framework took no account of
changes in the industry (such as technological innovations and inter
modal competition) and invited lawmakers to "revamp our regulatory
philosophy and practices" to accommodate these developments.[3] Statutory revision was also the theme of President Kennedy's 1962 Transportation Message, in which the Congress was informed that

> the management of the various modes of transportation is subjected to
> excessive, cumbersome and time-consuming regulatory supervision that
> shackles and distorts managerial initiative. Some parts of the trans-
> portation industry are restrained unnecessarily; others are promoted
> or taxed unevenly and inconsistently.

Regulatory reform, the message stated, should be geared towards
"greater reliance on the forces of competition and less reliance on
the restraints of regulation."[4] President Johnson, too, saw a need
(1965) for "greater emphasis on competition and private initiative
in interstate transportation,"[5] and his economic advisers spoke
approvingly (1967) of policy changes which "will permit the scope of
Government regulation to shrink in favor of greater emphasis on competition."[6] Criticism of Federal policies continued under President
Nixon, whose Administration proposed regulatory reform of surface

---

[1]U.S. Department of Commerce, Federal Transportation Policy and Program
(Washington, D.C.: U.S. Government Printing Office, 1960), p. 5.

[2]Senate Report no. 445, 87th Cong., 1st sess., (1961), p. 157.

[3]Ibid., p. 158.

[4]Congressional Record 108, part 5 (1962):5985.

[5]Economic Report of the President (Washington, D.C.: U.S. Government Printing Office, 1965), p. 19.

[6]Economic Report of the President (Washington, D.C.: U.S. Government Printing Office, 1967), p. 117.

transportation in 1971 and 1974. Much of the transportation industry, observed his Council of Economic Advisers,

> is subject to Federal and State regulation instituted under conditions
> that no longer exist. Such regulation today may be one factor that
> interferes with an efficient use of resources in transportation, and
> it appears that regulatory patterns may have to be reexamined if the
> industry is to contribute its full potential to the Nation's welfare.[1]

Referring particularly to air transportation, the Council noted:

> the substitution of service competition for rate competition tends to
> result in excess capacity. Fares higher than a more openly competitive
> market would establish have not, therefore, led to correspondingly high
> rates of return. Through the inducement to excess capacity, overinvest-
> ment in facilities and planes occurred. Costs were thereby increased,
> and the financial performance of the companies, even with sheltered
> fares, has recently been unsatisfactory. Faced with some excess capacity,
> airlines have asked the CAB to approve intercarrier agreements to reduce
> flight frequencies in selected markets. Such a remedy tends to treat
> the symptoms of the problem without removing the cause. The original
> cause of the excess capacity was regulatory restriction of price competi-
> tion. If price competition had not been inhibited, the incentive for
> airlines to provide excess capacity would have been reduced.[2]

"Overregulation" of the transportation sector was similarly deplored
by Gerald Ford, during whose brief presidency several reform bills
were submitted to the Congress.[3]

Unlike his predecessor, whose legislative initiatives had
dealt only with surface transportation, President Ford developed
reform proposals which also encompassed the airline industry. His
Aviation Act of 1975, the President believed, eliminated the "artificial constraints" of the "present promotional and protectionist
regulatory system" and would help to "strengthen the Nation's economy through greater reliance on competition in the marketplace."[4]
The proposal's principal provisions centered on liberalized entry
and greater pricing flexibility and included the following points:

1. The Board's power to suspend as "unjust or unreasonable" any rate above
   direct costs on the ground that the rate was too low was terminated.[5]
   (The agency's suspension powers vis-à-vis discriminatory and preferential
   rates remained unaffected.) The Act established a zone of reasonableness
   whereby rate increases were subject to suspension only if in excess of
   ten percent of the rate in effect twelve months prior to a new rate
   proposal. In the case of downward rate movements, suspensions were ruled

---

[1]Economic Report of the President (Washington, D.C.: U.S. Government Printing Office, 1971), p. 122.

[2]Ibid., p. 129.

[3]"Total Regulatory Reform Urged by Ford," Aviation Week and Space Technology 104, no. 20 (1976):34.

[4]Congressional Record 121, part 25 (1975):32177.

[5]S. 2551, 94th Cong., 1st sess., sec. 14(a), (1975).

out during the first and second year following enactment provided the decrease was less than twenty percent and forty percent, respectively, of the rate in effect on the day of enactment. Suspensions in subsequent years were to be permissible only where the rate had fallen below the direct costs of the service in question [1]

2. Supplementals were to be permitted to offer scheduled service [2]

3. The Board was to allow any "fit, willing, and able" certificated carrier to operate between any pair of points not receiving nonstop service without the carrier first having to satisfy the traditional public interest requirements.

4. Operators using equipment accommodating up to 56 passengers or 16,000 pounds of freight were to be exempt from certification requirements [3]

5. Various certificate restrictions dealing with, for instance, mandatory stops and single-plane service were to be eliminated over a five-year period [4]

6. Route abandonment was to be greatly eased, provided a carrier could demonstrate the unprofitability of the market(s) in question

7. Carriers were authorized to sell or lease part of their operating authority to other carriers (beginning January 1, 1978) without the Board invoking the traditional public interest criteria [5]

8. After January 1, 1981, the following annual maximum route enlargements were to be automatically approved:[6] (a) for the trunks and medium-sized combination airlines additional service of no more than five percent of the average scheduled number of available seat-miles operated by these carriers during the previous year, (b) in the case of the all-cargo companies a ten percent expansion based on the average scheduled number of available ton-miles operated in the preceding year, (c) for small combination carriers expansions of no more than ten percent of their previous year's average scheduled number of available seat-miles.

While the Ford Administration was working on its deregulation package several related developments were taking place. Hearings on the CAB's efforts to stabilize international air fares had been initiated by the Senate Subcommittee on Administrative Practice and Procedure during the second half of 1974. The scope of the hearings quickly expanded as subcommittee members began to look into a wide variety of issues, including the agency's approach to interairline capacity reduction agreements, its 1969-1974 domestic route moratorium, and the airline industry's illegal financial contributions to political campaigns.[7] A subsequent report, which strongly condemned

---

[1] Ibid., sec. 14(c).

[2] Ibid., sec. 6(a).

[3] Ibid., sec. 6(b).

[4] Ibid., sec. 6(c).

[5] Ibid., sec. 7.

[6] Ibid., sec. 9.

[7] U.S., Congress, Senate, Committee on the Judiciary, Oversight of Civil Aeronautics Board Practices and Procedures, Hearings before the Subcommittee on Administrative Practice and Procedure, Senate, 94th Cong., 1st sess., (1975). (Three volumes.)

Board practices in several areas, accused the agency of having been
overly concerned with the protection of the trunk carriers and thus
having produced substantial overcapacity and unnecessarily high
fares. Some of the other criticisms were: (1) the agency had failed
to pursue a consistent route policy; (2) the agency had disregarded
the views of parties to some of its route proceedings, having
reached major decisions prior to the holding of hearings; (3) numerous proceedings were being extended over an unreasonably long period
of time; and (4) the agency was attempting to shield its actions
from public view and, in some instances, from court review. In
addition, the report hinted at improper contacts between Board members and airline officials. Several of the report's suggested procedural and legislative reforms were not dissimilar to those found
in the Aviation Act of 1975. The Subcommittee concluded that the
CAB should be stripped of some of its authority over rates/fares,
entry/exit, and antitrust exemptions and recommended, inter alia,
the removal of route restrictions, a gradual policy of free entry,
abolition of rate floors, the setting of time limits on route proceedings, and the adoption of more stringent standards governing
antitrust immunity.[1]

The question of antitrust immunity was also of concern to the
Departments of Justice and Transportation, both of which supported
President Ford's effort to reduce Federal control over the airline
industry.[2] Approval of airline mergers and various interairline
cooperative agreements had traditionally been wholly the responsibility of the Board. The Justice Department, however, wished to dismantle some of the Board's antitrust exemption powers and transfer
these to the Federal courts. This contrasted with the position of
the Department of Transportation, where officials were pressing for
the retention of the agency as the chief arbiter of airline mergers.
The dispute had slowed progress on the Administration's airline bill
and its resolution in the latter part of 1975 enabled the White
House to send the bill to the Congress. Under the compromise agreed
to by the two departments, the CAB was to continue to oversee airline mergers, though its actions could now be challenged by the

---

[1]U.S., Congress, Senate, Committee on the Judiciary, Civil Aeronautics
Board Practices and Procedures, Subcommittee on Administrative Practice and
Procedure, Committee Print, 94th Cong., 1st sess., (1975), pp. 1-2.

[2]U.S., Congress, Senate, Committee on Commerce, op. cit., pp. 321-336;
Secretary of Transportation, A Study of National Transportation Policy (Washington,
D.C.: U.S. Government Printing Office, 1975), p. 7; U.S., Congress, House, Com-
mittee on Public Works and Transportation, Reform of the Economic Regulation of
Air Carriers, Hearings before the Subcommittee on Aviation, House of Representa-
tives, 94th Cong., 2d sess., (1976), pp. 1494-1655.

Attorney General.[1] In addition, the agency was instructed to attach
more importance to anticompetitive implications of merger approvals
and was deprived of authority to sanction various anticompetitive
intercarrier agreements.[2]

The entire airline industry (which had largely adopted a "wait
and see" attitude towards President Ford's initial pronouncements on
aviation reform) was jolted when, in the middle of 1975, the Civil
Aeronautics Board itself appeared to waver in its determination to
hold fast to its traditional regulatory course. In the first of two
reports the agency announced that free entry/exit and greater pricing
flexibility were to be introduced experimentally in several markets
in order to ascertain whether, as charged, regulatory constraints
had led to a suboptimal allocation of resources within the industry,
produced higher rates and fares, and discouraged service innovation.[3]
The agency rejected nonregulated intrastate airline operations as a
valid model for the national route system and, noting the limited
empirical evidence produced by the would-be deregulators,[4] expressed
the hope that its experimental approach would yield the data on
which to base future policy changes.

Reaction to the proposed experiment, even from those favoring
deregulation, was almost entirely negative. Critics termed the proposal a "decoy" and claimed the agency was merely attempting to halt
Congressional moves against its authority.[5] Delta Air Lines, which
along with other trunk carriers strongly opposed deregulation, considered free entry "antagonistic to the current national goals of
fuel and other resource conservation."[6] The experiment, according
to United Airlines, would provide little useful information, a view
also held by the Department of Justice and the Council on Wage and
Price Stability. The basic problem with the proposal was that a
carefully controlled experiment involving only several routes could
not serve as an accurate guide to the economic behavior of the deregulated industry as a whole. The CAB recognized that the carriers'
hostility towards deregulation made manipulation of the test results

---

[1]S. 2551, sec. 11.

[2]Ibid., sec. 12.

[3]40 FR, pp. 28774-28783.

[4]Ibid., p. 28773.

[5]Editorial, Wall Street Journal, July 17, 1975, p. 18.

[6]"Few Approve, Many Criticize CAB's Experimental Reforms," Aviation Week
and Space Technology 103, no. 12 (1975):25.

more than likely and, given the increasing doubts over the courts' willingness to uphold "an experiment which was simply an academic exercise unrelated to the Board's statutory, regulatory mission,"[1] quietly dropped its test proposal several months later.

A second study (Special Staff Report), also released in mid-1975, concluded that "the elimination of the threat of new entry in all markets at all times is the principal feature of the present regulatory regime which blunts the incentive for improving carrier efficiency"[2] and that "a system which permits entirely new entry and does not limit price competition would provide lower-cost, lower-priced service than the present scheme."[3] In view of the likelihood that the "economic effects of the present regulatory system will become progressively worse in years to come," the Special Staff panel noted, "the task of reforming economic regulation should be undertaken as soon as possible."[4] (This study, which was commissioned by the Board, did not reflect the official views of the agency.) The study recommended amendment of the Federal Aviation Act to remove (over a three- to five-year period) protective entry/exit and price restrictions and, while not calling for the outright abolition of the Board as some Department of Justice officials were doing, saw its future functions reduced to the administration of antitrust-type measures and the review of industry adherence to tariff publications. Since freight is a relatively minor revenue source for most airlines, the Special Staff panel felt the freight sector could absorb reforms in a shorter period and hence suggested deregulation of domestic all-cargo services over a two-year time span. In order to safeguard the interests of existing all-cargo companies, combination airlines were to be barred from financing freight operations with passenger revenues and free entry was to be limited for the first two years to low-volume markets and to freight having a minimum density of 17 pounds/cu. ft. At the end of the two-year period operators of all-cargo services were to enjoy unrestricted entry and exit rights and complete pricing freedom (discriminatory rates were to remain unlawful).[5]

---

[1]"CAB Experiment in Deregulation Not Possible, Staff Study Finds." Aviation Week and Space Technology 104, no. 3 (1976):26.

[2]Report of the CAB Special Staff on Regulatory Reform, p. 320.

[3]Ibid., p. 275.

[4]Ibid., p. 291.

[5]Ibid., p. 323.

In concluding that the air transportation industry is "natu-
rally competitive" and that it should not be placed under public
utility-type restraints, the Special Staff clashed strongly with
the Board, which continued to cling to the belief that no major
regulatory changes were warranted.[1] On the other hand, the Special
Staff study's overall orientation was in substantial agreement with
President Ford's airline bill, despite several significant differences.[2] The study's sweeping recommendations caused astonishment
within the CAB and helped to persuade many skeptics, both in the
Congress and in the business community, that the reform movement
could no longer be lightly dismissed.

Despite the growing strength of the reformers, President
Ford's Aviation Act of 1975 failed to win Congressional approval.[3]
Facing reelection (1976), many legislators, especially those from
sparsely populated states, were understandably hesitant to be associated with a bill which, it was feared, would lead to reductions
in scheduled air service. Various opponents of deregulation had
coalesced into an effective antireform lobby, and it was only as a
courtesy to the President that a reluctant Senator Warren G.
Magnuson (D. Wash.), Chairman of the Senate Commerce Committee, had
agreed to introduce the bill in the Senate. A liberal-conservative
coalition, which in mid-1975 seemed to fully support the President's
efforts, was splintering into various factions, with many Democrats
asking whether reforms should not be initiated by the regulatory
agencies themselves. The general feeling in the Congress towards
the end of 1975 and during much of 1976 was one of dissatisfaction
not so much with regulation per se as with the procedures and practices ("too legalistic, too rigid and too slow") of the regulators.[4]
(The idea that agency reforms would suffice to correct flaws in the
regulatory framework gained ground with the CAB's announcement that

---

[1] 40 FR, p. 28773.

[2] (1) The Special Staff Report urged abolition of price regulation over the
long term, whereas the bill retained maximum price limits. (2) The bill showed
greater leniency towards antitrust exemptions than did the Special Staff study.
(3) Of the two, the Special Staff study was more hospitable towards entry by new
operators and expansion by existing companies. The Aviation Act of 1975 displayed
more caution in this area, limiting annual expansions and seemingly favoring
existing carriers over new entrants.

[3] During its closing days the Ford Administration made another unsuccessful
attempt to enact reform legislation. See House Document no. 45, 95th Cong.,
1st sess., (1977).

[4] "The Reform Movement--Is It Running Out of Gas?" Traffic World 164, no. 2
(1975):31-32.

it was setting up an Advisory Committee on Procedural Reforms. However, if the agency believed this would ultimately deflect Congressional attention from regulatory affairs, it was to be disappointed,
for Senator Edward Kennedy [D. Mass.], who had chaired the aforementioned Senate Subcommittee on Administrative Practice and Procedure hearings, made it clear that, while procedural changes were
"vitally needed, . . . a fundamental redirection of the regulatory
effort--not simply procedural improvement--is required."[1]) Shifts
in Congressional opinion caused the Administration to draw back from
its earlier enthusiastic espousal of regulatory change and left it
wondering whether "there are any votes in reform."[2]

Among those objecting to deregulation were the International
Association of Machinists, the Airport Operators Council International (AOCI), and various other labor groups.[3] The stability
imposed by a firm regulatory structure, stated the AOCI on behalf
of airport managers, had facilitated long-term planning and financing of terminal operations and would be lost under deregulation.
Generally speaking, organized labor, an important financial contrib-
utor to the Democratic Party, envisioned rising unemployment as a
result of unchecked route realignments and other competitive measures.
Labor's arguments had a delaying effect on Congress and, when new
reform legislation was enacted in 1978, it contained significant
labor protection provisions.[4]

Destabilization of the industry was also on the minds of financial analysts who, testifying before the Aviation Subcommittee of
the Senate Committee on Commerce, Science and Transportation, noted
that investor confidence in the airlines, already at a low level,[5]
would plunge further should deregulation become a reality. During
the period 1965-1975 the average debt-to-equity ratio for the carriers had risen from 2.0 to 2.5, an increase lenders had tolerated
largely because of the carriers' protected route structure. Investment advisers appeared to feel that the aviation industry was in

[1]U.S., Congress, Senate, Committee on the Judiciary, Civil Aeronautics
Board Practices and Procedures, p. III.

[2]"The Reform Movement," p. 32.

[3]"AFL-CIO Still Opposed to Airline Deregulation," Journal of Commerce,
March 2, 1977, p. 3.

[4]Act of October 24, 1978, Pub. L. no. 95-504, 92 Stat. 1705. Also see
H. R. 8813, 95th Cong., 1st sess., sec. 27, (1977).

[5]"Worries Over Recovery Limit Gains for Investors," U.S. News and World
Report 79, no. 24 (1975):29.

need of improved CAB procedures rather than statutory amendments and attributed excess capacity not to the absence of price competition but to unfavorable market conditions.[1]

The most vehement protests, however, came from the trunks and local service carriers, whose representatives, while lavish in their praise of the private enterprise system, condemned the proposed dissolution of a regulatory regime which had "served the nation so well"[2] and had produced "the finest air transportation system in the world."[3] It may seem paradoxical that, at a time when governmental "interference" and "red tape" were under constant attack by the business community as a whole, a major industry should plead for the retention of Federal supervision. This contradiction, more apparent than real, is quickly disposed of if we consider the statement of an American Airlines official that "it would not be surprising if [following deregulation] as many as seven new airlines were to expand into the New York-Chicago market, already served by three airlines . . . making the market unprofitable for all."[4] Concern for the financial ramifications of deregulation was also voiced by the Air Transport Association of America (the Association represents the scheduled carriers), which, after noting the threat deregulation posed to the job security of airline workers and to existing service levels, acknowledged its members "were also worried about their profits."[5] Airline officials, reacting to the charge that fares and rates were at an unreasonably high level, pointed to the carriers' "seriously inadequate earnings" over much of the postwar period and invited their critics to reconcile this with the Board's alleged overprotection of their industry.

The trunklines were obviously loath to see any erosion of their industry share, which hitherto had been partially protected by entry restrictions. Profits, however, were not at the center of the industry's public statements. Indeed, probably because of a

---

[1]"Prospects of Easing Regulations Over Airlines Worrying Lenders." New York Times, March 26, 1977, p. 25; Remarks of Frederick W. Bradley, Jr., Vice President, Citibank, Airline Industry Seminar, Financial Analysts Federation, New York, July 28, 1976, mimeographed.

[2]James W. Callison, "Airline Deregulation--A Hoax?" Journal of Air Law and Commerce 41, no. 4 (1975):791.

[3]"Adams Urges Changes in Aviation Regulation," Journal of Commerce, April 4, 1977, p. 23.

[4]"Airline Rules Shift Snagged by Lobbying," New York Times, August 15, 1977, p. 30.

[5]"Ford Proposes Cut in Controls Over Airline Service and Fares," New York Times, October 9, 1975, p. 37.

barrage of criticism coming from various consumer interest groups,
overt references to profit margins were largely missing from the
industry's verbal counter-offensive, its leaders preferring to emphasize the public utility aspects of their business and their
ability to serve the traveling and shipping public adequately within
the existing regulatory framework. Among the major points these
defenders of the Federal Aviation Act made were:[1]

1. Continued route protection was essential, since the more profitable markets
   cross-subsidize less attractive routes. A reduction in profits due to
   competition from new entrants, said the trunks and local service carriers,
   would force them to reduce or abandon service between small-volume points
   and concentrate on the more attractive city pairs. Eastern Air Lines, for
   instance, suggested that about 160 of its routes required cross-subsidies
   and might have to be abandoned, and the Air Transport Association of America
   (ATA) indicated that service in as many as forty percent of all trunk and
   local carrier markets would be terminated.[2] (It is important to note that
   Congressional supporters of deregulation were not demanding the elimination
   of Federal subsidies for small carriers serving low-density markets. Indeed,
   Public Law 95-504, passed in 1978, extends the subsidy program.[3]) Various
   independent studies have discredited the airlines' projected route abandonments and suggest these figures were released largely for their political
   effect. Thus, an analysis of Eastern's claims revealed that only three
   (instead of 160) of its routes "may" require cross-subsidization.[4] A report
   issued by the General Accounting Office found the ATA's work "faulty" and
   concluded it "should not be relied on as an estimate of the consequences of
   a deregulated air transport system."[5]

---

[1]See: (1) AMERICAN AIRLINES. U.S., Congress, Senate, Committee on Commerce,
Science, and Transportation, Regulatory Reform in Air Transportation, Hearings
before the Subcommittee on Aviation, Senate, on S. 292 and S. 689, 95th Cong.,
1st sess., (1977), part 3, pp. 1409-1422. (2) BRANIFF INTERNATIONAL. Ibid.,
pp. 1214-1218. (3) CONTINENTAL AIRLINES. Ibid., part 2, pp. 584-589. (4) DELTA
AIR LINES. Ibid., pp. 861-872. (5) EASTERN AIR LINES. U.S., Congress, House,
Committee on Public Works and Transportation, Aviation Economics, Joint Hearings
before the Subcommittee on Investigations and Review and the Subcommittee on
Aviation, House of Representatives, 94th Cong., 2d sess., (1976), pp. 281-284.
(6) NATIONAL AIRLINES. U.S., Congress, Senate, Committee on Commerce, Science, and
Transportation, op. cit., part 3, pp. 1218-1227. (7) NORTHWEST AIRLINES. Ibid.,
pp. 1481-1492. (8) TRANS WORLD AIRLINES. Testimony of C. E. Meyer, Jr., remarks
made before the Senate Aviation Subcommittee, March 24, 1977, mimeographed;
Testimony of L. Edwin Smart, remarks made before the House Aviation Subcommittee,
October 12, 1977, mimeographed. (9) WESTERN AIR LINES. U.S., Congress, Senate,
Committee on Commerce, Science, and Transportation, op. cit., part 2, pp. 567-572.
(10) The local service carriers' objections to deregulation are found in Comments
of Eight Local Service Airlines on the Proposed Aviation Act of 1975, Docket 28490,
January 20, 1976. Also see below, p. 137, note 4.

[2]U.S., Congress, Senate, Committee on the Judiciary, Oversight of Civil
Aeronautics Board Practices and Procedures, I, p. 165.

[3]Pub. L. no. 95-504, sec. 33 (section 419 of the Federal Aviation
Act). See also S. 689, 95th Cong., 1st sess., sec. 17, (1977).

[4]Congressional Record 122, no. 117 (1976):S12983.

[5]Comptroller General of the United States, Comments on the Study: "Consequences of Deregulation of the Scheduled Air Transportation Industry" (Washington,
D.C.: General Accounting Office, 1977), p. 13. A similar conclusion was reached
by the Council on Wage and Price Stability, which declared that "the ATA simulation

2. Safety standards were likely to fall under deregulation, since smaller profits would lead to a reduced level of investment in safety. Safety, however, is the responsibility of the Federal Aviation Administration rather than the Civil Aeronautics Board, so a new role for the latter does not connote less Federal concern for safety standards. Also, of course, one wonders whether management would jeopardize a company's future by allowing it to acquire a reputation for lax safety controls. The Senate Subcommittee on Administrative Practice and Procedure stated flatly that statutory reform would in no way threaten carrier safety. Other studies support this position.[1] (The revised section 102 policy statement [1978] directs the Board to "consider . . . the assignment and maintenance of safety as the highest priority in air commerce."[2])

3. The rate of technological progress would be slower under deregulation, since companies would be less willing to assume the risks involved in investing in advanced equipment and facilities. Again, independent studies reject this line of reasoning. For instance, a CAB Special Staff Report notes that, in fact, under deregulation the new competitive climate "could be expected to bring increased carrier attention to bear on possibilities for cost reduction, and improved aircraft design is one obvious possible method of achieving this."[3]

4. The uncertainties inherent in deregulation would undermine the airlines' creditworthiness, making it impossible to attract the $15 billion in external financing the industry will require during 1975-1985 to meet debt commitments and proceed with its reequipment program. The U.S. Department of Transportation disputes this contention and notes that, while there might be certain short-term dislocations, only the inefficient operators will suffer under deregulation. The Department believes deregulation will actually ease financing problems because investment decisions will no longer be influenced by CAB rulings.

5. In the absence of Federal regulation the states would attempt to assert control over the carriers' interstate activities. The carriers' fear of a potentially confusing and contradictory set of state laws in place of Federal jurisdiction appears to have been shared by the Congress and rests in part on confrontations between the CAB and state public utility bodies in which the latter questioned the Board's prerogatives.[4] Public Law 95-504 makes clear that regulatory reform is not intended to affect Federal preemption.[5]

6. The termination of the Board's right to immunize intercarrier arrangements from the antitrust laws would disrupt the cohesion of the national air

---

provides no useful information about the likely effects of 'deregulation' since the system being simulated by the ATA bears no resemblance to the current U.S. air transport system." U.S., Congress, Senate, Committee on the Judiciary, Oversight of Civil Aeronautics Board Practices and Procedures, I, p. 394.

[1] Jordan, op. cit., pp. 49-53; Hardy K. Maclay and William C. Burt, "Entry of New Carriers into Domestic Trunkline Air Transportation," Journal of Air Law and Commerce 22, no. 2 (1955):133.

[2] Pub. L. no. 95-504, sec. 3 (section 102[a][1] of the Federal Aviation Act).

[3] Report of the CAB Special Staff on Regulatory Reform, op. cit., pp. 281-282. Also see William M. Capron, (ed.), Technological Change in Regulated Industries (Washington, D.C.: The Brookings Institution, 1971), pp. 159-160.

[4] People of the State of California v. Civil Aeronautics Board, 567 F. 2d 1 (D.C. Cir. 1977); U.S., Congress, Senate, Committee on Commerce, op. cit., pp. 905-906.

[5] See below, p. 203. See also Senate Report no. 631, 95th Cong., 2d sess., (1978), pp. 39-40.

transportation system, since it would expose to legal action a number of
cooperative agreements (e.g., Air Cargo Procedures Agreement, Airport
Scheduling Committee Agreements, and Small Packages Interline Agreements)
which the agency had earlier approved on the basis of public convenience
and necessity considerations.[1] This fear appears to have been misplaced,
for most agreements of this type are not anticompetitive in nature and,
indeed, are widely recognized as being in the public interest. Pressure
for change in this area had originated largely with the U.S. Department of
Justice, which, however, was concerned only to the extent that the Board
was encouraging anticompetitive actions on the part of the carriers. The
Department has argued that "price fixing, market allocation, and other
hard core antitrust violations are generally prohibited in the mainstream
of the American economy, and we see no reason to authorize them in the
airline industry."[2]

Despite the certificated route carriers' rejection of uncontrolled market entry/exit and unlimited pricing freedom, there was
broad agreement that some degree of regulatory change was both
necessary and desirable. However, views differed as to what that
degree should be and how it might best be achieved. Thus, while
local service airlines recommended adoption of a zone of reasonableness allowing unfettered annual upward and downward price adjustments of 10 per cent and 35 percent respectively, the larger
carriers believed maximum price fluctuations should be held to 15
percent. Also, the local service operators, aghast at the prospect
of unrestricted competition over their own routes,[3] had little
difficulty proposing free entry for the nation's fifteen leading
traffic markets, a position totally at odds with that of the trunklines.[4] The carriers' unanimity was further fractured by United
Airlines and Pan American World Airways. United was the only trunkline to openly support total deregulation during the early phase of

---

[1]U.S., Congress, Senate, Committee on Commerce, Science and Transportation,
op. cit., part 2, p. 1023 and part 4, pp. 1689-1705. Also see Statement of
William T. Seawell, March 24, 1977, pp. 8-9.

[2]U.S., Congress, Senate, Committee on Commerce, Science and Transportation,
op. cit., part 3, p. 1376.

[3]Unlike the local service operators, a number of transportation economists
believe that the quality of regular service between small communities is not contingent upon the maintenance of Board controls. Jordan, op. cit., pp. 131-132.
Also see George Eads, "The Effect of Regulation on the Cost Performance and Growth
Strategies of the Local Service Airlines," Journal of Air Law and Commerce 38,
no. 1 (1972), pp. 1-34.

[4]Association of Local Transport Airlines, Position on Legislative Proposals
for Regulatory Reform (Washington, D.C.: Association of Local Transport Airlines,
1977), p. 4; Also see: U.S. Congress, Senate, Committee on Commerce, op. cit.,
pp. 703-715; Testimony of Francisco A. Lorenzo, Chairman, Association of Local
Transport Airlines, remarks made before the House Aviation Subcommittee, October 11,
1977, mimeographed. The position of Hughes Airwest differed somewhat from that of
the other local service airlines. See The Need for Regulatory Reform, remarks
made by Russel V. Stephenson, General Manager, Hughes Airwest, before the National
Association of State Aviation Officials, Seattle, August 31, 1977, mimeographed.

the deregulation debate, arguing that the airline industry could not improve its financial performance so long as it remained shackled by Federal economic regulation.[1] This position was reiterated in 1976. (United Airlines is the nation's largest domestic air carrier. During Congressional hearings several opponents of deregulation noted that the company's stance reflected a need to solve its mounting excess capacity problem.) A year later the company adopted a more cautious tone and, while still endorsing increased competition its position now bore greater resemblance to that of the other trunk lines. Rate adjustments were to be exempt from Board review only if they fell within a specified zone of reasonableness. Also, United recommended that entry into scheduled air transportation be limited to two new carriers per year, with applications to be examined from the standpoint of the public convenience and necessity, and that incumbents be given the right to automatically extend their domestic routes by a predetermined amount every two years.[3] The other major carrier favoring substantial reform was Pan American World Airways. Long confined to international operations, the company welcomed any Congressional initiative which would finally allow it to move into domestic markets.[4]

Virtually all airline spokesmen insisted the Board was no longer able to properly handle its workload and urged Congress to make procedural expedition a major reform objective. (Of the principal route cases being considered by the CAB during the early part of 1975, over sixty percent had been initiated at least two years earlier.) There were also complaints that the Board's reporting requirements had become unduly burdensome and that the agency failed to utilize much of the statistical material at its disposal. Thus, the chairman of Northwest Airlines told Senate investigators that his company was devoting at least five man-days per month to the data requirements in the Domestic Air Freight Rate Investigation, above, and that "virtually nothing was being done by the Civil Aeronautics Board with the data to make it available in a usable format.

---

[1] Comments of Edward E. Carlson, Chairman, United Airlines, remarks made during a Cleveland civic luncheon, October 30, 1975, mimeographed. The CAB's target figure, a 12 percent return on capital, has never been achieved; the figure for the period 1972-1976 was 3.6 percent.

[2] U.S., Congress, House, Committee on Public Works and Transportation, Aviation Economics, p. 134.

[3] Statement of Richard J. Ferris, President, United Airlines, remarks made before the House Aviation Subcommittee, March 24, 1977, mimeographed; Remarks by Richard J. Ferris, The Wings Club, New York, March 16, 1977, mimeographed.

[4] Statement of William T. Seawell, Chairman, Pan American World Airways, remarks made before the House Aviation Subcommittee, October 12, 1977, mimeograph

The airline industry, continued Mr. Nyrop, "has been required for years to report data for which there is virtually no need or apparent use."[1]

Having reviewed the position taken by the trunklines and local service operators, let us consider now how other units of the air freight system reacted to the prospect of regulatory change.

Certificated all-cargo route carriers. Of the three airlines in this category, only the Flying Tiger Line fully supported total deregulation. During the decade 1967-1977, its domestic operations had seen seven unprofitable years, which the company attributed in part to the overall lack of pricing freedom. In addition, the company's domestic operating rights had been severely restricted by the CAB, and it was hoped that the lifting of entry controls would enable it to initiate service on a nationwide scale. Congressional investigators were told that air shipments were service- rather than price-sensitive and that the Board's rate and tariff controls should be reduced to the point where the agency retained authority only over discriminatory rates. Flying Tiger estimated that it would need about three years to restructure its domestic route network and requested that new entrants be held to the traditional public interest standards during this transition period.

The company's enthusiasm for regulatory reform was, as one would expect, based on self-interest. Thus, when in 1976 Senator Howard Baker (R. Tenn.) introduced legislation designed to enlarge the Board's certification exemption powers,[2] Flying Tiger opposed his bill (Baker's proposal was intended primarily to assist cargo commuter airlines, especially Federal Express, which has its headquarters in his state). Flying Tiger's objections caused Representative Glenn Anderson (D. Calif.), Chairman of the House Subcommittee on Aviation, to withhold his backing from the bill (Flying Tiger is based in California). Anderson's own reform bill (Air Service Improvement Act of 1977[3]) provided for equal treatment of section 401 and part 298 carriers, and Flying Tiger now "strongly" supported "basic reform" in the regulatory field.[4] (The U.S. Department of Transportation had also objected to Baker's private relief bill,

---

[1]U.S., Congress, Senate, Committee on Commerce, Science and Transportation, op. cit., part 3, p. 1490.

[2]S. 3684, 94th Cong., 2d sess., (1976).

[3]H.R. 8813.

[4]Statement of Joseph J. Healy, Executive Vice President, Flying Tiger Line, remarks made before the House Aviation Subcommittee, August 23, 1977, mimeographed.

since allowing commuter carriers to use larger aircraft under the
section 416 exemption would have given them an unfair advantage over
their certificated competitors. The Department also feared that the
bill, by splitting freight and passenger services into separate
issues, would weaken the drive for regulatory reform of passenger
transportation.[1])

For Seaboard World Airlines, an international all-cargo carrier, deregulation meant access to major domestic markets from which
it was excluded under the "old" regulatory scheme. The company,
however, was not uncritical of deregulation; it believed the Board
had frequently been unfairly censured and voiced agreement with
several of the points raised by the trunks and local service carrier

Airlift International, the third all-cargo carrier, viewed deregulation with considerable reserve. The company had long experienced financial difficulties and was concerned that unrestricted
competition would have a damaging effect on its future operations.

Commuter airlines. The deregulation movement had the whole-
hearted support of the all-cargo commuter operators, who devoted
much of their Congressional testimony to the Board's preoccupation
with the traveling public and its consequent failure to address the
problems of the freight industry. These companies were exempt from
the Board's certification and tariff filing requirements[2] and their
reform efforts were focused chiefly on raising their maximum permissible aircraft capacity without impairing their exempt status.
The 7,500-pounds payload rule, it was noted, was limiting commuters
to "multiple section flights with small aircraft in many markets
with resulting inefficiencies in ground operations, fuel utilization
and pilot utilization."[3]

Supplemental airlines. Although the supplementals were interested in substantial regulatory reform, they stopped short of calling for complete deregulation of air freight transportation. Thus,
they endorsed liberalized entry but asked for the retention of the
Board's public interest tests. Similarly, enhanced pricing flexibility was considered desirable but was to be kept within the bound

---

[1]Told the author by John W. Barnum, Deputy Secretary of the U.S. Department
of Transportation in the Ford Administration, 1978.

[2]See above, p. 23, note 4.

[3]U.S., Congress, House, Committee on Public Works and Transportation,
Aviation Regulatory Reform, p. 284. See also: U.S., Congress, Senate,
Committee on Commerce, Science, and Transportation, op. cit., part 1, pp. 489-494
Testimony of L. C. Burwell, Chairman, Pinehurst Airlines, remarks made before the
House Aviation Subcommittee, October 6, 1977, mimeographed; "Senate Passes Avia-
tion Package," Commuter Airline Digest 3, no. 9 (1977):1.

of a CAB-supervised zone of reasonableness. The main concern of this carrier group was "evenhanded" treatment of the scheduled and nonscheduled sectors of the industry, and, in this context, the companies were opposed to any measure which might perpetuate route protection for the trunks while loosening entry into the charter field. Relief was sought from a number of problems which had placed the charter specialists at a competitive disadvantage and which stemmed from the Board's perception of their limited role within the national air transportation system. One of these was the rule prohibiting split cargo charters, which in effect prevented small-volume shippers from using the supplementals' services (split passenger charters had been approved several years earlier). Another difficulty confronting these carriers was their inability to automatically carry freight over any route for which they held passenger authority. Freight exemptions had to be applied for on an individual basis, leading to delays and business losses. The carriers complained that the designation "supplemental" implied a "secondary or inferior status" and asked that it not be used in future legislation.[1]

Air freight forwarders. The deregulation controversy divided the forwarders into two groups. On the one side there were those who believed unrestricted price competition and free entry would result in "pricing chaos" and the possible collapse of the weaker airlines, thereby undermining the operational flexibility of the forwarders themselves. While generally in favor of a more liberal entry policy, these operators were unable to support any weakening of the CAB's traditional rate suspension powers. Also of concern was that joint loading agreements would be dissolved in the event that the Board was deprived of control over antitrust exemptions (this despite the fact that joint loading [chapter VI] is rejected by most forwarders) and that their archrivals, the commuter airlines, would (unlike the forwarders) not be subject to tariff filing requirements.[2]

Other forwarders, on the other hand, supported deregulation on the ground that existing Board controls were stifling the industry's growth. According to this group, the Board's interest focused mainly

---

[1] Statement of Edward J. Driscoll, President, National Air Carrier Association, remarks made before the House Aviation Subcommittee, October 5, 1977, mimeographed; see also U.S., Congress, House, Committee on Public Works and Transportation, Reform of the Economic Regulation of Air Carriers, pp. 1189-1198. In 1978 (Public Law 95-504, op. cit., sec. 2) the supplementals were renamed "charter air carriers."

[2] U.S., Congress, Senate, Committee on Commerce, Science, and Transportation, op. cit., part 3, pp. 1114-1119.

on the welfare of the passenger carriers, and Congress was urged to deregulate the freight sector independently of any action it might contemplate vis-à-vis the passenger field. Supporters of deregulation pointed to the combination airlines' reduction of all-cargo flights and hoped that reform legislation would help correct this problem by allowing commuter airlines to utilize larger aircraft.[1]

Air freight motor carriers. This group of carriers, which included both local pickup/delivery agents and ICC-regulated truckers, was totally opposed to deregulation, seeing it as a direct threat to its continued existence. Leaning heavily on figures supplied by the Air Transport Association of America, the motor carrier took the position that under deregulation "perhaps hundreds of airports" might be affected by route abandonments. Such a development would imperil various intermodal arrangements, e.g., joint air-surface rules and rates, and take its toll of the smaller trucking firms. (A related factor was that Federal Express, the leading commuter airline, was using its own pickup and delivery equipment and that other major commuters were likely to follow suit. This alone made it unlikely that the surface operators would support any measure which included enhanced operating rights for this carrier class.) The truckers had little confidence that the commuters could effectively replace the certificated route carriers in the abandoned markets. They considered the commuter airlines inherently unstable and did not believe that the close working relationship marking their dealings with the certificated airlines could be achieved with this airline class.[2]

New York-Newark interest groups. According to the Port Authority of New York and New Jersey, "radical regulatory change at this time would not appear warranted."[3] The Port Authority, which operates the three New York-Newark airports, believed the airlines should be exposed to greater competition, but not at the expense of the CAB's traditional public interest considerations. The reasons for its opposition to deregulation were similar to those presented by the trunklines and local service carriers and need not be restated. Two points, however, should be emphasized: (1) As many as one quarter of New York-Newark's domestic nonstop air routes were

---

[1]Ibid., part 4, pp. 1897-1898; John C. Emery, A Good Place to Start-- Deregulate Air Freight First! n.d., mimeographed.

[2]U.S., Congress, House, Committee on Public Works and Transportation, Reform of the Economic Regulation of Air Carriers, pp. 1346-1350.

[3]U.S., Congress, Senate, Committee on Commerce, op. cit., p. 1310.

being served wholly by local service airlines and/or commuters, and the Port Authority feared that carrier bankruptcies and route aban- donments would substantially weaken air service between its three airports and many small communities. (2) The Port Authority, one of the nation's leading airport managers, was uneasy about any measure which might impair its ability to raise capital. In this connection the agency told the Senate Aviation Subcommittee that deregulation could

> create serious financial problems for airport operators. The airport operator's large investment in facilities, his ability to raise investment monies for additional airport construction and his responsibility to pro- vide a diversity of airport services is basically supported by long-term leases and other financial commitments from his major airline tenants. Airport operators, airlines and other airport tenants have invested many billions of dollars in the nation's airports. The instability inherent in the proposed easy entry/exit air transportation system could threaten the security of these commitments and probably increase the financing cost of future airport development. The effect of a carrier failure on an air- port operator's finances would depend primarily on the lease arrangements and financial commitments to the operator. Because of increased competi- tive pressures to reduce costs, it cannot be assumed that a bankrupt carrier's leasehold could be leased in its entirety to another carrier or carriers.
> On the other hand, at some airports easy entry and exit could result in substantial airline demand for airport terminal space and other facilities. It would be exceedingly difficult for airport operators to reliably plan for or reasonably finance, any new or expanded airport facilities within this unstable environment. Of course, the airport operator could demand long-term lease agreements with new carriers. However, the newcomers, as well as the incumbent airlines, would be less likely to agree to long-term leases or to survive the term of the leases in the more competitive envi- ronment.[1]

The Port Authority's unhappiness with deregulation may be seen from another perspective. About thirty years ago the CAB approved freight rate equalization for New York and Newark, since "the air- ports located in those cities serve the same metropolitan area and a lower rate to one of them, would, as a practical matter, funnel all consignments to the New York City area through that airport."[2] This position was affirmed in the recent Domestic Air Freight Rate Investigation, above, wherein the Board concluded: "in situations where a city or metropolitan area is served by two or more airports, the [line-haul charge] should be calculated from the geographic mid- point of the airports."[3] Their new pricing freedom, the Port Author- ity feared, would enable the carriers to enhance the competitive

---

[1]U.S., Congress, Senate, Committee on Commerce, Science and Transportation, op. cit., part 4, p. 1988.

[2]Air Freight Rate Investigation--Directional Rates, (1950), p. 238.

[3]Domestic Air Freight Rate Investigation.

advantage of a particular terminal, should they so choose. This
would run counter to its long-term effort to operate the three terminals as complementary, rather than competitive, entities.

The Greater Newark Chamber of Commerce also opposed deregulation. The Chamber believed that deregulation would tempt the carriers to reduce (and in some cases eliminate) scheduled operations
at Newark, aggravating the city's unemployment problem.[1] Interestingly enough, this view clashed with that of Millicent Fenwick, U.S.
Representative from New Jersey's Fifth District. Said Mrs. Fenwick

> what is clear is that [entry] restrictions have substantially diluted
> carriers' incentives to provide conscientious and varied service. It is
> no accident that Newark Airport operates at only half of its capacity.
> Carriers do not fear competition and so can afford to concentrate services
> into La Guardia and Kennedy Airports where it may be more convenient for
> them, but it is not necessarily more convenient for all passengers. Entry
> restrictions deny consumers with proximity to Newark, the convenience of
> nearby service.[2]

As was indicated above, election year politics formed one of
the chief obstacles to enactment of major reform legislation in 197
Congressional involvement with other transportation issues (e.g.,
reorganization of the financially troubled railroads; aid for airport construction) also presented a problem since it reduced the
amount of time which could be devoted to airline deregulation. Muc
of 1977 was an equally frustrating period for reform-minded congres
men, who had to contend not only with the inherent complexity of
various interrelated deregulation issues but also faced determined
opposition from major sectors of the air transportation industry an
organized labor. Numerous mark-up sessions, Congress' preoccupatic
with other transport-related problems (such as aircraft noise control legislation), and low committee attendance combined to make
airline deregulation one of the most time-consuming issues to come
before the Senate Commerce Committee in recent years. Philosophica
differences dividing the House and Senate also hampered progress.
Thus, the Air Transportation Regulatory Reform Act of 1977,[3] cospon
sored by Senators Howard Cannon and Edward Kennedy (and hence
referred to as the Cannon-Kennedy bill), was given a cool receptior
in the House, where legislators believed it cut too deeply into the
CAB's authority. The House Aviation Subcommittee was concentrating
on the question of aircraft noise levels, and some of its members

---

[1]U.S., Congress, Senate, Committee on Commerce, op. cit. pp. 1233-1234.

[2]Ibid., p. 339.

[3]S. 689.

tended to view a Senate reform bill merely in terms of its usefulness as a channel for their own legislation dealing with more stringent Federal noise standards.

Quite apart from the fact that the House and Senate aviation
subcommittees had different priorities, cooperation between the two
was at times poor. Also, it was felt by some on the Senate side
that the chairman of the House Aviation Subcommittee did not fully
understand the various deregulation issues. A reorganization of the
Senate Commerce Committee changed its aviation subcommittee's membership, which again did little to speed regulatory reform.[1] A further
complication was the change in administration. Although President
Carter had made regulatory reform an election issue and despite his
subsequent assurance to the Congress that relief from "overregulation" of the American economy was one of his "major goals,"[2] the
new Administration failed to develop its own airline bill. Such an
initiative, according to the White House, was unnecessary since
Congress "has already moved substantially forward in dealing with
this important issue."[3] This position disappointed a number of
reformers who found the President insufficiently supportive of deregulation legislation. Similar criticism was leveled at the Department of Transportation. The new Secretary, Brock Adams, initially
expressed doubt about some of the reformers' claims (such as lower
rates under deregulation) but later had much praise for the Cannon-
Kennedy bill. Many thought the Secretary "has cheered the reform
movement from the sidelines, [but] has failed . . . to get involved
by lobbying his former colleagues in the House."[4]

One of the many witnesses to appear before the House and
Senate aviation subcommittees during 1976-1977 was John E. Robson,
Chairman of the Civil Aeronautics Board, under whose leadership the
agency had basically abandoned its antireform posture and who now
told the legislators that, "despite the incredible growth of the
domestic air transport system since 1938 and its considerable suc-
cesses, there are serious current problems and some clouds on the
horizon. . . . we are concerned that the present regulatory system

[1]Discussion between the author and Thomas G. Allison, Chief Counsel, Senate
Committee on Commerce, Science, and Transportation, 1977.

[2]House Document no. 92, 95th Cong., 1st sess., (1977), p. 1.

[3]"President Carter Supports Airline Deregulation Bill; Plans One Energy
Agency," Traffic World 169, no. 9 (1977):15.

[4]"Carter Renews Call To Free Airline Rein; Bill Faces Fight," New York
Times, June 21, 1977, p. 41.

may have great difficulty in coping successfully with the future."[1]
The rigidities of the existing regulatory structure made it difficult for the airlines to respond effectively to a worsening economic
climate, and

> a future Board might face inexorable, simultaneous public pressures for
> expanded service on the one hand and lower fares on the other, a road
> which could lead ultimately to financial disaster for the industry.
> . . . . We are sincerely concerned that future Boards may not be able to
> function effectively in an environment in which economic regulation would
> be subject to increasing attack both by a dissatisfied . . . public and
> a dissatisfied industry.[2]

Protective regulation, Robson acknowledged, "has induced costly inefficiencies through overscheduling, overcapacity, competition in
frills, equipment races and in other areas. It has not provided the
environment or the incentives for basic price competition."[3] He
agreed with those critics who had long complained about the CAB's
slowness in handling applications and petitions and stressed his
agency was doing all it could to correct the "regulatory lag" problem. Robson's testimony, it should be emphasized, reflected the
view of all Board members, who, in a statement to the two aviation
subcommittees, declared that

> the airline industry has achieved maturity. The economic circumstances
> which were responsible for the enormous expansion of the industry--rapid
> growth in demand, high rate of technological innovation, declining unit
> costs--have changed. A return to such favorable conditions is not forecast.
>   In light of these developments, and the difficulties which the Board
> foresees in averting severe long-term problems, including the ultimate
> possibility of the need for Government financial support to maintain the
> air transport system, the Board believes that the time has come for the
> Congress to change the orientation of the Federal Aviation Act. This
> might be pursued in one of two ways: by greatly tightening the regulatory
> hold over air transportation through very restrictive route and entry
> policies, legislation giving the Board authority to regulate schedules,
> equipment, service amenities, levels of service, and the like, or, on the
> other hand, by gradually removing the governmental controls over such
> fundamental management decisions as where carriers can operate (entry,
> exit) and at what prices. We believe that the latter approach offers the
> greatest potential benefits to the American public and recommend that
> Congress adopt it.[4]

In a sense the Board was now on trial, and it was inevitable
that some of Robson's testimony would take on a defensive character.

---

[1]U.S., Congress, Senate, Committee on Commerce, op. cit., pp. 347-348.

[2]Ibid., p. 376.

[3]U.S., Congress, House, Committee on Public Works and Transportation,
Aviation Regulatory Reform, p. 69.

[4]Ibid., p. 153; U.S., Congress, Senate, Committee on Commerce, op. cit.,
p. 386.

On the question of entry restrictions, for instance, he noted that, while it was true that no new trunk carriers had been certificated since the 1938 issuance of the grandfather permits (of the eighty or so certificate applications received since 1950 none had been approved[1]), additional competition had been encouraged through the creation of all-cargo, local service, and charter specialists. The agency's promotion of commuter service was also stressed, as was the fact that it had been the Congress, not the Board, which had terminated the supplementals' individually way-billed/ticketed operations.[2] With regard to regulatory lag, it was pointed out that the Federal Aviation Act's emphasis on the public convenience and necessity dictated a case-by-case approach involving hearings and other time-consuming procedures. The Act's policy declaration was termed "ambiguous" and Congress was told it would be "unfair" to expect the Board to oversee regulatory change without first giving it a new mandate and less cumbersome procedures.[3] "If Congress decides it wants a more competitive system," said Chairman Robson, "it ought to . . . change the law to insure that that is the direction in which regulation will go."[4] His idea (and those of the other Board members) of what that direction should be was set forth in a 17-point reform program, which was later formally introduced at the agency's request by Senators Howard Cannon (D. Nev.) and James Pearson (R. Kan.)[5] and Representatives Glenn Anderson (D. Calif.), William Harsha (R. Ohio), and Robert Jones (D. Ala.).[6] The Board's reform proposals were as follows:[7]

1. <u>Revision of the statutory declaration of policy</u>. Congress was urged to replace the Federal Aviation Act's section 102 policy statement with a declaration stressing Federal concern for increased competition in domestic air transportation. A principal objective of the new regulatory approach was to be "the phased and progressive transition to an air transportation system which will rely on competitive market forces to determine the variety, quality, and price of air services, through the facilitation and promotion of entry and potential entry of new carriers into all phases of air transportation, meaningful price competition, and optimal carrier efficiency."[8]

---

[1] Trans Caribbean Airways was a special case.

[2] See above, p. 26.

[3] U.S., Congress, House, Committee on Public Works and Transportation, <u>Aviation Regulatory Reform</u>, p. 74.

[4] Ibid., p. 75.

[5] S. 3536, 94th Cong., 2d sess., (1976).

[6] H.R. 14330, 94th Cong., 2d sess., (1976).

[7] U.S., Congress, Senate, Committee on Commerce, op. cit., pp. 385-398.

[8] H.R. 14330, sec. 3.

2. <u>Open entry into charter air transportation</u>. The Board believed this would
raise the efficiency of charter service and stimulate competition between
scheduled and supplemental operators. Licenses, issued on a showing of
fiscal fitness, willingness, and ability, would be used instead of the
traditional certificates of public convenience and necessity.

3. <u>Liberalization of charter rules</u>. The distinction between individually
ticketed transportation and group travel served no "necessary regulatory
purpose," and Congress was asked to exclude it from future reform legislation. A new definition of "charter," the Board suggested, should:
(1) be based on planeload transportation and (2) recognize that the agency's
obligation to protect "needed" scheduled flights could impose limitations on
the scope of charter service.

4. <u>Open entry into domestic air freight transportation and deregulation of air
freight rates</u>. Such a step would ensure that, "over the long run, rates
and service will be maintained at a level that market demand and cost conditions justify." Certificates would be replaced by licenses issued on the
basis of fitness, willingness, and ability. The lifting of entry and exit
restrictions was to apply to the all-cargo specialists as well as the passenger carriers' all-cargo services and was to be a gradual process (a two-
year transition period was recommended), giving the incumbents a chance to
adjust to the new circumstances. The Board would retain its authority to
move against discriminatory rates.

5. <u>Expansion of the unregulated commuter and air taxi zone</u>. The Board recommended a higher statutory ceiling (56 seats or a maximum payload capacity
of 16,000 pounds) for aircraft operating under the section 416 certification exemption. This was to permit commuters and air taxis to function
more efficiently in their essentially low-density traffic markets.

6. <u>Elimination of mandatory CAB jurisdiction in nonregulated zones</u>. The
Board's mandatory jurisdiction over section 408 arrangements (consolidations, mergers, etc.) would be removed from the industry's noncertificated
sectors (domestic all-cargo, supplemental, and commuter/air taxi operations),
enlarging management's freedom and reducing the agency's "expanding and
uncontrollable" workload. The Board would, however, retain residual authority in this area which it could assert at its discretion. Corporate agreements consummated without the Board's approval would not enjoy section 414
antitrust immunity.

7. <u>Amended procedures for domestic route applications</u>. Non-hearing procedures
were to be employed, except in the case of applications involving major
markets and complex choice-of-carrier decisions. Similarly, evidentiary
hearings were no longer to be required where an operator sought to delete
unused authority from his certificate. Carriers would have the right to
gradually expand their route network under expedited procedures with the
rate of growth based, for instance, on the size of their existing route
system. New route awards obtained through non-hearing procedures would
only become permanent following a specified trial period. Evidentiary
hearings, the Board told Congress, placed "a heavy burden of expense and
delay" on companies seeking certificate amendments. A staff shortage was
forcing the agency to limit the number of route applications which could
be set for hearing, thus accentuating the delay problem.

8. <u>Scheduled route authority for charter carriers</u>. The Board believed that
under section 401(d)(3) of the Federal Aviation Act supplemental operators
could not hold scheduled authority, and asked Congress to remove this
restriction. (This construction of section 401[d][3] was later rejected
by an appeals court, which ruled that a supplemental's request for scheduled rights had to be considered "on its merits."[1])

9. <u>Exit from unprofitable markets</u>. Termination of service between points
named in a carrier's certificate was to be permitted following ninety
days' notice. The Board would have the right to suspend the termination

[1]See above, p. 30.

for 270 days, giving it and the affected communities an opportunity to arrange for other air services (such as commuter flights).

10. <u>Changes in the Board's power to prescribe passenger fares.</u> The agency's authority over maximum fares was to remain unchanged, while its power to set minimum fares was to be confined to instances involving predatory pricing, discrimination, and failure to offer adequate service. It was hoped this might lead to lower fares, since fares at the level of direct costs would now be lawful and new entrants would not be required to base fares on industry averages. The Board believed its rule of ratemaking (section 1002[e])[1] contained internal contradictions and should be rewritten to clarify the new stress on competition.

11. <u>Establishment of mail rates by tariff filing.</u> Future mail rates were to be filed by the carriers rather than being set by the Board as provided under section 406 of the Federal Aviation Act.[2] The Board would thus no longer be compelled to hold costly and time-consuming evidentiary hearings, though it would have the power to investigate mail rates if called upon to do so by the Postal Service.

12. <u>Modification of the Postmaster General's powers.</u> The Postmaster General's authority under section 405(b)[3] was deemed to be inconsistent with the move towards greater competition, and the Board urged that it be deleted from the Act. That authority had only been exercised in rare instances, and it was believed that, in future, supplemental rather than scheduled carriers should be used to satisfy special Postal Service requirements. The Board also recommended that the Postmaster General be given greater authority to contract for the transportation of mail.

13. <u>Subsidy for small community service.</u> The Board hoped Congress would adopt new statutory language, defining subsidy eligibility in terms of service provided rather than carrier class, enabling noncertificated carriers to qualify for subsidy payments. A new subsidy program not tied wholly to local service carriers was considered essential if air service at small communities was to be improved.

14. <u>Termination of the subsidy eligibility of trunk airlines.</u> The Board recommended termination of the trunk carriers' subsidy eligibility, as well as that of any other carrier which had operated without subsidy over five consecutive years. The trunk's subsidy eligibility, initially a developmental tool, had become an anachronism which could no longer be justified given the industry's maturity.

15. <u>Modification of antitrust immunity.</u> Bowing to criticism of its extensive antitrust immunity authority, the Board recommended that this authority be restricted to "specifically approved" intercarrier arrangements and that it should no longer apply automatically to all aspects of any transaction approved on public interest grounds. The Board would have the right to define the scope of the immunity.

16. <u>Procedural expedition.</u> The Board would set up time limits for its decision-making process and would be obligated to explain in writing any failure to meet the new deadlines.

17. <u>Modification of the Board's exemption powers.</u> Congress was asked to amend section 416(b) of the Federal Aviation Act in order to give the Board greater operational flexibility. Under the proposed amendment the Board could, for example, exempt foreign air freight forwarders and foreign charter carriers from various regulatory provisions of the Act.

---

[1]See above, p. 10.

[2]See above, p. 18, note 1.

[3]See above, p. 17, note 3.

Despite its endorsement of substantial deregulation with respect to all-cargo, charter, and commuter transportation, the Board's
bill left intact the agency's traditional powers in a number of critical areas. In effect, the Board was requesting a new Congressional
mandate, which, while placing greater emphasis on competition, left
to the agency's discretion both the rate of change and the manner in
which change was to be effectuated. The suggestion that it become a
"cheerleader for total deregulation" was unacceptable to the Board.[1]
It emphasized that the "ultimate" regulatory regime could not be
predicted[2] and went out of its way to impress upon the Congress the
need for a cautious and closely monitored transition towards greater
competition. In the case of the all-important certificated combination (i.e., passenger-freight) flights, the transition was to be
gradual (7, above) or, in the words of the proposed policy statement,
"phased and progressive" (1, above). Congress was not given a specific transition period but was told "it would consume several
years."[3] Similarly, the Board, not the legislators, would decide on
the nature of antitrust exemptions and establish new procedural deadlines (15 and 16, above). Its reform proposals, the Board believed,
sufficed to protect the interests of both the public and the incumbent carriers. A continuation of its discretionary powers was necessary if it was to deal with "unforeseen perversities" and if it was
to have the flexibility to modify the pace and direction of reform
should this be shown to be desirable.[4] (The airlines derive about
ninety percent of their revenues from passenger transportation, and
the agency saw this sector of the industry as the most probable target for future unlawful activities. It was clearly less apprehensive
with regard to the more limited all-cargo field, where free entry
was contemplated following a two-year transition period [4, above].)
Not surprisingly, the Board took strong exception to several provisions of the Cannon-Kennedy bill, one of the principal pieces of
reform legislation claiming the Senate's attention in 1977.[5] The
bill, for instance, sought to: (1) grant the certificated carriers

---

[1]U.S., Congress, Senate, Committee on Commerce, Science, and Transportation,
op. cit., part 1, p. 134.

[2]Ibid., p. 124.

[3]U.S., Congress, House, Committee on Public Works and Transportation,
Reform of the Economic Regulation of Air Carriers, p. 319.

[4]Ibid., p. 318; U.S., Congress, Senate, Committee on Commerce, op. cit.,
p. 380; U.S., Congress, Senate, Committee on Commerce, Science, and Transportation, op. cit., part 1, p. 133.

[5]p. 689.

substantial discretionary route enlargements, (2) broaden the terms for court review of agency decisions, (3) remove the primary responsibility for antitrust exemptions from the Board to the Department of Justice, and (4) impose procedural deadlines on the agency (with applications considered granted where the Board failed to act within the prescribed period). On the other hand, a Republican version of the bill (Commercial Aviation Regulatory Reform Act of 1977, sponsored by Senators Baker and Pearson),[1] which essentially mirrored the Board's own proposals, was characterized as "an effective vehicle for regulatory reform."[2]

The CAB's long record of opposition to major regulatory change and its insistence on retaining extensive discretionary powers under a new mandate complicated its position as it attempted to persuade Congress to pass its reform package. Congressional investigators voiced doubt about the "depth" of the agency's proreform convictions and wondered whether future chairmen could be relied upon to pursue the drive towards greater competition. Chairman Robson replied that Congress' revised policy directive would leave his successors no choice in the matter,[3] but for many critics his assurances had a hollow ring. Thus, the White House and the Justice Department thought the Board's proposals gave the agency too much independence[4] and the Department of Transportation spoke of "backsliding by a future Board."[5] Robson, whose term was to expire in mid-1977, recognized his agency's credibility was now a major problem. "If you become convinced," he told the Senate Aviation Subcommittee,

> that the Board has been faithless to its existing mandate, you will naturally not want to entrust the administration of the transition toward a system placing greater reliance on market forces to the Board, but will want to write into the statute fixed dates and fixed actions which leave no administrative flexibility. . . . we can only convince you of the desirability of our . . . reform proposal if you believe that the Board will carry it out in accordance with the expressed intent of Congress.[6]

---

[1]S. 292, 95th Cong., 1st sess., (1977).

[2]U.S., Congress, Senate, Committee on Commerce, Science, and Transportation, op. cit., part 1, p. 126.

[3]U.S., Congress, House, Committee on Public Works and Transportation, Reform of the Economic Regulation of Air Carriers, p. 320.

[4]"CAB Seeks Broader Discretion," Aviation Week and Space Technology 104, no. 24 (1976):25.

[5]Remarks of Deputy Secretary of Transportation John W. Barnum, p. 4.

[6]U.S., Congress, Senate, Committee on Commerce, op. cit., p. 373.

Public Law 95-163: Deregulation of Interstate Air Freight Transportation

On November 9, 1977, President Carter signed into law legislation which essentially deregulated domestic air freight transportation (Public Law 95-163).[1] The new law, which originated in the House,[2] contains several provisions amending the Federal Aviation Act in the areas of policy, certification, and rates. These amendments and their implications are now discussed.

Policy. Public Law 95-163 states that, with respect to domestic all-cargo service, the following factors are in the public interest:

1. The encouragement and development of an expedited all-cargo air service system, provided by private enterprise, responsive to (A) the present and future needs of shippers, (B) the commerce of the United States, and (C) the national defense.

2. The encouragement and development of an integrated transportation system relying upon competitive market forces to determine the extent, variety, quality, and price of such services.

3. The provision of services without unjust discriminations, undue preferences or advantages, unfair or deceptive practices, or predatory pricing.[3]

This new policy declaration reflects Congress' intent that free market forces rather than Board-imposed controls are to determine the future growth and development of all-cargo service. Limited competition, i.e., "competition to the extent necessary" (section 102[d]),[4] is abolished as a policy goal for this type of service, relieving the Board of having to define the permissible level of competition on a market-by-market basis. Along with virtually unrestricted entry/exit rights, the amended Federal Aviation Act gives management the freedom to set rates as it sees fit. The Board, however, retains jurisdiction over discriminatory and preferential rates and, in view of the carriers' new pricing freedom, is specifically authorized to move against predatory rates.

The revised mandate, then, rests on the presumption that competition is in the public interest. It removes (in the domestic all-cargo field) one of the major difficulties facing the Board since 1938, namely its responsibility to simultaneously promote and control air transportation. All-cargo services provided under the

---

[1] Act of November 9, 1977, Pub. L. no. 95-163, 91 Stat. 1278.

[2] H.R. 6010, 95th Cong., 1st sess., (1977).

[3] Pub. L. no. 95-163, sec. 16 (section 102 of the Federal Aviation Act).

[4] See above, p. 6.

terms of the new law are exempt from the Federal Aviation Act's traditional section 401 certification requirements, and the agency will no longer evaluate route applications in terms of the 1938 public interest criteria to decide which carrier(s) should operate between any given city pair. The original legislation's contradictory policy objectives have been sharply criticized over the years. These contradictions are reduced, though not eliminated, under the new mandate. As before, the Board is called upon to resolve (without being given the necessary guidelines) potential conflicts between the shipping public's present and future needs. Similarly, no guidance is offered as to how the Board might best delineate national interests, on the one hand, and the interests of the shipping community, on the other.

Certification. The new law deprives the Board of virtually all of its former discretionary power regarding certificates of public convenience and necessity and directs the agency to issue all-cargo certificates "to any citizen of the United States who:"

1. Has a valid certificate issued under section 401(d)(1) of this title and who provided scheduled all-cargo air service at any time during the period from January 1, 1977 through the date of enactment [November 9, 1977] of this section [418]

or

2. (A) Operates pursuant to an exemption granted by the Board under section 416 of this title, and (B) provided scheduled all-cargo air service continually (other than for interruptions caused by labor disputes) during the 12-month period ending on the date of enactment of this section.

Furthermore,

3. After the three hundred and sixty-fifth day which begins after the date of enactment of this section, any citizen of the United States may submit an application to the Board for a certificate under this section to provide all-cargo air service.[1]

In the case of (1) and (2), above, grandfather certificates were to be applied for within 45 days of enactment and had to be issued within 60 days following an application's submission to the Board. Applications received after November 9, 1978 (3, above) were to be approved within 180 days unless the Board concluded that an applicant was not fit, willing, and able[2] and could not "comply with any rules and regulations promulgated by the Board." In all cases applications for all-cargo certificates were to "contain such

---

[1]Pub. L. no. 95-163, sec. 17 (section 418[a] of the Federal Aviation Act).

[2]See above, p. 15, note 5.

information . . . as the Board shall by regulation require."[1] The
agency was empowered to impose "reasonable conditions and limitations" on the new services,[2] which were, however, to be unrestricted
as to the points served or the rates to be charged. Where the new
all-cargo services are "not performed to the minimum extent prescribed by the Board," the agency "may by order, entered after notice and opportunity for a hearing," terminate the services.[3]

The first carrier to file an application for a nationwide all-
cargo grandfather certificate was the Flying Tiger Line. The company hailed enactment of the deregulation bill as "a landmark in the
history of commercial aviation in the United States" and promptly
announced it would purchase two additional DC-8-61s and extend its
operations to Atlanta, Charlotte, Cincinnati, Dallas-Fort Worth,
Houston, Miami, Portland, San Juan, and Washington-Baltimore.[4] Other
companies quickly followed suit, and, within a matter of days, all
the trunks and all-cargo operators eligible for a certificate under
the terms of (1), above, had submitted their certificate requests to
the CAB. The agency also accepted about sixty applications from
commuter carriers (2, above), including Federal Express, Freestate
Aviation, Great Western Airlines, Pinehurst Airlines, and Summit
Airlines. Only direct air carriers were eligible for grandfather
certificates, and applications submitted by forwarders were accordingly dismissed.

It is important to note that the deregulation provisions apply
only to domestic transportation. Free entry into international
markets is not contemplated under the amendments, giving those carriers holding international certificates a measure of protection as
they adjust to the changing domestic situation. (During the House
debate on H. R. 6010 Congressman Claude Pepper [D. Fla.] pointed out
that this placed the Miami-based Airlift International at a disadvantage, since it, unlike the other certificated all-cargo carriers
[Flying Tiger Line and Seaboard World Airlines], did not hold international authority. He expressed the hope that Airlift's request
for South American routes would be quickly granted by the Board.[5])

---

[1]The requirements are set forth in the CAB's Regulation ER-1028 (adopted November 16, 1977).

[2]These conditions include cargo/public liability insurance and new data reporting requirements.

[3]Pub. L. no. 95-163, sec. 17 (section 418[b] of the Federal Aviation Act).

[4]"Carter Signs Bill; Deregulates Airfreight," Tigereview 31, no. 7 (1977):1

[5]Congressional Record, November 2, 1977, p. H12045.

The transition period given the airlines before the open entry provision (3, above) was to come into effect was one year, a substantially shorter period than that requested by the Flying Tiger Line[1]
or recommended by the Board.[2]

Another aspect of Public Law 95-163 is that no capacity limitation is imposed on the equipment an applicant may use. This means
that air taxi operators can acquire substantially larger aircraft
than those permitted under the section 416 exemption.[3] Federal
Express, the largest carrier in this category and long a critic of
capacity restrictions, has already purchased (January, 1978) the
B-727-100. Such a step is beyond the financial reach of most air
taxi operators, many of whom, however, can now be expected to turn
towards larger and more economical turboprop aircraft. The relatively low financial barrier to entry for smaller companies indicates that deregulation could lead to an increase in competition in
some short- and medium-length markets and produce improved freight
services in these markets. (The trunklines have sharply reduced
their all-cargo flights in short/medium-length markets, leaving a
void which smaller freight specialists can be expected to fill.)
The substantial capital investment needed for long-haul service, on
the other hand, presents a formidable hurdle for potential newcomers
wishing to operate in these markets. Another problem facing would-
be entrants in long-haul markets is the apparently adequate level of
freight service which these markets receive.

The reader will have noted that under the terms of the new
certification provisions the supplementals were barred from applying
for grandfather rights. Their exclusion from automatic entry was
protested by the supplemental operators, who, it appeared, would
have to wait one year before filing their certificate applications,
which would then be evaluated in terms of the carriers' "fitness"
and ability to meet other possible regulations. (The Board took the
position that it lacked the authority to eliminate this distinction
between scheduled and nonscheduled carriers.[4]) It had been the legislators' intention to place the incumbent all-cargo operators on an
equal footing, and the exclusion of the charter specialists from the
first phase of the deregulation program was apparently an oversight

---

[1]See above, p. 139.

[2]See above, p. 148.

[3]See above, p. 23, note 4.

[4]Application of Evergreen International Airlines, Inc. for an Exemption
Pursuant to Section 416(b) of the Federal Aviation Act, Order 78-2-49.

on the part of Senator Howard Cannon, Chairman of the Senate Aviation Subcommittee. House and Senate conferees praised the contributions the supplementals were making to domestic air transportation and agreed the amendment's exclusionary language placed these carriers at a competitive disadvantage.[1] Subsequent legislation has corrected Cannon's error. It has removed the regulatory distinction between the scheduled and supplemental airlines and provides the "evenhanded" treatment the latter had earlier requested.[2] Under a new amendment enacted on March 14, 1978,

> any citizen of the United States who has a valid certificate issued under section 401(d)(3) . . . and who provided supplemental air transportation carrying only cargo at any time during the period from January 1, 1977, through . . . [November 9, 1977] may, during the forty-five day period beginning on April 1, 1978, submit an application to the Board for a certificate under . . . section [418] to provide all-cargo air service.[3]

The move to give the supplementals parity with the incumbent scheduled operators has been deplored by several legislators who believe the new entrants will divert business from the established scheduled carriers and ultimately weaken passenger services. One of those who expressed this fear was Representative Mark Andrews (R. N.D.), who cautioned his colleagues that

> if we keep nibbling more and more away at the scheduled airlines in the thinly populated areas that some of us represent, there is no way these scheduled airlines can continue to serve the small towns and cities in these areas, the towns of 15,000 and 20,000 population which the railroads have abandoned and no longer serve. The airlines cannot continue to serve these towns unless they also receive revenue from other sources such as cargo.[4]

Public Law 95-163 makes it possible for the forwarders to apply for the new section 418 certificates (after November 9, 1978) and thus to become direct air carriers. Financial considerations alone, however, rule this out as a viable option for all but the very largest of these companies. Forwarding depends on access to the entire commercial airfleet, and several forwarders have entered into charter arrangements with air taxi operators to replace scheduled all-cargo flights discontinued by the trunks. A number of

[1] Congressional Record, November 2, 1977, p. H12046; Congressional Record, November 3, 1977, p. H12139.

[2] See above, p. 141.

[3] Act of March 14, 1978, Pub. L. no. 95-245, 92 Stat. 156. April 1 was chosen as the effective date in order to give the scheduled all-cargo carriers additional time to acquire the type of equipment being used by the supplementals. Senate Report no. 638, 95th Cong., 2d sess., (1978), pp. 2-3.

[4] Congressional Record, November 3, 1977, p. H12139.

these charter programs will be terminated, the forwarders say, if, as predicted by the reformers, scheduled freight services improve under deregulation. The recent expansion of all-cargo air taxi service has been closely related to the reduction in the certificated combination carriers' all-cargo capacity. Deregulation offers the air taxis new growth opportunities and should make this carrier class more attractive to forwarders and other members of the shipping community.

In the past, Board approval of mergers between air carriers or between an air carrier and any other carrier (section 408), interlocking directorates (section 409), and intercarrier agreements (section 412) automatically extended antitrust immunity to the affected parties. Given its broad discretionary powers, the agency was able to subordinate anticompetitive factors to various public interest objectives of the Federal Aviation Act and thus, in effect, sanction anticompetitive measures which would have been considered unlawful in other sectors of the economy. Retention of its authority in this area had been considered essential by the Board, which feared that once its antitrust powers were transferred to the Justice Department "more orthodox antitrust factors" would take precedence over "legitimate air transportation considerations."[1] The Board's traditional antitrust powers are incompatible with the rationale behind Public Law 95-163, and, as a result, the agency has relieved forwarders and section 418 airlines from the provisions of sections 408, 409, and 412 of the Act. This means that the legality of the various activities covered by these provisions will now be judged, not in terms of Board-mandated public interest tests, but, rather, from the standpoint of generally accepted antitrust standards.

Pricing freedom. The Board has traditionally had the authority to "determine and prescribe" lawful domestic freight rates and tariff regulations where it concluded these were "unjust or unreasonable, or unjustly discriminatory, or unduly preferential, or unduly prejudicial."[2] Public Law 95-163 severely limits the agency's jurisdiction in this area. Thus, it may no longer "determine and prescribe" lawful rates, has no authority to cancel rates and regulations on the grounds of unreasonableness or unjustness, and has lost the suspension powers via which it was formerly able to prevent

---

[1] U.S., Congress, Senate, Committee on Commerce, Science, and Transportation, op. cit., part 1, p. 129.

[2] See above, pp. 9-10.

rates from taking effect. The amendment,[1] which applies both to
goods carried in pure freighters and in combination aircraft, gives
the certificated carriers unprecedented pricing freedom, enabling
them to change rates on a market-by-market basis without constant
reference to industry average costs.[2] This freedom, however, is not
absolute, for the Board retains jurisdiction over rates and practices
deemed discriminatory or prejudicial. In addition, the amendment
introduces a prohibition against predatory pricing.[3] In the event
that discrimination or predation are found to be taking place, the
CAB may order termination of the rates and/or practices in question.

A wide range of views exists on the subject of pricing freedom.
For instance, Emery Air Freight, one of the staunchest advocates of
deregulation, believes the new legislation will lead to lower freight
rates.[4] Others foresee destructive rate wars and a "shakeout"
throughout the industry.[5] The Board has taken a more cautious position, saying only that deregulation may "possibly" produce lower
rates than would otherwise be the case.[6] Various airline officials,
on the other hand, point out that, since fuel prices, labor costs,
etc., will continue to rise, major rate reductions should not be
expected. It is obviously not possible to state with certainty what
will happen to rates once deregulation comes fully into effect. It
should be noted, however, that one of the carriers' principal complaints against the Board has been that it has held their domestic
rates at unprofitable levels. This, together with the aforementioned
cost increases, makes it unlikely that the industry will see the low
rates which some reformers have so confidently predicted.

The Federal Aviation Act's tariff filing requirement (section
403), the Board believes, is inconsistent with the airlines' new
pricing freedom and contrary to the overall objectives of the deregulation legislation, and in the latter part of 1978 the requirement

---

[1]Pub. L. no. 95-163, sec. 18 (section 1002[d] of the Federal
Aviation Act).

[2]See above, pp. 60-61.

[3]A detailed discussion of this topic is found in Oliver E. Williamson,
"Predatory Pricing: A Strategic and Welfare Analysis," Yale Law Journal 87, no. 2
(1977):284-340.

[4]"Emery Lays Out Welcome Mat," Journal of Commerce, November 1977, p. 1

[5]"Decontrol May Bring an Air Freight War," New York Times, December 1977
p. 29; U.S., Congress, Senate, Committee on Commerce, Science, and Transportation,
op. cit., part 3, p. 1110.

[6]U.S., Congress, Senate, Committee on Commerce, op. cit., p. 388.

was eliminated for interstate air freight service. (In order to achieve parity among the carriers, the new rule was applied irrespective of whether shipments are carried in all-cargo or combination equipment.) At first glance this action appears to put the agency on a collision course with Washington's lawmakers, who, in a recent conference report, stated that they did

> not contemplate that the Board will exempt carriers from the requirement of filing tariffs. Tariffs provide valuable notice of rates to users of air transportation. Tariffs will be necessary for the Board to effectively carry out its duties to determine whether rates for the transportation of property are discriminatory, preferential, prejudicial, or predatory.[1]

(A more concrete expression of Congress' willingness to retain the tariff filing requirement is found in Public Law 95-163, section 10 of which expands the period of advance notice carriers must give the Board when wishing to modify their tariff rates.) In point of fact, however, termination of the section 403 tariff filing obligation does not conflict with the Board's revised mandate, for Public Law 95-163 also declares that

> any applicant who is issued a certificate under this section [418] shall, with respect to any all-cargo air service provided in accordance with such certificate, be exempt from the requirements of section 401(a) of this Act, and any other section of this Act which the Board by rule determines appropriate, and any rule, regulation, or procedure issued pursuant to any such section.[2]

The agency has responded to shipper and carrier protests[3] by noting that consumer dissatisfaction has not been a problem for commuter operators, who have always been exempt from the provisions of section 403. It believes "less restrictive ways" than traditional tariffs can be found to implement the goals of the House conferees and expects to meet its remaining responsibilities vis-à-vis unlawful rates by requiring airline officials to produce their waybills, rate sheets, and other documents for spot audits and for the investigation of shipper complaints. In the case of the forwarders, the Board has also determined that the requirement to file tariffs should be abolished. The tariff filing process, it was felt, imposed needless time restraints and higher costs on these operators while also reducing their pricing flexibility.[4] This decision has less

---

[1]House Report no. 773, 95th Cong., 1st sess., (1977), pp. 14-15.

[2]Pub. L. no. 95-163, sec. 17 (section 418[c] of the Federal Aviation Act). See also section 416(b) of the Federal Aviation Act.

[3]See below, pp. 388-389.

[4]Liberalized Regulation of Indirect Cargo Carriers, Docket 32318, EDR-350, p. 7.

significance than that concerning airline tariffs, since forwarders have long enjoyed substantial regulatory freedom and have suffered virtually no tariff rejections in recent years.

One further point needs to be made regarding the abolition of the tariff filing obligation. The Interstate Commerce Commission, as was discussed in chapter II, has in the past relied heavily on tariffs accepted by the Board for its determination of whether a pickup/delivery operation was a service "incidental to transportation by aircraft" and thus eligible for the section 203(b)(7a) certification exemption. Obviously, if no future tariffs are to be submitted to the Board, the Commission could base exemptions entirely on its own mileage criteria without any reference to its sister agency. It is not clear how this matter will be resolved. One possibility is that the Board may establish a master list naming all approved pickup and delivery points (with additional points added at its discretion), which, presumably, the Commission could utilize in much the same manner it has hitherto used the air carriers' tariffs. The implications Public Law 95-163 has for section 403(a) of the Federal Aviation Act are currently being examined by the Board, and it may well be that the agency will conclude its involvement in the delineation of pickup and delivery zones should be terminated.

Aviation, Winston Churchill once observed, was changing so quickly that one needed wings to keep up with it. Made over fifty years ago, this remark holds true for many aspects of the industry today. One of these is without doubt Congress' deregulation of air freight transportation, which, in the words of one Capitol Hill observer, took place "so quickly that if you were out of town for a couple of days you missed the whole thing."[1] The political considerations and legislative difficulties discussed above had made it clear that regulatory reform of the passenger sector was not possible in 1977. Freight service, on the other hand, was viewed as politically less sensitive, and on October 20 Senator Cannon added several freight deregulation provisions to a House bill (H.R. 6010) dealing primarily with the Federal aviation war risk insurance program. Cannon's omnibus amendment was agreed to by a conference committee on October 27 and was then rushed through both chambers where it was passed on October 28 (Senate) and November 2 (House). It was approved by President Carter on November 9.

The separate treatment given freight service reflected the view of both houses that freight and passenger operations are

---

[1]"Airline Maneuvering Intensifies in Wake of Cargo Deregulation," Air Transport World 15, no. 1 (1978):54.

basically different and that they should not be forced into the same regulatory mold.[1] Perhaps the most obvious difference between the two is that shippers tend to favor nighttime service, while most passengers travel during daylight hours. Passengers and freight generate different traffic patterns (freight movements, for instance, are generally one-way, as opposed to the two-way trips taken by most passengers), and, unlike the traveling public, shippers as a whole view air service as a supplemental or relatively minor transportation mode. The latter point means that in pricing their services (under deregulation) the airlines must bear in mind that most shippers can and do use surface modes of transportation, whereas these modes have ceased to be a realistic option for a large segment of the traveling public. Some legislators also seemed to feel that freight service deregulation could be viewed as an experiment which might serve as a guide for related action in the more controversial air passenger field. Congress' cautious approach to passenger transportation meant that proponents of airline deregulation had to wait another year before a passenger service reform bill was enacted into law (Public Law 95-504).

At the beginning of 1974 the then assistant director of the CAB's Bureau of Operating Rights, addressing a group of transportation specialists in Washington, D.C., assured his audience that he saw

> no effective pressure for deregulation in air transportation, none whatsoever. If the present situation is an accurate guide to the future, the Civil Aeronautics Board will continue to regulate the airlines indefinitely. So much for deregulation.[2]

Only three years later (January, 1977), however, the President's Council of Economic Advisers was able to report that

> the need for reform in air transportation is compelling and is now generally acknowledged. . . . The current issue appears to be not whether a change needs to be made, but rather how far and how quickly it should proceed.[3]

By the end of 1977 domestic all-cargo deregulation was an accomplished fact and a year later similar legislation was passed in the air passenger field. These developments, which surprised the

---

[1]Remarks of Senator Howard W. Cannon, Aero Club, Washington, D.C., April 26, 1977, mimeographed, p. 13; Congressional Record, October 20, 1977, p. S17533; Congressional Record, November 2, 1977, p. H12046.

[2]James C. Miller, (ed.), Perspectives on Federal Transportation Policy (Washington, D.C.: American Enterprise Institute for Public Policy Research, 1975), p. 205.

[3]Economic Report of the President (Washington, D.C.: U.S. Government Printing Office, 1977), p. 151.

regulators as well as the regulated, raise long-term questions not
only about future trends in domestic air transportation but about
the future of the Board itself. Of more immediate interest, however
are questions concerning the factors which precipitated these change
and toppled the Board from its position of near absolute power over
the U.S. air transportation industry. Several of these factors were
discussed earlier. Let us return briefly to the major points and
attempt to put them into perspective.

Probably the most important factor behind the deregulation of
all-cargo service was Congress' recognition that the authors of the
Federal Aviation Act were concerned primarily with passenger transportation and had not taken into account the special needs of the
shipping public.[1] Specifically, it was noted that Federal Express,
an unregulated airline, owed much of its success to the failure of
its certificated competitors to match its overnight services in various markets and that inadequate freight service by the certificated
combination airlines was forcing several leading forwarders to rely
increasingly on charter operations. Furthermore, rate and entry
restraints had excluded certain freight specialists from domestic
operations, while route and capacity restrictions had prevented
others from expanding their domestic route networks. Deregulation,
it was believed, would lead to lower rates, increased carrier flexibility and efficiency (larger aircraft, fuel conservation, etc.),
and greater service innovation. The other major element contributing
to the passage of Public Law 95-163 was the effective manner in which
the leading deregulation advocates, Federal Express and the Flying
Tiger Line, presented their case.[2] The importance of their role in
the deregulation movement was recognized by their opponents, one of
whom told the Senate Aviation Subcommittee that "the impetus for
free entry in the cargo field appears to be coming from Federal
Express. . . . We think inaction by an aspirant is hardly a reason
to amend a statute."[3] (The speaker represented Delta Air Lines,
which had terminated its scheduled all-cargo flights in 1973. He
was referring to Federal's unsuccessful attempt to be allowed to use
the DC-9-15 without losing its section 416 certification exemption.

---

[1]Congressional Record, October 20, 1977, p. S17533; Congressional Record,
November 2, 1977, p. H12044.

[2]Discussion between the author and David A Heymsfeld, Assistant Counsel,
House Committee on Public Works and Transportation, 1978.

[3]U.S., Congress, Senate, Committee on Commerce, Science, and Transportation
op. cit., part 2, pp. 931-932.

Federal Express had declined to seek a certificate of public convenience and necessity, arguing that the entire process [with the
outcome in doubt] could extend over a ten-year period.) These
factors alone, however, give us only a partial explanation for the
enactment of reform legislation, which, to be fully understood, must
be considered within a broader context. Air freight deregulation
was initially regarded not as an independent issue but, rather, was
viewed as part of regulatory reform of air transportation as a whole.
The early pressure for reform was directed more at the passenger
sector and was largely a reaction to a series of studies which indicated that protective regulation was responsible for high passenger fares. (One of the most important of these studies was released
at the beginning of 1977 by the General Accounting Office and stated
that air fares were from 22 to 52 percent higher than they would
have been in the absence of Federal regulation.) The Board's anticompetitive policies were condemned, as we have seen, by the White
House as well as by the Departments of Justice and Transportation,
and its position was further undermined once it became clear that a
number of liberal Democrats in the Congress would no longer automatically equate traditional regulatory practices with consumer protection.[1] Moreover, the mid-1970s saw a marked deterioration in the
relationship between the Congress and the Board. Robert D. Timm,
who became the Board's chairman in 1973, "consistently alienated the
Congress,"[2] his dealings with Washington's lawmakers displaying
extraordinary insensitivity towards his agency's need for allies on
Capitol Hill. The Board's difficulties did not stop there, for in
the mid-1970s the agency found itself enmeshed in political and
financial scandals involving its chairman and other leading officials.[3] These developments cost it much good will and, coming at a
time of eroding public confidence in established institutions,
caused Congressional investigators to examine its role far more
critically than would otherwise have been the case.

---

[1]Additional pressure came from the Ad Hoc Committee for Airline Regulatory
Reform, which included the American Conservative Union, Americans for Democratic
Action, Common Cause, the National Association of Manufacturers, the National
Taxpayers Union, and Sears Roebuck.

[2]"CAB Power Faces Crucial Test," Aviation Week and Space Technology 103,
no. 16 (1975):13.

[3]"CAB Member Is in Midst of Controversy Involving Stock Ownership by His
Wife," Wall Street Journal, May 19, 1975, p. 10; "CAB is Accused of Ignoring Its
Rules on Fiscal Disclosure," New York Times, September 17, 1975, p. 29; "Demoted
Chief of CAB Quits Agency at White House Request," New York Times, December 11,
1975, p. 36.

The Board's predicament and the reformers' assurance of lower air fares under deregulation have tempted various airline officials to see the entire question of regulatory reform in purely political terms. Addressing the Wharton School Graduate Association, C. E. Meyer, Jr., President of Trans World Airlines, recently declared that the Ford Administration,

> seeking a productive cause that would enhance its ability to win the 1976 election, . . . seized upon regulatory reform as an issue likely to win the support of conservative businessmen leaning towards the candidacy of Governor [Ronald] Reagan.

Warming to his theme, Meyer noted that it had long been

> liberal policy to advocate stricter regulation of business by government, supposedly in order to keep it honest. More recently, however, Mr. [Ralph] Nader and others have been heading the other way. They contend that the regulatory agencies have so fallen under the sway of the businesses they are supposed to control that they have failed in their mission, and now function mainly to shield business from the economic consequences of their inefficient management. . . . [President Ford's Democratic opponents were originally not favorably disposed towards deregulation.] Yet, some of them recognized the potential value of that cause, if it could be restructured to give it a wider public appeal. What it needed, they felt, was some liberal seasoning, with a dash of consumerism. That's precisely what it got from Senator Edward Kennedy, with a strong assist from the aforementioned Mr. Nader.

The reformers, Meyer continued, had "singled out" the airlines because of the latter's "relatively weak constituency." The air carriers "are highly visible, make good headlines and--because of the relatively higher price of their product compared with most other consumer goods--can be pictured as 'elitist.'"[1] Seaboard World's President, Richard M. Jackson, has spoken of "strange political winds . . . swe[eping] across the previously-stable airline scene," and of Congressional "zealotry . . . to get onto the consumerism bandwagon."[2] Eastern Air Lines, unconvinced that reform legislation would lead to lower fares/rates, stated that "now, as always, there is a great temptation to substitute political solutions for economic realities,"[3] and American Airlines believed it was "obvious that much of the fervor in Washington [for deregulation] stems from the political appeal of the promise of lower fares and

---

[1]C. E. Meyer, Jr., Business and the Regulatory Environment (New York: Trans World Airlines, 1978), pp. 6-7.

[2]Richard M. Jackson, The Second Generation Speaks Out (New York: Seaboard World Airlines, 1978), p. 9.

[3]U.S., Congress, House, Committee on Public Works and Transportation, Aviation Economics, p. 283.

lower rates."[1] Delta Air Lines, to give one other example, concluded that regulatory reform

> is being nurtured in the caldron of election year politics. . . . There
> is little doubt [that] the drive to force changes in CAB policy and
> procedure also reflects the general post-Watergate inquisition which,
> however productive in other areas, is of little value in judging the
> continued substantive soundness of the Federal Aviation Act.[2]

Significantly, Senator Kennedy (one of the most ardent champions of
statutory reform) also alluded to the circumstances surrounding
President Nixon's departure from office in his explanation of why
reform legislation, hitherto a seemingly unreachable goal, suddenly
lay within Congress' grasp. In a 1975 letter to the chairman of the
Senate Committee on the Judiciary, Kennedy noted that it had been

> difficult in the past to sustain public interest in regulatory reform
> over the time needed to investigate an agency, to formulate proposed
> reforms, and to enact them into law. The Congress tends to be guided by
> the public's sense of priorities. At present, however, the manifest
> lack of public trust in Government suggests that the public needs--indeed
> demands--changes that will make Government more responsive to the problems
> of this third century of American democracy.[3]

Virtually any major legislative effort lends itself to the
charge of having been politically motivated, and regulatory reform
is no exception. Both Democrats and Republicans recognized airline
deregulation as a potentially attractive issue, and it would be
naive to suppose party politics played no part in the assault on the
Board. In acknowledging this, however, we cannot conclude, as some
airline officials have done, that party interests alone ultimately
explain the success of the reform movement. Political considerations must be kept in perspective. That they played a role is beyond dispute; that role, however, should be seen within the context
of a broadly-based anti-Board campaign, which, as shown earlier,
included many members of the air transportation industry itself.

Not all the criticism directed at the Board has come from
opponents of regulation. Many of those in favor of a strong Federal
role in commercial aviation have also been sharply critical of the
agency, charging, inter alia, that its procedures have been too slow
and that its members lacked the competence required to deal with the
industry's problems. For instance, Robert E. Hotz, editor of the

---

[1]Fred H. McCusker, Airline Deregulation, remarks made to the Western
Traffic Conference, San Diego, May 16, 1978, mimeographed, p. 4.

[2]Callison, op. cit.

[3]U.S., Congress, Senate, Committee on the Judiciary, Civil Aeronautics
Board Practices and Procedures, p. III.

respected trade journal <u>Aviation Week and Space Technology</u> (and an
opponent of deregulation), has called the agency "a roosting place
for faithful party hacks and pensioners whom the electorate has
rejected."[1] He was referring, of course, to the fact that Board
members are named by the White House and all too frequently have
owed their appointment to political considerations rather than to
their expertise in the aviation field. Interestingly enough,
Alfred E. Kahn, who succeeded John E. Robson as the CAB's chairman
in mid-1977, was the first economist to ever hold that post. While
his credentials were widely praised, the appointment brought little
comfort to those who, like Delta Air Lines, remained convinced of
the Federal Aviation Act's "continued substantive soundness."
Their concern was understandable. Kahn, an outspoken advocate of
regulatory reform, supported the deregulation of freight service
and during Congressional hearings endorsed various other reform
measures including sunset provisions which foresee the eventual
abolition of the Civil Aeronautics Board.

Public Law 95-504: Deregulation of Interstate Air Passenger Transportation

Following the enactment of Public Law 95-163, Congress pressed
on with its effort to deregulate air passenger transportation. In
April of 1978 the Senate, by a vote of 83 to 9, passed the Cannon-
Kennedy-Pearson Air Transportation Reform Act of 1978 (S. 2493), and
on September 21 the House adopted (363 to 8) its own version of the
bill (H.R. 12611). About three weeks later, House and Senate conferees reached agreement on what was variously described as "a mile-
stone in aviation law" (Senator Magnuson), "a truly landmark bill"
(Senator Pearson), and "the most important piece of regulatory reform legislation ever acted upon" (Senator Kennedy) and sent their
compromise measure to the White House. There, an enthusiastic
President Carter thanked the legislators for "a wonderful bill" and
approved the Airline Deregulation Act of 1978 (Public Law 95-504) on
October 24. The Act, the President declared, was an important tool
in the nation's anti-inflation program and would place air transportation within the reach of a larger section of the traveling public.
The new legislation, he continued, was "a precursor to what the
Congress can help me do next year to minimize regulation of other
crucial industries, particularly in the transportation field."[2]

---

[1]Editorial, <u>Aviation Week and Space Technology</u> 102, no. 17 (1975):11.
Also see U.S., Congress, Senate, Committee on Commerce, op. cit., p. 443.

[2]"Airline Deregulation Act of 1978 (S. 2493)," <u>Weekly Compilation of Presidential Documents</u> 14, no. 43 (1978):1839.

Although dealing primarily with passenger service, Public Law 95-504 is of considerable interest here. Its automatic entry provisions will enable the trunks and local service airlines to restructure their route networks without Board approval and will lead to increased carrier participation in major passenger markets, such as New York-Chicago, New York-Los Angeles, and New York-Miami. The extra belly capacity added to these routes by new entrants could encourage the introduction of new freight rate discounts and slow the overall rise in freight rates.

The new law dissolves the Board's section 401 prerogatives and, using language similar to that of Public Law 95-163, stipulates that the "variety, quality, and price" of air transportation will in future be governed by competitive market forces. A revised section 102 policy declaration emphasizes this departure from the traditional public interest standards and defines as new policy objectives:

> the encouragement, development, and maintenance of an air transportation system relying on actual and potential competition to provide efficiency, innovation, and low prices, . . . [and] the encouragement of entry into air transportation markets by new air carriers, the encouragement of entry into additional air transportation markets by existing air carriers, and the continued strengthening of small air carriers so as to assure a more effective, competitive airline industry.[1]

The new legislation also shifts the burden of proof from applicants to those opposing new entry, expressly prohibits use of the President's section 801 powers "upon the basis of economic or carrier selection considerations,"[2] and exposes section 401 carriers to the antitrust tests generally applied to nonregulated industries. "Unjust discriminations, undue preferences or advantages, or unfair or deceptive practices" are declared unlawful. In addition, the legislation modifies the Federal guarantee of equipment loans, extending this program to charter airlines for the purchase of nonconvertible all-cargo aircraft. The law contains a ten-year air service guarantee for small communities, which, however, does not include all-cargo transportation.

The Federal Aviation Act's amended policy declaration appeared, in the view of some, to be too broad and ambiguous. Senator Pearson, for instance, discussing the new legislation, expressed the fear that "future Board members who may be opposed to deregulation could

---

[1] Pub. L. no. 95-504, op. cit., sec. 3 (section 102 of the Federal Aviation Act). These policy amendments apply only to domestic air transportation. The original policy declaration (shown on pp. 6-7) has been retained for foreign air transportation. (See Appendix.)

[2] Ibid., sec. 34 (section 801 of the Federal Aviation Act). (See Appendix.)

latch onto [the declaration's ambiguities] in order to stop the move toward competition." "How," Pearson wondered, "can we prevent that from happening?"[1] (It was, in fact, this very question which had prompted Congress to adopt the 1978 reform legislation. The Kahn-led Board was a vigorous supporter of deregulation, removing, some lawmakers felt, the need for further statutory change. Others, however, argued that reforms had to be formally codified if the reemergence of anticompetitive practices was to be prevented. Also, it was recognized "that certain institutional factors giving rise to an identity of interests between the CAB and the carriers which it regulates will remain present so long as the Board's powers are largely discretionary."[2]) Reassuring his colleague, Senator Howard Cannon pointed to the "limits" specified in Public Law 95-504, noting these made "any backsliding to the era of strict protectionism" impossible. Cannon's assertion was no exaggeration. Public Law 95-504 provides for an interim period of reduced Board control and sets: (1) December 31, 1981 as the termination date for the agency's route authority; (2) December 31, 1982 as the termination date for its fare authority; and (3) January 1, 1983 as the date on which the Board's section 408, 409, and 414 powers relating to interstate and overseas transportation are to be transferred to the U.S. Department of Justice. Moreover, January 1, 1985 is given as the date for the dissolution of Title II ("Continuation of Existing Board") of the Federal Aviation Act. This, however, does not necessarily mean that the Board will be abolished on January 1, 1985, for Public Law 95-504 also directs the agency to transmit to the Congress, "not later than January 1, 1984," an evaluation of the new legislation's impact on air transportation. The evaluation is to include

> a detailed opinion . . . as to whether the public interest requires continuation of the Board and its functions beyond January 1, 1985, and, if it is the Board's conclusion that it should continue to exist, detailed recommendations as to how the provisions of [the Federal Aviation Act] should be revised to insure continued improvement of the Nation's air transportation system beyond January 1, 1985.[3]

Public Law 95-504 is the culmination of a four-year effort by the Congress to deregulate air transportation. This effort established a number of "records," which included twenty mark-up sessions by the Senate Commerce Committee as well as eighteen days of hearing

---

[1]Congressional Record, November 9, 1978, p. S19559.

[2]Senate Report no. 631, p. 4; House Report no. 1211, 95th Cong., 2d sess., (1978), p. 4.

[3]Pub. L. no. 95-504, sec. 40 (section 1601[d] of the Federal Aviation Act).

by that body. In the House the Aviation Subcommittee held 36 days
of hearings and accepted the testimony of more than 200 witnesses.
The opening phases of the reform struggle were clouded by friction
between the Senate Aviation Subcommittee and the Senate Subcommittee
on Administrative Practice and Procedure (Senator Cannon, Chairman
of the Senate Aviation Subcommittee, felt his authority was being
challenged by the Administrative Practice and Procedure Subcommittee
and threatened to withhold funds from the latter) and by the suicide
of the Director of the Board's Bureau of Enforcement only days before he was to appear before an administrative practice and procedure
panel investigating election law violations by various airline officials. Later, tensions developed between the House and Senate aviation subcommittees. The House was giving priority to its airline-
aid legislation, and many felt the Senate's reform bill was being
held "hostage" by House members concerned primarily with passage of
their own legislation. In any event, virtually all concerned agreed
that airline deregulation had been one of the most complex issues
ever to come before their respective investigative committees.
Understandably, during the adoption of the final reform bill House
and Senate conferees yielded to feelings of euphoria, with many
sharing the view of Senator Harrison H. Schmitt (R. N.M.), who saw
"nothing but bright skies ahead for the airline industry."[1]   To
others, however, the skies appeared filled with storm clouds. For
instance, Senator Barry M. Goldwater (R. Ariz.), one of Congress'
most prominent foes of deregulation, believed this legislation
"open[ed] the door to a dog-eat-dog situation where the public and
the airlines will ultimately suffer the consequences."[2]   Goldwater
also questioned the sincerity of those commerce committee members
who foresaw significant advantages under deregulation:

> if the consumer was to gain substantial benefits, and if airlines were to
> become more efficient increasing net revenues, then it would be logical
> to expect that the mark-up sessions of the Committee would have reflected
> enthusiasm born of a better world to come. Instead, the atmosphere during
> the mark-ups more nearly resembled the distress of bathers approaching a
> river infested with piranha fish. . . . Doubt, distrust, and dissent [had
> characterized the Committee meetings]. Enthusiasm was conspicuous by its
> absence.[3]

Whether the Civil Aeronautics Board will actually cease to
exist on January 1, 1985, is, at this point, open to question. Many

---

[1] *Congressional Record*, October 14, 1978, p. S18800.

[2] Senate Report no. 631, p. 227.

[3] Ibid., p. 225.

airline officials, for instance, suggest that a major deterioration in the economic health of the carriers could cause the Congress to reconsider its deregulation policy. Moreover, Senator Cannon, discussing the conference report on deregulation, made clear the Congress might decide to "extend" the life of the agency. Alfred Kahn considers this unlikely. "The airlines industry," he insists, "will be knee-deep in the free-enterprise system and not returnable" to regulation.[1]

Concluding Remarks

In the latter part of 1977 Congress passed legislation essentially deregulating interstate air freight transportation (Public Law 95-163). The new law ensures that the "extent, variety, quality and price" of air freight service will in future be governed by competitive market forces, as opposed to Board-imposed public interest tests, and forms part of a wider deregulation effort which includes air passenger service and which may lead to the dissolution of the Board and to the transfer of its residual functions to other agencies of the Federal Government (Public Law 95-504).

A variety of interrelated factors sustained the reform movement and led to the enactment of reform legislation. Among these were: (1) the release of several academic and governmental studies pointing to lower fares/rates under deregulation; (2) the conviction that deregulation would enhance carrier efficiency and service innovation; (3) the failure of the certificated trunklines to adequately meet shipper needs in certain markets and the effectiveness with which some of the deregulation advocates exploited this point in testimony before Congressional investigators; (4) the feeling that a mature air transportation industry no longer required the regulatory safeguards deemed necessary in an earlier age and that the Board's procedures had become too cumbersome, legalistic, and time-consuming; (5) recognition and use of deregulation as a political issue; and (6) a lessening of support for the Board on Capitol Hill due in part to the improprieties of the agency's chairman and other officials.

The Civil Aeronautics Board had long been opposed to substantive statutory reform. However, under Chairman Robson, the agency began to acknowledge the validity of various of its opponents' criticisms and submitted reform proposals to the Congress. Robson himself was held in high regard by House and Senate investigators and

---

[1]"Carter Signs Airline-Deregulation Law; CAB Will Grant Routes More Generously," Wall Street Journal, October 25, 1978, p. 2.

there was little question as to the sincerity of his proreform convictions. In view of the agency's earlier history, however, and given the uncertainty over the direction a future chairman might take, the aviation subcommittees, not surprisingly, viewed with unease the Board's request for the retention of considerable discretionary authority. The Congress rejected many of the Board's recommendations, included (in the reform legislation) fixed dates to ensure strict agency compliance, and, going farther than even the staunchest reform advocates had believed possible, announced its willingness to dismantle the agency.

With the enactment of Public Law 95-163 air freight transportation has entered a transition period and it will be several years before a full evaluation of deregulation and its ramifications is possible. Elsewhere in this book (chapters VI, VII, and VIII) the reader will find the initial reactions of individual carriers to that law as well as to certain related developments. Here it will suffice to present a few generalizations regarding the significance deregulation holds for the carriers and the shipping public. Deregulation clearly enhances the operational flexibility of the carriers, enables individual companies to function more efficiently, and will provide shippers with additional airlift in a number of markets. While the new route freedom makes some loss of service a foregone conclusion, it should be remembered that both the Congress and the Board remain fully committed to a subsidy program for carriers serving small airport cities. The chaos which some industry observers foresee as a natural consequence of deregulation is unlikely to materialize. If, however, the nation's air transportation system is threatened by major disruptions, Congress will presumably intervene and reexamine the need for some form of public control.

Deregulation can be expected to contribute to greater intermodal integration. For instance, forwarders will be able to function as direct air carriers, and certain forms of air-surface coordination, formerly prohibited under section 408 of the Federal Aviation Act, will also become possible. Also, the Board's departure from the regulatory stage will leave only the Interstate Commerce Commission to define the scope of nonregulated pickup and delivery service, removing a source of potential conflict (between the regulators) and confusion (for the carriers). Public Law 95-163 has additional significance for the carriers in that it reduces their workload. Many operators had long chafed under what were generally considered onerous data collecting and reporting requirements. The modification or elimination of some of these requirements has received considerable support, particularly from smaller transportation companies.

Deregulation offers the airlines a broad range of pricing options, and in the first few months of 1978 a number of rate discounts were introduced. However, rates as a whole have tended to move upward, reflecting, in part, various inflationary pressures as well as the fact that rates had formerly been held at unrealistically low levels. (Administrative Law Judge Arthur S. Present, examining rates within the framework of the Domestic Air Freight Rate Investigation, above, concluded that they "should be increased on an average by 38.8 percent."[1]) The CAB remains unperturbed by rising rates and has expressed the view that rate increases will promote higher levels of service.

The agency's untroubled view of rising transportation costs is not shared by large segments of the shipping public. Similarly, many shippers dispute the claim that there is now no need to enforce the traditional tariff filing requirement, and such organizations as the National Industrial Traffic League and the Shippers National Freight Claim Council have threatened legal action to compel the Board to retain its rules regarding tariff filings and liability regulations. Abandonment of the tariff filing requirement, say these parties, will: (1) restrict the dissemination of price data, (2) lead to discrimination against small-volume shippers, and (3) destroy various standard freight classifications. The Board dismisses these contentions. It notes that price information will continue to be readily available through the carriers themselves and such sources as the Airline Tariff Publishing Company and emphasizes that volume-related price differentials are in the interests of greater carrier efficiency.

---

[1]Docket 22859, initial decision, April 15, 1975, p. 240.

PART II

AIR FREIGHT OPERATIONS AND SERVICES

IN NEW YORK-NEWARK

CHAPTER IV

RIVALRY AND COORDINATION AMONG THE

NEW YORK-NEWARK AIRPORTS

The activities of the New York-Newark region's air freight
industry focus on the region's three major air terminals, namely
John F. Kennedy International, La Guardia, and Newark International
airports. The Port Authority of New York and New Jersey became the
regional airport manager in 1947-1948, in which capacity it has
intervened in many Civil Aeronautics Board and Interstate Commerce
Commission proceedings pertaining to the region's air services. The
Port Authority has attempted "so far as practicable" to merge some
of the region's airport operations "in[to] a unified system" and to
reduce the bitter aviation rivalry which once marred the relationship between the cities of Newark and New York.

Rivalry Between Newark and New York City

The early rivalry between Newark and New York City for regional leadership in air transportation is part of U.S. aviation history.
The initial "winner" was the City of Newark, which, opening its airport in 1928 (making Newark Airport one of the oldest commercial air
terminals in the country), became, two years later, the busiest air
traffic center in the nation. As the most advanced air terminal in
the area, Newark Airport was designated the New York metropolitan
region's sole air mail terminus by the Post Office Department, a
crucial advantage at a time when postal contracts were the major
source of income for the fledgling airline industry. This, combined
with Newark Airport's proximity to major railroads and the ease with
which it could be reached from Manhattan, left New York City little
in the way of inducements with which to persuade the air carriers to
transfer operations to Brooklyn's Floyd Bennett Field (completed in
1931).

In 1935 New York City approached the Post Office Department
with a formal request that Floyd Bennett Field be named the metropolitan region's air mail terminus. Technical improvements at that
facility had proved insufficient to lure the airlines away from
Newark Airport, and the city recognized that a favorable ruling by

the postal authorities was essential if commercial aviation was to
be attracted to its terminal. The Department's decision, made know
several months later, was a sharp disappointment for New York, for
it confirmed the status of Newark Airport as the region's only air
mail terminal. The proposed switch, it had been concluded, would
simply involve the Post Office Department in major expenses without
bringing tangible benefits to passengers or improvements in mail-
handling procedures.[1]

The Department's decision was greeted with enthusiasm in
Newark, where officials were following with apprehension New York
City's drive to become the region's major air traffic hub. Newark
had invested substantial sums of money in its airport and, unable
to compete financially with its powerful neighbor, viewed with alar
any possible transfer of carrier activities to New York's municipa
air terminal. Newark's Mayor M. C. Ellenstein, the leading champi
of Newark Airport, had articulated his city's fears on a number of
occasions. For instance, in a 1934 radio address he denounced New
York's ambitions as unfair competition, which, if successful, "wou
automatically force all air mail carriers operating out of the Eas
to remove to the Long Island field." New York City's efforts were
"in disregard of the comity that should exist between neighboring
cities," the product of "vain ambition and not monetary concern."[2]
Newark, insisted Ellenstein,

has made every possible concession to the companies now operating out of
Newark Airport to retain their patronage. It cannot hope to compete with
New York in its financial resourcefulness. On the other hand, it cannot
afford to give away an airport in which its people have invested more than
$5 million.[3]

In April of 1935 Ellenstein carried his spirited defense of
Newark Airport to Washington, D.C., where his testimony contribute
to the Post Office Department's denial of air mail rights to New
York City. During January of 1936 he again appeared before the De
partment, which was then considering a second New York City applic
tion for air mail rights. This, too, was rejected.[4] At the same
time a Mayor's Airport Committee was formed to help mobilize publi
support for the mayor's cause. A pamphlet issued in this connecti

[1]"Air Mail Rejects Bennett Field Site," New York Times, August 25, 1935,
p. 1.

[2]"Airport Fight Widens," Newark Star Eagle, November 26, 1934, pp. 1-2.

[3]Harold Stein, (ed.), Public Administration and Policy Development (New
York: Harcourt, Brace and Company, 1952), pp. 154-155.

[4]"Farley Again Bars City Airport Plea," New York Times, March 22, 1936,
p. 1.

cautioned Newark residents that

> the campaign against the Newark Airport by New York officialdom recently
> has increased in vigor. For that reason it has become urgently imperative
> that the persistent and insidious efforts now being made to challenge
> Newark's claim to supremacy in airport facilities be combatted with re-
> newed energy.[1]

The driving force behind New York City's efforts to become a
leading air traffic center was its mayor, Fiorello H. La Guardia.
A pilot during World War I, the mayor had many connections in the
airline industry and brought to his confrontation with Ellenstein a
keen, personal interest in aviation matters. An early incident--
which won him nationwide attention if not support--illustrates the
determination which was to characterize his battle for a major New
York airport. Landing in Newark after a flight from Chicago, the
mayor refused to disembark, maintaining that his ticket showed New
York City as the destination point. Only after it had carried him
to Floyd Bennett Field in Brooklyn did La Guardia leave the aircraft.[2] Floyd Bennett Field, La Guardia lamented on another occasion, had "everything except tenants," and, without awaiting the
outcome of the Post Office Department's investigation, he went on
to say: "I don't want to destroy any airport of any other city . . .
my job is to build an airport for the city [New York] and I'm going
to do that regardless of whose toes I step on. There is no reason
in the world why we shouldn't have an airport in the city."[3]

The Post Office Department's second ruling was, for La Guardia,
only a temporary setback. Undeterred, he embarked with characteristic energy on another project, namely the construction of a new
municipal airport in Queens. Larger and substantially more elaborate than Floyd Bennett Field, it was built on the site of a privately owned aerodrome on which the city had held a lease since December
of 1934[4] and which came under its full control during the early part
of 1936. The new airport, fittingly named after the mayor, was to

---

[1]Port of New York Authority, Statements by Honorable John F. Sly, Austin J.
Tobin, Fred M. Glass for the Port of New York Authority before the Joint Legisla-
tive Committee of Senate and House Assembly of the State of New Jersey (New York:
Port of New York Authority, 1952), p. 32.

[2]La Guardia's ticket had been filled in with a pen; tickets of the other
passengers were stamped "Chicago to Newark." Not surprisingly Ellenstein denounced
this incident as a "setup." "La Guardia Balks at Air Landing Here, Ends Flight in
New York," Newark Sunday Call, November 25, 1934, p. 1.

[3]"Mayor Urges Need for Airport Here," New York Times, May 10, 1935, p. 10.

[4]"City Takes Lease on Queens Airport," New York Times, December 5, 1934,
p. 25. The lease, commented the Times, marked a new step in the "drive to make
New York City instead of Newark the eastern air terminus of the country."

cost close to $50 million by the time it was formally dedicated in October of 1939. Matters were not allowed to rest there, for New Yorkers were already being assured that the growth in air traffic would soon prove to be too much for the new terminal's capacity. "It is time," La Guardia said even before the airport's official opening, "to look around and see what to do next"[1] and, again, two years later, "I am convinced that after the war we will need another airport to take up the increased demand for domestic and transatlantic traffic and to take care of the air freight business."[2] The city did "look around" and in April of 1942 started building a second major airport in Queens. This terminal, Kennedy (Idlewild) Airport, was opened in July of 1948.

La Guardia Airport was technically more sophisticated than Newark Airport, was closer to the center of Manhattan, and was considered by various authorities the safest air terminal in the country.[3] The dependence of the air carriers on postal revenues (a form of subsidy) was now no longer anything like what it had been during the industry's infancy, and, against this background, four of the largest airlines (American, Eastern, TWA, and United) requested the Civil Aeronautics Authority (CAA) to authorize a transfer of their base operations from Newark to La Guardia Airport. In its application for certificate amendments, American Airlines asked that New York City be included as an additional point on two of its routes; the other companies wished to see New York recognized as a new terminal point, with Newark serving only as an intermediate point. On November 7, 1939, over the bitter objections of Ellenstein and his supporters, the Civil Aeronautics Authority declared that La Guardia Airport would henceforth serve the New York metropolitan region jointly with Newark Airport. La Guardia's designation as a coterminal for the region was required, since

> the use of two airports for regularly scheduled air transportation service to and from the metropolitan district, located so as to be readily accessible to the centers of population on each side of the Hudson River, is necessary at the present time.

Furthermore, noted the CAA, La Guardia's new status was in accord with the policy objectives of the Civil Aeronautics Act, since it would

---

[1]"Mayor Is Honored for New Airport," New York Times, October 4, 1939, p. 30.

[2]"New Airport Data Due Next Week," New York Times, November 29, 1941, p. 33.

[3]"Pilots Find Field Safest in the U.S.," New York Times, October 16, 1939, p. 21.

encourage and assist the development of an air transportation system
properly adapted to the future needs of the foreign and domestic commerce
of the United States, the postal service and the national defense.[1]

This decision, airline officials were told, in no way relieved them
of the responsibility of providing "adequate" service at the Newark
terminal. To its wider audience the CAA said that in shaping its
decision it had "placed the greatest emphasis upon the distribution
of population and of economic and commercial interest" and had acted
"in almost complete disregard of any considerations of political
boundaries."[2] Subsidiary factors in La Guardia's favor were its
seaplane base facilities (which could be used for transatlantic
flights) and congestion at Newark Airport, especially during bad
weather.

The reaction to the Civil Aeronautics Authority's order was
instantaneous and came from several directions. American Airlines
moved its corporate headquarters from Chicago to New York, virtually
all commercial carriers became tenants at the new facility, and
within weeks Newark's airport was registering a sixty percent decline in the number of scheduled stops. In New York, of course,
these developments were hailed; in Newark, whose airport was now
"virtually reduced" to the level "of an emergency landing field,"[3]
they provoked consternation in business, civic, and political circles. A tenacious Mayor Ellenstein, claiming the Civil Aeronautics
Authority had "prejudged" the issue, traveled once more to Washington,
D.C., where he enlisted the support of New Jersey's senators and representatives for a Congressional investigation into the matter. Both
Ellenstein and La Guardia subsequently presented the merits of their
respective terminals to a subcommittee of the Senate Commerce Committee, their appearance before that body quickly falling to the level
of an acrimonious exchange.

The subcommittee hearings (March, 1940) did nothing to change
the situation. Ellenstein's assertion that American Airlines' move
to La Guardia Airport was the result of "collusion" between the
carrier and New York City officials was not upheld, and the subcommittee voted four to one against opening a full Senate investigation.[4] Its majority report made clear that the Civil Aeronautics

---

[1]"CAA Decision on North Beach Pleases Mayor," Brooklyn Eagle, November 8,
1939, p. 28. Also see above, p. 6.

[2]Ibid.

[3]"Promises Airport Inquiry," Newark Evening News, February 9, 1940, p. 2.

[4]"Inquiry Refused on Airport Shift," Newark Evening News, March 15, 1940,
p. 1.

Authority's decision-making process had been within the law and that the agency had not been improperly influenced by extraneous considerations.[1] The dissenting vote was cast by Senator Barbour of New Jersey, who, even before the commencement of the hearings, had suggested that political pressures ruled out impartiality on the part of the Civil Aeronautics Authority.[2] There was now little Ellenstein could do. A halfhearted attempt to reverse the CAA's order through the U.S. Circuit Court of Appeals at Philadelphia was abandoned, and, faced with a sharp drop in airport revenues (due to the decline in traffic), the mayor was reduced to threatening closure of Newark Airport unless the airlines provided $135,000 for the fiscal year. He was not spared the final humiliation, for airline officials balked at having to give, in effect, an annual income guarantee to keep the terminal open. A modified proposal, "more than the airlines deserve, considering the shabby treatment they have given Newark,"[3] was rejected, and with the city's closing of the air control tower (May 31, 1940) commercial aviation came to a halt at Newark Airport.

National defense needs led to the reactivation of Newark Airport as a Federally controlled facility in 1942.[4] After the war, surrender of the Federal lease was endorsed by the New York Regional Office of the War Assets Administration, this paving the way for the Port Authority to take over the administration of the terminal (the agency's lease became effective on March 22, 1948). Ellenstein, now a Newark city commissioner, attempted to block the inevitable to the very end and, when outvoted by his fellow commissioners, called the transfer "the most stupendous mistake" in Newark's history.[5] The La Guardia and Kennedy terminals had come under Port Authority control on June 1, 1947, and, with the three facilities finally under common jurisdiction, a long and bitter quarrel dividing the two municipalities came to an end. Future New York-Newark airport operations, the Port Authority emphasized, would be characterized by "cooperation and not competition." Such a commitment was vital "if the metropolitan district is to win and hold the same degree of

[1]"CAA Absolved of Bias," New York Times, March 20, 1940, p. 20.

[2]"Airlines' Experts Back North Beach," New York Times, September 13, 1939, p. 27.

[3]"Bargain Day for Airport," Newark Evening News, April 20, 1940, p. 1.

[4]The army's cargo operations at Newark Airport are outlined in "Air Cargo for the Far Corners of the Earth," Air Transport 2, no. 5 (1944):37-39.

[5]Newark, N.J., Board of Commissioners, Minutes of Meetings, October, 1947, p. 19.

preeminence as an air center that we enjoy in transportation by land and sea."[1]

Coordination of Regional Air Services by the Port Authority of New York and New Jersey

The New York-Newark airports are under the jurisdiction of the Port Authority of New York and New Jersey.[2] The Port Authority, or to give it its pre-1972 name, the Port of New York Authority, is a self-supporting public corporation established in 1921 by joint resolution of the states of New York and New Jersey.[3] In article I of their compact[4] the parties "agree to and pledge, each to the other, faithful cooperation in the future planning and development of the port of New York."[5] Article II defines the Port of New York District, the region to which the compact applies. It covers an area of roughly 1,500 square miles within an approximately 25-mile radius measured from New York City's Statue of Liberty (figure 3). Article III identifies the Port Authority as the instrument through which the two states' controlling objectives--the protection and promotion of the Port District's commerce and the development and operation of various transport-related facilities--are to be effectuated.

The Port Authority does not possess the power of taxation, cannot "pledge the credit of either state,"[6] but may "borrow money and secure the same by bonds."[7] New projects are undertaken only

---

[1]Port of New York Authority, Summary of Proposal for the Development of New York City Airports, p. 15.

[2]The Port Authority has been studied extensively. See, for instance: Erwin W. Bard, The Port of New York Authority (New York: Columbia University Press, 1942); Frederick L. Bird, A Study of the Port of New York Authority (New York: Dun and Bradstreet, 1949); Robert Igoe, "An Administrative Review of the Individual Functions and Overall Performance of the Port of New York Authority" (doctoral dissertation, New York University, 1962).

[3]New York, New Jersey Port and Harbor Development Commission, Joint Report with Comprehensive Plan and Recommendations (Albany: J.B. Lyon Co., 1920). The Compact Between New York and New Jersey for the Creation of a Port Authority and the Comprehensive Development of the Port forms part III of the Joint Report.

[4]Entered into pursuant to chapter 154, Laws of New York, 144th sess., (1921), and chapter 151, Laws of New Jersey, 145th Leg., (1921).

[5]New York, New Jersey Port and Harbor Development Commission, op. cit., part III, article I.

[6]Ibid., article VII.

[7]Ibid., article VI. To date the Port Authority has borrowed more than $3 billion for its various projects. Airport investments come to: Kennedy--$670 million; La Guardia--$208 million; Newark--$400 million.

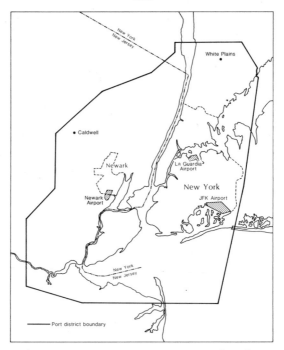

Fig. 3.   The Port of New York District

after it has been concluded that they will ultimately become self-supporting.[1] Its personnel are career public servants, who, however, are not part of the municipal or state civil services. Only such projects as have been authorized by the New York and New Jersey state governments are carried out by the agency. It is directly answerable to the two state legislatures, which may or may not adopt proposals sponsored or otherwise supported by it. All of its actions are subject to gubernatorial veto.[2]

In a strictly legal sense the Port Authority consists of a board of twelve commissioners, who constitute "a body corporate and politic." Each state governor appoints six commissioners, who must in turn be confirmed by the respective state senate. The board authorizes bond issues, makes budgetary decisions, issues the final directives relating to new projects, and sets overall agency policy. Commissioners may be removed for cause by the governor of New York

---

[1] The exception has been the Port Authority Trans-Hudson System.

[2] Some recent examples of the use of these veto powers are found in: "Byrne Is Vetoing Routine Actions by Port Authority," New York Times, May 26, 1977, p. B2; "Port Body Action to Bar Concorde for Noise Level in 1985 Vetoed by Byrne," New York Times, December 28, 1977, p. B2.

or, in the case of New Jersey, the senate.

The board of commissioners elects an executive director, who forms the link between it and the administrative staff. He presents board decisions to the staff, advises the board of staff recommenda-tions, and, more generally, is charged with the day-to-day running of the agency. Reporting to him are the directors of the following "line and staff" departments: line departments--Aviation (consisting of subdivisions dealing with airport management, economics, planning, public services, and technical services), Marine Terminals, Rail Transportation, Terminals (bus and truck), Tunnels and Bridges, and World Trade; staff departments--Administration, Comptroller, Engi-neering, Finance, General Services, Law, Management Services, Medi-cal, Personnel, Planning and Development, Public Affairs, and Treasury.

It goes without saying that at the time of the Port Authority's creation air transportation played no appreciable role in the eco-nomic life of the region. The compact does, however, in listing transportation facilities of concern to the agency, refer to "air-craft suitable for harbor service" (it fails to mention air terminals under "terminal facility").[1] Of perhaps greater interest is the document's recognition of future innovations and the Port Authority's potential involvement with "every kind of transportation facility now in use or hereafter designed for use for the transportation or carriage of . . . property."[2] In this connection the two signato-ries concurred on the agency's right to petition at any level of government "for the adoption and execution of any physical improve-ment, change in method, rate of transportation, system of handling freight . . . or transfer of freight, which, in the opinion of the Port Authority, may be designed to improve or better the handling of commerce" within the Port District.[3]

One of the most striking examples of what might have been en-visioned in terms of a new transportation facility or system "de-signed to improve or better the handling of commerce" came in 1947. In that year the states of New York and New Jersey passed an amend-ment to their compact of 1921, authorizing the Port Authority to "establish, acquire, construct, rehabilitate, improve, maintain and

---

[1]New York, New Jersey Port and Harbor Development Commission, op. cit., part III, article XXII.

[2]Ibid.

[3]Ibid., article XIII.

operate air terminals"[1] within the Port of New York District. This
legislation, designed to promote the goals of the 1921 agreement,
recognized the need for close bistate cooperation in the field of
air transportation and expressed the resolve of the parties to
"encourage the integration of . . . air terminals so far as practicable in a unified system."[2] The Port Authority was to pay no taxes
for the airports under its control[3] and was invested with the power,
subject to certain provisos, to apply directly to the Federal Government for airport-related financial aid. Details relating to terminal
construction and financing and the setting of rates and charges were
made entirely the responsibility of the agency,[4] which could also,
upon its own discretion, enlarge the terminals through the right of
eminent domain or condemnation.[5]

Uppermost in the minds of those advocating a new form of airport administration were financial considerations. Newark International Airport ("International" was added in 1972), which was being
operated by its owner, the City of Newark, New Jersey, had cost taxpayers, during the period 1928 to 1944, an average of $415,000 per
year. Maintenance costs were accelerating sharply and the city's
consulting engineers, reviewing the situation, recommended that
Newark invite the Port Authority to assume control over its air and
sea terminals and not attempt further development of these on its
own. Their report took note of the Port Authority's "very large
financial resources," its expertise in the transportation field, and
the desirability of integrating Newark's transportation facilities
with those of New York City. Surveys of the region's airport requirements had been undertaken by the Port Authority in 1927,[6] the
mid-1930s, and again in 1944, and, when the City of Newark asked it
in December of 1945 to state the conditions under which it could
operate and modernize the terminals, the agency, following additional

---

[1]New York, Laws, 170th sess., ch. 802, sec. I, (1947); also New Jersey,
Laws, 171st Leg., ch. 43, sec. I, (1947).

[2]Ibid.

[3]Ibid., sec. V.

[4]Ibid., sec. X.

[5]Ibid., sec. XV.

[6]Port of New York Authority, Tentative Report of Deputy Manager on an Airport for the New York Metropolitan District (New York: Port of New York Authority,
1927). This early investigation, which concluded the region should have "one or
more thoroughly modern" air terminals, found that one way this could be achieved
was through joint action by the states of New York and New Jersey.

studies, responded with a plan under which it would assume ownership of the city's air and marine terminals and run them at no expense to the taxpayer.[1]

Newark city officials showed little enthusiasm for the Port Authority's proposal, their objections focusing primarily on the initial cash payments the city was to receive for the facilities and on various subsequent annual payments the agency would make in lieu of taxes. Two city commissioners, Keenan[2] and Brady,[3] thought these so inadequate that they felt the city's interests would be better served if the airport were subdivided into lots and sold to industrial developers. The community at large, on the other hand, viewed the agency's terms more positively:[4] Port Authority acquisition of Newark Airport was espoused by the Democratic Party during its 1946 New Jersey senatorial campaign,[5] and various municipal groups such as the Merchants Association of Newark,[6] the Newark Real Estate Board,[7] and the Chamber of Commerce[8] urged acceptance of the agency's proposal. Doubts over Newark's ability to finance future terminal development caused New Jersey's State Director of Aviation to bluntly advise the city to withdraw from "the airport business."[9]

With four of Newark's five city commissioners openly protesting the financial provisions of the Port Authority's proposal, it was clear the agency would have to adopt a new approach if the discussions were to be kept alive, and this it did with an offer to raise the cash payments for the airport from $7.5 million (over a thirty-year period) to $9.2 million (for the same period). The revised

---

[1]Port of New York Authority, Development of Newark Airport and Seaport (New York: Port of New York Authority, 1946). The Port Authority was to make payments to Newark of $1 million per year over a five-year period, followed by $100,000 annually for as long as it owned the facilities.

[2]"Planning Board Group Favors Airport Offer," Newark Evening News, August 6, 1946, pp. 1-2.

[3]"Brady's Statement," Newark Evening News, August 8, 1946, p. 2.

[4]Reservations were however expressed by the Newark Taxpayer's Association. See "Stress Study of Port Plan," Newark Evening News, August 14, 1946, p. 1.

[5]"For Tube Purchase by Port Authority," New York Times, June 19, 1946, p. 24.

[6]"Newark Groups Back Port Authority Plan," New York Times, August 11, 1946, p. 47.

[7]"City Delay Seen on Port Decision," Newark Star-Ledger, August 14, 1946, p. 1.

[8]"Quick Port Action: Control by Authority Spurred by Chamber," Newark Star-Ledger, August 17, 1946, p. 1.

[9]"Decision on Port by Sept. 15 Seen," Newark Star-Ledger, August 19, 1946, p. 1.

figure, as well as the replies to various questions troubling the
city commissioners (such as the placing of responsibility for airport police and fire protection), stirred no interest and were unanimously rejected on September 17, 1946. Not wishing to rule out
further negotiations, however, the city submitted a substantial
package of counterproposals, which included a new airport price of
$10.4 million. Also:[1]

1. The Port Authority's deferred payment plan was rejected; full payment was
   to be made at the time of the transfer

2. Port Authority payments (in lieu of taxes) were to begin immediately and
   were not to be considered part of the purchase price

3. Title search fees and title clearance costs were to be paid by the Port
   Authority

4. Newark was to be compensated for tax losses suffered through future additional
   land acquisitions made by the agency

5. The city refused to be legally bound to provide various services (e.g., fire
   protection) at the airport. Such services were to be the responsibility of
   the Port Authority

6. The city rejected as too low the Port Authority's offer of $1 million in the
   event that airport subsoil tests fell short of expectations (Disappointing
   test results would have jeopardized the agency's projected expansion program)

7. Newark's seaport facilities were to be treated as a separate matter and were
   not to be included in the airport negotiations.

These proposals were rejected "with deep regret" by the Port Authority's Board of Commissioners, who feared that under the city's plan
the airport could not be operated on a self-supporting basis.

In June of 1947 Newark was offered an entirely new terminal
proposal by the Port Authority. Patterned after a formula under
which the agency was acquiring control of New York City's airports,
the proposal called for agency management on a leasehold rather than
a direct ownership basis. As before, the Port Authority refused to
view Newark's airport and seaport as separate issues (it proposed to
allocate $59 million for the airport's enlargement over an initial
five- to seven-year period, about $12 million for the seaport) and,
with congestion at La Guardia a growing problem, now intimated that
undue delay would lead it to examine other suitable airport sites in
northern New Jersey.[2]

This time the city commissioners proved to be more receptive.
The airport (about eighteen percent of the city's area) would not
be permanently lost, Newark could expect (over the life of the lease)
revenues in excess of twice its total terminal investment, and

---

[1]"Text of City's Port Proposal," Newark Evening News, September 18, 1946,
p. 21.

[2]"Port Authority May Shop Elsewhere for Air Field," Newark Evening News,
June 6, 1947, p. 5.

additional land acquired by the Port Authority would revert to the
city with the termination of the lease. The hesitation of Mayor
Vincent J. Murphy, who was pressing for a revenue split of 75-25 in
Newark's favor, was overcome when the Port Authority acceded to this
demand.[1] Although its precise impact cannot be gauged, the Port
Authority's potential interest in other New Jersey airport sites
presumably also helped nudge the commissioners towards acceptance of
the agency's terms; certainly the prospect of a second New Jersey
air terminal serving the New York metropolitan area (thus competing
with Newark) must have been an unsettling one. Even at this point,
however, the commissioners were far from united. Brady was unable
to shed his earlier reservations, while one of his colleagues,
Ellenstein (who enlivened the proceedings with an attack on Mayor
Murphy[2]), spoke darkly of Port Authority "propaganda agencies" and
their campaign to conceal the proposal's full financial implications.[3] Public hearings on the subject, representing more a gesture
towards Ellenstein's sensibilities than a desire to elicit additional information, were held in mid-October, and, later in the month,
the city commissioners, by a vote of three to two, accepted Port
Authority jurisdiction over both transportation terminals.[4]

Meanwhile, on August 2, 1946, a letter from Mayor William
O'Dwyer of New York had been received by the Port Authority. Written within days of the release of the agency's initial offer to
Newark (a "coincidence" which did not go unnoticed), it called on
the agency to submit a proposal for the future "financing, construction, rehabilitation and operation" of New York City's airports.
Echoing the sentiments of the Newark engineering group, the letter
acknowledged that Port Authority management of the air terminals
would spare New York the "tremendous burden of future airport financing and . . . would make the terminals available without cost
to the city's taxpayers."[5] This was a complete turnabout for the
mayor, who only several months earlier had defended his city's willingness to proceed alone with the development of municipal air

---

[1] The Port Authority had initially hoped to see a 50-50 revenue split during
part of the lease period.

[2] Murphy was accused of being the willing tool of the Port Authority.

[3] "Delay Is Hit in Port Deal," Newark Evening News, June 19, 1947, p. 1.

[4] Port of New York Authority, The City of New York and the Port of New York
Authority: Agreement with Respect to the Newark Marine and Air Terminals (New York:
Port of New York Authority, October 22, 1947).

[5] "Port Board Asked for Airfield Plan," New York Times, August 3, 1946,
p. 27.

terminals, insisting that the people of New York would reject "an abject surrender of the city's planning powers" to an agency subject to the vetoes of the governors of New York and New Jersey.[1] There was no need, O'Dwyer had said, for a regional approach to airport planning (which would include Newark), since air traffic competition and coordination in the metropolitan area could be supervised by the Federal Government through the Civil Aeronautics Administration. In any event, the Port Authority's Board of Commissioners agreed to the mayor's request and, towards the end of the year, came forward with a proposal under which the agency would assume full responsibility for the city's airports, operating these on a self-supporting basis.

New York City was at this time considering several avenues of approach to its airport problems. One of these was the Port Authority, another was direct financing and development by the city, and a third was the newly-organized New York City Airport Authority, a quasi-independent municipal agency which would finance terminal development outside the city's debt limit. The mayor's office had only just received the Port Authority's proposal when a counterproposal reached it from the City Airport Authority.[3] Its report, which differed from that of the Port Authority in a number of ways,[4] contained one section devoted entirely to criticisms of Port Authority involvement in the future running of the city's air terminals. The major points were:[5]

1. Since the City Airport Authority functioned within the guidelines imposed by New York's charter and its members were appointees of the mayor, the city retained some control over its activities. On the other hand, making the airports the responsibility of the Port Authority would mean removing them totally from the city's jurisdiction

2. The Port Authority would not be able to make the projected rental payments to New York because it had based these on unrealistically high traffic predictions

3. The Port Authority's plans for the development of Kennedy (Idlewild) Airport were overly elaborate and costly

4. The Port Authority intended keeping La Guardia Airport open to traffic during the forthcoming redevelopment phase. The City Airport Authority viewed this as impractical, proposing instead the temporary closing of the terminal

---

[1]"O'Dwyer Fights Plan for Airport Control," New York Times, February 9, 1946, p. 28.

[2]Port of New York Authority, Summary of Proposal for the Development of New York City Airports (New York: Port of New York Authority, December 18, 1946).

[3]New York City Airport Authority, Airport Program for New York City (New York: New York City Airport Authority, January 13, 1947).

[4]The details are found in the references cited here.

[5]New York City Airport Authority, op. cit., chapter VII.

5. Several options were included in the Port Authority's airport plan (e.g., the agency could purchase the facilities at the end of the lease term). New York, according to the City Airport Authority, would become "a sure loser" because the Port Authority would only exercise the options if convinced of their profitability

6. The City Airport Authority foresaw major legislative delays before the Port Authority could act on airport matters. On the other hand, its own legal status was such as to allow it to "move promptly" in this direction.

The Port Authority immediately responded to this attack on "our figures, our engineering conclusions, and even our motives" and in a lengthy rebuttal drew the mayor's attention to the City Airport Authority's "inaccurate and unrealistic financing and development plan."[1] More damaging perhaps was the position taken by a group of investment bankers, who criticized the City Airport Authority's revenue estimates and raised doubts as to the marketability of its bonds. Also opposing the City Airport Authority were airline representatives, who, fearing that the agency's failure to provide for nonaviation revenue sources imposed an unacceptable financial burden on their companies, condemned its entire proposal as "patently inadequate and incapable of realization."[2] In the end it was the Port Authority which prevailed.[3] After protracted dissension and confusion within the ranks of the city administration and following the submission, by the Port Authority, of a revised form of its earlier plan, the terminals came under the agency's control.[4] Administrative transfer was effectuated through leasehold agreements entered into by the Port Authority and the municipal government. Title to the terminals remains with the municipality during the life of the leases (fifty years), at the end of which airport bonds issued by the agency will be retired. (A similar arrangement holds for Newark Airport.)

Its many pronouncements on the subject leave no doubt that the Port Authority had long recognized air traffic as an important component of the commercial life of the New York metropolitan area, and, in taking on the new role of airport manager, the agency was acting

---

[1] Port of New York Authority, Considerations Submitted to the Mayor of the City of New York by the Port of New York Authority, in Answer to the Attacks Made by the City Airport Authority upon the Port Authority's Report Entitled: "Summary of Proposal for the Development of New York City Airports," January 15, 1947, mimeographed.

[2] "City Delays Action on Airport Plans," New York Times, January 16, 1947, p. 2; "Airport Control Assailed by Airlines," New York Times, January 20, 1947, p. 26.

[3] The City Airport Authority was dissolved in 1947.

[4] New York, N.Y., Board of Estimate, "Board of Estimate; Port of New York Authority--Approval of Agreement Relative to Municipal Air Terminals," Journal of Proceedings, 3 (1947):3183-3218.

entirely in the spirit of the 1921 compact. It seems reasonable
also to suggest that the agency became more favorably disposed
towards this costly, long-term commitment as a result of being under
pressure to justify both its considerable financial reserves and its
opposition to lower tolls on its tunnels and bridges.[1] Self-
interest, too, may have tinged its approach to the question of air
transportation, for in the absence of new projects the Port Authority will, in time, see its role reduced to the point where it remains only a toll collector.[2] The demise of its planning, developmental, and promotional functions would presumably invite legislative
review of the agency's activities and lead to a reshaping of its
organization and purpose.

Construction contracts awarded by the Port Authority during
its first full year as an airport operator came to about $12 million.
Since that time developmental and maintenance programs have encompassed runway extensions, subsoil stabilization projects, construction of buildings, fuel storage and lighting systems, accessibility
studies and traffic surveys, to name but a few. Some indication of
the growth the three airports have seen in the period 1950-1977 is
given in table 3.

In performing its duties vis-à-vis air transportation the Port
Authority is not restricted to the management and operation of terminals. The authors of the 1921 compact had empowered the agency to
intervene in any proceeding affecting the commerce of the Port District, and subsequent legislation has affirmed the agency's right to
present its views to the various Federal and state regulatory bodies
(or any other governmental authority having jurisdiction, directly
or indirectly, over some aspect of the Port District's economy),
whenever it feels their deliberations touch on the region's commercial interests. In this connection the Port Authority had already
intervened as early as 1944 in fourteen Civil Aeronautics Board proceedings dealing with the establishment of direct air service between New York-Newark and foreign cities. Since that time, it has
appeared before the CAB (and the ICC) on numerous other occasions.
A few of these are now shown, accompanied by some brief comments on

---

[1] The "exorbitant" tolls charged by the Port Authority were cited by New
York's Mayor O'Dwyer as one of the reasons for his initial reluctance to have the
agency assume new (i.e., aviation) financial responsibilities. "O'Dwyer Fights
Plan for Airport Control."

[2] See Editorial, New York Times, May 23, 1977, p. 26.

the position taken by the agency.

Air Freight Forwarder Case (decided 1948).[1] The Port Authority wished to see the forwarder industry operate under the fewest possible regulatory constraints and fully supported the Board's issuance of "letters of registration," as opposed to certificates of public convenience and necessity.

New York City Area Helicopter Service Case (1951).[2] New York Airways[3] was authorized by the CAB to provide scheduled helicopter service: (1) between the region's airports, and (2) between the airports and several other local points. The Board's action was endorsed by the Port Authority.

Transatlantic Cargo Case (1954).[4] The continuation of an earlier case (United States-Europe-Middle East Cargo Service Case[5]), this proceeding resulted in temporary certification of Seaboard's all-cargo service between several coterminals (New York, Philadelphia, and Baltimore) and a number of airports in Western Europe. The Port Authority was an advocate of such service, citing, as it has done in similar situations, a "strong community of interests" between the areas at issue. Favorable Board action was considered necessary in order to reverse a trend which had seen the proportion of U.S.-flag carrier all-cargo transatlantic flights fall from 81 percent in 1949 to 30 percent in 1952.

Air Freight Renewal Case (1955, 1956).[6] All-cargo service between the Port District's airports and other U.S. points was strongly supported by the Port Authority.

Service to Puerto Rico Case (1957).[7] Involved here was a review of passenger and all-cargo flights between New York-Newark and Puerto Rico, which led to a permanent certificate for Eastern Air Lines and a renewal of Riddle's certificate. The Port Authority was greatly interested in a strengthening of existing services between the Port District and the Commonwealth.

Intra-Area Cargo Case (1959).[8] The Port Authority welcomed the CAB's decision allowing the Flying Tiger Line to initiate intra-area flights, as this enabled the carrier to link the Port District with other points in the NE United States.

New York-San Francisco Nonstop Service Case (1959).[9] Here transcontinental nonstop service by a third carrier was authorized by the CAB. This action had the support of the Port Authority, which stated that its surveys indicated that there was a need for the additional service.

Transpacific Route Case (1961).[10] Additional air service between New York and Asia was favored by the Port Authority.

Domestic Cargo-Mail Service Case (1962).[11] Continued certification of the all-cargo carriers was recommended by the Port Authority.

Motor Transportation of Property Incidental to Transportation by Aircraft (1964).[12] The proposal of American Trucking Associations, Inc. that air terminal areas be made coextensive with section 203(b)(8) commercial zones[13] was firmly rejected by the Port Authority.[14] This proposal, if adopted, would have placed Newark Airport outside the New York air terminal area and was incompatible with a major

---

[1]See above, p. 84, note 2.

[2]15 CAB 259 (1951).

[3]See below, p. 234.

[4]21 CAB 671 (1954).

[5]15 CAB 565 (1952).

[6]See above, p. 16, note 1; p. 17, note 1.

[7]26 CAB 72 (1957).

[8]See above, p. 12, note 6.

[9]29 CAB 811 (1959).

[10]See above, p. 47, note 1.

[11]See above, p.20, note 6.

[12]See above, p. 105, note 4.

[13]See above, p. 106, note 4.

[14]Statement Pursuant to Proposed Rule-Making on Behalf of the Port of New York Authority, Docket MC-C-3437, November 15, 1961.

TABLE 3

THE NEW YORK-NEWARK AIRPORTS: 1950-1977

Terminal	1950	1955	1960	1965	1970	1975	1977
Kennedy							
Plane movements[a]							
Domestic passenger	5,259	65,848	141,893	212,936	176,464	137,254	144,668
Overseas passenger	7,667	27,700	44,468	58,649	93,155	74,000	73,987
Domestic all-cargo	14	2,094	6,470	10,899	20,069	12,829	13,975
Overseas all-cargo	154	1,738	3,753	6,378	13,708	16,527	14,934
Air taxi	-	2,677	8,878	32,284	34,816	27,196	30,373
Domestic supplemental	611	1,212	1,653	1,564	3,919	2,847	3,444
Revenue cargo (tons)[b]							
Freight							
Domestic	2,194	30,459	77,751	236,271	371,453	380,935	463,983
Overseas	5,617	22,585	60,304	180,958	388,093	585,931	727,100
Mail	2,770	18,113	44,117	85,630	143,882	140,548	144,227
Airport employment	2,507	12,757	28,506	33,382	43,003	39,452	39,471
Airport payroll ($1,000)	-	71,397	191,000	283,000	490,000	670,000	770,000
La Guardia							
Plane movements[a]							
Domestic passenger	119,886	166,147	128,814	100,634	231,845	222,939	236,642
Overseas passenger	9,520	926	0	0	232	0	0
Domestic all-cargo	2,744	4,722	1,325	2	2	3	5
Overseas all-cargo	0	0	0	0	0	0	0
Air taxi	-	8,517	13,889	26,000	17,248	25,036	36,566
Domestic supplemental	4,925	4,220	2,588	176	128	19	23
Revenue cargo (tons)[b]							
Freight							
Domestic	38,842	53,164	30,672	14,224	39,815	50,822	48,936
Overseas	4,870	72	0	0	0	0	0

Mail	14,916	20,844	13,466	2,822	24,119	32,127	37,011
Airport employment	8,188	8,257	7,394	5,182	7,354	8,542	8,078
Airport payroll ($1,000)	–	44,422	55,000	48,000	90,000	160,000	170,000

Newark

Plane movements[a]

Domestic passenger	51,247	75,541	103,902	126,156	141,784	99,520	107,392
Overseas passenger	0	4	9	479	3,873	4,276	5,426
Domestic all-cargo	12,429	5,715	5,501	7,334	8,166	3,470	1,490
Overseas all-cargo	0	0	0	0	2	107	7
Air taxi	–	3,263	6,546	21,728	16,820	29,245	28,958
Domestic supplemental	5,515	3,231	3,657	4,623	2,698	1,605	5,037

Revenue cargo (tons)[b]

Freight

Domestic	51,361	38,266	58,313	98,212	156,109	108,894	104,471
Overseas	86	1	0	783	1,192	3,296	4,202
Mail	3,104	4,256	10,557	13,704	37,401	34,650	38,948
Airport employment	1,498	3,442	3,988	5,093	6,561	5,920	5,082
Airport payroll ($1,000)	–	19,382	29,000	44,000	75,000	100,000	95,000

SOURCE: The Port Authority of New York and New Jersey.

[a]The first four categories cover scheduled flights only.

[b]Two-way traffic.

Port Authority objective, namely the unification of airport operations within the Port District.[1] Instead, the Port Authority urged the Interstate Commerce Commission to continue to apply its section 203(b)(7a) exemption to pickup/delivery points accepted by the Civil Aeronautics Board. A reduction in the size of the New York-Newark terminal area, the Port Authority emphasized, would deprive a number of local shippers and receivers of the benefits inherent in a single through bill of lading and lead to higher transportation costs. (During this period about half the shipments handled at the New York-Newark airports were subject to the air carriers' minimum pickup/delivery charge of $2. The minimum charge of the motor common carriers, on the other hand, was about $3.90 per shipment.) The trucking organization's proposal, as we have seen (chapter II), was not adopted by the Commission.

Interpretation of Operating Rights Authorizing Service at Designated Airports (1969).[2] In May of 1969 the ICC received a petition from several truckers (including Air Delivery Service, Bayshore, Con-Ov-Air, and Harbourt [figure 6, chapter VI]) authorized to operate between the New York-Newark airports and points in New Jersey and Pennsylvania, requesting continued recognition of their certificates even though some of the air-surface freight exchanges might take place at off-airport locations. In view of the fact that a number of airlines and forwarders were establishing terminal facilities beyond the boundaries of the airport named in the truckers' certificates, the Commission granted the request. The Commission noted that requiring the motor carriers to apply for new certificates of public convenience and necessity covering individual off-airport freight buildings would unnecessarily disrupt air freight services and accordingly issued a general rule of construction, under which off-airport terminal facilities were included in the truckers' operating authority. This action was strongly endorsed by the Port Authority. It informed the Commission of changing land use patterns around the New York-Newark airports and argued, as had the petitioners, that the construction of warehouses, air carrier terminals, and other freight-related facilities beyond the airport boundaries called for a reinterpretation of the motor carriers' operating rights.[3]

Transpacific Route Investigation (1969).[4] The Port Authority welcomed the initiation of scheduled all-cargo service and was in favor of additional combination carrier service.

Agreement Adopted by IATA Relating to North Atlantic Cargo Rates (1973).[5] In this proceeding the CAB found that existing North Atlantic cargo rates were "unduly and unreasonably" preferential to New York and "unduly and unreasonably" prejudicial to a number of competing gateway cities, and thus unlawful. New rates were to be based on mileage flown, a position the Port Authority supported. The Board overturned the initial decision of its examiner, who had recommended that New York be common-rated with several of its competitors. The imposition of common rates would have improved the competitive position of Baltimore, Philadelphia, and Washington and was opposed by the Port Authority.

New England Service Investigation (1974).[6] As its name suggests, this case involved an examination of air transportation in New England. Long concerned with the deteriorating quality of air service in the region, the Board concluded that a "vigorous governmental response" was required if New England's "chronic" air service problems were to be resolved. An evaluation of three possible solutions—(1) expanded operations by commuter carriers; (2) expanded operations by Delta Air Lines, the region's major certificated airline; and (3) certification of

---

[1] See above, p. 184.   [2] 110 MCC 597 (1969).

[3] Statement on Behalf of the Port of New York Authority in Support of Proposed Amendment of Section 1041.23, 49 CFR, Docket MC-C-3437 (Sub.-no. 4), August 8, 1969.

[4] See above, p. 47, note 3.   [5] See above, p. 55, note 3.

[6] Docket 22973, Order 74-7-70.

other regional carriers, resulted in the adoption of option (3) and led to the certification of Air New England. The Board's action, to the extent that it ensured continuation of air service between various New England communities and the terminal point of New York-Newark, had the support of the Port Authority. However, the Port Authority favored a different approach, believing that the service problems of the low density, short-haul markets at issue could best be solved through the use of more commuter flights. It also feared that certification (by reducing the number of commuter carriers) would lead to operational complications at La Guardia (the terminal at which most of the commuters providing service between New England and the Port District were based). In testimony before the CAB the Port Authority explained: "La Guardia is one of four airports designated as High Density Traffic Airports by the Federal Aviation Administration. . . . Under the High Density Traffic Airports Regulation the airlines are limited to 48 scheduled IFR operations per hour between 0600 and 2400 hours at La Guardia. The carriers serving the High Density Traffic Airports have established Airline Scheduling Committees to allocate the available slots at the four airports. For over a year, virtually all of the 48 airline hourly slots have been taken at La Guardia Airport between 0800 and 2159 hours. It would be very difficult for an additional certificated airline or airlines to get slots during these hours. More importantly, additional slots gained at La Guardia for the operation of the predominantly small planes which will operate in the New England markets would probably mean slots lost by the incumbent airlines which operated planes with an average 100.3 seat capacity at La Guardia this summer. Five years from now the average airline movement at La Guardia is expected to have 153 seats."[1]

Service to Omaha and Des Moines Case (1975).[2] Here the Board's attention focused on (1) the monopoly position held by United Airlines over routes linking Omaha and Des Moines, on the one hand, and terminal points on the East Coast and West Coast, on the other, and (2) the need for competitive service over these routes. The Port Authority took no position on the need for additional air service in the Des Moines/Omaha-East Coast market but viewed with concern the Board's inclination to name a specific airport as the route's eastern terminal. In view of the changing conditions at its three airports (runway congestion, availability of aircraft ramp space, etc.), the Port Authority noted, it was vital that airlines retained the flexibility to switch flights from one terminal to another.[3] The CAB agreed and, in its order authorizing additional air service, designated "New York-Newark" as the route's eastern terminal.

Transatlantic Route Proceeding (1978).[4] Approved by President Carter in 1978, the Board's major recommendations in this case were: (1) renewed certification of existing transatlantic services; (2) approval of transatlantic flights by additional U.S. airlines; (3) the naming of a number of U.S. airport cities as new international gateways. (Somewhat similar proposals had earlier been submitted to President Ford. These were rejected on the grounds that they failed to "address adequately" the economic issues involved and placed too much emphasis "on a single European gateway."[5] This gateway was London, and Mr. Ford clearly wished to delay affirmative action pending the outcome of an Anglo-American air services agreement then being negotiated. Another possible reason behind

---

[1] Cited in Brief of The Port Authority of New York and New Jersey to Administrative Law Judge Greer M. Murphy, Docket 22973, January 15, 1973, p. 5.

[2] Docket 18401.

[3] Brief of The Port of New York Authority to Examiner Richard A. Walsh, Docket 18401, February 7, 1969, pp. 2-3.

[4] Docket 25908, Order 78-1-118.

[5] The President's letter is found in the CAB's Order 77-1-98.

the President's move was his "reluctance to antagonize any particular bloc of voters before the 1976 elections."[1]) Continued certification of the existing scheduled and supplemental transatlantic services had the Port Authority's support, and at its suggestion "New York" was redesignated as "New York-Newark" in the U.S.-flag transatlantic airlines' route certificates. In another area, however, namely the designation of eleven U.S. cities as new transatlantic coterminals, the Port Authority's efforts suffered a significant setback. (The Board's action has a number of implications for New York-Newark. For instance, it threatens to erode the region's position as the nation's leading transatlantic gateway and may lead to the loss of jobs at its three airports.) Additional coterminals, the Board believed, were required because of congestion at existing East Coast international airports. The Port Authority conceded that congestion and delays at its airports had been a problem during the 1960s but insisted major improvements had removed these difficulties as a basis for the Board's action.[2]

Concluding Remarks

The Port Authority was established jointly by the States of New York and New Jersey in 1921. Its mandate enables it to represent the economic interests of the Port District (an area with a radius of about twenty-five miles, measured from the Statue of Liberty) before various governmental bodies, and in this context it has frequently intervened in Civil Aeronautics Board and Interstate Commerce Commission proceedings in order to influence decisions concerning the District's air traffic. On becoming an airport operator (in the late 1940s) the Port Authority set itself the goal of eliminating the rivalry between the Cities of Newark and New York for regional dominance in air transportation and of transforming the three terminals "so far as practicable in[to] a unified system." Thus, for example, it has urged (1961) that the ICC not accept a proposal of American Trucking Associations, Inc. calling for smaller air terminal areas, as this would have removed Newark from the New York-Newark air terminal area. Similarly, whenever the CAB has thought of naming a specific Port District airport as a service point in one of its route proceedings, the Port Authority has requested that the point be designated as "New York-Newark" in order to strengthen the carriers' service interchangeability at the three airports. The Port Authority has supported those of the Board's actions tending to increase the number of scheduled and supplemental flights between New York-Newark and other air traffic centers. It

---

[1]"Overseas Routes for 11 New Cities Get Approval from the President," New York Times, December 22, 1977, p. D11.

[2]Brief of The Port Authority of New York and New Jersey to Associate Chief Administrative Law Judge Ross I. Newmann, Docket 25908, September 9, 1974, pp. 14-18.

has not failed to protest Board decisions where these appeared to favor other airport cities at the expense of New York-Newark.

The position of the New York-Newark air terminals within the national air traffic hub system is shown in table 4. Of the approximately 640 certificated air service points in the United States, 156 have been designated as air traffic hubs (1977). These are defined by the Federal Aviation Administration as "cities and Standard Metropolitan Statistical Areas requiring aviation services" and form the basis for most of its economic and operations research work. Depending on their percentage of the total number of enplaned passengers by U.S. domestic certificated route carriers, air service points fall into four categories: (1) large hub (here the percentage is one or more); (2) medium hub (0.25 to 0.99 percent); (3) small hub (0.05 to 0.24 percent); and (4) nonhub (below 0.05 percent). On the basis of this classification there are 25 large hubs, 39 medium hubs, and 92 small hubs in the United States. The first group, which includes New York and Newark, accounts for 68.1 percent, the second group for 18.4 percent, and the third group for 10.2 percent of total U.S. passenger enplanements. It should be noted that an air traffic hub, since it is an urban area rather than a specific airport, can contain more than one air terminal, and in fact this is the case with twelve of the nation's 25 large hubs. Thus, for example, the New York City hub consists of Kennedy and La Guardia airports and two heliports, the San Francisco-Oakland hub of two airports and two heliports, and the Los Angeles hub of three airports. The overall impact of the heliports is negligible, as each accounts for no more than 0.01 percent of total U.S. passenger enplanements. Table 4 makes clear that the "preeminence" of which the Port Authority spoke in the 1940s has been achieved. The New York-Newark airports lead the nation's air traffic hubs in three of the five transportation categories shown, namely scheduled aircraft departures, enplaned freight, and enplaned priority mail. They are marginally behind Chicago with respect to passenger enplanements and are in third place (after Chicago and Atlanta) when ranked according to enplaned priority (express) shipments.

Congestion at the New York-Newark air terminals has been of concern to local, state, and U.S. authorities for much of the period considered in chapter IV. Congestion at Newark played a role in the designation of La Guardia (1939) as one of the New York region's coterminals, and during the 1940s capacity problems in New York were a factor in the Port Authority's interest in acquiring New Jersey terminal facilities. In 1959 the Port Authority predicted that it

TABLE 4

THE LEADING U.S. AIR TRAFFIC HUBS
(12 months ended June 30, 1977)

Rank	Hub	Transportation Category	Percent of U.S. Total
		Scheduled Aircraft Departures (thousands)	
1	New York-Newark	300	6.3
2	Chicago	286	6.0
3	Atlanta	214	4.5
4	Los Angeles	150	3.1
5	Dallas-Ft. Worth	144	3.0
6	Washington	125	2.6
		Enplaned Passengers (thousands)	
1	Chicago	18,647	8.0
2	New York-Newark	18,151	7.8
3	Atlanta	14,109	6.1
4	Los Angeles	10,724	4.6
5	Dallas-Ft. Worth	8,167	3.5
6	Washington	7,183	3.1
		Enplaned Freight (revenue tons)	
1	New York-Newark	413,899	12.7
2	Chicago	341,866	10.5
3	Los Angeles	326,698	10.0
4	San Francisco	179,344	5.5
5	Seattle	136,443	4.2
6	Miami	128,099	3.9
		Enplaned Priority (Express) Shipments (revenue tons)	
1	Chicago	7,069	18.3
2	Atlanta	3,932	10.2
3	New York-Newark	3,215	8.3
4	Los Angeles	2,912	7.5
5	San Francisco	2,355	6.1
6	Miami	1,262	3.3
		Enplaned Priority Mail (revenue tons)	
1	New York-Newark	90,996	10.9
2	Atlanta	72,442	8.6
3	Chicago	71,441	8.5
4	Dallas-Ft. Worth	40,019	4.8
5	Los Angeles	38,703	4.6
6	Washington	29,326	3.5

SOURCE: Civil Aeronautics Board.

NOTE: These figures (which include originations and transfers) are for U.S. carriers only and cover domestic and international service.

would be "utterly impossible for the existing . . . [New York-Newark]
airports to handle the air traffic of 1975,"[1] and in 1971 Governor
Nelson Rockefeller, addressing the State Legislature in Albany,
voiced concern over Kennedy's "inadequacy and . . . current congestion" and urged development of Stewart Airport (Orange County) as
the region's fourth major air terminal.[2] Two years later, a planning group, in a report to the Metropolitan Transportation Authority,
endorsed Stewart's future role as a major regional terminal, since
"the demand for air transportation services in the greater New York
Metropolitan region will continue to grow, and, beginning in the year
1980, will begin to exceed the ability of existing major airports to
provide accommodations for the demand."[3]

It is now generally accepted that earlier traffic forecasts
relied, in part, on erroneous assumptions. Recent studies indicate
that runways, taxiways, and airspace at the three New York-Newark
airports suffice to meet the requirements of the region's anticipated
air traffic for the foreseeable future and that Stewart Airport will
be needed as a subregional facility only. This scenario takes into
account Newark's present underutilization as well as greatly reduced
aircraft movement projections. The latter reflect, inter alia, the
changing outlook for the tri-state region's economic growth, rising
fuel prices, technological changes (larger aircraft), and the
growing importance of other U.S. airport cities as international
gateways.[4]

---

[1]Port of New York Authority, A New Major Airport for the New Jersey-New
York Metropolitan Area (New York: Port of New York Authority, 1959), p. 16.

[2]New York, Public Papers of Governor Nelson A. Rockefeller, 1971, p. 1256.

[3]TransPlan, Inc. and Seelye Stevenson Value & Knecht, Inc., A Study for the
Development of Stewart Airport, Summary Report (New York: TransPlan, Inc. and
Seelye Stevenson Value & Knecht, Inc., 1973), p. 11.

[4]Tri-State Regional Planning Commission, Public Policy Toward Aviation
(New York: Tri-State Regional Planning Commission, May, 1978).

CHAPTER V

AIRPORT OPERATIONS AND SERVICES

In chapter IV we saw how the Port Authority of New York and
New Jersey became an airport operator and noted its attempts to
influence the outcome of various Federal freight-related regulatory
proceedings. Here the agency is examined further, particularly with
reference to its ability to promulgate laws which may affect the
flow of traffic at its terminals.

An air freight center must, if it is to operate effectively,
provide a broad range of services and facilities. A general classification of these services includes the following: (1) services
provided or supervised by the airport manager, e.g., administration,
maintenance, and security; (2) services provided by air carriers,
brokers, forwarders, and truckers; and (3) governmental services,
e.g., import/export controls, quarantine and veterinary services,
and postal services. A number of these services are discussed in
this chapter.

Management

The Port Authority exercises control over its various airport
operations through general managers at Kennedy and Newark and a
manager at La Guardia. It is they who, in an overall sense, bear
the responsibility for the daily administration of their respective
terminals. They are appointed by the director of the Port Authority's Aviation Department and are answerable to him.

At Kennedy Airport, the largest of the terminals both in terms
of traffic volume and area, four divisional managers are responsible
to the general manager. Their divisions cover: aeronautical services, business administration, plants and structures, and public
services.

In the case of aeronautical services, the area of immediate
concern is the condition or quality of structures and facilities
directly bearing on air transportation. For this reason close contact is maintained with the Federal Aviation Administration on a
wide range of safety-related matters. Aeronautical services personnel would, for instance, be involved in the formulation of regulations concerning the spacing of a new type of runway lighting system.

It is this division which, through committees including pilot and airline representatives, passes on the usability of runways under any particular set of conditions.

The duties of the business administration division are far narrower than its name might suggest. It negotiates the terms of all leases and licenses for the use of airport property; these are then submitted to the Port Authority's Law Department, where they are formally drawn up. An example here would be an air carrier's lease for a cargo building. Formerly, revenues generated by the airport came within the purview of this division but are now handled directly by the office of the general manager.

The plant and structures division is further subdivided into planning, construction, and maintenance sectors. It has responsibility for the upkeep of Port Authority buildings and joint-use facilities such as the international arrivals building, runways, taxiways, parking lots, etc. The contract for work done on a joint use structure is prepared by the Port Authority's Engineering Department, which also releases the contract for bidding. This procedure differs somewhat from that followed where an airport tenant wishes to erect a cargo or passenger building for his exclusive use. Here the tenant makes his own arrangements with a contractor who may only proceed with the work once the "go ahead" has been given by the division. Although the airports are run independently of their city-owners, terminal buildings must conform to the relevant city building codes. Frequently the Port Authority's design criteria are more stringent than those of the two cities or the agency may impose entirely new specifications not called for under city law. A builder must meet all the stated requirements and will have his work examined by the division to ensure that he does so.

At this point it may be well to stress that the relationship between the Port Authority and the individual airline is as that between landlord and tenant. The carrier (or other airport tenant) does not own the building(s) used. Should he desire a modification (such as an enlargement) of his facility, all pertinent details must be submitted to the plant and structures division. Only after its approval has been obtained may work on the alterations be initiated.

The public services division has control over a number of areas which, while closely affecting airport users, are not directly connected with air transportation. Police protection may be cited as an example.

Differences in organizational structure at the two other airports are more a matter of form than of substance and reflect the reduced level of activity found there. At Newark there are three

divisions under the general manager's office. Two of these, business administration and plant and structures, have counterparts at
Kennedy. The third, the operating services division, is subdivided
into three sections: an operations unit, a terminal service unit,
and the police unit. Together these encompass the services provided
or supervised by Kennedy's aeronautical services and public services
divisions. At La Guardia the manager's office consists of four
units. These, headed by supervisors, cover: administrative, operations, police, and building maintenance functions. The administrative unit's work includes the negotiating of leases, though these,
before they can take effect, must be approved by Kennedy's business
administration division. Under the operations unit are subsumed the
functions of Kennedy's aeronautical services division and public
services division.

As an airport operator a local public agency is able, under
certain circumstances, to promulgate rules which may have an impact
on the movement of air traffic. Local rules, the U.S. Department of
Transportation has stipulated, must be reasonable, nondiscriminatory,
and in harmony with Federal legislation. The Department's position
has won the support of Congress[1] and has been affirmed by the Supreme Court.[2] The regulatory role of local public bodies remains
unaffected by Public Law 95-504 (Airline Deregulation Act of 1978).
Indeed, fearing that airline deregulation might encourage greater
assertiveness on the part of airport managers, Congress added the
following section to the Federal Aviation Act:

> no State or political subdivision thereof and no interstate agency or
> other political agency of two or more States shall enact or enforce any
> law, rule, regulation, standard, or other provision having the force and
> effect of law relating to rates, routes, or services of any air carrier
> having authority under title IV of [the Federal Aviation Act] to provide
> interstate air transportation.[3]

This amendment to the Federal Aviation Act appears to have caused
some initial confusion. "I am concerned," Senator Kennedy said
shortly before the final Senate vote on the deregulation bill,

> that long recognized powers of the airport operators to deal with noise
> and other environmental problems at the local level may be inadvertently
> curtailed by this section. Am I correct in stating that actions of the
> airport operators, presently accepted as valid exercises of proprietary

---

[1] Senate Report no. 1353, 90th Cong., 2d sess., (1968), pp. 6-7; Senate
Report no. 1160, 92d Cong., 2d sess., (1972), pp. 10-11; House Report no. 842,
92d Cong., 2d sess., (1972), p. 10.

[2] Douglas v. Seacoast Products, 431 U.S. 265 (1977).

[3] Pub. L. no. 95-504, sec. 4(a) (section 105[a][1] of the Federal
Aviation Act).

powers, are not intended to be interpreted as 'relating to . . . routes or services' of air carriers and are not intended to be preempted by the powers created by this section?[1]

The question was answered by Senator Howard Cannon, Chairman of the Senate Subcommittee on Aviation:

> that is correct. It was not the intent of the Senate conferees to limit in any way the normal exercise of the existing proprietors' powers to place nondiscriminatory restrictions on the operations at an airport, subject to constitutional and statutory limitations.[2]

Under various agreements linking the Federal Government and the Port Authority, the latter receives Federal aid for approved terminal development projects, such as:

> improving, or repairing a public airport or portion thereof, including the removal, lowering, relocation, and marking and lighting of airport hazards, and including navigation aids used by aircraft landing at, or taking off from a public airport, and including safety equipment required by rule or regulation for certification of the airport . . . , and security equipment required of the [Port Authority] by the Secretary [of Transportation] by rule or regulation for the safety and security of persons and property on the airport, and including snow removal equipment, and including the purchase of noise suppressing equipment, the construction of physical barriers, and landscaping for the purpose of diminishing the effect of aircraft noise on any area adjacent to a public airport.[3]

The disbursement of Federal funds hinges on the Port Authority's ability to meet various legal obligations, one of which is that its airports "will be available for public use on fair and reasonable terms and without unjust discrimination."[4] The relationship between the Federal Government and the Port Authority may be seen as a partnership in which the former has virtually preempted economic and safety regulation of air transportation, leaving the Port Authority with rule-making powers which essentially complement Federal action. Despite the extensiveness of Federal jurisdiction, the agency retains some leeway, for the government

> has not so pervasively regulated the movement of aircraft that [it] has excluded the existence of areas of proper airport regulation. Direct conflict between Federal regulation and local law of course results in the invalidation of the local provision. . . . However, . . . there is room for the operation of Port Authority regulations which have the effect of curtailing activities not forbidden by Federal regulation, and, indeed, contemplated as specifically permissible by Federal regulation, in the absence of other competent prohibition.[5]

---

[1]*Congressional Record*, October 14, 1978, p. S18799.

[2]Ibid.

[3]49 U.S.C. 1711.

[4]Ibid., sec. 1718.

[5]*Aircraft Owners and Pilots Association v. Port Authority of New York*, 305 F. Supp. 93, 104-105 (E.D. N.Y. 1969).

A recent test of the Port Authority's regulatory power involved the Anglo-French Concorde, whose owners, the British and
French governments, had let it be known in 1970 that they hoped to
obtain landing rights for the aircraft at Kennedy Airport. The
initial response of the Port Authority was that the SST would have
to conform to the same noise standard (the 112 PNdB [perceived noise
in decibels] rule) applied to subsonic aircraft using that facility.
Subsequent Concorde test results persuaded the U.S. Department of
Transportation to allow transatlantic Concorde operations, and, in
a decision of February 4, 1976, the Secretary of Transportation,
William T. Coleman, authorized Concorde service at Kennedy. Flights
were to be conducted for a sixteen-month trial period, during which
the aircraft's noise and vibration emissions were to be further
evaluated. Support for such a trial program was also forthcoming
from President Carter and the Federal Aviation Administration.
Washington's guarded pro-Concorde stance contrasted sharply with
the situation in the New York area, where hostility towards the SST
had been growing steadily. Supersonic flights were assailed on
environmental grounds by residents of Queens and Nassau counties,
special interest groups, the mayor of New York, and various New York
state lawmakers, and, on January 5, 1976, the New York State Legislature passed a bill banning the Concorde from Kennedy Airport.
This action, however, had little significance, since similar legislation was not enacted by the New Jersey Legislature.

On March 11, about five weeks after Secretary Coleman's ruling,
the Port Authority announced a ban on Concorde operations at Kennedy
for at least six months. This move, it was explained, was based on
environmental considerations as well as the question of agency liability in the event of SST-related damage suits.[1] The 112 PNdB rule
was not applied to the Concorde because of what were termed the
latter's "unique" noise characteristics. The agency agreed with
Coleman that an assessment of the aircraft's noise and vibration
emissions under actual operating conditions was necessary and retained several consultants for the purpose of monitoring the plane's
environmental impact on communities near airports in Dallas, Washington, London, and Paris. Subsequent test results for these cities
were rejected by the agency, which for the next few months repeatedly
extended the original six-month ban while attempting to devise an
anti-Concorde noise formula which would not expel various subsonic
aircraft from its air terminals. Unwilling to accept further

---

[1]Port Authority of New York and New Jersey, Kennedy International Airport--
Concorde Operations, resolution of March 11, 1976, mimeographed.

exclusion from the New York market, British Airways and Air France instituted legal proceedings, and in May of 1977 Federal District Judge Pollack made known his initial decision in British Airways Board v. The Port Authority of New York and New Jersey.[1]

The district court's ruling was a major disappointment for Concorde opponents, for it voided the Port Authority's ban of March 11, 1976, stressing that in any "irreconcilable conflict" between the Federal Government and a local public agency the latter had to yield under the Supremacy Clause of the Constitution. The court also noted that "the leading Federal act governing air commerce is the Federal Aviation Act of 1958. The statute is broadly drafted and as expressed leaves no doubt of adequate statutory authority to land the Concorde at JFK."[2] Judge Pollack's decision was based on the principle of Federal primacy. This narrow interpretation caused considerable irritation within the Executive Branch which, while favoring Concorde operations, was hesitant to invoke Federal supremacy lest this expose the government to damage suits at some later point. The Carter Administration thus argued before the U.S. Court of Appeals in Manhattan (following the Port Authority's appeal of the lower court's decision) that the agency's ban on Concorde landings at Kennedy was "unfair, dilatory, arbitrary and unreasonable."[3] The government's brief affirmed the right of airport proprietors to set their own noise standards but emphasized the Port Authority's repeated failure to reach a final decision and its seeming refusal to take the aircraft's latest noise abatement procedures into consideration. The Administration feared that the agency's position might weaken relations with two major European allies and spoke of the potential loss of advanced technical knowledge to the United States.

The government's contention that airport operators had the right to establish local noise rules, provided these were fair, nonarbitrary, and nondiscriminatory, was upheld by the U.S. Court of Appeals (June 14), which urged the Port Authority to cease its procrastination and "fix reasonable noise standards with dispatch."[4] The district court's order was overturned and the case was remanded to the lower court for a decision on the reasonableness of the

---

[1] 431 F. Supp. 1216 (S.D. N.Y. 1977).

[2] Ibid., p. 1220.

[3] "U.S. Brief Opposes Port Authority Ban on Concorde Flight," New York Times, June 7, 1977, p. 1.

[4] British Airways Board v. The Port Authority of New York and New Jersey, 558 F. 2d 75, 86 (2d Cir. 1977).

gency's actions. Complying, the district court held evidentiary
hearings and released its second opinion on August 17. This ruling,
too, dealt a sharp blow to the hopes of New York's anti-Concorde
forces. The agency, the court found, had been unable to demonstrate
that Concorde service, as authorized by the Department of Transportation, "would appreciably or intolerably worsen present [environ-
mental] conditions" and had sponsored research projects which were
"redundant and irrelevant" as a basis for developing new noise
standards.[1] "The conclusion is inescapable," Judge Pollack declared,
that the Port Authority

> has no intention of taking the responsibility of setting the present or
> another noise standard applicable to the Concorde. Its failure and
> excessive delay in doing so are unreasonable, discriminatory and unfair
> and an impingement on commerce and on the national and international
> interests of the United States.[2]

The case was now returned to the appeals court, which affirmed the
district judge's findings on September 29. The court noted that the
Concorde was able to satisfy the Port Authority's 112 decibel rule
and that SST-induced vibrations were comparable to vibrations emitted by other aircraft using Kennedy, such as the B-747 and DC-10.
The Port Authority had dismissed various Federal studies supporting
Concorde service, had failed to develop a nondiscriminatory noise
ndex, and "had . . . grasped [at] . . . excuse[s] for nonaction."[3]
his "abdication of responsibility," the court implied, was the
result of local political pressure. The agency was enjoined from
continuing its Concorde ban but was told it remained free to develop
a nondiscriminatory noise standard which might exclude supersonic
aircraft from its air terminals.

This was not the end of the controversy. In June the legislature in Albany had passed a bill enabling New York state residents
to sue the Port Authority for SST-related property damage, following
which Governor Hugh Carey and other state officials continued their
campaign against the Concorde. The governor vowed he would veto
agency approval of Concorde landings and threatened to defy the
Supreme Court if it left standing (which it did in October) the
appeals court's final order. His concern, he insisted, was for the

---

[1]British Airways Board v. The Port Authority of New York and New Jersey,
437 F. Supp. 804, 817 (S.D. N.Y. 1977).

[2]Ibid., p. 818.

[3]British Airways Board v. The Port Authority of New York and New Jersey,
564 F. 2d 1002, 1009 (2d Cir. 1977).

"health and security" of the people of New York.[1] Critics saw his
motivation in less lofty terms, calling his performance "a cheap b
for votes."[2] Towards the end of the year the agency's Board of Co
missioners voted to adopt new, nondiscriminatory noise rules which
would have barred the Concorde from the New York-Newark airports i
1985. However, Governor Brendan Byrne of New Jersey, long interested in attracting the Concorde to Newark's relatively underutilized airport, vetoed this action.[3]

Freight-Related Services

Of the several U.S. Government departments which are involve
in some phase of airport activity, the two whose work is most germane to this study are the Department of the Treasury and the Depa
ment of Agriculture. The first of these, through its Bureau of
Customs, has responsibility for the assessment and collection of
duties payable on items brought into the United States. At both
Kennedy and Newark the Bureau's Cargo Section employs some forty
inspectors who check that no discrepancies exist between manifests
and the items actually carried. The frequency with which inspec-
tions are carried out varies with commodity and country of origin.
The inspectors are supported by the Import Specialists Unit (with
staff of about 65 at Kennedy, a lesser figure at Newark), which
advises on the correct duty rate for specific commodities, annual
import quotas, etc. Another unit of the Bureau of Customs, the
Administrative Division, acts as the clearing house for most of th
paper work connected with the collecting of duties. In addition i
helps to enforce the rules and regulations of about 150 other governmental bodies. For example, the division, with a total staff a
Kennedy and Newark of around seventy, ensures on behalf of the Wil
life Section of the Department of Agriculture that there is no com
mercial traffic in skins and feathers of endangered species and on
behalf of the National Safety Board that safety features on import
vehicles meet the necessary Federal requirements. Other aspects o
the Bureau's work are its sealing of goods only passing through th
United States (and thus duty-free as long as the Bureau's seal remains unbroken) and its supervision of privately owned off-airport
bonded warehouses.

---

[1]"Carey Doubts the Supreme Court Can Overrule Governor on SST," New York
Times, October 13, 1977, p. B2.

[2]Editorial, New York Times, October 14, 1977, p. A26.

[3]"Port Body Action to Bar Concorde for Noise Level in 1985 Vetoed by Byr

Veterinary programs form an integral part of an international airport's activities and are maintained at Kennedy through the U.S. Department of Agriculture's Veterinary Service. Essentially, the staff, one veterinarian and four inspectors, combat the entry into the United States of animals carrying or suspected of carrying diseases posing a threat to U.S. livestock. Certain species originating in given areas are automatically barred from entering the United States. Others, especially ruminants, are examined at the airport but must then be transferred to the Department of Agriculture's quarantine station at Clifton, New Jersey, for more extensive observation.[1] The general procedure is that, when an animal is expected at the airport, the airline or importer notifies the Veterinary Service, which dispatches a staff member to meet the plane. The airport has two mobile holding pens in which are carried out such preliminary checks as blood tests and the disinfection of hooves. A number of animals destined for zoos need not be quarantined and receive their airport check while confined in a crate. Should an animal be diseased, or should it have been sent from a prohibited region, the importer is given the choice of returning it to the country of origin or destroying it.

Since the import regulations of a number of countries call for a governmental health check in the country of origin (to be performed not more than 24 hours prior to the time of entry), the Department of Agriculture also provides services and facilities (it has twelve horse stalls, for example) which enable American exporters to meet foreign trade requirements.

Although important, the traffic in live animals is not great. For instance, in 1977 380 cattle, 893 horses, and 49 swine entered the United States via Kennedy. Some export figures for the same year are: 904 cattle, 551 horses, and 76 swine.

Newark Airport has no staff or facilities to deal with this type of traffic. When the occasional animal is shipped from Newark, medical checks are administered by personnel from Kennedy or Clifton's quarantine station.

Inspection of fruit, vegetable, and plant imports is handled by the Department of Agriculture's Plant Protection and Quarantine Programs Unit. It has about 65 inspectors at Kennedy and maintains a facility there for the treatment (chemical dips, fumigation, etc.) of imports. During 1977 about five million plants of nursery stock

---

[1]A new quarantine station is being built at Stewart Airport, Orange County. A description of this facility is found in "Quarantine Center for Animals to Move to State," New York Times, August 9, 1975, p. 21.

were examined. The unit also supervises the cleaning and disinfecting of animal crates and handles much of the paperwork relating to the inspection by Department of Agriculture-approved off-airport personnel of imported meat and other animal products.

At Newark incoming plant material is checked by nine inspectors. Importers must move their products to the Port Authority's fumigation chamber in Port Newark for treatment.

Terminal Facilities

The freight facilities at the New York-Newark airport complex are among the most modern and extensive of their kind in the world. Of the three airports, Kennedy has by far the largest number of cargo buildings and related services, with Newark in second place. Only about five percent of New York-Newark's air freight is handled at La Guardia, which is not normally served by all-cargo aircraft.

Expansion of freight facilities at the area's three air terminals, especially at Kennedy, has been considerable in recent years. Kennedy's freight center, opened in 1956, originally covered 89 acres; in the late 1970s its area was 400 acres.[1] Again, in 1956 the center's then four cargo buildings and one cargo service building covered some 300,000 square feet, while today its 24 buildings have a combined area of 2.5 million square feet. Thirteen buildings have been constructed by tenants, the remainder by the airport's manager, the Port Authority of New York and New Jersey. Development of these facilities has cost the Port Authority $39 million; tenants have invested a further $69 million.

Of the eleven U.S. scheduled combination carriers which are presently tenants at Kennedy's freight center, nine are direct lessees and two (Allegheny and Braniff) are sublessees. Airlift International, Flying Tiger, and Seaboard World Airlines also lease space at the center, as do a number of supplemental and commuter airlines. In addition, about twenty foreign-flag carriers are direct lessees, while a further seventeen are sublessees or have contractual arrangements with other airlines, which, employing their own personnel, handle freight operations on their behalf. Nonairline tenants include forwarders (about 35 in all), customs house brokers, cartage companies, and agencies of the Federal Government. The freight center has postal and banking facilities and relies on its own power substation.

---

[1]This figure includes loading ramps, parking space, etc., and constitutes about eight percent of the entire airport.

Newark's considerably smaller freight facilities include three cargo buildings (each has an area of about 36,000 square feet) and one cargo service building. This freight center (29 acres) was opened in 1959 and has to date seen Port Authority investments of about $3 million. At La Guardia, the smallest of the three airports, five hangars have truck loading/unloading docks. As already noted, this terminal has no all-cargo service, and shipments must be moved from the hangars to the passenger area for loading into combination aircraft.

Two terminals, those of Lufthansa German Airlines and Emery Air Freight, are used below to illustrate various facets of the freight-handling process.

Officially inaugurated in 1973, Lufthansa's freight terminal at Kennedy Airport was constructed at a cost of $12 million; installations cost an additional $4.3 million. Since the carrier was responsible for the construction work, no rent is paid the Port Authority for the use of the building per se. The Port Authority does, however, receive close to $11,000 per month for use of the land occupied by the facility. The company's lease has a life of 20 years.

The building, a model of which is shown in figure 4, covers an area of 137,000 square feet and has a height of about 60 feet. Initially it had a handling capacity of 74,000 tons of freight per year, which is expected to rise to 260,000 tons in 1985. This anticipated growth has been taken into account in a number of ways. For example, the enclosed tarmac storage system (22 in figure 4), which holds igloos, pallets, and 10-foot and 20-foot containers (40-foot containers will be accommodated at a later point) and runs along half the building's airside, can, when required, be extended (20) to double its capacity. Similarly, the towcart stacker (13), shown with two aisles in use, will be expanded in stages until all six aisles are operational. On the landside, eight truck docks (area 2) are partially subleased to Argentina's national carrier, Aerolineas Argentinas, an arrangement which can be terminated following an increase in Lufthansa's traffic volume. A similar situation applies to spare office space(7).

In 1972 Lufthansa began using the Boeing 747 freighter on its North Atlantic flights, the first airline to do so. This aircraft, seen in figure 4 receiving freight via a special loading bridge (21), can accommodate the entire range of containers currently in use, including the 8' x 8' x 40' model. Upon leaving the loading bridge, containers enter the aircraft's main-deck compartment through a nose

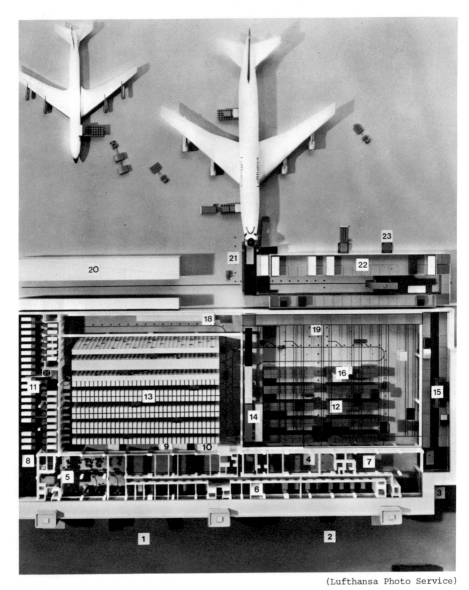

(Lufthansa Photo Service)

Fig. 4. Lufthansa's freight terminal at Kennedy Airport

door and are moved to their final position by a series of electrically powered casters and rollers. A system of locks secures the
freight. In the aircraft's lower hold, electrically driven pneumat-
ic wheels similarly bring unitized goods to their assigned position.
The lower deck consists of two sections, which together can hold
thirty LD-1 or LD-3 containers, and one compartment (800 cubic feet)
for noncontainerized items. Lower-deck freight leaves the terminal
building from airside transfer stations (23), is brought to the aircraft on mobile equipment, and is placed into the aircraft through
three doors on the freighter's right side. Only two men are required to oversee the entire loading process, which can be completed
in little more than half-an-hour.

Loading and unloading of the aircraft is computer-controlled.
An operator feeds a container's number into a computer, which,
through comparison with a predetermined loading plan, releases or
holds the merchandise in question. Transducers and sensors form
part of a computer-controlled balance mechanism, which transmits
(to the operator) a series of center of gravity and weight readings
and automatically stabilizes the aircraft during all phases of loading and unloading.

About 75 percent of the airline's freight is carried in all-
cargo aircraft. In addition to one 747, Lufthansa uses the Boeing
707 freighter in New York and has four tarmac positions available
for these smaller machines (one of which can be seen being loaded
in the upper left-hand corner of figure 4). The remaining freight,
that is, the other 25 percent, is transported in the freight section of all-purpose aircraft, which are loaded at the airline's passenger terminal in another section of the airport. Any lower-hold
pallet or container used in the 747 freighter can be carried in the
passenger version of the same aircraft or in the 707 freighter.
Freight ground-handling equipment used in the main-deck loading/un-
loading of the 707 and DC-8 is compatible with the 747's lower-lobe
system.

One of the pivotal features of the entire facility is the
elevating transfer vehicle (ETV). This device, which moves along
the entire 270-foot long track of the tarmac storage area (22), is
able to carry two 8' x 8' x 10' containers or one 8' x 8' x 20'
container and raise these for storage in one of 225 compartments
situated on four levels. A computer determines the precise location
in which any given unit is to be stored. The ETV, which has a maximum horizontal speed of 24 feet per minute and a vertical speed of
52 feet per minute, can transfer the 747's full inbound (import) and
outbound (export) main-deck loads between the loading dock (21) and

storage compartments in under 50 minutes.

Those of the inbound containers which must be broken down before their contents can leave the building travel from area (22) along a series of conveyors into break-down (also build-up) stations, of which there are five (area 19). Here the freight, depending on size and nature, is placed into towcarts and pallets. The latter, used for shipments heavier than 440 pounds and oversize items generally, are held in storage area (12) before being transferred to the terminal's landside. The towcarts (each holds about 1,300 pounds of freight), on the other hand, are moved to the ten-story towcart stacker (13), currently the tallest in the industry, for temporary storage. Consisting initially of 1,300 bins, the stacker will, when fully operational, be served by computer-controlled storing and retrieving cranes. Small shipments (one to four pounds) move to a separate upper level storage area (11). In addition, the towcarts (which travel along a single 1,200-foot long chain track conveyor with the chain countersunk in the floor) can be automatically guided to several other specific points within the building. These include the U.S. Customs office (8) and area (9), where are located rooms and facilities for imports requiring special attention (e.g., rooms for live animals, restricted articles, and especially valuable shipments, and refrigeration and deep freeze facilities). Outgoing shipments remain in area (9) until the next flight, incoming shipments until the next business day. All imported freight, irrespective of where it has been stored, is removed by truck from pickup area (1) or the special transfer station (3). The latter is used for incoming and outgoing ten- and twenty-foot containers.

Exports, which arrive in trucks in areas (2) and (3), fall into two categories: those already containerized (these move directly into storage while awaiting the next flight) and those requiring unitization. Pallets and containers are built up in area (4). In the absence of proper documentation, etc., containerization must be postponed and goods transferred to the towcart stacker (13) or storage area (12). From there they are moved to a build-up position in area (19) and used to "top off" partially filled containers.

Since frequent use of the word "storage" may have evoked a picture of large quantities of freight being stowed for considerable periods of time, a clarification is in order. A freight manager derives satisfaction not from being able to store freight but from transferring shipments as rapidly as possible from the terminal's landside to its airside, and vice versa. Anything tending to interfere with the movement of freight, such as, for instance, special handling requirements, must be dealt with quickly if the facility is to function efficiently. An air carrier has no control over the landside arrival of freight, which, in the case of Lufthansa, comes to over 200 shipments per day. Most of these, however, are brought to the terminal between three and five hours prior to departure time, which is sufficient to ensure that they will leave New York on the next flight.

Several areas/facilities of the terminal, numbered in figure 4, have not been specifically referred to in the foregoing discussion. These are: upper level offices (5 and 6), the control center for all storage operations (10), an upper level storage area for 40-foot containers (14), a storage area for 10-foot and 20-foot containers (15), upper level storage space for 10-foot containers (16), and the steering control system for pallets kept in the tarmac storage area (18).

Emery's terminal at Kennedy Airport is larger than that of any other forwarder. Built in 1963, the terminal initially had an area of 40,000 square feet, which in 1967 was expanded to 48,000 square feet. Emery has long applied computer technology to its freight-handling problems. Its New York station, as all its domestic offices, contains communications terminals, which are connected with central processing units located at Emery's headquarters in Wilton, Connecticut. Its On-Line Air Freight Control System (EMCON), which "keeps track of all shipments in Emery service," serves a wide variety of purposes. For instance, prior to 8 A.M. EMCON checks all shipments, flight schedules, etc., and notifies local Emery offices of any problems or "unusual circumstances" likely to arise during the day. Destination points can be alerted before the arrival of a given flight, permitting preestablishment of truck delivery manifests and other documents. Also, computer-produced manifests reduce paperwork and computer edits of the manifests help to route shipments correctly. Another advantage of EMCON is that it permits local personnel to make consolidation decisions based on advance traffic flow information. The shipping public has direct access to the EMCON network, and a telephone enquiry enables a shipper to establish "instantly" the location of any given shipment, its actual arrival time, the name of the person accepting the shipment, etc.

Concluding Remarks

The Port Authority of New York and New Jersey, a local public agency, is the manager of the three New York-Newark airports. The agency has the right to introduce regulations affecting traffic flows at its terminals, provided such regulations do not conflict

with the intent of Congress, that is, with the various provisions of
the Federal Aviation Act and other pertinent Federal legislation.
This junior role in the regulatory sphere is illustrated by the attempt of the agency to ban SST flights at Kennedy Airport, an attempt overruled by a Federal judge on the ground that the action was
unreasonable and discriminatory, and as such imcompatible with the
policies of the Federal Government. The New York-Newark air terminals form part of the national airport system, and, according to a
Federal directive, must be "available for public use on fair and
reasonable terms and without unjust discrimination."

More freight is enplaned in New York-Newark than in any other
U.S. airport center (table 4). The region's preeminence, both in
the field of domestic and international air transportation, reflects
in large measure a concerted drive by the Port Authority and various
airport tenants to create some of the most advanced and extensive
air freight facilities found anywhere today. Tenants include airlines, forwarders, brokerage firms, and agencies of the Federal
Government, who together offer the shipping public a comprehensive
range of freight-related services.

CHAPTER VI

INTEGRATION AND COMPETITION WITHIN THE

NEW YORK-NEWARK AIR FREIGHT SYSTEM

The preceding chapters have dealt, wholly or in part, with
various aspects of the regulatory process working within the air
freight system. The question may be asked, what is the result
the interaction between the regulators and the regulated in terms
of the scope and nature of the freight services available to ship-
pers/receivers using the New York-Newark airports? Chapter VI
provides a partial answer. It presents and examines various of
these services from the standpoint of the carriers' desire to
compete, on the one hand, and their need to cooperate and to coordinate, on the other.

The New York-Newark Air Terminal Area:
General Considerations

An air carrier's terminal area has traditionally been defined
as the zone within which its trucking operations have been recognized by the CAB as bona fide pickup and delivery service. We know
from chapter II that in the case of the New York-Newark airports
the Board, acting in response to requests made by various carriers
(especially indirect carriers), has accepted pickup and delivery
points lying substantially beyond the boundaries prescribed by its
conventional 25-mile formula. At the same time, certain carriers
(e.g., forwarders and their agents and Air Cargo, Inc. agents)
linking these points with the airports and carrying shipments
"having an immediately prior or immediately subsequent movement by
aircraft"[1] have been exempted from the ICC's certification requirements. For these points (to say nothing of those within the
25-mile zones) "services in connection with . . . air transportation"
(CAB) are the same as services "incidental to transportation by
aircraft" (ICC). The scheduled airlines have shown less interest
than the forwarders in enlarging the scope of their pickup and
delivery activities and their pickup and delivery zone lies wholly
within that of the forwarders'. The relationship between the pickup

---

[1] See above, p. 106.

and delivery boundaries and the traditional 25-mile zones is shown in figure 5.

The New York-Newark air terminal area[1] encompasses thirty counties (wholly or partially) in the states of Connecticut, New Jersey, and New York, covers an area of approximately 6,600 square miles, and has a population of about 17.3 million (1977). Slightly more than sixty percent (by weight) of the freight leaving its airports by air (i.e., outbound freight) originates within its boundaries; conversely, about sixty percent of the inbound air freight is trucked to destination points within the area (table 15, chapter VII). It may be thought of as a functional region having as its nodal point the airport complex consisting of John F. Kennedy International, La Guardia, and Newark International airports.

The air terminal area contains the New York-Newark-Jersey City Standard Consolidated Statistical Area, the nation's foremost manufacturing region. Here are found representatives of virtually all of the over 400 industries recognized by the United States Bureau of the Census. On the basis of employment, the leading industry groups are: apparel, printing and publishing, electrical and electronic equipment, food and kindred products, textile mill products, fabricated metal products, chemicals, and nonelectrical machinery. The area is also one of the nation's most important transportation centers. Scheduled steamship services, for instance, link it with about 380 foreign ports. Over 400 long-haul trucking concerns (to mention only those with terminals/offices in New York-Newark) operate between it and points throughout the United States. It supports regular air service to about 350 domestic and 350 foreign airport cities.

Air Cargo, Inc.

The overall responsibilities of Air Cargo, Inc. (ACI) and its relationship with the airlines and the Civil Aeronautics Board were discussed in chapter I, where we saw how a series of contracts

---

[1] The New York-Newark air terminal area as defined here is the zone in which the indirect air carriers may offer pickup and delivery service. (Strictly speaking, there is no one single air terminal area, since the points served by one operator may differ from those served by another.) It includes, but is not to be confused with, the smaller zone within which the Air Cargo, Inc. agents are active. Its boundary (figure 5) is a generalized line based on the pickup and delivery tariffs of several of the major forwarders, namely: Airborne, Air Express International, Burlington Northern Air Freight, CF Air Freight, Emery, PIE Air Freight Forwarding, USAIR Freight, and WTC Air Freight. The Newark 25-mile zone has been measured from Newark's municipal boundary; the New York 25-mile zone from New York City's municipal boundary.

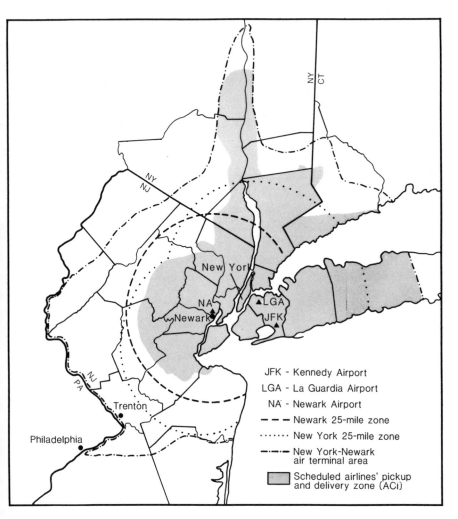

Fig. 5. The New York-Newark air terminal area (1976)

and agreements between ACI and various surface carriers enable
the scheduled airlines to offer a combined air-surface movement
between points not directly linked by air service. The two distinct
types of surface operations involved, local pickup and delivery
work, and long-haul service, are now examined with respect to New
York-Newark. Also outlined is the corporation's contribution to
inter-airport transportation.

Pickup and Delivery Service

As the contracting agent for the airlines, ACI negotiates on
their behalf the rates, points to be served, coordination of motor
and air schedules, and other particulars pertaining to motor transportation. (An antitrust exemption has traditionally protected
these arrangements.[1]) Individual airlines are free to set their
own rates if dissatisfied with those negotiated by ACI. Air Cargo,
Inc. agents are able to execute one airbill for the entire
door-to-door movement, an important consideration from the shipper's
standpoint. Pickup and delivery service may not be lawfully performed for an airline under the ICC's commercial zone exemption.[2]

Of the ten local cartage contractors serving ACI's New York-
Newark air terminal area (1976), eight carry general merchandise,
the other two restricting themselves to perishable items. Their
agency status confers several advantages: (1) contractors are
assured of prompt payment (they are paid by ACI rather than by
members of the shipping public), (2) their liability (in the event
a consignment is lost or damaged) is covered by ACI's own policy,
(3) agents are recognized by shippers as the only local motor
carriers having contractual agreements with the scheduled airlines.
Agency status, however, also has a major drawback, for, as one
pickup/delivery carrier once complained to the ICC, agents "are
entirely dependent upon the whims of [ACI, which] . . . under the
terms of [its] agreement[s], could terminate the agency contract[s]
and thus put [agents] out of business."[3] (A number of agents now
also hold authority as long-haul carriers and are thus shielded
from the "whims" of ACI.) It is this loss of independence which

---

[1] Big Bear Cartage, Inc. v. Air Cargo, Inc., 419 F. Supp. 982 (N.D. Ill.
1976); Frank W. Scroggins v. Air Cargo, Inc., 534 F. 2d 1124 (5th Cir. 1976).
The corporation's antitrust immunity has not covered activities not expressly
approved by the Board. Breen Air Freight, Ltd. v. Air Cargo, Inc., 470 F. 2d
767 (2d Cir. 1972).

[2] See above, p.106, note 4.

[3] Commodity Haulage Corp. Common Carrier Application, 69 MCC 527, 528 (1957)

has caused the forwarders, who in 1961 were given the right to become cartage contractors, to generally shun Air Cargo, Inc. (In addition to participating in ACI's overall pickup/delivery program, two of the system's leading freight carriers, American Airlines and United Airlines, have entered into exclusive arrangements with individual ACI agents. Trucks leased under these arrangements give the airlines greater control over surface operations. Also, the trucks are marked with the pertinent airline's name, giving the latter additional exposure in the market.) Each agent serves a particular region within ACI's pickup and delivery zone, which is divided into ten rate areas; pickup and delivery charges are uniform for points lying within a specific rate area. Table 5 summarizes the rates.

Let us briefly consider the work of the zone's foremost pickup and delivery agent, ACI's Trucking Division (the Division differs from other agents in several respects; its operations, however, illustrate various aspects of pickup and delivery service as a whole). The Division is the zone's largest cartage agent both in terms of traffic handled and number of trucks (about fifty) and is unique in that it is the only trucking concern owned outright by ACI. Its activities are restricted to four New York City boroughs: Bronx, Brooklyn, Manhattan, and Queens. It handles about 200,000 shipments per year and makes, on an average day, 130 pickup stops and 225 delivery stops. Manhattan accounts for roughly half the Division's traffic volume, with the other half more or less equally distributed among the three other boroughs. Shipments are picked up within about two hours of the time a consignor's call has been received. The emphasis is on pickups in the afternoon and deliveries in the morning, with a weight ratio (pickup:delivery) of 3:2 being achieved (this imbalace is greater with most other agents). The prime departure time for all-cargo aircraft is from 11 P.M. to 4 A.M., and any special processing or handling of freight (e.g., containerization) leaving on night flights must be accomplished well before that time. The average weight of an unconsolidated outbound shipment, both for the four-borough area and for ACI's pickup and delivery zone as a whole, is about 190 pounds.

About 35 percent (by weight) of the Division's outbound traffic has been containerized by shippers (most other agents report considerably lower figures), the LD-3 (table 7) being the most popular container type. The Division states it can load/unload an LD-3 container in half the time required to handle 200 pounds of loose freight. It will containerize loose freight for shippers if

222

TABLE 5

ACI PICKUP AND DELIVERY RATES IN THE NEW YORK-NEWARK AIR TERMINAL AREA

Rate Area	Airport	Minimum	Rate in Dollars per 100 Pounds[a]			
			100	1000	2000	5000 pounds
Connecticut						
Fairfield Co.	JFK & La G	8.90	4.0	3.80	3.55	2.50
New Jersey						
Bergen Co.	Newark	6.95	3.40	2.90	2.60	1.75
Essex, Hudson, Morris, Passaic, Union Cos.	Newark	6.75	3.35	3.20	3.05	2.20
Middlesex, Somerset Cos.	Newark	6.75	3.40	3.25	3.00	2.40
New York						
Bronx, Brooklyn, Queens	JFK & La G	8.75	5.90	4.85	4.60	3.10
Manhattan	JFK & La G	9.95	6.70	4.85	4.60	3.10
Staten I	Newark	8.75	4.30	3.95	3.75	2.65
Dutchess, Orange, Putnam, Rockland, Ulster, Westchester Cos.	JFK & La G	8.90	4.00	3.80	3.55	2.50
Nassau Co.	JFK & La G	7.95	3.50	3.05	2.90	1.95
Suffolk Co.	JFK & La G	8.30	3.65	3.25	3.05	2.15

SOURCE: Air Cargo, Inc.

[a] Effective September, 1976. The first column shows the minimum charge; the remaining columns show the rate per 100 pounds for various weight brackets.

requested to do so and assesses a charge of 60 cents per 100 pounds for the service. Shippers, however, must solve their own routing problems; they are given a blank airway bill and the Division (that is, ACI) thus avoids any bias towards a particular airline. If difficulties subsequently arise and a shipper wishes to trace a consignment, he will be referred to the originating airline. The Division does not complete export/import documents, nor does it offer various other specialized services commonly associated with brokers and forwarders.

Air Cargo, Inc. has a pronounced interest in encouraging the use of containers, and at present an estimated ten percent (by weight) of its outbound New York-Newark traffic is containerized by shippers. The figure is growing by about ten percent annually. These numbers are modest, for only a small proportion of shippers generates traffic in such volume that containerization is justified. Containerization faces another hurdle since relatively few air shippers have the physical facilities required for container operations. Generally speaking, ACI agents will perform container pickup/delivery service only if truck-bed platforms are between 44 and 52 inches above street level. Where platforms do not conform to this specification, shippers and consignees must provide their own container-handling equipment.

Since, in average terms, about eighty percent of the total time taken in moving an air freight shipment from consignor to consignee is spent on the ground, any technique which results in more efficient ground handling is of interest to all those connected with the air freight industry. Containerization is clearly one such technique. A major aid to intermodal integration, containerization has an impact on virtually every sector of the industry. Thus, for instance, it is of concern to the shipper because it can lead to a significant lowering of his transportation bill. Savings are realized in several areas: (1) transportation rates, (2) packaging, (3) terminal handling, (4) terminal space requirements, (5) damage, (6) loss and theft, and (7) insurance rates. Containerization eases congestion at transportation interfaces and, by raising stacking efficiency, contributes to higher freight densities and revenue payloads for the airlines. Air Cargo, Inc. has built incentive discounts into its container pickup and delivery rates, as can be seen from a comparison of tables 5 and 6. The chief physical properties of the major container types are shown in table 7, which also indicates the type of aircraft for which the containers have been designed. Table 7 also gives some idea of

TABLE 6

ACI CONTAINER PICKUP AND DELIVERY RATES IN THE NEW YORK-NEWARK AIR TERMINAL AREA

Rate Area	Airport	Rate for Given Container Type in Dollars[a]									
		A-1 / A-1	B	B-2	D	FTC	LD-1	LD-3	LD-7	LD-11	QD / E
New Jersey											
Bergen Co.	Newark	77.00	45.00	25.00	15.00	37.50	43.00	37.50	77.00	65.00	6.95
Essex, Hudson, Morris, Passaic, Union Cos.	Newark	86.50	50.75	26.50	16.75	41.50	45.00	41.50	77.00	66.25	6.75
Middlesex, Somerset Cos.	Newark	88.00	59.00	31.00	17.00	43.50	43.50	43.50	88.00	68.00	13.00
New York											
Bronx, Brooklyn, Queens	JFK	71.00	57.50	31.50	18.75	39.75	46.75	39.75	71.00	71.00	8.75
Manhattan	JFK	71.00	57.50	31.50	81.75	39.75	46.75	39.75	71.00	71.00	9.95
Dutchess, Orange, Putnam, Rockland, Ulster, Westchester Cos.	JFK	95.00	60.00	33.00	22.00	49.00	50.75	49.00	95.00	70.00	8.90
Nassau Co.	JFK	80.00	53.10	28.35	17.00	40.00	45.00	40.00	80.00	63.00	7.95
Suffolk Co.	JFK	85.00	56.70	29.70	18.00	44.00	49.00	44.00	85.00	67.00	8.30

SOURCE: Air Cargo, Inc.

[a] Effective September, 1976. Multiple container rates are also available. Weight specifications for the various containers are shown in table 7.

how various containers are built up into larger units, and
lists, for each container type, the airlines' minimum chargeable
load.

Air/Truck Service

Interline agreements between ACI and fourteen over-the-road
trucking concerns form the basis of ACI's air/truck service, a
cooperative effort under which truckers and scheduled airlines
exchange traffic with each other. The actual transfer takes place
at the airports, and, within this context, all three of New York-
Newark's air terminals are recognized as "interchange airports."
From the shipper's viewpoint, one of the most attractive features
of this service is its utilization of a single shipping document
(air/truck airbill), relieving him of the necessity of completing
separate surface and air way bills. (The truckers must purchase
the air/truck bill from the air carriers. Some truckers reject
this arrangement, and here separate documents must be used for the
air and surface segments of a through movement.) Rates and tariffs
are also greatly simplified, because for the purpose of this program
the commodity classifications of the airlines and surface operators
are unified, charges being quoted under a common FAK (freight all
kinds) formula. The air/truck program has traditionally involved
the two major regulatory bodies discussed in this book, the CAB
and the ICC. The former (prior to deregulation) approved the air
portion of a through movement while the latter has sanctioned the
surface haul. The liability imposed on motor carriers by the Commission is generally greater than the liability of the air carriers.
The ICC's released rate orders have enabled surface operators in
the air/truck program to limit their liability and align their
rates with those of the airlines.

Combination rates are used to compute the total charge for
an interline shipment. Thus, an entire door-to-door movement could
have the following components (not all necessarily apply in every
instance): (1) the motor carrier intercity charge, (2) the motor
carrier valuation charge, (3) the air carrier intercity charge,
(4) the air carrier valuation charge, and (5) ACI's pickup and
delivery charge. Additional charges, such as for the collecting
of C.O.D. payments, may also be assessed. It is the responsibility
of the delivering carrier (provided his tariff includes this
service) to collect the amount due, which is then remitted to the
shipper. If for some reason a delivery cannot be made, the originating carrier contacts the shipper and assists in any way possible

TABLE 7

CONTAINERS HANDLED AT THE NEW YORK-NEWARK AIRPORTS

Aircraft	Type	Owner		Cubic Capacity	External Dimensions and Cubic Displ.	Minimum Chargeable Pounds	Weight		Allowable Tare (lbs.)	Handling Features for Shippers
							Maximum Gross Weight			
FREIGHTERS	A-1	Airline Provided		393 cu. ft.	L 88" W 125" H 87" cu. displ. 425 cu. ft.	3,000	13,300		Actual Weight	Dolly Transporters Available. Can be Pallet & Net
	A-2	Airline Provided		440 cu. ft.	L 88" W 125" H 87" cu. displ. 475 cu. ft.	3,200	12,500		Actual Weight	Dolly Transporters Available Can be Pallet & Net
	B	Shipper Provided	(Insert for "A")	Varies	L 84" W 58" H 76"-45" cu. displ. 197.70 cu. ft.	1,800	5,000		200	Forkable
	B-2	Shipper Provided	(Insert for "A")	Varies	L 42" W 58" H 76"-45" cu. displ. 98.85 cu. ft.	900	2,500		100	Forkable
	D	Shipper Provided	(Insert for "A")	Varies	L 58" W 42" H 45" cu. displ. 63.44 cu. ft.	500	2,000		63	Forkable
	FTC	Airline Provided		151 cu. ft.	L 81" W 60.4" H 62.75" cu. displ. 171.5 cu. ft.	3,200	4,500		Actual Weight	Forkable

	Provided	Shape	Volume	Dimensions				Notes
WIDE BODIES								
ARA or M-1	Airline Provided		572 cu. ft.	L 125" W 96" H 96" cu. displ. 666 cu. ft.	4,400	15,000	1,241	Picked up or delivered on conventional truck trailer chassis.
M-2	Airline Provided		1077 cu. ft.	L 240" W 96" H 96" cu. displ. 1280 cu. ft.	12,363	25,000	2,116	Picked up or delivered on conventional truck trailer chassis.
LD-3 LD-1	Airline Provided		150 cu. ft.	L 79.0" L 62.0" W 60.0" H 64.0" cu. displ. 166.0 cu. ft.	1,100	3,500	Actual Weight	Dolly Transporters Available
LD-N	Shipper Provided	(Insert for LD-3)	Varies	L 56" W 55" H 57" cu. displ. 101.6 cu. ft.	900	3,160	100	Forkable
LD-7 LD-9	Airline Provided		355 cu. ft.	L 125" W 88" H 63" cu. displ. 401 cu. ft.	2,800	10,400	Actual Weight	Dolly Transporters Available
LD-11 LD-5	Airline Provided		265 cu. ft.	L 125" W 60" H 64" cu. displ. 277 cu. ft.	1,800	7,000	Actual Weight	Dolly Transporters Available

TABLE 7—Continued

Aircraft	Type	Owner		Cubic Capacity	External Dimensions and Cubic Displ.	Minimum Chargeable Pounds	Weight Maximum Gross Weight	Allowable Tare (lbs.)	Handling Features for Shippers
STANDARD BODIES	QD	Shipper Provided		Varies	L 39.5" W 27.5" H 21" cu. displ. 12.0 cu. ft.	100	400	13	Side Handles Recommended
	E	Shipper Provided		Varies	L 42" W 29" H 25.5" cu. displ. 17.97 cu. ft.	130	500	18	Side Handles Recommended

SOURCE: Air Cargo, Inc.

NOTE: Dimensions and weights are approximate and may vary from airline to airline.

to resolve the problem at hand. The responsibility for lost, delayed, or damaged merchandise rests with whichever carrier had custody of the consignment at the time of its loss, etc. Originating carriers bear the responsibility for any improper documentation resulting in the refusal of connecting carriers to accept shipments for further transportation.

About fifty percent (by weight) of the freight system's outbound traffic carried by ICC-regulated motor carriers is accounted for by truckers associated with the air/truck program. The average weight of an outbound shipment is of the order of 210 pounds, making it about 20 pounds heavier than its ACI counterpart in the pickup and delivery zone. The truckers' customers are located in outlying areas (relative to the air terminals) and in the course of their business operations are essentially oriented towards surface modes for their regular transportation needs. Their consignments normally differ appreciably in terms of bulkiness, density, nature and value of the product, etc., from those of shippers specializing in air transportation. Thus, when these off-line shippers use air transportation (frequently to fill special orders or because of an emergency situation, etc.), their shipments tend to be somewhat heavier than those tendered by regular air shippers.

Roughly ten percent (by weight) of the truckers' outbound traffic has been containerized by shippers; containerization is encouraged through the use of discount rates but remains the responsibility of the shipper. Most truckers will offer advice on routing matters if requested to do so, though the scope of such advice is necessarily curtailed by their limited field of responsibility. Truckers, unlike forwarders, do not have door-to-door responsibility and cannot offer their customers a comprehensive tracing service. Also, documentation (domestic and foreign), labelling, etc., are usually left to the shipper.

The air/truck program connects about 430 points with one or more airports in New York-Newark, the distribution of points served being approximately: (1) Connecticut--12 percent, (2) New Jersey--40 percent, (3) New York--17 percent, (4) Pennsylvania--30 percent, and (5) the Washington, D.C. area--1 percent. (The service areas of individual truckers are depicted in figure 6.[1] Washington, D.C. is not included.) In general, the communities involved are small: 63 percent have a population figure below 5,000; 17 percent between

---

[1] Figure 6 is based on pickup/delivery tariffs. The areas, shown in generalized form, represent operating territories within which the truckers offer regular runs to and from the New York-Newark air terminals.

5,000 and 10,000; and a further 15 percent between 10,000 and 50,000. About 5 percent of the points have a population in excess of 50,000. Since some of the larger centers are airport cities, the question arises, why are the truckers' shipments not diverted to their air terminals instead of being hauled to New York-Newark? Several answers suggest themselves: (1) the local airports offer only a limited number of flights and do not have direct connections with major air freight markets, (2) the local airports do not have all-cargo service, (3) the local airports are not served by overseas flights. A consignor could, if he chose, enplane a shipment at a local airport (say, Albany) and then have it transferred to another flight at Kennedy Airport. Ordinarily, however, there would be little inducement for him to do so, since the Albany to New York truck schedules dovetail with Kennedy departure times making possible next day delivery at the destination airport city.

Air Cargo, Inc. emphasizes that its connecting truckers are specialists, that is, they are "not truckmen otherwise involved in business not related to air freight." This specialization is not their's alone, for many other ICC-approved truckers hauling shipments to and from the airports operate throughout the New York-Newark area, making this sector of the air freight industry far more competitive than figure 6 would suggest. (For instance, about six motor carriers specializing in air freight operate in R & G Air Freight's service territory.) Also, of course, the New York metropolitan area is served by numerous other over-the-road carriers (some 1,200 trucking concerns, for example, connect New York-Newark with points throughout Connecticut; about 2,500 with points in New Jersey), which, while not normally concerned with air freight, might make an occasional trip to one of the airports. Additional competition is provided by "gypsies" (truckers operating unlawfully without ICC authority), who, in the words of one ACI trucker (Con-Ov-Air), "select the best accounts in the area" and offer rates which might be as much as seventy percent below those of the regulated motor carriers.

The competitive situation is further complicated by the growth of the New York-Newark air terminal area, which has made it possible for the forwarders to offer pickup and delivery service at points once served exclusively by ICC-regulated truckers (figure 2). Their attitude towards the air terminal area divides the truckers into two categories: those who consider the area too large and are actively opposed to it, and those who do not view forwarder pickup/delivery rights as excessive. These two viewpoints reflect a

231

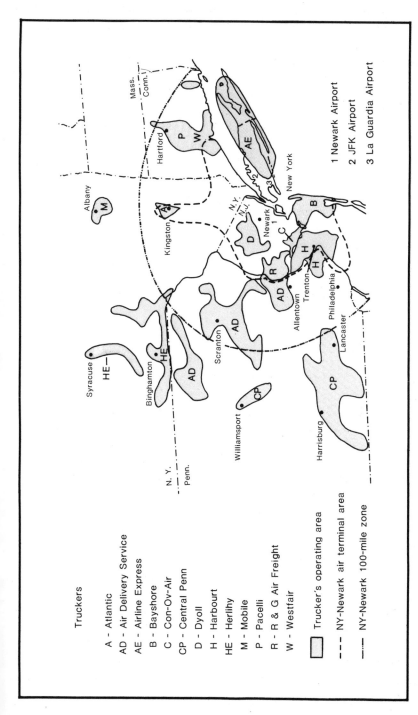

Truckers

A - Atlantic
AD - Air Delivery Service
AE - Airline Express
B - Bayshore
C - Con-Ov-Air
CP - Central Penn
D - Dyoll
H - Harbourt
HE - Herlihy
M - Mobile
P - Pacelli
R - R & G Air Freight
W - Westfair

▨ Trucker's operating area

--- NY-Newark air terminal area

—— NY-Newark 100-mile zone

1 Newark Airport

2 JFK Airport

3 La Guardia Airport

Fig. 6. Operating areas of ACI truckers serving the New York-Newark airports (1976)

difference in the relationship the forwarders have established with the individual motor carriers. Thus, where forwarders use their own trucks, they compete with the motor carriers; on the other hand, if they use the truckers' equipment, they are looked upon as customers. Motor carriers objecting to the size of the air terminal area include: Air Delivery Service, Atlantic Air Freight, Central Penn, Dyoll, Harbourt, R & G Air Freight, as well as a number of non-ACI truckers. They contend that the scope of forwarder operations has been enlarged to the point where bona fide pickup and delivery work, performed in conjunction with airline schedules, has been transformed into independent line-haul service. Strict adherence to the CAB's conventional 25-mile pickup/delivery zone would remove the forwarders as competitors from all outlying service areas and would be openly welcomed by these motor carriers. As indicated above, not all truckers are adversely affected by the forwarders' activities. For Bayshore Air Freight, for instance, forwarders have become important customers and the company has entered into agency agreements with several of these indirect carriers.

In northern and central New Jersey forwarder competition has become particularly acute. Dyoll Delivery Service, for example, referring to a practice found in much of the New York-Newark air terminal area, notes that several of the larger forwarders (e.g., Airborne, Emery, and WTC), using their own trucks "make special runs to customers in our areas [especially Morris County, N.J.] to pick up or deliver several thousand pounds of freight; yet, when not worth their while, they will call on Dyoll to deliver or pick up minimum shipments for them."[1] In other instances forwarders haul freight across northern/central New Jersey before releasing it to truckers in the vicinity of the Pennsylvania-New Jersey boundary for onward transportation. This, too, represents a loss for truckers, who in the absence of the forwarders would undertake the entire surface movement themselves. The case of Harbourt Air Freight Service is especially helpful in illustrating (from the truckers' viewpoint) the harmful impact of trucker-forwarder rivalry. This trucking company, which was unsuccessful in its attempt to halt penetration of its operating territory by Emery and other forwarders (chapter II), has seen its market share fall from close to ninety percent to about thirty percent. At one time Emery alone accounted for twenty percent of the company's gross annual revenues; with the

---

[1]Verified Statement of Roger Doll for Dyoll Delivery Service, Inc., Docket MC-C-3437 (1977), p. 5.

xpansion of the Newark air terminal area in the late 1960s, however,
mery withdrew most of its traffic from Harbourt. This action,
long with other business losses, brought the company close to
ankruptcy (1971). It survived, but had to reduce its twice-a-day
uns to/from the New York-Newark air terminals to once per day for
ewark and Kennedy and to a "call basis only" for La Guardia. In
ddition, Harbourt raised its rates and began to develop revenue
ources outside the air freight industry.

Forwarders offer the shipper single-entity responsibility and
an quote door-to-door rates. This gives them considerable flexi-
ility in rate-making, since low surface rates can be offset through
n adjustment of those charges pertaining to the air portion of a
hrough movement. Their air rates, in other words, can serve as a
ushion for ground services provided at rates designed to attract
raffic which might otherwise be tendered directly to the long-haul
otor carriers. In accusing the forwarders of unfair competitive
ractices, the truckers point to the disparity between their own
verall financial situation and that of the forwarders, and speak
f their inability to compete with the latter on an equal basis.
Table 8 compares gross annual revenues of several of the leading
orwarders and ICC-regulated motor carriers serving the New York-
ewark airports.) The forwarders deny that their surface rates are

TABLE 8

TRUCKER V. FORWARDER REVENUES (1976)

	Truckers		Air Freight Forwarders	
arrier	Total Rev-enues ($)	Air Freight Revenues ($)	Carrier	Revenues ($)
an's Auto	1,700,000	714,000	Emery	296,944,000
erek	1,628,643	1,628,643	Airborne	130,482,000
arbourt	900,000	870,000	Air Exp.Int.	96,894,000
ayshore	744,000	724,000	Burlington	72,214,000
& G	609,484	609,484	United Parcel	55,876,000
yoll	316,266	227,266	WTC	51,395,000
irp.Tr. Serv.	201,135	184,493	Profit by Air	34,192,000

SOURCES: Company statements.

established at uneconomical levels as contended by many trucking
fficials. Similarly, they reject the charge that they use their
wn trucks (or those of contractors) solely to serve large-volume
oints while calling on the motor common carriers to handle their
relatively unprofitable accounts. Their protestations, however,
inspire little confidence, for it remains a fact that the forwarders

are highly selective in the pickup/delivery points they choose to serve with equipment under their direct control. Also, the forwar ders' rates (for shipments of up to about fifty pounds[1]) appear to be consistently lower than those of the regulated truckers, who, depending totally on surface transportation, can be expected to align their charges more closely with the true cost of ground serv

Inter-Airport Transportation

A shipment flown to, say, Newark Airpot may have to be transferred to an aircraft leaving from one of the system's two other airports. Air Cargo, Inc.'s Trucking Division provides a "shuttle" service between the three airports, the airlines absorbi the cost of the inter-airport movement. The Trucking Division doe not hold an ICC certificate and thus cannot operate as a long-haul motor carrier. Inter-airport truck runs are intended to meet the needs of ACI's airline owners as a whole and, where they fail to satisfy a particular carrier's requirements, they have been replaced or supplemented by that carrier's own trucking arrangemen

The airports are also linked through the helicopter flights New York Airways. The company is affiliated with Air Cargo, Inc. is the only carrier whose pickup and delivery functions are effec- tuated through an air, rather than a ground, movement. Its aircra (three Sikorsky Mark II helicopters) travel from La Guardia to Kennedy airport in five minutes, from La Guardia to Newark in eigh minutes, and from Newark to Kennedy in ten minutes. Flights which commence at 6:43 A.M. and terminate at 10:07 P.M. (Winter schedule 1975) arrive at each of the three airports at approximately 30-min intervals.

Each of the helicopters, which carry passengers, is equippe with six cargo bins ranging in capacity from 26.5 cubic feet to 33.6 cubic feet. The company transports some 35,000 pounds of inter-airport freight per month and does not accept units weighing over 150 pounds or exceeding 20 in. x 25 in. x 60 in. The average weight of a shipment is 28 pounds.

New York Airways' work is restricted to inter-airport (and heliport) service. Its trucks may not be used to carry merchandis in off-airport situations. After freight has been removed from a helicopter, the consignees (airlines, forwarders) are notified of i

---

[1] A few truckers report a higher figure. (For ACI's local pickup/deliver agents the figure is about 25 pounds.)

rrival; in the case of off-airline consignees, the company contacts trucker who handles the onward transportation.

Joint Air-Truck Service

Section 1003 of the Federal Aviation Act authorizes the airlines to "establish reasonable through service and joint rates" with CC-regulated surface carriers. A few airlines have taken advantage f the Section 1003 provisions, establishing single factor through ates with individual trucking concerns. Generally offered only t selected points within a motor carrier's operating territory Harbourt [figure 6], for instance, has joint air-truck agreements ith the Flying Tiger Line and United Airlines, covering about 12 oints and 40 points, respectively), joint air-truck rates are romotional in nature, tending to be lower than combination rates. nother advantage for the shipper is that the door-to-door charges re found in a single publication. The Flying Tiger Line and United irlines are the two principal air carriers offering joint air-truck ates at points in the tri-state area; Flying Tiger provides these ates in conjunction with about seven motor carriers, United ith two.

Despite their promotional features, joint air-surface opera-ions have met with only limited acceptance. This, many truckers eel, is due to the airlines' insufficiently vigorous marketing trategy. Also, a number of truckers have declined to participate n the service, citing difficulties in reaching intercarrier agree-ent on rates. Another hurdle the service faces is the unwillingness f some truckers to set up a separate rate regime for selected points n their operating territory. The airlines, too, appear less than nthusiastic about this form of air-surface coordination, and only our have joint air-truck rate tariffs on file with the Board (1977). ne of these, Flying Tiger, has stated that it may dismantle its oint air-surface program ("Skyroad"), citing such drawbacks as: (1) he difficulties posed by lack of trucker interest, (2) the program's imited applicability (mainly large-volume traffic points are nvolved), and (3) the time needed to prepare and file tariffs. In he course of Congressional hearings (1977) the company advocated egislation permitting the common ownership of direct air and sur-ace carriers. Flying Tiger has indicated that, as a result of leregulation, it will seek new contractual arrangements with ong-haul motor carriers.

The advantages of an industry-wide joint air-motor rules ariff, covering, inter alia, acceptance rules, claims procedures,

declared value rules, liability limits, and shipping documents,
have been recognized by the Civil Aeronautics Board, which in June
of 1977 authorized joint air-motor rules tariff discussions between
motor carrier officials and airline representatives. A consolidate
air-motor rules tariff has long been advocated by various members
of the air freight industry but, given the many practical difficulties facing any joint enterprise involving so many carriers, remain
as yet a distant goal. One of the major difficulties here appears
to be the carriers' inability to reconcile their differences
regarding liability rules. Another problem is the reluctance of the
airlines to antagonize the forwarders who, generally speaking, are
opposed to an expansion of joint air-truck services. It should als
be noted that Congress' deregulation of air freight transportation
represents an additional complication since it has stripped the
Board of the right to accept or reject tariff rules on the basis of
their justness/reasonableness, leaving individual carriers free to
introduce rules which had earlier been declared unlawful. The
initial air-truck tariff discussions have brought together official
of the Air Freight Motor Carriers Conference and representatives of
Airlift International, American Airlines, Continental Airlines,
Delta Air Lines, Flying Tiger Line, Seaboard World Airlines, Trans
World Airlines, and United Airlines. As the Airline Tariff Publish
ing Company pointed out to the Board in a letter of February 25,
1977, any joint air-truck rules tariff which may finally be adopted
can only be "as nearly uniform as the best interests of the individual participating carriers will permit."

Substitute Service

Under certain circumstances, direct and indirect air carriers
may utilize motor carrier service in lieu of air transportation.
Such substitutions are not to be confused with other forms of
air-surface transportation, from which they differ in a number of
ways. Thus, whereas the air-truck through movements discussed abov
may involve any point (provided it has been approved by the ICC and
until recently, the CAB), motor-for-air substitutions can be offere
only between airport cities. Their scope is substantially greater
than that of pickup and delivery service, and they are excluded fro
the joint board provisions of the Federal Aviation Act's section
1003. Also, under substitution rules all routing arrangements are
the responsibility of the air carrier (unless otherwise specified b
the shipper), and it is its tariff which applies to the entire
movement.

237

The Board's statutory authority over substitute transportation
is based on sections 204(a)[1] and 403(a)[2] of the Federal Aviation
Act. Its stance vis-à-vis such transportation, however, can be
viewed in a somethat broader context. Substitutions offer advantages to both the shipping public and the air carriers. They, for
instance: (1) encourage the use of air transportation by connecting
airport cities with larger air traffic hubs having superior air
service, (2) enable air carriers to offer single-entity responsibility between more points, (3) enhance the air carriers'
operational flexibility, and (4) can contribute in certain cases to
lower rates because participating carriers are not subject to the
expense of maintaining joint air-truck tariffs. The agency recognizes these advantages and its acceptance of substitutions
represents a response to Congress' directive that it encourage and
promote the nation's air transportation industry. The Supreme
Court has held that substitutions are supportive of the national
transportation policy and has affirmed their legality.[3]

The earliest detailed consideration of surface-for-air substitute service arose out of the Flying Tiger Line's desire to suspend
its flights at Philadelphia and truck that city's freight to Newark
airport (1957). Philadelphia, an intermediate point on Flying
Tiger's transcontinental route, was a relatively small generator of
air freight, and the company, then in the process of replacing its
C-46 equipment with the larger Lockheed Constellation, concluded
the city's shippers could be served more effectively via Newark
airport. Flying Tiger had been providing C-46 feeder flights
between Philadelphia and Detroit; at the latter point traffic was
transshipped and flown to the West Coast, making possible
second-morning delivery in Los Angeles. Under the proposed service
Philadelphia's freight was to be trucked to Newark, loaded into the
new aircraft at about 11 P.M., and flown to California, with a
resulting first-morning delivery in the Los Angeles area. A service

[1] "The Board is empowered to perform such acts, to conduct such investigations, to issue and amend such orders, and to make and amend such general or
special rules, regulations, and procedure, pursuant to and consistent with the
provisions of this Act, as it shall deem necessary to carry out the provisions
of, and to exercise and perform its powers and duties under this Act." 72 Stat.
743, 49 U.S.C. 1324.

[2] See above, p. 111, note 3.

[3] American Trucking Associations, Inc. v. Atchison, Topeka and Santa Fe
Railway Co., 387 U.S. 397 (1967). At issue here was the right of motor and water
carriers to participate in TOFC ("piggyback") service.

control system had been set up at Newark and was to ensure that
Philadelphia shippers were allotted the same departure priority as
shippers in the New York-Newark area. Flying Tiger's use of truck
hauls between Philadelphia and Newark Airport, the CAB concluded,
served the public interest, and the substitution was duly authoriz
The agency's decision, which rested on

> such matters as general practices in the industry, the distance of the airp
> from the community to be served, the availability of other airports, the
> speed, convenience, and frequency of the service that can be offered to the
> community through one or the other airport, the relative cost to the carrie
> of serving the community through the available airports, etc.,[1]

was immediately challenged by the City of Philadelphia but was
sustained by a Federal court of appeals, which ascribed the city's
opposition largely to the fact that its "pride ha[d] been hurt" by
the loss of Tiger's direct service at Philadelphia International
Airport.[2]

A number of criticisms regarding substitute motor-for-air
transportation were voiced at the time the Board made known its
Flying Tiger decision. Some of these have surfaced again in
connection with more recent proceedings and are of interest here
because they illustrate the misconceptions which continue to surro
various aspects of substitute service. The Board's critics have
contended that: (1) in approving long-distance surface hauls the
CAB is arrogating to itself the right to regulate surface
transportation; (2) since the airlines involved do not hold appropriate ICC authority, they should be barred from offering surface
transportation; (3) an airline must serve a certificated point
through the airport nearest to that point; and (4) the authorized
substitute movement does not constitute air transportation within
the meaning of the Federal Aviation Act. In turning to points
(1) and (2), it should be stressed at the outset that the CAB has
issued no overall distance rule regarding the surface segment of a
air-surface movement. Absence of a formal mileage restriction,
however, does not mean that substitutions of unlimited scope can
or will be automatically approved. Thus, in accepting Flying Tige
Philadelphia-Newark truck haul, the agency rejected any suggestion
"that substantial surface transportation is available to air carri
for the performance of air transportation service at all times and

---

[1] The Flying Tiger Line, Inc., Air-Truck Service, pp. 244-245.

[2] City of Philadelphia v. Civil Aeronautics Board, 289 F. 2d 770, 773
(D.C. Cir. 1961).

ithout limit."[1]   When, several years later, Trans World Airlines
equested approval of substitute service between Kennedy Airport,
n the one hand, and Norfolk and Charleston, on the other (distances
f 291 and 639 miles, respectively), the company was told that
urface hauls of such magnitude were incompatible with its certifi-
ate obligation.   The CAB's ruling in cases of this type has not
inged on an applicant's status vis-à-vis the Interstate Commerce
ommission.   Rather, sections 204(a) and 403(a) of the Federal
viation Act serve as the basis for the Board's approval of
ubstitutions, and it has been emphasized on several occasions that
uch approval is not to be construed as a challenge to the
ommission's authority over interstate surface transportation.   The
oard's position, clearly set forth in Flying Tiger, is that it is

> not asserting jurisdiction over the motor carrier [performing the substitute
> service] . . . . Whether the . . . truck haul should be considered as
> incidental to air transportation within the meaning of the Interstate
> Commerce Act, and thereby exempt from economic regulation under that statute,
> is a matter for the Interstate Commerce Commission.[2]

imilarly, in the aforementioned Trans World Airlines proceeding the
oard pointed out that, despite the application's dismissal, the
irline, "of course," remained "free to provide the integrated
ervices by means of joint arrangements with a surface carrier
olding such authority from the ICC as may be required."[3]   Other
riticisms ([3] and [4] above) were that termination of Flying
iger's operations at Philadelphia International Airport weakened
he quality of Philadelphia's air services and represented a viola-
ion of the company's operating authority.   Here the Board was able
o reply that the city's shipping public supported the
hiladelphia-Newark truck haul and that it (the Board) had "never
. . suggested that the availability of an airport located nearer
o the certificated community than is the second airport actually
eing used in and of itself causes the service to lose its character
s air transportation to the certificated point."[4]

Although the Board has made clear that it is not assuming
urisdiction over the surface segment of an air-surface movement,
he curious belief persists that the agency views the motor haul as
f it were, in fact, air transportation.   This misconception

---

[1] The Flying Tiger Line, Inc., Air-Truck Service, p. 256.

[2] Ibid., p. 245.

[3] Order E-24026.

[4] The Flying Tiger Line, Inc., Air-Truck Service, p. 244.

appears to have its roots in the interpretation of section 101 of the Federal Aviation Act as given in City of Philadelphia v. Civil Aeronautics Board, above. Section 101(10) states that "'air transportation' means interstate, overseas, or foreign air transportation or the transportation of mail by aircraft." An elaboration is provided in section 101(24), which describes interstate, overseas and foreign air transportation as

> the carriage by aircraft of persons or property as a common carrier for compensation or hire or the carriage of mail by aircraft, in commerce between [various points] . . . whether such commerce moves wholly by aircraft or partly by aircraft and partly by other forms of transportation. (Emphasis added.)

The court held that "whether . . . partly by aircraft and partly by other forms of transportation" pertained to the definition of "interstate air transportation" and concluded "that the California-Newark-Philadelphia movement of freight is air transportation notwithstanding the 90-mile link between Newark and Philadelphia served by truck."[1] The Board's traditional position, of course, has been that (in certain instances) the surface portion of an air-truck movement constitutes a service "in connection with . . . air transportation."[2] As part of a recent clarification the agency emphasized that "air transportation" is restricted to "carriage by aircraft" and that "whether . . . partly by aircraft and partly by other forms of transportation" was a reference "only to the phrase 'in commerce between.'"[3]

A number of issues touching on motor-for-air substitutions were recently examined by the Board. The agency's investigation was launched as a result of new tariff rule proposals filed by several air freight forwarders and reflected concern that various air carrier practices lay outside the scope of permissible substitute service. Thus, a tariff rule issued by Airborne Freight Corporation informed shippers that the forwarder "will utilize" surface transportation

> in emergency conditions arising from the inability of the direct air carrier to perform air transportation due to adverse weather conditions, equipment failure or other causes beyond the control of the direct air carrier . . . When under the performance of this rule it becomes necessary to utilize other than air transportation no reduction or refund of charges will be made

---

[1] City of Philadelphia v. Civil Aeronautics Board, p. 774.

[2] See above, p. 111, note 3.

[3] Substitution of Other Services for Air Transportation Rule Proceeding, Order 75-3-37, p. 4.

[4] Order E-26605, p. 1.

Another forwarder, Emery, described its proposed use of substitutions in the following manner:

> when, for any reason, including temporary suspension of air service, refusal or inability of air carrier to perform services requested, embargoes, strikes or other causes, diversion of shipments to other means of transportation is necessary, the forwarder shall have the right to use his best judgment as to the means of transportation to be selected. No reduction or refund of charges will be made when, under the provision of this rule, it becomes necessary to utilize other than air transportation in order to expedite the shipment.[1]

These and other substitution rules immediately raised two questions: could shippers be compelled to pay air rates even though surface transportation was used? and could surface transportation be utilized "for any reason"? In its replay (1975) the Board defined the lawful parameters of substitute service and declared that the charges were to be "the air freight charges from origin to destination via the route shown on the airbill."[2] The agency's enquiry indicated that lower truck rates had not tempted air carriers to unnecessarily divert traffic to surface transportation. Furthermore, average air carrier costs were not lowered through the use of surface modes, and it was concluded that the use of air charges was not "unjustly discriminatory, unduly preferential, or unduly prejudicial." At the same time, however, it appeared that shippers were not always made aware that their consignments might be transferred from air to surface vehicles, and air carriers were accordingly ordered to include the following notice in their shipping documents: "To expedite movement, shipment may be diverted to motor or other carrier as per tariff rule unless shipper gives other instructions hereon."[3]

Table 9 summarizes the circumstances under which direct and indirect air carriers may substitute surface for air transportation. For instance, adverse weather, equipment failure, strikes, as well as other emergency conditions beyond a forwarder's or direct air carrier's control may be the cause of "occasional" substitutions. A distinction is drawn between this category and "regular" substitutions, which, under certain conditions, are also lawful. In an industry letter released June 13, 1977, the CAB's Bureau of Enforcement cautions air carriers that it intends to take action against violations of the substitution rules. These include the charging of air rates where the entire movement has been by truck and the regular use of surface vehicles in markets lacking adequate airlift.

---

[1] Ibid., p. 2. [2] Order 75-3-37, p. 10.

[3] Order 75-5-37, p. 3.

TABLE 9

SUBSTITUTE SERVICE

Extent of Substitution	Frequency of Substitute Service		
	Occasional		Regular
	"True" emergency: bad weather, mechanical failure, strikes, etc.	Oversized freight, restricted items, unforeseen backlog, etc.	Unrestricted
Entire origin to destination	Permitted	Not Permitted	Not Permitted
Accompanied by prior or subsequent air movement	Permitted	Permitted	Permitted[a]

SOURCE: Order 75-3-37.

[a]This service is permitted as long as the carrier also provides some service by aircraft between the points between which regular substitute service is used.

Initially the substitution rules applied only to domestic transportation, leaving untouched the international airlines' unrestricted use of truck service between their authorized gateways and interior U.S. cities. Such a situation, needless to say, was unacceptable to the domestic trunklines, which, anxious to capture this surface traffic, petitioned the CAB to limit the scope of substitutions on the domestic segment of international air freight movements. The petitioners noted that several IATA meetings had failed to reform the substitution practices of international carriers and attributed this to the "intransigence and self-interests of those IATA carriers which benefit greatly from unlimited substitution in this country."[1] Long a critic of the International Air Transport Association, the Board needed little encouragement to move once more against that organization. Like the trunklines, it deplored the absence of "reasonable" IATA substitution rules and commented on the "obvious abuses that can occur without proper rules."[2] Its domestic substitution rules, the agency concluded, were equally applicable to air-surface movements having foreign

[1]Petition for Investigation, Docket 29525, July 16, 1976, p. 3.

[2]Order 76-11-9, p. 2.

origins or destinations, and in December of 1976, these rules were extended to international traffic.

There is considerable uncertainty as to the Board's future authority over surface-for-air substitutions. Continued supervision of these substitutions would appear to run counter to Public Law 95-163, passage of which, along with the agency's termination of the carriers' tariff filing obligation, removes the basis for judging the lawfulness of domestic substitute service. On the other hand, international transportation is unaffected by the recent deregulation legislation, ensuring that, for the time being at least, the status quo will be maintained with respect to substitutions on the domestic section of international freight movements.

Virtually all of the trunks and all-cargo carriers serving the New York-Newark airports concede that domestic shipments moving to/from the airports are subject to "occasional" substitution ("regular" substitutions are common for international traffic), the most frequently given reasons being bad weather and oversized shipments. American Airlines also offers the service regularly between Philadelphia and New York; involved here are 20 ft. containers which the company is unable to fly out of Philadelphia International Airport and which are trucked to Kennedy Airport for onward transportation. The major forwarders, too, will occasionally divert air shipments to surface carriers. The principal airport cities receiving/originating New York-Newark's substitute shipments are Albany, Baltimore, Boston, Hartford, Philadelphia, Pittsburgh, and Washington, D.C. Only about two percent of the domestic tonnage carried to/from the New York-Newark airports by long-haul truckers is substitute traffic.

We have already seen that, in order for a surface movement to fall within the ambit of section 203(b)(7a) of the Interstate Commerce Act, the movement must as a rule be confined to the air carrier's air terminal area. Where an emergency arises, however, the Commission waives its usual mileage restrictions and the Act's regulatory provisions do not apply:

> transportation of property by motor vehicle is transportation incidental to transportation by aircraft if it constitutes substituted motor-for-air service, performed at the expense of the direct air carrier or air freight forwarder, on a through air bill of lading, in emergency situations arising from the inability of the direct air carrier to perform air transportation due to adverse weather conditions, equipment failure, or other causes beyond the control of the direct air carrier.[1]

---

[1] Motor Transportation of Property Incidental to Transportation by Aircraft (1964), appendix III.

It is the inability of <u>airline officials</u> to control a particular situation that is the decisive factor here. In other words, for the certification exemption to come into force, weather conditions, etc., must be considered "adverse" not by the forwarders or their agents but by airline representatives. Lack of airlift due to the oversoliciting of freight is not recognized as an emergency situation. The National Bus Traffic Association and the National Association of Motor Bus Owners have labelled the Commission's attitude towards emergency substitutions "prohibitory and capricious" and have demanded that air carriers and truckers be enjoined from offering this service unless they hold appropriate ICC authority. This position has been rejected by a U.S. district court on the ground that "an emergency situation justifies specialized treatment."[1]

The Air Freight Forwarders

The regulatory constraints acting on the air freight forwarder industry were examined in chapter II. In this chapter the focus is on the forwarders' transportation role and on their relationship with various direct carriers. The first of these two areas is emphasized in this section, which is divided into three parts. The first part is concerned with the role of forwarders generally and serves as an introduction to their <u>modus operandi</u> and to the services they offer the shipping public. The second part examines the work of several of the leading forwarders in the New York-Newark air terminal area. A number of conclusions and generalizations concerning forwarder service in New York-Newark form the final part.

Function of the Air Freight Forwarders

The air freight forwarders serve both as consolidators and as expeditors.[2] They receive small shipments from the shipping public, assemble as many of these as possible into larger consignments, and then tender these to the airlines for carriage to destination airports. There, they or their agents "break bulk" and the individual shipments are then carried to the appropriate consignees. Unlike the certificated airlines, forwarders have not been restricted to specific routes. Their permissible operations have been nationwide and, if they held international authority, worldwide in scope.

---

[1] <u>National Bus Traffic Association v. United States</u>, 249 F. Supp. 869, 873 (N.D. Ill. 1965); affirmed <u>per curiam</u>, 382 U.S. 369 (1966).

[2] See above, p. 81.

Depending on the specifications of the consignor, forwarders will furnish either door-to-door or airport-to-airport service. (In New York-Newark the forwarders handle roughly 98 percent of their traffic on a door-to-door basis.) Also provided are: insurance service, assembly service, armed surveillance, documentation, labelling, packaging, and storage. The major portion of a forwarders' revenues are generated through the consolidation process, which, by converting small shipments into larger units, enables him to exploit the airlines' tapering rate structure. Some examples of the "spread," that is, the difference between what forwarders charge their customers and are in turn charged by the airlines, are presented in table 10. Forwarders issue their own

TABLE 10

DOMESTIC SPREADS OF SELECTED AIR FREIGHT
FORWARDERS (July - December 1974)

Forwarder	Average Spread per 100 Pounds ($)
Airborne Air Freight	19.16
CF Air Freight	14.88
Emery Air Freight	17.03
United Parcel Service	7.89
Group of nine forwarders[a]	12.52

SOURCE: Docket 26907, initial decision, p. 48.

[a]Air-Land Freight Consolidators, Amerford, Associated Air Freight, Behring, Jet Air Freight, Profit by Air, Shulman, Trans-Air Freight System, and WTC.

tariffs and, by offering single-carrier responsibility, relieve shippers of most of the paperwork which routing procedures ordinarily entail. They provide a comprehensive transportation service (with emphasis on the small package field), forming a link between shippers, airlines, surface carriers, and receivers.

Passage of Public Law 95-163 will enable the forwarders to acquire and operate their own aircraft. However, as noted earlier,[1] only a few companies have the financial resources to purchase/lease this equipment so that, for the vast majority, deregulation will leave unchanged their established relationships with the airlines. Forwarders may choose not to own any vehicles at all, as surface operations can be conducted through independent motor carriers. In actual practice most of the major forwarders are also truck fleet

[1]See above, p. 156.

owners, thus ensuring their independence with respect to pickup and delivery work. Their ability to operate through established airlines (as opposed to operating their own aircraft) has long been regarded by most forwarders as one of the strengths of their industry. It has enabled them to bypass numerous capital expenditures and has provided relief from such problems as excess capacity and directional imbalance. The forwarders have traditionally enjoyed greater flexibility than the airlines, whose route structures were subject to CAB approval. This flexibility has not been restricted to routing matters. Forwarders, for instance, do not require fixed maintenance bases and have been able to lease warehouse space on a short-term basis. Burlington Northern Air Freight, for example, has continually outgrown its facilities during the period 1972-1977 and now leases "fourth generation" warehouse space.

In many areas a forwarder finds it expedient to operate through an agent. In some cases this will be an "exclusive" agent whose chief function it is to develop outbound traffic for his principal. In addition, he may also perform other duties such as billing, consolidation, and pickup service. Another kind of agent used is "nonexclusive" and specializes in carrying freight from the airport to receiving points within the air terminal zone.

Complete familiarity with the entire transportation network is central to the function of the air freight forwarder. Factors hostile to the uninterrupted flow of traffic, such as physical bottlenecks, labor disputes, etc., require his constant attention, and, in order to monitor the progress of shipments as they move from origin to destination, some of the larger forwarders have acquired sophisticated electronic communications equipment. Irrespective of how many direct carriers enter a given situation, a consignment released to a forwarder travels under a single air waybill, namely his own. It is his door-to-door responsibility which makes him especially valuable to shippers, most of whom are probably unaware of the identity of the underlying carriers hauling their consignments. The forwarder ensures that the schedules of the direct carriers chosen in any particular case mesh but clearly has no control over freight following its transfer to a surface operator or airline. However, having offered single-entity responsibility, it is he who, in the event of legal action (arising from damage, loss, etc.), will be considered (by shippers) to have had full responsibility for a consignment from the time it left the shipper's loading dock to the moment delivery was made at the point of destination.

Between sixty-five and seventy percent of the domestic two-way traffic moving through the New York-Newark airports is tendered to the airlines by the forwarders. For international shipments the figure, if IATA agency traffic is included, is somewhat higher. In order to strengthen international air freight forwarding, closer cooperation between forwarders in North America and Western Europe has long been urged by officials of the Fédération Internationale des Associations de Transitaires et Assimilés (FIATA),[1] who also stress the need for greater contact between FIATA members, appropriate governmental agencies, and business organizations. With the same objective in view, they would like to see the emergence of a more intimate dialogue between FIATA and the International Air Transport Association.[2]

From the shippers' viewpoint the forwarder is a carrier; from the airlines' perspective he is a shipper. Forwarders point out that they are, by far, the airlines' major customers of freight space and assert that, as a consequence of their promotional activities and constant search for new markets, the airlines, both domestically and internationally, are carrying greater quantities of freight than would otherwise be the case. Their special position in the air freight industry, many forwarders feel, is not being given sufficient recognition by airline executives.

Indirect air carriers contend that their service is superior to that offered by the airlines in conjunction with ACI. In support of this they cite a number of factors, including their ability to offer door-to-door responsibility between more points than can the airlines, their greater willingness to serve off-line customers, and their interest in making "special runs" directly to the customer. In addition, they believe that competition among themselves is important in that it reduces shippers' costs and helps to make the freight industry more innovative. Their superior service, according to the forwarders, rests ultimately on the fact that they are

---

[1] Founded in 1926, FIATA is an international organization representing the interests of freight forwarders in all transportation modes. It maintains liaison with the International Air Transportation Association on a number of issues, especially technical matters, rates, and commission levels. Its membership encompasses 50 national associations in 42 countries, over 900 individual forwarding companies in 83 countries, and a number of port (air and sea) authorities. Ninety-eight percent of Western Europe's air freight forwarders belong to FIATA. Letter to the author from W. Zeilbeck, Director of FIATA's Air Freight Institute, Zurich, 1976.

[2] Herbert Braunagel, "Die gegenwärtige Lage der Luftfracht vom Luftfracht-Spediteur aus generell betrachtet," Wirtschaft und Technik im Transport 40, no. 192 (1972):142-143.

freight specialists. This contrasts with the combination airlines, which, receiving roughly ninety percent of their revenues from the traveling public, remain essentially passenger-oriented. This orientation, say the forwarders, stifles freight-related initiatives the airlines might otherwise take and raises doubts about their present and future commitment to freight transportation.

The view which forwarders have of themselves is, not unnatural-ly, a positive one; it is, however, one not shared by all sectors of the freight system. We have already seen that many truckers have few kind words for the forwarders, whom they accuse of "raiding" their profitable accounts and of "abusing" the shipping public in various ways. (Harbourt, for instance, has complained to the ICC that some forwarders, while charging customers their own high tariff rate, have used Harbourt's lower-priced service and pocketed the difference.) The truckers also note that the forwarders are only able to offer extensive service to outlying points because they know that the truckers, as ICC permit-holders, must perform the actual surface transportation if called upon to do so.

The truckers are not alone in their criticism of forwarder activities, for airline spokesmen, too, express concern about the indirect carriers, with whom they enjoy a relationship which, while outwardly cordial, is beset by a number of problems. There can be no question, however, that the present situation is a marked improvement over that of an earlier period during which the scheduled airlines, arguing that their own ground services sufficed to meet shippers' needs, attempted to persuade the Civil Aeronautics Board to strip forwarders of their operating permits (chapter II). While it would be difficult today to find airline representatives who openly advocate the abolition of the forwarder industry (quite the contrary, many concede that, were the forwarding concerns dissolved, "the airlines would be in a very poor position to attempt to handle the freight business on a direct basis"[1]), the central dilemma characterizing the airline-forwarder relationship remains unresolved. The basic problem is that, despite their interdepen-dence, forwarders and airlines are competitors. Putting it rather more bluntly than many of his colleagues in the aviation field, John H. Mahoney, a vice president of Seaboard World Airlines, has called the forwarders the airlines' "deadliest competitors" and

---

[1] Remarks made to the author by James R. Rohm, Manager-Cargo, Market Development, United Airlines.

has spoken candidly of the airlines' "fear" of the indirect carriers. This fear centers on the forwarders' growing dominance of freight markets and the power this gives them to influence airline rates and, in effect, to play off one airline company against another, a threat presumably made more urgent by the various deregulation measures recently enacted into law.

In New York-Newark roughly sixty-five percent of the domestic outbound freight handled by the airlines is received from forwarders, and one readily encounters airline officials who speak of "pressure" being exerted by the forwarders against the direct carriers. One example of what is meant here is a forwarder's request for a later time-of-tender, which, if granted, could force the airline to reschedule its own departure time. The unspoken threat is that if the airline in question refuses to cooperate, the forwarder's business might be offered to a competing carrier. Also of concern to the airlines is that, because of the large proportion of freight coming from the forwarders, airline yields are lower than they would be if more unconsolidated shipments were received directly from the public. As in the case of the truckers, account "raiding" between the forwarders and airlines is not unknown.

The forwarders, of course, have their own complaints against the airlines. For example, they have stated on various occasions that modifications in the latter's weight breaks structure were designed to destroy or weaken forwarding,[2] charges airline officials categorically deny. Many of the larger forwarders feel the airlines are not providing the necessary incentives for large-scale consolidations and recommend the reinstatement of various high weight breaks. (Emery, for example, would like to see the return of weight breaks at the 5,000- and 10,000-pound levels.) Another criticism concerns the airlines' specific commodity rates, which, in the course of the Domestic Air Freight Rate Investigation, above, the forwarders urged the Board to disallow on the grounds that these were discriminatory and tended to weaken the industry's pre-containerization efforts. Forwarders are also opposed to recent trends in airline scheduling, particularly cutbacks in nighttime

---

[1] John H. Mahoney, Intermodal Action--The Challenge of Today, speech given at the National Conference and Shipper's Dialogue (1974), p. 13.

[2] See, for instance: "San Juan Prelude," Air Transportation 50, no. 3 (1967):15; and "A Rate Fracas Bubbles Up," Cargo Airlift 58, no. 1 (1971):20. Also see above, p. 12.

freighter service.[1] Finally, forwarders believe the airlines
should restrict themselves to providing airport-to-airport transportation.   They would be delighted to see the direct air carriers
terminate their pickup/delivery operations and certain other
ground activities such as assembly service.

Although the Air Freight Forwarders Association once briefly
supported the Board's policy of unrestricted (free) forwarder entry
into the market "on the ground that at the present early stage in
the development of the air freight industry, a continuing flow of
new blood into forwarding is most likely to promote development of
new and efficient forwarding techniques,"[2] its position today is
that the CAB's licensing policy militates against the interests of
established forwarders and should be terminated.   In this connection
the Association has petitioned the CAB to

> impose an immediate moratorium on the grant of new air freight forwarder
> authorizations, and contemporaneously to institute an investigation of
> competition in the air freight forwarding industry for the purpose of perma-
> nently certifying a selected number of existing forwarders based on the
> criteria of public convenience and necessity.[3]

The Association might have spared itself the trouble, for the answer
(1976) was a predictable "no."[4]   The Board has consistently held
that an aggressive, outward-looking forwarding industry is indispensable to the well-being of air freight transportation as a whole
and remains unalterably attached to the belief that the vitality
of the forwarder community is best assured through a policy of free
entry.   Every unit of freight generated by forwarders must ipso

---

[1]Rapidly rising fuel costs, Federal antinoise legislation, and growing
support on the part of local and state authorities for aiport noise curfews are
among the factors which have caused the trunklines to increasingly question the
viability of their freighter operations.   United Airlines, for example, estimates
it will have to spend about $40 million to retrofit its DC-8 freighters if these
aircraft are to meet Federal noise regulations.   "Noise polluters" have come under
attack in the New York State Legislature, where a transportation committee has
"recommend[ed] that the FAA mandate a program of retrofitting the engines of
older aircraft. . . . We also suggest that consideration be given to basing
takeoff charges in part on the amount of noise emitted by a jet during takeoffs
with the scale of charges favoring the quietest aircraft. . . . The charges
also could be related to the time of day with the highest charges applying at
night."   New York, Select Legislative Committee on Transportation, Transportation
Progress in New York State, Legislative Document no. 25, 1974, p. 48.

[2]Air Freight Forwarder Investigation, p. 548.

[3]Air Freight Forwarders Association, Petition to the Civil Aeronautics
Board for a Moratorium on the Admission of New Forwarders and for Certification
of the Air Forwarding Industry (Washington D.C.: Air Freight Forwarders
Association, 1973), p. 1.

[4]Order 76-11-148.

facto be carried in an aircraft, and it would have been strange
indeed had the Board retreated from its free entry rule at a time
when the forwarders' traffic share and revenues were reaching a new
peak. Also, the Association's plea for a protectionist policy came
at a time when the CAB, under Chairman Robson, was beginning to
question the need for various public interest tests and was recom-
mending that the Congress consider a relaxation of controls over the
freight sector. Nor can it be said that the Association advanced
its case by attributing to the Board's free entry policy the forwarder industry's alleged fragmentation "into wafer thin pieces,"
when in fact the ten leading operators (several of whom were
Association members) accounted for some seventy percent of total
domestic forwarder revenues.

The Air Freight Forwarders Association and many individual
forwarders contend that the unchecked growth of the forwarder
population has led to a saturation of the market and has weakened
forwarders generally. Destructive competition, it is claimed, by
reducing the average volume of freight handled per forwarder, is
impeding the growth of the industry's containerization program.
Critics of the Board emphasize that after some thirty years it is
time to dispel the uncertainties inherent in an industry functioning
under permits (which could be withdrawn) and to replace these with
permanent certificates for "a selected number" of operators. Citing
reluctance on the part of investors to involve themselves with a
partially government-controlled industry lacking an "official"
permanent status, industry spokesmen state that investment capital
will be more readily attracted once a permanent status has been
secured by forwarders, who will then themselves be emboldened to
make greater financial commitments to their business. Forwarders
are quick to point out that permanent certification, accompanied
by stringent screening procedures of new applicants, would deny
entry into their ranks to those lacking the financial qualifications
and the necessary motivation. The industry's image has been tar-
nished by a number of bankruptcies and the abuses of many fly-by-
night operators. Illegal acts include the misclassification of
merchandise, demanding payment for services not required or actually
rendered, deviation from published rates, etc. In order to purge
the industry of these practices the Air Freight Forwarders Association has adopted a code of ethics[1] but feels its full implementation
can come about only with the Board's imposition of fitness tests.

---

[1] AFFA Code of Fair Trade Practices, Agreement 17003, Order E-19984.

The Board recently (March, 1978) adopted a regulation which will make it possible for forwarders to tender their traffic to other forwarders. Under a policy of long-standing these operators had been compelled to utilize "the services of a direct air carrier;" however, deregulation of domestic air freight transportation caused the agency to review its stance towards the forwarders and it concluded this restriction had become redundant. Several carriers (American Airlines, Flying Tiger Line, Trans World Airlines) have protested the Board's action on the grounds that the involvement of more than one forwarder in a given through movement will confuse shippers and hinder tracing operations and claims settlements. In addition, it is feared this form of forwarder cooperation will unduly strengthen the major operators, who, with their enhanced consolidations, will depress airline yields and be in a better position to manipulate the direct air carriers.

Most of the major forwarders do not object to the Board's new regulation, although they are quick to note that they themselves have no intention of working through other forwarders (i.e., their competitors). Others oppose the measure on the ground that it enables a weak company to enlarge its operations and survive in the marketplace. The smaller forwarding concerns tend to favor the regulation, since it permits them to give their traffic to the leading forwarders and thus provides access to the latter's over-night charter flights. They also feel, as does the Board, that since most shippers currently do not know which underlying carriers a forwarder uses, the new rule could hardly create the type of confusion predicted by some of the airline companies. The Board believes the new rule gives forwarders and shippers "increased flexibility and availability of services" and, as part of its ongoing review of the industry, has announced that it will eliminate the distinction between domestic and international service in future forwarder authorizations and that further changes in its definition of "air freight forwarder"[1] may be forthcoming. The forwarders, however, have been cautioned that the agency "in no way intends to avoid its responsibility to monitor closely their operations and the impact on the shippers of [a] more freely operating market." Should it become necessary to introduce new regulatory requirements (e.g., new claims procedures), "the Board will not hesitate to do so."[2]

---

[1] See above, p. 81.

[2] ER-1046.

Selected Forwarders in the New
York-Newark Air Terminal Area

Having examined forwarder service from a general standpoint, we now turn to a consideration of some individual companies. The five companies discussed below are among the largest air freight forwarders in the New York-Newark air terminal area and, though few in number (about 100 forwarders maintain terminals/offices in the area), they account for some fifty percent of its total forwarder-consolidated air freight tonnage. A high degree of concentration, far from being unique to New York-Newark, is characteristic of the industry. The companies are presented alphabetically. The figures throughout this subsection are for the year 1975.

Air Express International (AEI). With annual revenues in excess of $90 million, Air Express International is one of the nation's major forwarders. It derives the overwhelming proportion of its operating revenues--as do all leading indirect air carriers--from the price differential between what its customers pay for airport-to-airport transportation and what it, as a customer of the airlines, is charged for that service by the latter. The company's operating expenses can be broken down into the following categories: air transportation purchases--74.7 percent, station freight handling--16.3 percent, pickup and delivery--9 percent (administrative and marketing expenses have been omitted). Of the $59 million paid the airlines in 1975, 86 percent was spent on international flights. This sets AEI apart from the other forwarders profiled here, whose work in contrast is slanted far more heavily towards domestic operations.

The company's total domestic and international consolidated outbound traffic at New York-Newark (its leading consolidation center) makes it the area's fifth largest forwarder. About eight millions pounds or one third of the total is domestic traffic. Two components constitute the outbound traffic flow: (1) surface-to-air traffic, which consists of shipments picked up by the forwarder in the air terminal area, shipments hauled by over-the-road truckers, and (rarely) packages delivered to the forwarder by the consignor; and (2) shipments which were flown to New York-Newark from other airport cities (air-to-air transfers) and are resorted and reconsolidated there. A consolidated outbound load leaving, say, Kennedy Airport will normally be made up of (1) and (2), and it follows that this load is greater than that which the company actually receives from customers in and around the air terminal area.

Of the domestic outbound traffic, 70 percent (by weight) originates "locally" (1, above), the remainder coming from other airports. The average weight per locally received shipment is 133 pounds and the average weight per consolidation 430 pounds. With respect to international traffic, only 40 percent is received from local customers. The average weight per international shipment is 254 pounds, substantially below the average weight per international consolidation (2,987 pounds). The company containerizes about 75 percent (by weight) of its domestic outbound traffic; for international traffic the figure is about 50 percent. Roughly 80 percent (by weight) of AEI's domestic traffic enplaned at New York-Newark is carried by the trunklines, with about half this tonnage being loaded into all-cargo aircraft. The local service airlines account for about 15 percent of the domestic outbound traffic; all-cargo route carriers and commuters for 3 and 2 percent, respectively.

New York-Newark, as previously noted, is AEI's most important consolidation center. It is also the company's leading destination point, receiving about 7 million pounds of freight for delivery to local consignees. The second and third major destination stations are, respectively, Chicago (3.7 million pounds) and Los Angeles (2.3 million pounds).

AEI makes specific commodity rates available between New York-Newark and some fifty domestic points (international specific commodity rates are also offered). These rates are of special interest here because, being promotional in character, they are indicative of the company's desire to enhance (or retain) its competitiveness for certain types of traffic in particular markets. Examples of actual price levels are given in the next subsection; suffice it here to show a few of the company's major domestic traffic routes together with some of the principal items covered by its specific commodity rates:

I. From New York-Newark to

(1) Chicago: automobile parts, chemicals and pharmaceuticals, electrical machinery, telephone and telegraph equipment; (2) Los Angeles: automobile parts, chemicals, electronic equipment, photographic paper, printed matter; (3) Miami: automobile parts, chemicals and pharmaceuticals, electronic equipment, photographic paper, toilet preparations; (4) San Francisco: automobile parts, electrical and electronic equipment, pharmaceuticals, telephone equipment.

II. To New York-Newark from

(1) Chicago: cosmetics, medicines, office equipment, printed matter, telephone equipment; (2) Los Angeles: aerospace vehicle equipment, automobile parts, electrical machinery, foodstuffs, precision and calibrating equipment; (3) Miami: computers and parts, drugs and medicines, kitchen equipment, office machinery; (4) San Francisco: electrical and electronic equipment, drugs, office machinery, optical instruments, toilet preparations.

Generally speaking, AEI would like to see an enlargement of the New York-Newark air terminal area. It owns about twenty trucks for local pickup and delivery work and holds ICC forwarder authority, so that traffic moving under its responsibility can be interlined with ICC-regulated truckers operating beyond its pickup/delivery zone. As already emphasized, an air freight forwarder's authority for this type of traffic is restricted to shipments "having an immediately prior or subsequent movement" by aircraft.[1] Truckers performing the connecting-line service act as agents of AEI and handle (in New York-Newark) roughly 20 percent of its outbound and 20 percent of its inbound surface traffic.

Airborne Freight Corporation (AFC). The corporation is the second largest air freight forwarder in the United States. Transportation revenues constitute roughly 97 percent of its total revenues; operating expenses are made up of: air transportation-- 55 percent, pickup and delivery--22.5 percent, station freight handling--also 22.5 percent. International traffic consumes 30 percent of its total transportation expenses.

In terms of its consolidated outbound traffic at New York-Newark (roughly 24 million pounds), AFC is the area's sixth major air freight forwarder. Sixty-six percent of the combined consolidated outbound load represents domestic traffic. Fifty-five percent and sixteen percent, respectively, of the domestic and international outbound traffic is generated locally. The average weight of a domestic shipment originated in the area is 70 pounds, of a consolidated load tendered to the airlines 367 pounds. The corresponding weights for exports are 159 pounds and 1,530 pounds. About 65 percent of its domestic and 70 percent of its international traffic is containerized. Airborne tenders 75 percent (by weight) of its New York-Newark domestic freight to the trunk carriers; about 60 percent of the load is carried in passenger, the remainder in all-cargo equipment. Roughly 10 percent of its domestic traffic is moved by the local service airlines and a further 10 to 15 percent by the certificated all-cargo operators. About 2 percent is handled by commuter airlines.

The corporation charges its customers specific commodity rates on about sixty percent of the domestic traffic enplaned in New York-Newark and offers these rates between the area's air terminals and about fifty U.S. airport cities. Some examples are:

---

[1] See above, p. 116, note 1.

I. From New York-Newark to

    (1)Atlanta: clothing and footwear, electrical and electronic equipment, printed material; (2) Chicago: clothing and footwear, electrical and electronic equipment, phonograph records; (3) Los Angeles: clothing, computers and parts, electronic equipment, magnetic tape, phonograph records, printed material; (4) San Francisco: clothing and footwear, electronic equipment, printed material.

II. To New York-Newark from

    (1) Atlanta: automobile and truck parts, clothing and textile articles, electrical machinery, printed material; (2) Chicago: aircraft and surface vehicle parts, electrical and electronic equipment, medical equipment, pipe and pipe fitting; (3) Los Angeles: automobile and tractor parts, clothing and footwear, electrical equipment, medical supplies, optical instruments, printed material; (4) San Francisco: electrical equipment, hand tools, office equipment, printed matter, vegetables.

Airborne received an Interstate Commerce Commission freight forwarder permit in 1972 and thus is able to assume carrier responsibility for shipments trucked beyond the boundaries of pickup/delivery zones. In the case of New York-Newark, between five and ten percent of the freight trucked to and from the airports is carried across the boundary of this zone.

Emery Air Freight. Emery is firmly established as the nation's leading indirect air carrier. Its operating revenues of $237 million are more than twice those of its nearest rival and form about one fifth of the revenues produced by the entire U.S. air freight forwarder industry (1975). It is by far the largest forwarder in New York-Newark, where it accounts for approximately seventeen percent of the total forwarder traffic received by the airlines. The company is widely considered to be the "senior member" of the air freight forwarder community. It has undertaken a considerable amount of research into various aspects of the freight industry and has introduced a number of marketing and freight-handling techniques which have been adopted by air freight forwarders as a whole.

Transportation revenues account for 99 percent of Emery's combined operating revenues. Operating expenses consist of: air transportation--63 percent, pickup and delivery--15.6 percent, station freight handling--21.4 percent. Approximately 40 percent of the company's air transportation bill is spent on international flights.

Of Emery's total domestic consolidated traffic tendered to the airlines throughout the United States, 50 million pounds or about 13 percent is enplaned in New York-Newark, making the area the most important consolidation point in its national network. Chicago is in second place with 37 million pounds and is followed by Los

Angeles with 21 million pounds. If international shipments are
added, the figures for New York-Newark and the other two cities
become, respectively, 76, 43, and 22 million pounds.

The average weight of a domestic shipment received from
customers in the New York-Newark area is 78 pounds, the average
weight of a consolidation about 900 pounds. Roughly 80 percent of
the consolidated outbound domestic tonnage represents surface-to-air
traffic, the remainder being air-to-air transshipments. Turning to
international commerce, the average weight of a customer's shipment
is about 120 pounds, of a consolidated load 2,780 pounds. Here
only about 20 percent of the traffic originates locally. About 80
percent of Emery's total outbound traffic has been containerized.

Approximately fifty percent of the domestic freight tonnage
enplaned by Emery in New York-Newark moves under its specific
commodity rates (the figure is considerably higher in the case of
several other major forwarders), which are offered between the area
and about 56 U.S. airport cities. A few of its most important
routes, along with examples of the commodities in question, are now
given.

I.   From New York-Newark to

(1) Chicago: clothing-on-hangers, computer terminals and parts, motion
picture film, office equipment; (2) Dallas: computer terminals and parts,
drugs and pharmaceuticals, surgical instruments, textile products; (3)
Los Angeles: costume jewelry, drugs and pharmaceuticals, footwear, motion
picture film, phonograph records; (4) Seattle: aircraft parts, computer
terminals, leather goods, textile articles.

II. To New York-Newark from

(1) Chicago: costume jewelry, drugs and pharmaceuticals, phonograph records,
surgical instruments, textile products; (2) Dallas: clothing-on-hangers,
costume jewelry, leather goods, motion picture film; (3) Los Angeles:
aircraft parts, clothing, drugs, film projectors, surgical instruments;
(4) Seattle: aircraft parts, video tape.

The company has two consolidation stations in the area, one at
Kennedy Airport, the other at Newark Airport. In New York it uses
about seventy of its own trucks for pickup and delivery work. Emery
holds ICC freight forwarder authority and can therefore offer
through-service to/from outlying points under rates appearing in its
own tariffs. It is estimated that in the case of the New
York-Newark airports about five percent of both its inbound and
outbound truck shipments are hauled across the boundary of the
air terminal area.

United Parcel Service (UPS). The company's forwarder activities generated revenues of $72 million in 1975, making it the

nation's fourth largest indirect air carrier. Transportation
revenues account for virtually its entire operating revenues. Its
chief operating expenses can be broken into air transportation purchases (about 73 percent) and pickup and delivery (about 27 percent)
Unlike the other companies discussed here, UPS does not hold
international forwarder authority. Another point of distinction is
that it does not offer specific commodity rates.

United Parcel will not accept packages weighing more than
fifty pounds or having a combined length and girth in excess of 108
inches. Its small-package emphasis combined with various other
service features have helped to make the company the chief competito
of the U.S. Postal Service. United Parcel, unlike the Postal Servic
offers free insurance up to $100 per parcel and will make three
attempts to deliver any one parcel. It guarantees third-day
delivery for a 900-mile route and fifth-day delivery for a 2,000-mil
route; the delivery range for the Postal Service, on the other hand,
is roughly 300 miles (third day) and 1,000 miles (fifth day).

Generally speaking, UPS does not use New York-Newark as an
air-to-air transfer point. After Los Angeles, New York-Newark is
its major originating point (about 41 million pounds), the average
weight of a locally-received package being nine pounds. The compan
is an ICC-authorized trucker and is therefore able to use its own
equipment to carry freight beyond the limits of its pickup and
delivery zones. In New York-Newark about ten percent (by weight) of
its two-way traffic is moved across the boundary of this zone.

WTC Air Freight. In 1975 WTC had revenues of $44.6 million;
transportation revenues contributed about 97 percent of this figure.
Air transportation purchases, pickup and delivery, and station
freight handling made up 58 percent, 21 percent, and 21 percent,
respectively, of its total operating expenses. International flights
accounted for only three percent of the company's air transportation
purchases.

New York-Newark is WTC's leading consolidation point; of its
total load tendered to airlines throughout the United States, this
area accounts for 33 percent. The average weight of a domestic
shipment received locally is about 220 pounds, of an outbound
consolidation 1,866 pounds. For international traffic these figures
are, respectively, 230 pounds and 950 pounds. About 60 percent (by
weight) of the company's outbound domestic traffic at New York-Newark
has been containerized.

Of WTC's total domestic traffic received from shippers in the
New York-Newark area, roughly 85 percent moves under its specific

commodity rates, which are offered between the area and about 50 U.S. airport cities. Some of the more important routes, along with examples of commodities covered by these rates, are shown below.

I. From New York-Newark to

> (1) Chicago: drugs and pharmaceuticals, footwear, office equipment, printing plates and dies; (2) Los Angeles: aerospace vehicle parts, costume jewelry, electrical equipment and machinery, medical equipment, textiles; (3) San Francisco: aerospace equipment, automobile parts, clothing and footwear, drugs, electronic equipment, printing plates and dies; (4) Seattle: aerospace equipment, automobile parts, clothing, drugs, footwear, medical equipment.

II. To New York-Newark from

> (1) Chicago: automobile parts, clothing, drugs and chemicals, electrical equipment, printing plates and dies; (2) Los Angeles: aircraft and automobile parts, clothing and footwear, drugs, electrical and electronic equipment, office equipment; (3) San Francisco: clothing, drugs and pharmaceuticals, printing plates and dies; (4) Seattle: clothing.

Over 80 percent (by weight) of WTC's outbound domestic freight at New York-Newark's airports is carried by trunk airlines. All-cargo carriers move about 15 percent; only about 2 percent is carried by local service airlines and commuters. The company maintains 2 consolidation facilities in the New York-Newark area, where it owns 25 trucks for pickup and delivery work. It holds, since 1972, an ICC freight forwarder permit, thereby extending its carrier responsibility to points beyond the pickup and delivery zones. Less than five percent of its New York-Newark traffic is trucked across the boundaries of this zone.

Concluding Remarks

Importance of the forwarders. About sixty-five percent (by weight) of New York-Newark's domestic surface-to-air traffic is tendered to the airlines by the forwarders; for international shipments the figure is somewhat higher. The forwarders' share of the system's total freight volume has been rising steadily and is causing unease among airline officials, who believe this trend is making the direct air carriers' freight operations increasingly vulnerable to forwarder pressure and/or control. Since consolidations move under volume rates, the airlines also feel the forwarders are responsible for an erosion of their yields. Despite the reservations many airline executives have about the forwarders, they do not deny that the latter are of crucial importance to their freight business, and a close working relationship exists between individual airlines and the major forwarding concerns. Knowing that in some instances their packages, as part of a forwarder's

large-volume, regular traffic, will be handled more expeditiously
by the airlines than they would as individually tendered units, many
shippers will work through the indirect carriers rather than giving
their business directly to the airline companies.

In view of the fact that forwarders are able to offer their
customers single-carrier door-to-door responsibility, the latter need
not handle routing problems nor need they deal with the various surface and air carriers providing the actual transportation, and it is
this which makes forwarders particularly attractive from a shipper's
standpoint. Forwarders also perform the necessary documentation and
provide a complete tracing service. Their expertise in the preparation of various international documents (export license applications,
consular invoices, declarations of value, etc.) is especially
important to the smaller company (which is unlikely to have its own
traffic department) and is a major reason for their prominent role in
international transportation.

In high-volume areas the large forwarders generally have more
flexibility in their pickup and delivery work than is true of ACI's
local cartage agents, who tend to operate under a more tightly
structured schedule. An important exception is ACI's Trucking
Division, which, in its four-borough service area (Bronx, Brooklyn,
Manhattan, and Queens), will make "special runs" if requested to
do so.

Traffic characteristics. The average weight of a domestic
outbound consolidated load varies (1975) from 1,866 pounds (WTC Air
Freight), 900 pounds (Emery), and 430 pounds (Air Express International) to virtually insignificant amounts for numerous smaller
companies. Some examples of the average weight of a domestic
shipment received from customers in the New York-Newark area are:
220 pounds (WTC Air Freight), 133 pounds (Air Express International),
78 pounds (Emery), and 70 pounds (Airborne). Generally speaking,
international shipments and consolidated loads have higher average
weights, reflecting differences between domestic and international
rate structures.

About 15 percent (by weight) of all traffic tendered to U.S.
forwarders worldwide (exclusive of IATA agency traffic) has been
received from customers in the New York-Newark area. The size of
this market (both as an originating station and as a transshipment
point) and the consequent potential for significant consolidations
make the area one of the nation's most attractive air traffic centers
for many forwarders and explain the marked growth in the number of
operators active there. Of the system's twenty leading forwarders
(1977), 17 rank New York-Newark as one of their three most important

originating stations; for 15 it is their most important air-to-air
transfer point. Approximately 25 percent of the system's total
consolidated outbound forwarder tonnage has arrived in New York-
Newark by air and must be resorted and reconsolidated for onward
transportation.

Virtually all of the system's major indirect air carriers hold
an ICC freight forwarder permit and can thus assume door-to-door
responsibility (under a single freight bill) for shipments trucked
beyond the limits of their pickup and delivery zone. Most of the
leading forwarders are dissatisfied with the size of the New York-
Newark air terminal area and advocate its enlargement or abolition.
Approximately 10 percent (by weight) of the forwarders' two-way
air-surface traffic is interlined with long-haul truckers and
carried across the boundary of this area (1975).

Joint loading. Joint loading is defined as

> the pooling of shipments and their delivery to a direct air carrier for trans-
> portation as one shipment in accordance with the . . . tariff rules of the
> direct carrier, pursuant to an agreement between two or more indirect
> carriers of the same subclassification . . . or between one or more air
> freight forwarders and one or more cooperative shippers associations.[1]

Permitted since 1955 (domestically) and 1959 (internationally),
joint loading has never held much appeal for the forwarders, and only
three of the system's twenty leading forwarding concerns participate
in this activity (1977), which they restrict to a few foreign markets for which, acting alone, they lack the volume for profitable
operations. The traffic in question is small, involving only two
percent of their combined outbound consolidated tonnage.

By pooling their shipments forwarders are able to obtain lower
air rates, and the CAB originally hoped this would lead to reduced
rates for shippers. The forwarder community, however, is highly
competitive and its members have little interest in a cooperative
venture which could strengthen the position of a rival. In a joint
loading arrangement, for instance, one forwarder may learn the
identity of his partner's customers, inviting subsequent account
"raiding." Another problem centers on the time advantage enjoyed by
whichever indirect carrier is the first to unload and the last to
enplane his shipments.

Joint loading agreements between shippers associations and
forwarders were authorized in 1977 and are among several steps
initiated by the Board to reduce the regulatory differences between
these two groups of indirect carriers. The Air Freight Forwarders

---

[1]ER-994.

Association has taken exception to this action on the ground that it might encourage shippers to withdraw their business from a forwarder, form an association, and then seek to joint load with that forwarder. The Board considers this unlikely. The new rule has also been protested by several scheduled airlines which fear the associations' new freedom will prompt them to transfer their freight from scheduled to charter operations. As the Board has noted, however, the number of shippers associations operating under its regulations is small, so that, even if some traffic diversion did occur, its impact on the scheduled carriers' revenues would be negligible.

The Board's new rule is unlikely to lead to large-scale cooperation between the two classes of indirect carriers. The associations' freight, where tendered directly to the airlines, is lost to the forwarders, and it is unrealistic to suppose that the latter have any interest in an arrangement which may bolster the position of the cooperatives. One example will suffice to illustrate the competitive relationship between the two factions. In mid-1976, WTC Air Freight, a forwarder, amended its specific commodity rates for the New York to Honolulu route, reducing these by 25 percent (at the 1,000-pound weight break) and 32 percent (at the 2,000-pound weight break) below the then prevailing levels. Among the affected items were clothing and other important components of the Hawaii Air Cargo Shippers Association's New York to Honolulu traffic. Unable to match WTC's new rates, the Association turned to the CAB for relief, urging it to dismiss the rates on the grounds that they were noncompensatory and were designed purely to capture the Association's traffic. The Board, however, concluded that the rates, though substantially below those of the Association, were not unreasonable and refused to order their cancellation. The new rates, the agency argued, were justified because of the lower average costs of WTC's large-scale containerization program.

Competition. Of the nation's approximately 350 authorized air freight forwarders (1975) about 200 are involved in the system's two-way traffic. A high level of concentration characterizes the industry. For instance, 5 companies account for roughly 50 percent (by weight) of New York-Newark's outbound forwarder traffic; the leading 20 companies account for over 90 percent. About 50 percent of the system's consolidated domestic outbound forwarder tonnage is generated in New York City; for overseas shipments the figure is about 40 percent. Although New York-Newark maintains regular air service with over 300 U.S. cities, 10 markets contribute approximately 70 percent of the system's domestic two-way forwarder traffic. The cities in question are: Atlanta, Chicago, Dallas-Fort Worth, Denver, Detroit, Houston, Los Angeles, Miami, San Francisco, and Seattle. Competition over these major routes is intense and, again, is marked by a high degree of concentration. Over 70 percent of the New York to Chicago forwarder traffic flow, for example, is generated by only five companies; a similar situation holds with respect to Los Angeles and San Francisco.

As was shown above, forwarders make considerable use of specific commodity rates. (More than half of New York-Newark's twenty leading forwarders apply specific commodity rates to over sixty percent of their outbound domestic traffic.) An important competitive tool, these discount rates are offered for a wide range of commodities, frequently over as many as 50-60 of the system's routes. (This, incidentally, contrasts with the airlines, many of which have sharply reduced their own use of specific commodity rates.) A number of forwarders have attempted to establish them- selves as transportation specialists for particular types of freight moving between given city pairs. Specific commodity rates were (and are) widely used to capture and hold the traffic in question. Recently, however, there has been a determined effort on the part of some of these companies to move towards the more profitable (and less cyclical) general commodity business.

In chapter II we examined the strained relationship between so-called independent forwarders and forwarders affiliated with long-haul surface carriers and noted the attempts of the former to block their competitors' entry into the market. Unless remedial action was taken, the major independent operators told the Civil Aeronautics Board, surface carriers would soon dominate the air freight forwarder industry. Moreover, it was alleged, the financial resources of the affiliates (or, more to the point, the resources of the parent companies) left the independents at a competitive disadvantage, undermining their position and that of the industry as a whole. Certainly in the New York-Newark air terminal area this gloomy scenario has not materialized: at the beginning of 1976 only five affiliates were active in the region, a far cry from the massive entry by surface interests foreseen in the late 1960s. These five operators account for about five percent of New York-Newark's surface-to-air forwarder traffic. Even so small a percentage draws criticism from some independents, who say the fact that most of this traffic (about 90 percent) is generated within the air terminal area shows the five companies have no interest in developing new sources of business and are content to expand their operations in the terminal area at the expense of the independents. To this the afffiliates reply that the long-term development of their business at points outside the pickup and delivery zone is feasible only so long as they are not excluded from the more profitable operations within the zone.

The independents have often accused the long-haul carrier affiliates of predatory price cutting, a charge which cannot be sustained within the context of this study. Table 11 lists forwarder pickup and delivery rates within the New York-Newark air terminal area's leading freight producing/consuming sector, namely the Bronx, Brooklyn, Manhattan, and Queens. For instance, for a package (at the 100-pound weight break) picked up in Manhattan and carried to Kennedy Airport, the rate for the leading independent ranges from $3.50 to $6.30, for the affiliates from $3.65 to $6.70. The minimum charge for one shipment varies from $7.00 to $12.15 (independents) and $7.95 to $9.10 (affiliates). In the case of a single shipment picked up in Newark and trucked to Newark Airport, the figures are: (1) minimum charge--$5.95 to $7.25 for the independents and $6.75 to $7.45 for the affiliates, (2) rate for a 100-pound shipment--$3.00 to $3.75 (independents) and $3.35 to $3.50 (affiliates). Rates and charges for more than one shipment similar fail to demonstrate predation on the part of the affiliate group. Airport-to-airport specific commodity rates for the two groups are compared in table 12. In the case of each group the average minimum charge per shipment and the average rate per 100 pounds (at the 100-pound weight break) is given for several major commodities carried over some of the system's principal domestic routes. Here again the data do not show that the affiliates are engaged in predatory rate cutting.

Charter traffic. The chartering of aircraft by forwarders was initially authorized in the Air Freight Forwarder Case, above, and in the International Air Freight Forwarder Investigation, above, the basic supporting arguments being: (1) chartering provided forwarder with greater operational flexibility, (2) lower charter rates could be passed on to shippers, and (3) lower charter rates would win new customers for the air freight industry. In 1970, Shulman, then one of the nation's major forwarders, entered into an agreement with Airlift International, under which the latter was to provide charter flights from New York to Los Angeles five days per week over a one-year period. This arrangement was challenged by the Flying Tige Line, one of Airlift's competitors in the New York-Los Angeles marke causing the Board to reexamine its existing policy, particularly wit reference to chartering on a regular basis. The agency was especially concerned that forwarders, in negotiating rates, could reap "undue" advantages by playing competing airlines off against each other and that regular charter service might be developing at the expense of scheduled traffic. The ensuing Air Freight Forwarders' Charters Investigation, however, found these fears to be unfounded, and in a 1977 decision unrestricted chartering of aircraft, whether on a sporadic or regular basis, was upheld.[1]

As with so many Board proceedings, the issues in question divided the air freight industry into opposing factions. The Flying Tiger Line and several trunks (American, Delta, Pan American, Trans World, and United) thought unrestricted forwarder charters undermined scheduled air transportation and requested the imposition of various limitations, including (for each situation in which chartering was contemplated) formal Board authorization and a showing of inadequacy with regard to scheduled services. These companies also claimed the Board's unrestricted charter policy unlawfully removed the statutory distinction between scheduled and nonscheduled air transportation and rejected the suggestion that forwarder charters would attract additional traffic from surface shippers. As one might expect, their views clashed with those of the forwarders and the supplemental carriers, both groups arguing in favor of unfettered chartering on public interest grounds (cost reductions, encouragement of containerization, expansion of freight service to secondary markets, etc.). This approach was also adopted by Airlift International and the U.S. Department of Justice, which stated that traffic diversion from scheduled to chartered flights was too insignificant to justify the introduction of restrictive charter regulations.

The Board's willingness to allow unlimited forwarder charters has so alarmed the Flying Tiger Line and Pan American World Airways that they have petitioned the agency to reconsider its conclusions in the Air Freight Forwarders' Charters Investigation. Congress' removal of unregulated individually ticketed/waybilled point-to-point authority from the supplementals,[2] it is argued, was intended not only to establish a statutory barrier between charter and scheduled operations but was also to protect scheduled air transportation from the charterers. Individually waybilled charter services of the forwarders are qualitatively no different than the services of the scheduled airlines and, say the two carriers, pose "too great a potential threat to the scheduled system to be implemented without some safeguards against deterioration of scheduled service."[3]

---

[1] Docket 23287, Order 77-7-25 [2] See above, p. 26.

[3] Joint Petition of the Flying Tiger Line, Inc. and Pan American World Airways, Inc. for Reconsideration of Order 77-7-25, Docket 23287, August 2, 1977, p. 11.

TABLE 11

GENERAL COMMODITY PICKUP AND DELIVERY RATES: INDEPENDENT FORWARDERS
V. LONG-HAUL CARRIER AFFILIATES (July – August 1977)

Forwarder	Borough	Number of Shipments	Pickup		Delivery	
			Minimum Charge per Shipment ($)	Rate per 100 Lbs.[a] ($)	Minimum Charge per Shipment ($)	Rate per 100 Lbs.[a] ($)
Independent Forwarders						
Airborne	Bronx, Brooklyn,	1	7.00	3.50	7.75	3.50
	Manh. and Queens	5	1.80	3.50	7.75	3.50
		10 and over	1.65	3.50	7.75	3.50
Air Express	Bronx, Brooklyn,	1	7.05	3.65	7.05	3.65
	Manh. and Queens	4 and over	2.25	3.65	2.25	3.65
Emery	Bronx and Brooklyn	1	7.85	4.00	7.85	4.00
		5	3.85	4.00	7.85	4.00
		10 and over	3.14	4.00	7.85	4.00
	Manh. and Queens	1	7.50	3.75	7.50	3.75
		5	2.92	3.75	7.50	3.75
		10	2.26	3.75	7.50	3.75
		25 and over	0.95	3.75	7.50	3.75
WTC Air Freight	Bronx, Brooklyn, Queens	1 and over	10.00	5.25	10.00	5.25
	Manhattan (zone A)	1 and over	9.95	4.65	9.95	4.65
	(zone B)	1 and over	12.15	6.30	12.15	6.30
Long-Haul Carrier Affiliates						
CF Air Freight	Bronx	1 and over	7.95	3.50	7.95	3.50
	Brooklyn and Queens	1 and over	8.75	5.90	8.75	5.90
	Manhattan	1	7.95	6.70	8.95	5.05
		5	2.20	6.70	8.95	5.05

		1.40	6.70	8.95	5.05
10		1.25	4.85	8.95	5.05
11 and over					
PIE Air Freight	All boroughs	8.30	3.65	8.30	3.65
	1 and over				
USAIR Freight	All boroughs	9.10	4.75	9.10	4.75
	5 and over	3.00	3.80	9.10	4.75

SOURCES: Forwarder pickup and delivery tariff.

NOTE: The table shows the regular pickup and delivery rates and charges between New York City airports and points within four of the city's boroughs (these rates and charges do not apply to several points specifically named in the forwarders' pickup and delivery tariffs). Not included are various rates and charges which apply in the case of specific commodities. Where more than one shipment is involved, lower charges apply only if all shipments are picked up at one time at one address. Only a limited range of charges (based on the number of shipments) is shown.

[a]Minimum weight 100 pounds.

TABLE 12

SPECIFIC COMMODITY RATES: INDEPENDENT FORWARDERS V. LONG-HAUL CARRIER AFFILIATES (Airport-to-Airport, July 1977)

Commodity	Route	Average Minimum Charge per Shipment ($)		Average Rate per 100 Lbs. ($) (min. wt. 100 lbs.)	
		Independent Forwarders	Long-Haul Carrier Affiliates	Independent Forwarders	Long-Haul Carrier Affiliates
	From New York-Newark to:				
Pharmaceuticals . . .	Atlanta	7.75	7.25	24.90	26.50
Electrical & electronic equipment . . .	Chicago	7.21	7.80	28.46	38.00
Pharmaceuticals . . .	Chicago	7.62	7.75	25.01	30.59
Textiles & footwear . . .	Chicago	7.36	7.70	23.87	30.08
Office equipment . . .	Dallas	7.50	7.75	38.40	45.05
Electrical & electronic equipment . . .	Los Angeles	7.21	7.75	64.44	63.65
Pharmaceuticals . . .	Los Angeles	6.87	7.50	46.58	58.08
Clothing (not on hangers) . . .	San Francisco	7.52	7.00	55.93	64.71
	To New York-Newark from:				
Automobile parts . . .	Atlanta	7.11	7.00	32.13	26.00
Electrical & electronic equipment . . .	Chicago	7.00	6.10	33.32	32.18
Pharmaceuticals . . .	Chicago	7.50	5.86	31.40	29.61
Textiles & footwear . . .	Chicago	7.47	7.75	23.38	28.10
Electrical & electronic equipment . . .	Dallas	6.58	6.83	34.20	36.58
Aircraft & aerospace vehicle parts . . .	Los Angeles	7.30	7.50	43.25	47.97
Motion picture film . . .	Los Angeles	7.29	7.75	34.79	44.45
Pharmaceuticals . . .	Los Angeles	7.19	7.50	36.41	51.30
Textiles and footwear . . .	Los Angeles	7.30	7.44	40.93	46.48
Printed matter . . .	San Francisco	7.05	7.75	41.25	46.65

t seems highly improbable that the Board will reverse itself in
his matter. Indeed, it has already addressed the petitioners'
rincipal contentions in the aforementioned Charters Investigation
ecision, noting that Congressional action against individually
icketed/waybilled authority was directed at the supplemental air-
ines, not the forwarders. In the same proceeding the agency also
cknowledged that traffic diversion

> is an important policy consideration in defining the proper limits, consis-
> tently with the public interest, of cargo charters operated by air freight
> forwarders. Our conclusions, however, . . . are that forwarder charters
> have not had sufficient impact on scheduled services to warrant any
> restrictions.[1]

eregulation makes it even less likely that a carrier will be able
o count on the Board's aid in combating the competitive inroads of
ther carriers. An early indication of this is the language in a
ecent Senate bill dealing with regulatory reform of the air
assenger field: "the diversion of revenue or traffic from another
ir carrier is not in itself inconsistent with the public convenience
nd necessity."[2]

Drawing on data for 1973 and 1974, the Board has examined the
otential for charter service in 23 major markets. Its Air Freight
orwarders' Charters Investigation (which took into account only
quipment used by the certificated airlines and assumed a forwarder
reakeven point of 60,000 pounds per day)[3] found only one domestic
oute, New York to Los Angeles, to be charterworthy and concluded
hat, despite their potential advantages, regular charter flights
ould not be expected to grow significantly in the foreseeable
uture. The charter breakeven load factors for several aircraft
ypes are given in table 13, which shows, for example, that over a
ong-haul route (New York to Los Angeles) the Flying Tiger Line
ust carry at least 66,300 pounds of freight per day to break even;
or a medium-length route (New York to Chicago) the company would
equire a minimum of 47,100 pounds daily. (The breakeven load fac-
or [column H] represents essentially a comparison of charter and
cheduled rates. In a number of short- and medium-length markets

---

[1]Order 77-7-25, p. 9.

[2]S.2493, 95th Cong., 2nd sess., sec. 5, (1978).

[3]The Board concedes that this figure is in dispute. A detailed account of
he investigation appears in Order 77-7-25.

TABLE 13

COMPUTATION OF CHARTER BREAKEVEN LOAD FACTORS (1974)

A	B	C	D	E	F	G	H	I
Airline[a]	Aircraft	Charter Rate per Mile[b] ($)	Total Charter Charge[c] ($)	Aircraft Capacity (Lbs.)	Charter Rate per Cwt.[e] ($)	Forwarder Av. Sched. Rate per Cwt.[f] ($)	Breakeven Load Factor[g] (%)	Breakeven Pounds per Day[h]
From New York to Los Angeles								
AI	DC-8-63F	6.35	15,716	90,000	17.46	28.75	60.7	54,630
FTL	DC-8-63F	6.30	15,593	100,000	15.59	23.53	66.3	66,300
TWA	B-707	4.55	11,261	75,260	14.96	27.89	53.6	40,339
UA	DC-8-50F	--	10,784	76,240	14.14	25.25	56.0	42,694
From Los Angeles to New York								
AI	DC-8-63F	6.35	15,716	90,000	17.46	18.98	92.0	82,800
FTL	DC-8-63F	6.30	15,593	100,000	15.59	16.66	93.6	93,600
TWA	B-707	4.55	11,261	75,260	14.96	18.42	81.2	61,111
UA	DC-8-50F	--	10,784	76,240	14.14	17.84	79.3	60,458
From New York to Chicago								
FTL	DC-8-63F	6.30	4,618	100,000	4.62	9.81	47.1	47,100
TWA	B-707	4.55	5,000[d]	75,260	6.64	11.23	59.1	44,479
UA	B-727QC	--	3,912	40,220	9.73	9.27	105.0	42,231
UA	DC-8-50F	--	4,425	76,240	5.80	9.27	62.6	47,726
From Chicago to New York								
FTL	DC-8-63F	6.30	4,618	100,000	4.62	10.98	42.1	42,100
TWA	B-707	4.55	5,000[d]	75,260	6.64	10.50	63.2	47,564
UA	B727QC	--	3,912	40,220	9.73	12.57	77.4	31,130
UA	DC-8-50F	--	4,425	76,240	5.80	12.57	46.1	35,147

SOURCE: Docket 23287, initial decision, appendix 21.

$1,750/departure.

... $1,750, mile × $1,750/departure. Rates for United Airlines' B-727QC: $2.95/mile +

c Charter rate per mile times mileage of 2,475 for New York-Los Angeles and 733 for New York-Chicago.

d Trans World Airlines' minimum charter charge, tariff CAB no. 270, 1st. revised page 13.

e Col. D divided by col. E, times 100.

f 1973 forwarder average scheduled rate/cwt. adjusted to reflect the following scheduled freight yield increases: Airlift International--19.54 percent; Flying Tiger Line--6.82 percent; Trans World Airlines--6.82 percent; Trans World Airlines--15.98 percent; United Airlines--12.86 percent (for the quarter ended December 31, 1974, over the fourth quarter of 1973; Trans World Airlines--third quarter of 1974 over the third quarter of 1973).

g Col. F divided by col. G, times 100.

h Col. E times col. H, divided by 100.

high departure costs form part of the charter rate, and here scheduled transportation could be less expensive even though the shipper might offer the charter airline a full-plane load. United Airlines' 105 percent breakeven load factor for its B-727QC illustrates such a case.) The forwarders generate sufficient traffic to sustain medium- and long-haul charter flights over a mere five routes (table 14), only two of which (Chicago-Los Angeles and Los Angeles-New York) satisfy the 60,000-pound weight requirement in both directions. Table 14 assumes that the leading forwarders are interested in charter operations and are willing to pool or joint load their freight in order to realize the resultant economies of scale. Such an assumption, however, has no basis in fact; United Parcel Service (UPS) is satisfied with scheduled transportation and does not intend to enter the charter business, and the other operators, for reasons discussed above, refuse to joint load their domestic traffic. This, then, leaves only one route (New York to Los Angeles) for which a forwarder, acting alone, has enough traffic to meet not only his own breakeven point but also that of the underlying certificated airline.

The early 1970s, the period on which the Board's study is based, saw the beginning of a substantial reduction of the trunk carriers' overnight freighter flights, particularly in short- and medium-length markets. This forced the major forwarders to reexamine their position towards charter service, and in 1975 four companies Air Express International, Emery, Shulman, and WTC Air Freight--were chartering aircraft for some of their outbound domestic freight at New York-Newark, with most of this traffic going to Atlanta, Chicago Los Angeles, and San Francisco. Company spokesmen stressed that charter operations were being used primarily to compensate for the inadequate scheduled freight lift provided by the trunks, not because they were financially attractive. They enabled the companies to provide next-day delivery, rather than the second- or even third-day delivery associated with much of the freight carried in the bellies of daytime passenger aircraft, and thus to meet established tariff commitments.

The most extensive charter program is that instituted by Emery in 1976 ("Emery Air Force"), linking New York-Newark with about th other cities, including Atlanta, Charlotte, Chicago, Cleveland, Dallas, Dayton, Detroit, Hartford, Kansas City, Memphis, Miami, Ne Orleans, and Pittsburgh. The service is two-way and utilizes aircraft ranging from the DC-8 and Lockheed Electra to the Skyvan and Beech 18. Roughly forty percent (by weight) of Emery's total outb

TABLE 14

AVERAGE DAILY TRAFFIC OF THE INDIVIDUAL
FORWARDERS IN THE DOMESTIC "CHARTER POTENTIAL" MARKETS[a]

Route[b]	Forwarder	Outbound Traffic (lbs.)		Inbound Traffic (lbs.)	
		Total 1973 (1,000)	Average Daily[c]	Total 1973 (1,000)	Average Daily[c]
Chicago- Los Angeles	Airborne	1,659	6,610	2,726	10,861
	Emery	1,922	7,657	1,431	5,701
	UPS	24,718	98,478	28,547	113,733
	WTC	--	--	2,564	10,215
	Total	28,299	112,745	35,268	140,510
Chicago- New York	Airborne	1,668	6,645	1,794	7,147
	Emery	4,472	17,817	5,036	20,064
	Shulman	--	--	3,849	15,335
	UPS	1,120	4,462	1,915	7,629
	WTC	1,147	4,570	5,113	20,371
	Total	8,407	33,494	17,707	70,546
Chicago- San Francisco	Airborne	1,219	4,857	2,186	8,709
	Emery	1,318	5,251	--	--
	UPS	16,114	64,199	7,238	28,837
	WTC	2,909	11,590	--	--
	Total	21,560	85,897	9,424	37,546
Los Angeles- New York	Airborne	3,188	12,701	2,371	9,446
	Emery	2,820	11,235	3,358	13,378
	Shulman	2,657	10,586	16,583	66,068
	UPS	22,179	88,363	29.910	119,163
	WTC	4,372	17,418	11,093	44,195
	Total	35,216	140,303	63,315	252,250
New York- San Francisco	Emery	1,919	7,645	1,299	5,175
	Shulman	1,216	4,845	--	--
	UPS	17,776	70,821	6,284	25,036
	WTC	6,585	26,235	--	--
	Total	27,496	109,546	7,583	30,211

SOURCE: Docket 23287, initial decision, appendix 22.

[a]Includes only forwarders having in excess of 5,000 pounds of traffic per day (260-day working year).

[b]All routes meet the assumption of breakeven at 60,000 pounds total forwarder traffic per day.

[c]Total 1973 traffic divided by 251 days per year.

domestic freight at New York-Newark's airports (1977) is carried in chartered aircraft. The trunks show no interest in restoring their nighttime freighter service to the level of the early 1970s, and Emery may soon expand its charter program. Airborne, another leading forwarder, and one of Emery's major competitors, has adopted a similar strategy in the face of inadequate overnight trunk service. The company's efforts focus on next-morning delivery and, to this end, it has entered (June, 1977) into a contractual arrangement with Midwest Air Charter (an Ohio-based air taxi), under which the latter provides Airborne with night flights between New York-Newark and Atlanta, Baltimore, Boston, Charlotte, Chicago, Cleveland, Dallas, Hartford, Indianapolis, Jacksonville, Oklahoma City, Philadelphia, Pittsburgh, Richmond, St. Louis, San Antonio, and Tulsa. The Airborne-Midwest contract specifies the aircraft to be used (Aerostar, Aztec, Citation, Hansa, Lear, and Twin Beach) and sets 12:00 A.M. to 4:30 A.M. as the time limit for the two companies' New York freight exchanges. In the wake of deregulation the larger forwarders may wish to purchase and/or lease aircraft (Air Express International, Airborne, Burlington, Emery, and WTC Air Freight have already indicated an interest in doing so). This, added to the forwarders' growing interest in chartering, will further lessen their dependence on the trunklines.

Since the trunks carry the major portion of the forwarders' traffic, it is the performance of this carrier class which is of greatest concern to the forwarders, and it is trunkline officials at whom the forwarders' major complaints have been directed. The main forwarder criticism in New York-Newark, as perhaps in other leading airport cities, centers on insufficient scheduled nighttime airlift. The forwarders are united in their condemnation of the trunks' gradual abandonment of freighter service and, irrespective of the size of their consolidations, they insist this development restricts their operations and hampers the air freight industry's expansion. (An all-cargo carrier such as the Flying Tiger Line, of course, does not gear its schedules to the needs of the traveling public. It serves relatively few markets, however, and cannot be regarded as an alternative to the trunk carriers.) The charge of inadequate trunk nighttime service, used effectively during the deregulation debate, puts the forwarders at odds with airline officials, many of whom contend that the majority of air shippers have no need of overnight service and are not opposed to seeing their consignments carried in combination aircraft during daylight hours. The combination carriers' all-cargo services have produced massive financial losses,[1] and, say the trunks, the use of combination equipment has not resulted in a qualitatively inferior service for shippers and receivers.

Competition from Federal Express, a small-package airline formed in 1973, has provided and continues to provide much of the impetus for the charters and related contractual arrangements initiated by some of the leading forwarders. They maintain that the ability to offer their customers overnight transportation and next-day delivery (as Federal is doing) is essential to their business and dismiss the combination carriers' position as proof that these have no interest in the promotion of freight traffic. Emery estimates that if deprived of all overnight air transportation it would lose fifty percent of the domestic tonnage it originates in the New York-Newark area; Airborne puts its potential loss at seventy-five percent.

Shippers Associations

An air shippers association is a special form of indirect air carrier. The Civil Aeronautics Board permits such an organization to function provided it is

> a bona fide association of shippers, operating as an indirect air carrier on a non-profit basis, which: undertakes to ship property for the account of such association or its members, by air, in the name of either the association or the members, in order to secure the benefits of volume rates or improved services for the benefits of its members, and utilizes for the whole or any part of such transportation either the services of a direct air carrier . . . or those of an air freight forwarder.[2]

Association members pool their freight, paying lower airline rates than would apply to smaller shipments tendered individually. Where the volume of freight generated by members is so small as to preclude worthwhile consolidations, an association may represent its members simply as a shipping agent. Associations are controlled by their members as a whole, and, in overseeing their activities, the Board ensures that individual members or groups of members do not dominate or control association affairs.

Authority to function as indirect air carriers was granted the associations in 1955. This decision, which formed part of the Air Freight Forwarder Investigation, above, met with opposition from the

---

[1] Colin Hugh McIntosh, The Economics of Air Cargo: An Analysis of Profits Unnecessarily Diminished (Washington, D.C.: ATW Marketing Services, 1977), tables 6 and 8.

[2] ER-1046.

276

forwarders, who, perceiving these organizations as a threat to their own operations, pressed the Board to require the associations to prove that a public need existed for their services. The agency refused to impose such a restriction, viewing it as an unwarranted governmental intrusion into the private sector, and instead ordered the cooperatives to furnish information enabling it to assess the scope and nature of their activities. They were required to tender their freight to direct air carriers, were confined to domestic operations, and were to remain independent of any kind of forwarder influence or control. The latter point is of particular importance, since effective control of an association by its members was, and remains, the crucial distinction between it and a forwarder.

The situation remained essentially unchanged until, in 1977, Novo Airfreight, a forwarder, approached the Board with a request for a declaratory order authorizing utilization of air freight forwarders by cooperative shippers associations.[1] (Novo's request reflected the company's desire to win the business of various film distributors, who were then considering formation of a shippers association. Air Express International, a competitor whose major customers included a number of film companies, promptly assailed Novo's plea, calling it a private relief bill and "a device to attempt to recoup lost business.")[2] While denying the petition for a declaratory order, the agency nevertheless agreed to review the position of the associations and, in March of 1978, it announced that henceforth they could tender their traffic to forwarders as well as airlines. This new ruling, which had the support of the American Institute for Shippers' Associations, Inc., was intended to enhance the "efficiency and flexibility" of the air freight industry and, to the extent that it eased market entry for small associations, was in harmony with earlier Federal deregulation legislation. As part of its justification for this action the agency has noted that the associations' maturity now makes it less likely that they will fall under the control of the forwarders. Its confidence in their resilience, however, remains qualified, and association members were presumably reassured to receive the agency's pledge of "continuing supervision . . . to ensure the independence of the cooperatives."[3]

---

[1] Petition of Novo Airfreight, Docket 30783, April 25, 1977.

[2] Comments of Air Express International to Petition of Novo Airfreight, Docket 30783, June 13, 1977, p. 2.

[3] ER-1046

Reference must also be made to two other regulatory changes affecting shippers cooperatives. Towards the end of 1975 the Hawaii Air Cargo Shippers Association filed a petition in which it sought approval to charter aircraft on the same terms as might a forwarder. The state of Hawaii was at this time threatened by a longshoremen strike, and the Association, anticipating a substantial diversion of freight from sea to air transportation, was fearful that the state's scheduled airlift would be unable to absorb the additional traffic. Shippers cooperatives had traditionally been excluded from the charter market, and the Association protested the Board's unjust discrimination "in favor of one class of indirect air carriers (forwarders) to the detriment of another class of indirect air carriers (associations)."[1] A notice of proposed rule-making was subsequently issued (May, 1976), followed a year later by new regulations equalizing the charter rights of the two carrier groups.

Charter authority for the cooperatives was welcomed by the supplemental carriers[2] but has been deplored by the Flying Tiger Line and several trunk carriers. In a plea to the CAB not to grant the requested charter authority, Flying Tiger noted that such authority

> will for the first time permit associations of produce shippers to shift to charter operations large amounts of eastbound perishable traffic which now sustains scheduled freighter service in that direction. It would be only a matter of time before the diversionary impact of westbound forwarder charters operating in conjunction with eastbound produce shippers association charters would become so acute as to result in a severe degradation of the level of scheduled freighter service.[3]

The threat of traffic diversion was not taken seriously by the Board, given the small number of associations in existence. Similarly, the agency remained unmoved by the Hawaii association's discrimination charge, which, it pointed out, had no validity in view of the basic differences between the two carrier groups.[4] It has explained its action in terms of (1) its desire to simplify the general charter regulations and (2) the absence of any need to maintain a statutory distinction between forwarders and associations with respect to chartering.

---

[1] Petition for Rule Change to Allow Hawaii Air Cargo Shippers Association to Charter, Docket 28256 (1975), p. 3.

[2] Comments of Member Carriers of the National Air Carrier Association, Docket 28256, June 10, 1976.

[3] Comments of the Flying Tiger Line, Inc., Docket 28256, June 10, 1976, p. 3.

[4] See above, pp. 9-10.

The second change was made in March of 1978 and permits the cooperatives to participate in overseas transportation, from which they were previously barred because at the time international operations by indirect carriers were being authorized (1958) there appeared to be no public need for their services. With the receipt by the Board of several association applications for international rights, this prohibition could no longer be upheld and international authority was accordingly extended to the cooperatives. The action, warmly applauded by the supplemental airlines, has been severely criticized by the Flying Tiger Line on the ground that it is injurious to its scheduled international operations. Flying Tiger foresees an erosion of its yield (since consolidations move under lower rates) and believes the search for more favorable transportation rates will tempt shippers to tender their pooled traffic to charter specialists. The company also predicts the formation of shipping cartels for particular commodity groups.[1] (A number of forwarders, fearing business losses, have also criticized the Board's move.) The CAB (as well as the American Institute for Shippers' Associations, Inc.) has rejected Flying Tiger's contentions. It notes that various "commercial difficulties" tend to hinder the formation of shipping cartels and points out the associations do not enjoy immunity from Federal antitrust laws.

There were only two major air shippers associations active in the New York-Newark area during the mid-1970s. They are discussed here not so much because of their contribution to the freight system's traffic flow, which must be considered minor, but because they represent actual examples of shipper cooperation. The larger of the two (in terms of traffic volume) is the Hawaii Air Cargo Shippers Association, which was established as a mechanism by which shippers might transport freight between Hawaii and the U.S. mainland. Detailed traffic figures for the New York market have not been released, though the Association does say that of its total Hawaii-New York tonnage 99 percent moves from New York to Honolulu. All of its traffic is containerized (the containers used are types LD-3, LD-7, and LD-11); in New York it maintains an account with ACI's Trucking Division, which performs the containerization. During 1977 the Association, which has about 500 members, shipped a total of 3.2 million pounds of freight—clothing, other textile articles, and foodstuffs were among the major items—and received from its membership revenues of $1.3 million.

---

[1]Comments of the Flying Tiger Line, Inc., Docket 31272, December 7, 1977.

The other cooperative, the Jewelers Shipping Association, has been formed to allow members to pool their costume jewelry traffic. In 1975 it handled 1.9 million pounds of air freight and generated revenues of $0.5 million. One quarter of its nationwide membership of 1,400 is located in the New York-Newark area and produces about 300,000 pounds of freight annually. Its principal destination points (from New York-Newark) are: Chicago, Dallas, Los Angeles, and San Francisco. Consolidations are performed by the Association itself. Both it and the Hawaii organization estimate membership brings individual shippers, on average, savings of fifteen percent on their transportation bills.

Air-Sea Service

The Atlantic Container Line (ACL), in conjunction with Eastern Air Lines and the Flying Tiger Line, offers shippers a United States-Europe scheduled air-sea through service for LTL traffic. The monthly two-way volume ranges from 750,000 to one million pounds (1975). The export:import ratio is 3:2 with Scandinavia and the United Kingdom accounting for about forty percent of the total traffic. The service is about five years old. Its appeal, in the words of an ACL brochure, lies in the fact that it "is cheaper than all air and faster than all surface."

Let us consider the manner in which this joint program works in practice. Shipments are flown to New York-Newark from points in the United States and are then carried by truck to the Atlantic Container Line's Elizabeth (N.J.) terminal. Here they are containerized prior to being shipped to European destinations. Generally, goods will leave at the announced sailing time if brought to the terminal before 5 P.M. on the day preceding departure. The ocean containers have characteristic markings and are given priority treatment at destination points. Conversely, the contents of containers arriving at Elizabeth is trucked to the air terminals, where the imports are reassembled. Approximately fifty percent of the import traffic is recontainerized for the flights to destination airports. Air and sea movements are coordinated through use of a single document, the Atlantic Container Line Datafreight Receipt, which is a nonnegotiable through bill of lading. "Nonnegotiable" in this context means that ownership of the merchandise cannot be changed while goods are in transit.

A great deal of enthusiasm surrounded the early phase of coordinated air-sea service; traffic volume for 1974 was 178 percent above that of the previous year, and airline and ACL personnel viewed future developments with confidence. Despite a promising beginning, however, traffic growth has failed to live up to expectations, causing one participant, American Airlines, to withdraw from the program (May, 1977). Although the company continues to praise the intermodal principles involved, the disappointing freight volume made it impossible to justify special truck runs between Kennedy Airport and Elizabeth. The attempts of another air carrier, Flying Tiger, to interest additional shipping lines in coordinated air-sea service have not been successful.

Concluding Remarks

The two major underlying themes of the present chapter, competition and integration (cooperation, coordination), are encountered to some extent throughout this study. (Where referring to carriers, "cooperation" usually implies that only one transportation mode is involved, whereas "coordination" relates to two or more modes.) Thus, competition among airline classes was considered in chapter I, where we also saw how the Board, in pursuing a number of national/ public policy objectives, resorted to various anticompetitive measures. Chapter II reviews competition between forwarders and certificated truckers, with particular reference to the air terminal area, a discussion that is taken up again in chapter VII. Also examined in chapter II is the Board's initial use, in its own proceedings, of several ICC decisions, and the two agencies' cooperation in the matter of the 25-mile exempt zone as well as their joint acceptance of many additional pickup and delivery points. Chapter III introduces the reader to Public Law 95-163 and to the carriers' responses to the prospect of unlimited competition. Chapter IV outlines the early aviation rivalry between the cities of Newark and New York and notes the efforts of the Port Authority to establish a unifed airport system. Competition among the airlines serving New York-Newark is investigated in chapter VIII, wherein are also given examples of interairline cooperation.

Chapter VI has presented a number of air freight services available to the New York-Newark shipper and receiver, examining these in the light of various competitive and integrative considerations. The attitude of most carriers towards competition is that there is too much of it. The shipper, on the other hand, welcomes carrier competition in that it broadens his range of service options and contributes to lower transportation rates. Some degree of

ntegration, of course, is accepted by all and recognized as
indispensable if the system is to function as an interlocking whole.
The principal examples of integration and competition discussed in
chapter VI may be summarized as follows:

I. Integration

    1. Pickup/delivery service: airline cooperation in the setting up and
        running of Air Cargo, Inc.; air-surface coordination
    2. Air-truck service (joint and combined)
    3. Surface-for-air substitutions
    4. Single-entity door-to-door forwarder service
    5. Shipper cooperation (associations)
    6. Air-sea service (involves air, land, and water carriers)

II. Competition

    1. Trucker v. Trucker
    2. Trucker v. Forwarder
    3. Forwarder v. Airline
    4. Forwarder v. Forwarder
    5. Forwarder v. Shippers Association

The air freight industry faces a period of uncertainty, and it
would be unrealistic to think of the various freight services within
a static framework. Some of these services, to say nothing of the
competitive and integrative factors on which they rest, are currently
undergoing reexamination, making it likely that a number of carriers
will soon experiment with new approaches to air freight transportation. Thus, for instance, deregulation makes possible new forms of
carrier mergers and acquisitions and hence new patterns of
air-surface integration. Also, Public Law 95-163 may encourage
greater use of motor-for-air substitute service. Another potential
change focuses on several airlines' dissatisfaction with Air Cargo,
Inc. and the possible emergence of new pickup and delivery programs.

CHAPTER VII

THE NEW YORK-NEWARK AIR TERMINAL AREA:

CONSTANCY OR CHANGE?

In May of 1977 the Interstate Commerce Commission released a
proposal calling for the blanket enlargement of pickup and delivery
zones. Highly controversial, the proposed 100-mile zone has been
greeted with much enthusiasm in some quarters, while encountering
strong resistance in others. The revised mileage rule, introduced
briefly in chapter II, is now examined at length, with particular
reference to the New York-Newark situation.

Commodity Flows in the New York-Newark
Air Terminal Area

A number of functional relationships characterizing the air
freight system were analyzed in the previous chapter. The significance of these linkages lies in their facilitation of freight
movements, and we turn now to a consideration of such movements
within the New York-Newark air terminal area[1] (nationwide traffic
flows are examined in chapter VIII). Figures 7a and 7b show, respectively, total freight flows (by county) between the Kennedy and Newark
air terminals, on the one hand, and points within 100 miles of these
facilities, on the other. This zone accounts for approximately 70 percent
(by weight) of the system's total two-way traffic and is large enough
to accommodate changes in the scope of pickup and delivery operations
as contemplated (1977) by the Interstate Commerce Commission. Also

---

[1]The data on which part of this chapter is based have been derived from
unpublished material made available by the Aviation Economics Division of the Port
Authority of New York and New Jersey. The Division's statistical information was
generated through an air freight survey (conducted during the two-year period
1973-1974), in which were examined the shipping documents covering all traffic
(exclusive of "express" traffic) moving on various predetermined flights. The
sampling rate was: (1) for all-cargo aircraft--one out of every 120 flights, and
(2) for combination aircraft--one out of every 1,600 domestic flights and one out
of every 400 overseas flights. The information abstracted from the airbills
included: commodity mix, forwarder traffic share, origin and destination (according to shipper/consignee postal ZIP codes), shipment weight, etc. The survey, in
which 43 scheduled airlines and 282 forwarders participated, resulted in a freight
sample in which all scheduled direct flights to and from Kennedy and Newark airports were represented. Extrapolation of the sample yielded a total two-way air
freight tonnage which was eight percent below the actual 1973-1974 figure as
reported by all carriers. (La Guardia Airport handles less than five percent of
the region's air freight and was not included in the survey.)

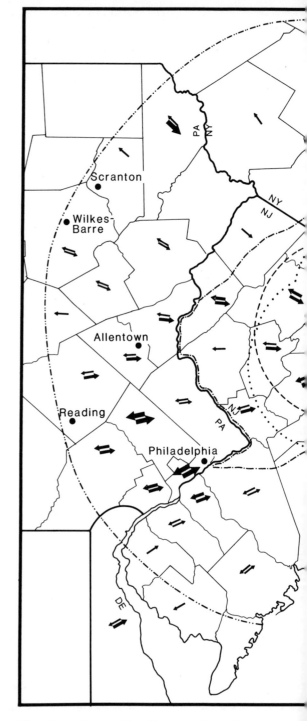

Fig. 7a. Commodity flows to/from Kennedy Air

285

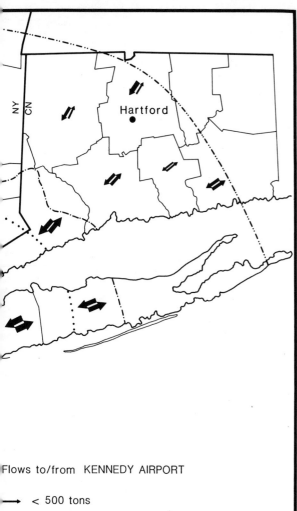

Flows to/from KENNEDY AIRPORT

→ < 500 tons
➡ 500-4,999 tons
➡ 5,000-19,999 tons
➡ 20,000-100,000 tons
➡ > 100,000 tons

---- Newark 25-mile zone
······· New York 25-mile zone
—·—· New York-Newark air terminal area
—··—· New York-Newark 100-mile zone

commodities   (January 1973 - December 1974)

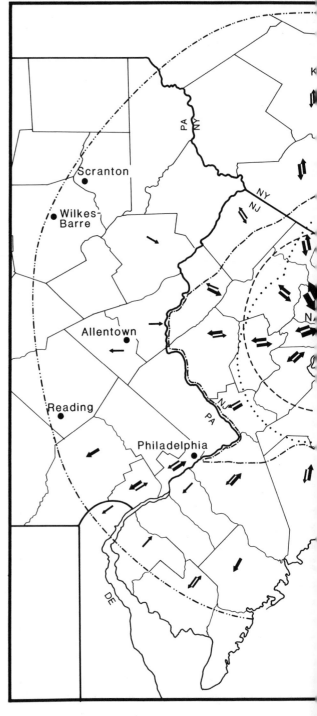

Fig. 7b. Commodity flows to/from Newark Airport

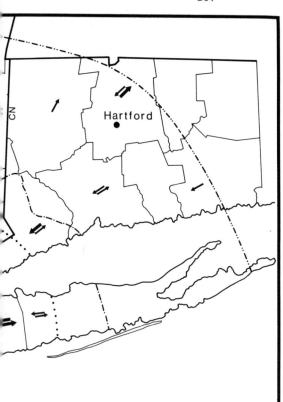

ws to/from NEWARK AIRPORT

< 500 tons
500-4,999 tons
5,000-19,999 tons
20,000-100,000 tons
> 100,000 tons

Newark 25-mile zone
New York 25-mile zone
New York-Newark air terminal area
New York-Newark 100-mile zone

ommodities   (January 1973 - December 1974)

shown are the conventional 25-mile pickup and delivery zones, as
well as the actual New York-Newark air terminal area within which
nonregulated carriage of air freight by certain carriers has been
accepted by the Civil Aeronautics Board and the Interstate Commerce
Commission.[1]

New York City is far and away the system's most important pro-
ducer and consumer of air freight, accounting for about 44 percent of
the total (table 15). New York's dominance is due largely to the
part played by Manhattan, which alone is responsible for some 30
percent of the system's traffic. Queens, another New York City
borough, though greatly overshadowed by Manhattan, remains an important air freight center in its own right and generates about 10
percent of the total two-way traffic. By comparison, Newark, the
air terminal area's second largest city, plays only a modest role;
it accounts for less than 5 percent of the total tonnage. Other
relatively important freight producing/consuming areas are: (1) the
industrialized counties of northeastern New Jersey;[2] (2) Nassau,
Suffolk, and Westchester (New York); and (3) Fairfield (Connecticut).
The heavy concentration of air freight shippers and receivers in and
around New York City can be illustrated from another perspective:
about 62 percent of the inbound and 60 percent of the outbound
traffic centers on the New York 25-mile zone. A substantially
larger area, the New York-Newark 100-mile zone, captures only an
additional 6 percent of the inbound and 8 percent of the outbound
traffic.

Figures 7a and 7b are of interest not only because of what they
tell us about the spatial distribution of local freight origins and
destinations, but because the freight movements reflect important
differences in the services provided at the system's two principal
airports. Mere proximity to an airport is, of course, not enough
to ensure a shipper's use of air transportation; rather, shippers
look to the quality and range of the services the airport offers or,
putting it another way, to the terminal's ability to satisfy their
particular requirements. Of the traffic handled by the two airports
almost 90 percent moves through the Kennedy facility. A major
reason for this imbalance is that practically all overseas freight
(about 50 percent of the system total) is channeled through Kennedy

---

[1] See above, p. 117.

[2] Bergen, Essex, Hudson, and Union counties account for about 70 percent
of New Jersey's air freight traffic.

Airport.[1] Only about 50 percent of the outbound overseas traffic originates within the New York-Newark air terminal area, underscoring Kennedy's role as the leading East Coast gateway for air shipments coming from all parts of the United States. Kennedy's commanding lead over Newark rests not only on its position as the region's major international airport; in the domestic sphere, too, various service characteristics combine to give it a substantial competitive advantage. Thus, roughly 80 percent of the system's scheduled domestic all-cargo flights leave from Kennedy, as do 75 percent of the wide-body passenger-cargo flights. In addition, the two terminals can be distinguished on the basis of markets served. For instance, Kennedy is the principal facility for scheduled transcontinental departures, offering about 85 percent of the direct flights to the major West Coast points (Los Angeles, San Francisco, Seattle).

Within the New York-Newark air terminal area virtually all freight moved to and from the airports is carried by truck. Of the tonnage transported between points outside the terminal area and the airports, however, roughly two-thirds is carried by air (air-to-air transfers), the remainder by truck (air-truck transfers). About 50 percent of the air-to-air tonnage represents international traffic. In the case of air-truck transfers, on the other hand, international traffic is relatively more important and comes to about 80 percent. Of the domestic air-truck transfers only about 20 percent are handled at Newark Airport. The reason for this low figure is that four-fifths of the long-haul truck tonnage is transferred to/from all-cargo aircraft (i.e., to/from night flights), the majority of which are routed through the Kennedy terminal. Kennedy's advantages over Newark are reflected in its greater ability to attract traffic from points located beyond the boundaries of the air terminal area. Thus, of the total outbound traffic at Kennedy, only about 60 percent originates within the air terminal area; for Newark, the figure is about 85 percent.

Flows for all those commodities constituting at least five percent of the system's total two-way tonnage are depicted in figures 8a through 12b. The commodities are: apparel (Standard Industrial Classification--23), chemicals and allied products (SIC--28), electrical and electronic machinery (SIC--36), nonelectrical machinery (SIC--35), and printed material (SIC--27). The

---

[1] Almost all scheduled overseas all-cargo flights and wide-body passenger-cargo flights leave from Kennedy Airport.

TABLE 15

ORIGIN AND DESTINATION OF FREIGHT
MOVING THROUGH THE KENNEDY AND NEWARK AIR TERMINALS
(Scheduled Flights: January, 1973 - December, 1974)

| | Kennedy Airport | | | |
| | Domestic Freight | | Overseas Freight | |
	tons	% of total	tons	% of total
	Inbound Traffic			
Consignee Destination				
Newark	11,983	3	1,683	0.4
Newark SMSA[a]	16,184	4	5,802	1
New York City	215,995	49	192,827	45
Bronx	13,456	3	4,078	1
Brooklyn	5,968	1	7,268	2
Manhattan	136,360	31	130,354	30
Queens	60,209	14	51,004	12
Staten I.	2	–	123	–
New York SMSA[b]	227,462	52	212,835	50
New York 25-mile zone[c]	271,844	62	249,978	58
NY-Newark air terminal area[d]	275,792	63	253,293	59
NY-Newark 100-mile zone[e]	292,889	67	274,259	64
United States	440,086	100	427,779	100
	Outbound Traffic			
Origin of Shipper				
Newark	11,488	3	4,635	1
Newark SMSA[a]	14,643	4	9,501	2
New York City	168,984	49	247,810	42
Bronx	4,612	1	4,112	1
Brooklyn	5,255	1	11,811	2
Manhattan	118,703	35	191,317	32
Queens	40,387	12	40,563	7
Staten I.	27	–	7	–
New York SMSA[b]	183,008	53	258,799	44
New York 25-mile zone[c]	233,033	68	295,289	50
NY-Newark air terminal area[d]	243,453	71	299,658	51
NY-Newark 100-mile zone[e]	267,404	78	336,770	57
United States	343,092	100	592,575	100

SOURCE: The Port Authority of New York and New Jersey.

[a]Includes Essex, Morris, Somerset, and Union counties.

[b]Includes New York City and the following counties: Bergen, Putnam, Rockland, and Westchester.

[c]Measured from New York City's corporate limits.

[d]See above, p. 218, note 1.

[e]The zone's northern and eastern boundaries have been measured from La Guardia Airport; its southern and western boundaries from Newark Airport.

TABLE 15--Continued

| Newark Airport | | | | Both Airports | | | | Domestic & Overseas Freight | |
| Domestic Freight | | Overseas Freight | | Domestic Freight | | Overseas Freight | | | |
tons	% of total	tons	% of total	tons	% of total	tons	% of total	tons	% of total
				Inbound Traffic					
21,194	19	0	0	33,177	6	1,683	0.4	34,860	4
30,952	28	0	0	47,136	9	5,802	1	52,938	5
27,678	25	0	0	243,673	44	192,827	45	436,500	45
212	0.2	0	0	13,668	2	4,078	1	17,746	2
376	0.3	0	0	6,344	1	7,268	2	13,612	1
22,829	21	0	0	159,189	29	130,354	30	289,543	30
4,215	4	0	0	64,424	12	51,004	12	115,428	12
46	-	0	0	48	-	123	-	171	-
36,347	33	0	0	263,809	48	212,835	50	476,644	49
86,964	79	0	0	358,808	65	249,978	58	608,786	62
89,776	81	0	0	365,568	66	253,293	59	618,861	63
97,683	88	1	0.5	390,572	71	274,260	64	664,832	68
110,398	100	200	100	550,484	100	427,979	100	978,463	100
				Outbound Traffic					
27,045	18	163	29	38,533	8	4,798	1	43,331	4
47,468	32	163	29	62,111	13	9,664	2	71,775	7
46,330	31	28	5	215,314	44	247,838	42	463,152	43
142	0.1	0	0	4,754	1	4,112	1	8,866	1
948	0.6	0	0	6,203	1	11,811	2	18,014	2
40,956	27	28	5	159,659	32	191,345	32	351,004	32
4,092	3	0	0	44,479	9	40,563	7	85,042	8
192	0.1	0	0	219	-	7	-	226	-
56,392	37	28	5	239,400	48	258,827	44	498,227	46
123,364	82	191	34	356,397	72	295,480	50	651,877	60
127,294	85	191	34	370,747	75	299,849	51	670,596	62
134,162	89	555	100	401,566	81	337,325	57	738,891	68
150,589	100	555	100	493,681	100	593,130	100	1,086,811	100

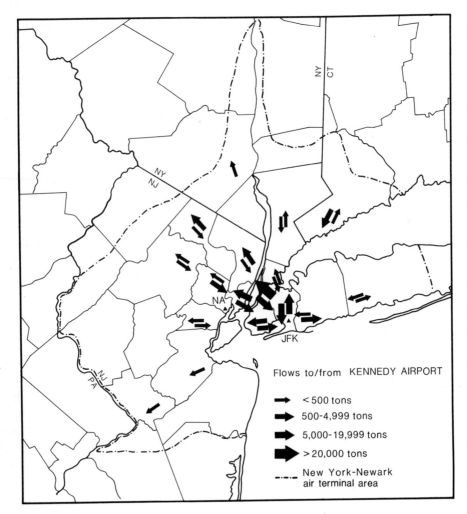

Fig. 8a. Commodity flows in the New York-Newark air terminal area to/from Kennedy Airport: Apparel (January 1973 - December 1974)

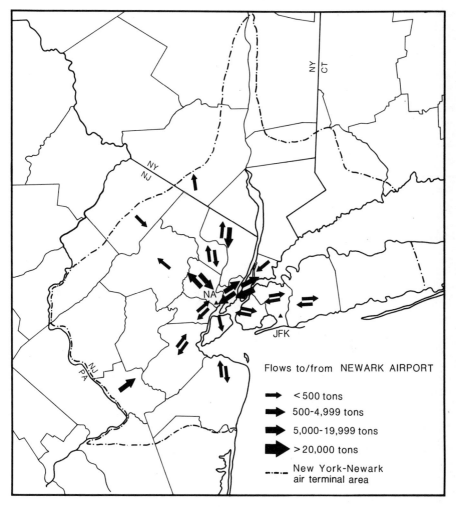

Fig. 8b. Commodity flows in the New York-Newark air terminal area to/from Newark Airport: Apparel (January 1973 - December 1974)

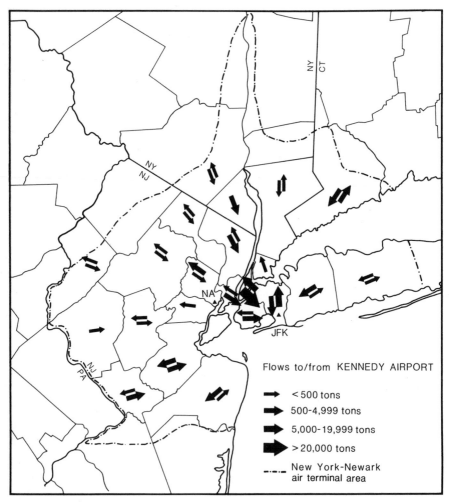

Fig. 9a. Commodity flows in the New York-Newark air terminal area to/from Kennedy Airport: Chemicals (January 1973 - December 1974)

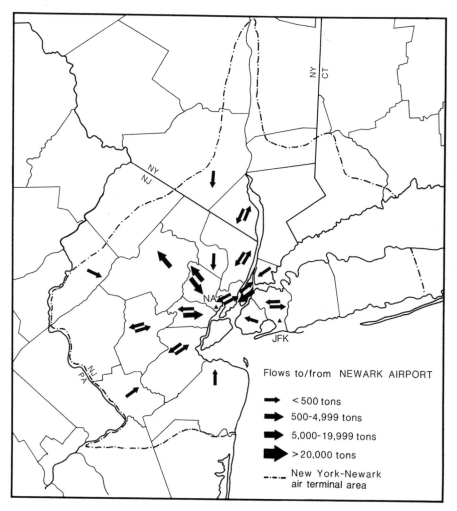

Fig. 9b. Commodity flows in the New York-Newark air terminal area to/from Newark Airport: Chemicals (January 1973 - December 1974)

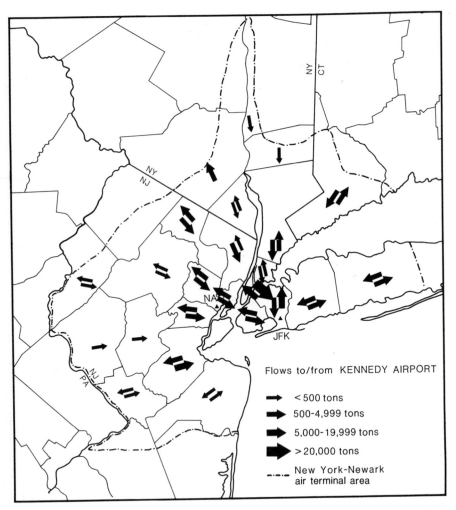

Fig. 10a. Commodity flows in the New York-Newark air terminal area to/from Kennedy Airport: Electrical and electronic machinery (January 1973 - December 1974)

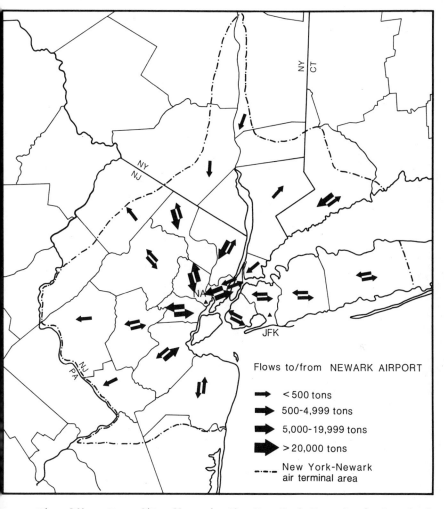

Fig. 10b. Commodity flows in the New York-Newark air terminal area to/from Newark Airport: Electrical and electronic machinery (January 1973 - December 1974)

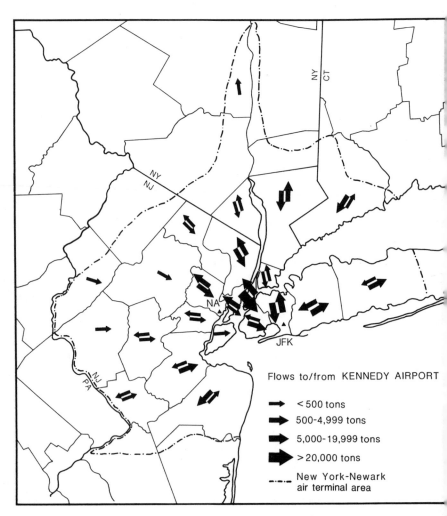

Fig. 11a.   Commodity flows in the New York-Newark air terminal area to/from Kennedy Airport: Nonelectrical machinery (January 1973–December 1974)

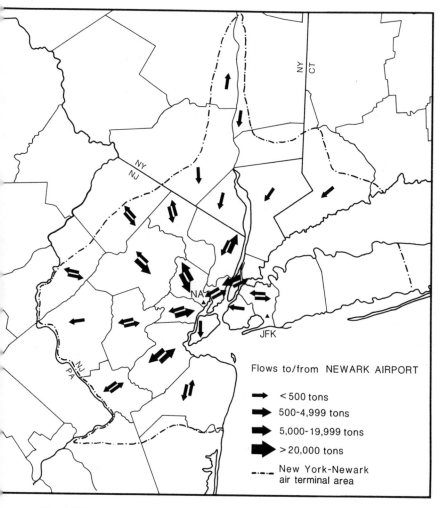

Fig. 11b. Commodity flows in the New York-Newark air terminal area to/from Newark Airport: Nonelectrical machinery (January 1973 – December 1974)

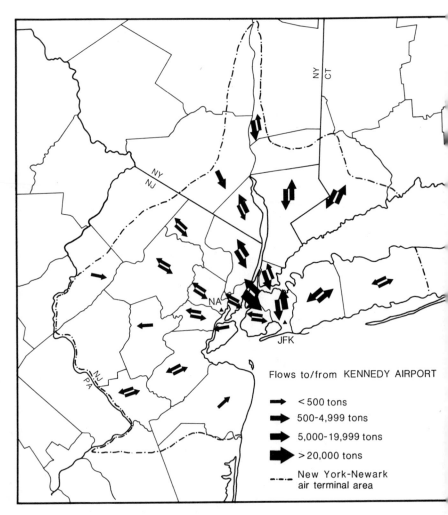

Fig. 12a. Commodity flows in the New York-Newark air termina
area to/from Kennedy Airport: Printed material (January 1973 -
December 1974)

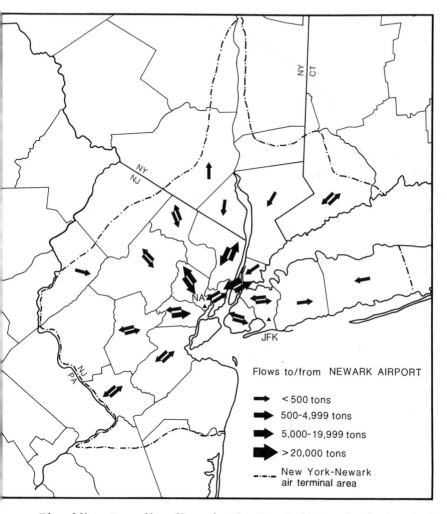

Fig. 12b. Commodity flows in the New York-Newark air terminal
area to/from Newark Airport: Printed material (January 1973 –
December 1974)

flow patterns generated by these groups are broadly comparable to
that outlined for the combined commodity mix and are not discussed
individually. It is worth noting that this small number of commodi
ties accounts for about fifty percent of both the air terminal area
tonnage and the system's overall tonnage. As before, New York City
position as the leading origin and destination point is unchallenge
the city accounting for fully two-thirds of the terminal area's
five-commodity traffic.

Responses to a Changing Regulatory Environment

The ICC and the CAB have in the past approved pickup and
delivery service between certain airports and specified points lyir
beyond the conventional 25-mile air terminal areas. Such authoriza
tions, as was shown earlier in the case of Newark, have aroused
much criticism and have usually been accompanied by efforts on the
part of competing carriers to reverse the relevant agency ruling(s)
The controversy surrounding the scope of pickup and delivery servic
has been heightened by the Interstate Commerce Commission's willing
ness to enlarge the radius of air terminal areas from 25 to 100
miles[1] (chapter II). The proposed radius sharply increases the si
of those areas within which nonregulated motor transportation of ai
shipments is permissible and is strongly opposed by various partie
especially those who operating under licenses issued by the ICC,
believed themselves protected against competition from nonregulate
carriers.

The Commission's stance has sent shock waves through the ran
of the licensed air freight truckers and has drawn the most strenu
objections from this carrier group. (Some specific examples of th
effects competitive inroads by forwarders have had on truckers
operating within the existing air terminal area were given in the
previous chapter and need not be recapitulated.) Enhanced pickup
and delivery rights, truckers state, will simply accentuate their
current problems, destabilize the entire fabric of air
freight-related ground service, and remove the ICC as the guaranto
of fair rates and practices.[2] The truckers are holders of certifi
cates of public convenience and necessity and as such have had to

---

[1] The Commission believes the new terminal areas should include all point
within section 203(b)(8) commercial zones any part of which is intersected by t
100-mile radius.

[2] The Commission approves the rates and the rules and regulations under
which the certificated truckers operate.

demonstrate: (1) a need for their service[1] and (2) that they were financially and operationally capable of undertaking the service. Furthermore, under the terms of their permits they are legally bound to serve without discrimination all points indicated in their certificates. Within the enlarged zone new entrants would not have to meet these certification requirements, would enjoy freedom from rate regulation, and would be able to serve points on a selective basis.

Adoption of the 100-mile zone, argue the regulated motor carriers, will unleash a rate war in which they will lose their most lucrative accounts to noncertificated truckers and will be left with relatively unprofitable traffic, i.e., poorly located shippers and small-volume and infrequent shippers. (The regulated truckers believe that their expensive union contracts, insurance coverage, and investment in specialized equipment would make it impossible for them to compete with the new entrants on an equal footing.) Since the larger accounts now subsidize service to less attractive points, the truckers may be compelled to increase rates or offer a reduced level of service. Service is expected to deteriorate further because of the presumed absence of specialized skills and equipment on the part of many new entrants. (These charges of unfitness are almost certainly exaggerated and bring to mind the early campaign of the scheduled airlines to discredit another group of uncertificated entrants, the forwarders. Certification alone, of course, does not guarantee competence and safe practices. In this connection it is of interest to note that with regard to freight loss, damage, and delay, the CAB's Office of the Consumer Advocate receives more complaints against the airlines than against the forwarders.) A motor carrier's certificate represents an investment, the value of which at any given moment depends on market conditions (the cost in legal fees, etc., of these certificates lies in the area of $6,000 to $8,000; one certificate was recently sold for almost $200,000). An expanded air terminal area, it is feared, will jeopardize the value of the certificates. A number of truckers are convinced the new rule makes profitable operations impossible and will drive them into bankruptcy. They note that the ICC has an avowed interest in assisting the small businessman, a designation for which they qualify (table 8). Certificate holders find the Commission's

---

[1]See, for instance, Wallkill Air Freight Corporation Common Carrier Application, 125 MCC 639 (1975). Here the Commission concluded that motor carrier service between the New York-Newark airports and Dutchess, Orange, and Ulster counties was adequate and denied Wallkill's certification request.

objectives "incongruous" and believe that by virtue of its actions "we will be assisted out of business."[1]

The possible collapse of some of the trucking companies and retrenchment on the part of others are of particular concern to the Teamsters Union. The union, of course, can be expected to oppose any measure which might have a negative impact on the size of its membership, and it comes as no surprise that the Teamsters hope the ICC will not adopt the 100-mile rule. Union spokesmen see the expanded zone as "a dumping ground for unsafe vehicles and unqualified drivers"[2] and, somewhat unexpectedly, point to the environmental damage additional truck movements will cause. Presumably of greater concern to the union is the fact that the small, independent trucker who are expected to invade the regulated operators' service territories will prove resistant to unionization.

The Commission's detractors contend that the introduction of the 100-mile air terminal area amounts to nothing less than de facto deregulation of truck movements to and from airports. The validity of this argument will be examined below. For the moment, let us note that the agency's proposal signals regulatory changes which appear be more quantitative than qualitative in nature. Thus, the section 203(b)(7a) exemption would continue to apply only to direct and indirect air carriers and their agents; truckers acting on their own behalf or as agents for shippers and receivers would be required to seek ICC authority as before. (The legality of a trucker's operation hinges essentially on the way in which he is reimbursed. In other words, where a trucker, operating without a certificate, paid by the consignor or consignee, rather than out of the revenue the air carrier receives for the combined air-surface movement, the motor haul is unlawful and the trucker is subject to disciplinary measures.[3])

Illegal truck operators, or "gypsies" as they are derisively called, appear to be active in most parts of the New York-Newark air terminal area. Their rates, of course, have not been approved by the Interstate Commerce Commission and are below those charged by the regulated truckers. Their existence is made possible by the fact that most air carriers will not reject their freight since it

---

[1] Verified Statement of Robert M. Van Why, Sr. for R and G Airfreight, Inc. Docket MC-C-3437, August 31, 1977, p. 10.

[2] Comments of Teamsters Union, Docket MC-C-3437 (1977), p. 3.

[3] See above, p. 108.

will then be tendered to a competing carrier. If there is one other issue which unites the regulated truckers as much as does their hostility towards expanded pickup and delivery zones, it is their belief that the ICC has failed utterly in its attempts to curb, let alone eliminate, illegal motor transportation. The Commission's inept handling of the problem within existing air terminal areas, say the truckers, merely convinces them that enlarged areas will foster a greatly increased level of illegal activity. Using data obtained under the Freedom of Information Act, American Trucking Associations, Inc. (ATA is a national non-profit organization representing the trucking industry) has outlined the problem as it exists in and around several major air terminal areas. In the case of Kennedy and La Guardia airports it was found that, of eighteen ICC enforcement proceedings completed during the period April, 1976 to July, 1977, thirteen involved nonregulated carriers. This, however, covers only a small proportion of those violating the Interstate Commerce Act in this region. The Commission could, according to ATA, "easily" remove the gypsies "through a comprehensive and committed enforcement effort" and should not expand terminal areas "and thereby countenance past illegal operations."[1]

The motor service provided by the gypsies is not the only unlawful activity grafted on to the air freight system. Kennedy Airport has the dubious distinction of leading the nation's air terminals in the value of goods reported stolen by the airlines.[2] The District Attorney for Queens, John J. Santucci, puts the value of Kennedy's annual freight losses (most of which are attributed to organized crime) at $10 million. This estimate is higher than the figures released by airline representatives who, along with insurance companies and officials of the Port Authority of New York and New Jersey have been accused by Mr. Santucci of falsifying crime statistics, a charge these parties deny. Santucci's assertion is supported by the Waterfront Commission of New York Harbor, which recently accused the airlines of "knowingly" misleading the Congress with respect to the scope of their New York-Newark freight losses. New York-Newark's "uniquely severe" theft situation, the Waterfront Commission has concluded,

> is simply a facet of the larger problem of organized crime and conditions at the airports cannot improve until a governmental body vested with

---

[1] Supplemental Comments of American Trucking Associations, Inc., Docket MC-C-3437, October 14, 1977, p. 4.

[2] See above, p. 55, note 4.

sufficient powers to break the grip of organized crime over the airports intervenes to regulate the airports.[1]

The Waterfront Commission's concern is shared by the Federal Bureau of Investigation, which is examining the attempts made by organized crime to win control of various air freight trucking operations in the New York-Newark area. Of particular interest to the Bureau are the motor-for-air substitutions discussed in the previous chapter.

The possibility that a new pickup and delivery zone will tempt organized crime to make further inroads into the air freight industr has been forcefully raised by several certificated truckers, who believe this alone should cause the ICC to reconsider its proposal. As one New York trucker told the Commission, the enlargement "will invite infiltration of Long Island trucking by elements of the underworld . . . and hand [his business] over to the mob."[2] The District Attorney's office has taken no official position on this controversy, though it does not reject the suggestion that the pro-jected enlargement may strengthen criminal activities in and around Kennedy's freight center. Clearly, the extent to which a new air terminal area might encourage organized crime activities is and will remain a matter of conjecture. In any event, the "infiltration" feared by many New York truckers is, in the view of some officials, already an accomplished fact. Deplorable though the situation may be, it falls within the province of various law enforcement authori-ties and should not, it would seem, be used as an argument to deter an administrative agency from the exercise of its legitimate functions.

Most of the truckers raising formal objections to the Commis-sion's revised mileage rule have done so through the Air Freight Motor Carriers Conference and the Irregular Route Common Carrier Conference, both of which are affiliates of American Trucking Associations, Inc. These organizations have protested the 100-mile proposal, calling it unwarranted, counterproductive, and a renuncia-tion of the Commission's regulatory duty. The three trade groups believe a sufficient territorial enlargement can be achieved by adhering to the traditional 25-mile concept, but adding all portions of those ICC commercial zones which are intersected by the 25-mile

---

[1] Waterfront Commission of New York Harbor, Report on True Extent of Cargo Thefts at the New York-New Jersey Airports, March 7, 1975, mimeographed, p. 34.

[2] Letter sent to the ICC by Francis P. O'Brien, President, Direct Airport Service, Inc., June 22, 1977.

boundaries.[1] Such an extension, say these parties, is more in
accord with the pattern of pickup and delivery service offered by
the scheduled airlines, while also taking into account urbanization
and commercial development in outlying areas. For most airport
cities this proposal signifies an extension of existing pickup and
delivery zones. If applied to New York-Newark, however, it leads
to the loss of a significant portion of the air terminal area (i.e.,
parts of Hunterdon, Sussex, and Warren counties in New Jersey; parts
of Dutchess, Orange, Putnam, Suffolk, Ulster, and Westchester counties in New York; and part of Fairfield county in Connecticut).[2]
Reductions would similarly be imposed on several other major air
terminal areas.

Air Freight Motor Carriers Conference, Inc. and the Irregular
Route Common Carrier Conference have suggested that important similarities exist between their proposal and the position taken by the
scheduled certificated airlines and in this they are substantially
correct. Air Cargo, Inc., the scheduled certificated airlines'
ground service organization, has endorsed the 25-mile formula from
the beginning, and over the years its members have filed relatively
few requests for pickup and delivery rights to points beyond the
conventional air terminal areas. Where such requests have been made
the airlines have shown considerably more restraint than the forwarders (figure 5), preferring to handle traffic to/from outlying points
through ACI's air/truck program.

The scheduled certificated airlines (with the exception of the
all-cargo carriers) have given the Commission's proposal little
support. A 100-mile terminal area is viewed with alarm, since it
would invite nonregulated truckers to compete directly with the
airlines for freight moving between airports which are within 100
miles of each other. Traffic diversion would be an especially
serious matter for local service carriers whose routes consist essentially of short segments. For instance, one local service airline,
Ozark, estimates it will lose at least $180,000 annually if the

---

[1]American Trucking Associations, Inc., however, also states that "ideally"
the air terminal areas should be adjusted on an individual basis. Representations
of the Air Terminal Zone - Special Project Group, Air Freight Motor Carriers
Conference, Irregular Route Common Carrier Conference, Docket MC-C-3437, I, 1977,
p. 55; Comments of American Trucking Associations, Inc., Docket MC-C-3437,
September 19, 1977, p. 25.

[2]The Commission, of course, has no interest in reducing the size of the
air terminal area and has already rejected such a proposal with respect to air
passengers. See Exempt Zone--La Guardia and Kennedy International Airports, 111
MCC 284 (1970).

100-mile rule is enforced.[1] The airline companies make the point
that surface movements which compete with air service are not
"incidental" to that service and must therefore be excluded from the
section 203(b)(7a) exemption. They recognize, however, that urban
growth makes some zonal expansion desirable and recommend that the
new pickup and delivery zones have a radius of 35 miles.[2] A 35-mile
radius leaves only 31 markets (as opposed to over 300 at the 100-mile
level) in which nonregulated truckers can compete directly with the
scheduled certificated air carriers and thus "would have a minimal
adverse impact on air transportation."[3] In the case of New
York-Newark, a 100-mile zone would enable the motor carriers to
compete with the airlines between the system's three airports and
airports in: (1) Allentown, (2) Hartford, (3) Philadelphia, (4)
Reading, (5) White Plains, and (6) Wilkes-Barre-Scranton (figure 7a);
a 35-mile radius eliminates all but White Plains. Eastern Air Lines
opposes even a ten-mile extension. It believes the new, nonregulated
surface operators will weaken the established motor carriers and,
"once economics deteriorate, service does the same."[4] There is one
other reason behind the combination airlines' resistance to the
100-mile zone. Generally speaking, an ACI agent handles about thirty
shipments per day, leaving the airport between 9 and 10 in the
morning and returning between 5 and 6 in the evening. Such a work
pattern imposes its own limitation on the distance the agent can
travel if the normal standards of the service are to be maintained.
Air Cargo, Inc. believes that beyond a 35-mile air terminal zone its
pickup and delivery service would "probably" not be "administratively
practical and economically feasible."[5]

Unlike the certificated combination carriers, the major
all-cargo airlines (Airlift International,[6] Federal Express,[7] Flying

---

[1] Comments of Ozark Air Lines, Docket MC-C-3437, August 5, 1977, p. 3.

[2] Unlike the Air Freight Motor Carriers Conference, the airlines do not wish
to see the largest air terminal areas reduced in size.

[3] Representations of Air Cargo, Inc., on Behalf of the Scheduled Certificated
Airlines of the United States, Docket MC-C-3437 (1977), p. 15.

[4] Letter written by Jerry Schorr, Director of Cargo Sales, Eastern Air Lines,
to the ICC, August 12, 1977.

[5] Representations of Air Cargo, Inc., p. 17.

[6] Letter to the author from Robert A. Blanks, Vice President, Marketing and
Sales, Airlift International, October 31, 1977.

[7] Comment of Federal Express Corporation, Docket MC-C-3437 (1977).

Tiger Line,[1] and Seaboard World Airlines[2]) have responded to the
Commission's proposal with enthusiasm. Their criticism of the ICC
lies on the other side of the spectrum, for they consider even a
100-mile limit unnecessarily restrictive. The suggestion, made by
Federal Express, that the section 203(b)(7a) exemption should apply
regardless of the length of the surface movement can clearly not be
accepted by the Commission, which recognized long ago that automatic
approval of all pickup and delivery distances favored by the airlines
was incompatible with its statutory responsibilities.[3] It has also
been suggested (Flying Tiger Line) that adoption of the 100-mile zone
is needed in order to remove the disproportionate burden placed on
the all-cargo operators in the Substitution of Other Services for
Air Transportation Rule Proceeding, above. The substitution regulations, according to the Flying Tiger Line, imposed a greater
hardship on the all-cargo carriers than on the combination airlines,
and the latter's failure to endorse the 100-mile radius reflects
their reluctance to see the operating conditions for the two carrier
classes equalized. In point of fact, however, the various substitution restrictions have applied equally to both airline groups.
The combination airlines, serving more markets than the all-cargo
carriers, were formerly able to make greater use of substitute
truck service; whatever advantage this may have given them has been
largely removed as a result of Congress' relaxation of the traditional entry/exit criteria.

Important differences separate the surface arrangements on
which the major all-cargo airlines rely. Irrespective of these
differences these carriers are agreed that the conventional pickup
and delivery limits have impeded the growth of the air freight
industry and that their removal will enable them to serve their
customers more effectively. Enhanced operational flexibility,
argue the all-cargo parties, is now more important than ever before.
They note that the last few years have seen a significant cutback
in the number of all-cargo flights offered by the combination airlines and that, as a consequence, shippers in many markets are
almost entirely dependent on them for overnight air transportation.

An airline cannot hold itself out as having responsibility for
a combined air-surface movement where the consignor (or consignee)

---

[1] Comments of the Flying Tiger Line, Inc., Docket MC-C-3437 (1977).

[2] Information given the author by Wendell R. Stevens, Vice President,
Marketing, Seaboard Airlines, 1977.

[3] See above, p. 105.

is located outside its air terminal area. An enlargement of this area means the airline can extend single-entity responsibility to more of its customers and offer shippers/receivers at off-line locations a complete tracing system, enhanced security, and less paperwork. An additional benefit to shippers could come in the form of lower rates, since an airline serving off-line points directly (either by using its own equipment or through an agent) would be free to consolidate shipments instead of having to waybill separately each shipment otherwise carried by an independent motor common carrier. The case of Federal Express illustrates this situation. Although the company, the nation's leading all-cargo commuter airline, owns or leases about 650 pickup and delivery vans, it must still use ICC-regulated motor carriers for the roughly ten percent of its total shipments which originate/terminate outside its pickup and delivery zones. A 100-mile New York-Newark air terminal area, for instance, would enable it to utilize its own vehicles between the airports and : (1) Long Branch-Asbury Park, New Jersey; (2) New London-Norwich, Connecticut; (3) Poughkeepsie, New York; and (4) Scranton, Pennsylvania. Federal Express estimates that rates based on consolidations rather than on individually way-billed shipments would save customers at these locations between $8.00 and $10.00 per shipment. Low traffic levels rule out the use of company vans for most points within the expanded zone, but here Federal Express believes that competition from the new surface carrier entrants will also lead to lower rates.

In contrast to Federal Express, Airlift International does not use its own vehicles for pickup and delivery and leaves surface operations mostly in the hands of forwarders and large-volume ship-pers. Both these groups favor expanded air terminal areas, and it follows that Airlift, too, supports the ICC's proposal. In an expanded area Airlift would probably make greater use of ACI agents, whom it considers "more reliable" than independent motor common carriers. The Flying Tiger Line, on the other hand, is interested in achieving maximum control over surface operations and, to further this objective, recommended appropriate legislative action. The weaknesses of its "Skyroad" service were discussed in chapter VI. An improved air-surface program, says Flying Tiger, is now possible since the recent statutory reforms, in effect, permit all-cargo airlines to enter surface transportation via extensive contractual arrangements with ICC-regulated motor common carriers.

Probably the greatest support for the abandonment of the 25-mile rule-of-thumb has come from the forwarders, for whom the enlargement of air terminal areas has long been a principal objective. We have already noted (chapter II) that at the time of the Commission's reexamination of the section 203(b)(7a) exemption (1964) the certificated route air carriers, through Air Cargo, Inc., urged continued adherence to the 25-mile principle, while the forwarders pressed for the adoption of a 125-mile limit. Since then virtually all of the requests for greater pickup and delivery rights have originated with the indirect carriers (table 16).

TABLE 16

PICKUP AND DELIVERY APPLICATIONS FILED WITH
THE CIVIL AERONAUTICS BOARD

Year	Applicant (A--airline F --forwarder/s)	Airport City	Points Granted
1965	F	Detroit	0
1966	F	Boston	1
	F	Chicago	0
	F	Cleveland	34
	F	Dallas	6
	F	Indianapolis	1[a]
	F	Kansas City	14
1967	F	Boston	45
	F	Buffalo	1
	F	Houston	avw
	F	Newark	47
	F	Wichita	1
1968	F	Atlanta	8[a]
	F	Charlotte	2
	F	Newark	108
1969	F	Los Angeles	14
	F	Philadelphia	1
1972	F	Dover	avw
	A	Portland	avw
1973	F	New York-Newark	avw
	F	Reno	1
1974	F	Hartford	1
	F	Minneap.-St. Paul	1
	F	Philadelphia	0
1975	F	various cities	0
1976	F	Orlando	15
1977	F	Tampa	1

SOURCE: Civil Aeronautics Board.

avw--application voluntarily withdrawn.

[a]Negated (fully or in part) by subsequent action of the Interstate Commerce Commission.

Applications for Puerto Rican points are not shown.

Requests for zonal enlargements have involved not only small airport cities (e.g., Charlotte, Dover, Reno) but also larger ones including those which, because of the existence of certain grandfather points, have long had air terminal areas extending well beyond the conventional 25-mile limit. About fifty percent of all new pickup and delivery applications (1965-1977) have focused on Newark Airport, resulting in an air terminal area which in some counties has reached the Pennsylvania border. Even so the major forwarders are dissatisfied with the scope of their pickup and delivery rights and believe the zone should be further enlarged.[1] The certificated airlines, on the other hand, have filed no pickup and delivery requests for New Jersey points. In the case of New York and Connecticut, however, their tariffs name about forty points which are outside Kennedy Airport's 25-mile zone. Pickup and delivery service for these grandfather points predates the 1964 CAB-ICC agreement and, following the adoption of the revised exemption regulations, was permitted to remain in effect.

The forwarders have long prided themselves on their ability to offer customers a complete door-to-door transportation service. They, contend, however, that their capacity to "truly" serve the shipping public is contingent on their being able to utilize their own equipment for pickup and delivery work.[2] Thus, their justification for seeking greater pickup and delivery authority is based on a claim of better service for those customers who must currently rely on ICC-regulated truckers. This commitment to improved service has not been devoid of self-interest. In the past, ICC certification exemptions were based in part on whether or not the underlying air carriers were subject to the tariff filing provisions of the Federal Aviation Act. Many forwarders opposed the Board's decision to terminate the carriers' tariff filing obligation (chapter III) and expressed the hope that the Commission would continue to be guided by Board-approved tariffs, since this would have implied that such potential competitors as cooperative shippers associations and air taxi operators would not be able to automatically take advantage of the enlarged pickup and delivery zones.[3] Federal Express and the Flying Tiger Line, two leading supporters of Public Law 95-163,

---

[1] See above, p. 261.

[2] Comments of Members of the Air Freight Forwarders Association of America, Docket MC-C-3437, August 8, 1977, p. 4.

[3] Supplemental Comments of Members of the Air Freight Forwarders Association of America, Docket MC-C-3437, September 19, 1977, p. 3.

similarly opposed the Board's decision, claiming it conflicted with Congress' recent call for the "encouragement and development of an integrated transportation system."[1] These operators feared that the Board's action jeopardized the growth of single-carrier door-to-door service, since in the absence of Board-approved pickup/delivery tariffs the ICC might at some future stage adopt a more restrictive section 203(b)(7a) exemption standard. "It would be ironic," states Federal Express, if elimination of the tariff filing requirement left a "regulatory 'gap' into which another, less enlightened regulator might step."[2]

Two branches of the Federal Government, the Department of Justice[3] and the Department of Transportation,[4] have also voiced support for a redefinition of pickup and delivery rights. Both parties, however, say a 100-mile limit serves no useful purpose and suggest the "incidental" exemption ought to apply to any surface movement having an immediately prior or subsequent movement by aircraft, irrespective of the distance pickup/delivery vehicles must travel to/from airports. Such a construction of the "incidental" exemption, argues the Department of Justice, is not at variance with the Interstate Commerce Act since section 203(b)(7a) of the act fails to specify a mileage restriction. This line of reasoning, of course, represents a complete reversal of the ICC's approach under which pickup and delivery service of unlimited scope has been consistently rejected.

Both departments believe enlarged pickup and delivery zones will result in improved services for shippers and receivers and thus are in the public interest. Larger zones "should," according to the Justice Department, produce lower freight rates and will reinforce the recent tendency to construct new airports at greater distances from cities. Also, the Department of Transportation predicts enlarged pickup and delivery zones will not have an adverse effect on the regulated motor carrier industry. It recognizes that certain aircraft container rates are lower than LTL truck rates but feels the long-haul truckers would suffer no appreciable traffic diversion, since these lower air rates are restricted to shipments carried in the belly

---

[1] See above, p. 152.

[2] Comments of Federal Express Corporation, Docket 33093, September 11, 1978, pp. 4-5.

[3] Comments of the United States Department of Justice, Docket MC-C-3437, September 23, 1977.

[4] Comments of the United States Department of Transportation, Docket MC-C-3437, September 19, 1977 and September 15, 1978.

space of combination aircraft, which, by their nature (schedules, volume limitations, etc.), are frequently found to be unacceptable by potential air shippers.

Another controversy arising out of the 100-mile proposal is the question of how redefined air terminal zones are to be measured. In the past, pickup and delivery distances have been measured from either the airport or the airport city limits, whichever yielded the larger area. The Commission, however, now feels this dual approach should be eliminated and replaced by one based solely on airport distances. This has won the support of the Justice Department, which has emphasized that, since city boundaries are not referred to in section 203(b)(7a) of the Interstate Commerce Act, the revised mileage standard would be "consistent with the statutory language."[1] Several truckers also favor the adoption of a single mileage standard, believing this would eliminate unnecessary confusion.[2] The retention of the dual mileage formula, on the other hand, has been strongly urged by the Civil Aeronautics Board, which has pointed out that

> while traffic does move to and from airports, the Board assesses public need with regard to the city. The location of the airport is an accident of geography and only rarely is a particular airport noted in a certificate. Since airports are not centralized, discrimination could result between localities otherwise equally situated with respect to the [certificated] points served by a particular airport.[3]

The freedom to measure pickup and delivery distances from either the airport or airport city greatly enhances the carriers' operating flexibility, and it comes as no surprise that most of the freight system's airlines, forwarders, and truckers are opposed to the Commission's suggestion. Certainly this greater flexibility and the carriers' ability to offer equitable treatment to potential pickup/ delivery points lying on opposite sides of an airport city argue for the continuation of the dual mileage rule regardless of any changes which may be made in the size of the air terminal areas. Also, it would seem that a new definition of these areas ought to

---

[1] Comments of the United States Department of Justice, p. 9.

[2] Comments on Behalf of Kerek Air Freight Corporation, Airport Transportation Service, Inc. and R and G Airfreight, Inc., Docket MC-C-3437, August 31, 1977.

[3] Civil Aeronautics Board, Comments of the Civil Aeronautics Board on the Proposal of the Interstate Commerce Commission, p. 5. These remarks were made prior to the enactment of Public Law 95-163. The new section 418 certificates (chapter III) do not name airports or airport cities.

take into account a special situation such as exists in New York-Newark. Traditionally, pickup and delivery boundaries have been defined separately for New York City's Airports and the Newark facility (although, as a practical matter, the carriers have generally disregarded this distinction).[1] The three airports serve the same metropolitan region, and a revised formula should reflect this reality by providing for one terminal area for all three airports.

The Proposed 100-Mile Pickup and Delivery Zone: Further Considerations

It is difficult to reconcile the 100-mile proposal (1977) with the Commission's traditional practice of authorizing air terminal area changes only on an individual basis, and then but for "compelling reasons." The Commission is obviously correct in saying that the air freight industry has seen a number of important changes since the 25-mile rule was instituted. However, some of these (such as the growth in traffic and the movement of manufacturers into suburban and semirural areas, to say nothing of various logistical problems facing the industry) have long been recognized, and one wonders whether the need for the 100-mile zone is really more "compelling" today than it was, say, during the period 1970-1975, in which the agency concluded on several occasions[2] that the Kenny formula, as codified in 1964, should be upheld. The Commission has recently received several petitions which, it claims, demonstrate a need for enlarged pickup and delivery zones. The list of petitions[3] is in some ways a curious one. Only two requests were directly concerned with air freight; in a third case a terminal area reduction was sought, and yet another focused on a local oddity, a small island only part of which fell within the exempt zone. Whatever one may think of the Commission's rationale, there is little doubt that from

---

[1] In parts of Connecticut, for instance, a 100-mile pickup/delivery zone, measured separately for Newark and New York, results in a boundary displacement of about eighteen miles.

[2] For instance, see: Motor Transportation of Property Incidental to Transportation by Aircraft (1970); Philadelphia International Airport, Philadelphia, Pa.--Exempt Zone, 123 MCC 228 (1975).

[3] Exempt Zone--Philadelphia International Airport, 113 MCC 189 (1971); Exempt Zone (Passengers)--Savannah, Ga., Airport, 114 MCC 804 (1971); Philadelphia International Airport, Philadelphia, Pa.--Exempt Zone; Miami and Fort Lauderdale, Fla.--Air Terminal Areas, 125 MCC 519 (1976); Exempt Zone (Passengers)--Chicago, Ill., O'Hare Airport, 126 MCC 332 (1977).

the agency's standpoint the proposal is well-timed. The ICC has
long perceived a need to streamline its internal procedures and ease
its workload; clearly a blanket enlargement of the type envisioned
is a step in this direction. Also, a number of recent actions have
been aimed at loosening regulatory constraints within the
transportation field. The 100-mile proposal is in harmony with this
development and comes at a time when legislative and business
circles are showing increasing willingness to abandon many of the
regulations which have governed U.S. transportation during most of
the postwar era.

A number of the Commission's critics have questioned its right
to repudiate the traditional 25-mile distance rule. This concern
is misplaced, for the agency's authority to modify its exemption
criteria is founded in law and is not at issue. As was noted in
Air Dispatch,

> the determination of the scope of [the section 203(b)(7a)] exemption from
> economic regulation must logically fall on the Commission. Whether this
> determination is accomplished on an ad hoc basis as in Kenny and the cases
> following that decision, or by use of the rule making power does not alter
> the right to make such a determination.[1]

The Supreme Court, too, has concluded that

> regulatory agencies do not establish rules of conduct to last forever; they
> are supposed, within the limits of the law and of fair and prudent adminis-
> tration, to adapt their rules and practices to the Nation's needs in a
> volatile, changing economy. They are neither required nor supposed to regulate
> the present and the future within the inflexible limits of yesterday.[2]

The question facing us here is not whether the ICC may modify the
25-mile rule-of-thumb, but whether, in the words of the Supreme
Court, the 100-mile radius is "within the limits of the law." Put
another way, does the proposal represent a reasonable interpretation
of section 203(b)(7a) and will its implementation be consonant with
the intent of Congress? Table 17 indicates that the answer is "no."
(Unlike table 15, which includes air-to-air transshipments, table 17
is concerned solely with air-surface traffic.) Both 100-mile zones
capture so overwhelming a proportion of their respective airport's
traffic that it is difficult to escape the conclusion that for these
two airports the 100-mile proposal amounts to de facto surface

---

[1] Air Dispatch, Inc. v. United States, p. 453.

[2] American Trucking Associations, Inc. v. Atchison, Topeka and Santa Fe
Railway Co., p. 416.

TABLE 17

THE 25-MILE V. THE 100-MILE PICKUP/DELIVERY ZONE
(Scheduled Flights: January 1973 – December 1974)

Origin/Destination	Inbound Freight		Outbound Freight		Two-Way Traffic	
	tons	% of total	tons	% of total	tons	% of total
Kennedy Airport						
New York 25-mile zone[a]	521,822	81	528,322	73	1,050,144	77
NY-Newark air terminal area[b]	529,085	82	543,111	76	1,072,196	79
New York 100-mile zone[c]	566,118	88	597,932	83	1,164,050	85
United States	644,566	100	718,966	100	1,363,532	100
Newark Airport						
Newark 25-mile zone[d]	85,163	86	119,590	87	204,753	87
NY-Newark air terminal area[b]	89,776	91	127,485	93	217,261	92
Newark 100-mile zone[e]	96,632	98	134,138	98	230,770	98
United States	98,871	100	136,709	100	235,580	100

[a] See table 15, note c.

[b] See above, p. 218, note 1.

[c] Measured from La Guardia and Kennedy airports.

[d] Measured from Newark's corporate boundaries.

[e] Measured from Newark Airport.

carrier deregulation.[1] In the absence of nationwide air freight
traffic data it would be presumptuous to attempt a detailed charac-
terization of the effect the Commission's proposal will have on oth
air traffic hubs. That, in any case, is not the objective of this
study. What we should note, however, is that Kennedy's unusual
service characteristics, e.g., the availability of scheduled
all-cargo and wide-body combination flights, the large number of
points served (both domestic and overseas), and the frequency of it
flights, make it an atypical airport and render it exceptionally
attractive for long-haul truckers of air freight. The more modest
service levels found at Newark,[2] on the other hand, while still
differing markedly from those of numerous other air traffic hubs,[3]
make its freight patterns somewhat more representative of the
situation at most of the nation's larger airport cities. A 100-mil
pickup/delivery zone would remove regulatory constraints from about
98 percent of Newark's two-way air-surface traffic (table 17), and
it seems realistic to suggest that the practical effect of the
100-mile rule on a nationwide basis will also be de facto deregulation of the surface operators.[4]

---

[1]Table 17 shows that about 85 percent and 98 percent of the freight
handled at Kennedy and Newark, respectively, would be affected by the new
deregulatory measure. (In actual fact the proportion of deregulated traffic wou
be a little higher because the new rule would exempt not only points within 100
miles of an airport, but also those section 203(b)(8a) commercial zones any part
of which is intersected by the 100-mile radius. Additional exempt points beyond
this area could also be included at the Commission's discretion.) For purposes
of this comparison, figures are also given at the 25-mile level (traffic within
these zones is totally deregulated) and for the New York-Newark air terminal are

[2]See above, p. 289.

[3]For instance, Newark, unlike most other airports, offers some scheduled
all-cargo flights.

[4]This position is supported by the following:
1. Systems Analysis and Research Corporation---"a 100-mile periphery would
encompass areas substantially inclusive of the tributary areas of most major
airports." Systems Analysis and Research Corporation, Intermodal Movement of Ai
Cargo, I (Washington D.C.: Systems Analysis and Research Corporation, 1975), p.
133
2. National Small Shipment Traffic Conference and Drug and Toilet Preparation
Traffic Conference---"[we] are unaware of any significant amount of motor carria
incidental to movement by aircraft that involves distances of greater than 100
miles [from airports]." Comments of the National Small Shipment Traffic Confere
and Drug and Toilet Preparation Traffic Conference, Docket MC-C-3437, September
19, 1977, p. 5
3. U.S. Department of Justice---"expansion of the exempt zone to 100 miles will
probably not require the Commission to consider revision of the zone's boundarie
for a considerable period of time, if ever." Comments of the United States
Department of Justice, p. 10.

Although the distance factor has never been the sole determinant of the applicability of section 203(b)(7a), the Commission has rejected all previous attempts to have the 25-mile rule permanently set aside and has repeatedly affirmed its validity. Obviously, it can be argued that to distinguish between long-haul and pickup/delivery services on the basis of a 25-mile boundary (or some other limit) is arbitrary, and that the motor service to and from points lying, say, three miles beyond that boundary need be no less a bona fide pickup and delivery service than truck movements confined entirely to the air terminal zone. The agency recognizes that in many instances the essential attributes of the motor services being rendered on both sides of the dividing line may be identical but has insisted that "the only workable delimitation [between exempt and regulated transportation] must be, of necessity, the boundary of the terminal area itself."[1] Requests for exceptions to the 25-mile principle have been examined on a case-by-case basis and approved (or denied) in the light of local circumstances. This narrow interpretation of the exemption's scope has been consistently applied throughout the life of section 203(b)(7a). No less signifi-cant than this consistency has been the Commission's belief that in interpreting the exemption narrowly it was effectuating the intent of Congress. In the words of the agency (1964):

> our interpretation of the [section 203(b)(7a)] exemption conforms to the general practice of constructing strictly any exemption[2]

and

> we would not be complying with the congressional mandate were we to adopt, in the absence of a clear legislative directive, a regulation which would greatly increase the scope of exempt transportation at the expense of those motor carriers which are subject to the economic regulation of the Interstate Commerce Act.[3] (Emphasis added.)

More recently the Commission again refused to discard the 25-mile rule in favor of a broader exemption, pointing out that for it to do so would be to "ignore the statutory mandate inherent in the Interstate Commerce Act."[4] (Emphasis added.) Section 203(b)(7a)

---

[1] Motor Transportation of Property Incidental to Transportation by Aircraft (1970), p. 15.

[2] Motor Transportation of Property Incidental to Transportation by Aircraft (1964), p. 91.

[3] Ibid., p. 86.

[4] Motor Transportation of Property Incidental to Transportation by Aircraft (1970), p. 16.

became part of the Interstate Commerce Act in 1938, and, although th
Act has since been amended a number of times, the exemption itself
remains intact.   The significance of prior statutory construction
has frequently been examined by the Supreme Court, which has

> held in many cases that . . . a long-standing administrative interpretation,
> applying to a substantially reenacted statute, is deemed to have received
> congressional approval and has the effect of law.[1]

The U.S. Department of Transportation, the Flying Tiger Line,
and various other parties claim that a 100-mile air terminal area
will not harm the regulated motor carrier industry.   This assertion
has little meaning, for, in considering the possible repercussions
of the Commission's action, we are concerned not with the motor
carrier industry per se but, rather, with those truckers who depend
primarily on traffic carried to and from air terminals.   Obviously,
the effect of additional competition on this admittedly small
segment of the trucking industry will be uneven and will depend in
part on how desirable new entrants find individual truckers' service
areas.   The air freight truckers as a whole fear that the effects of
large-scale deregulation will be disastrous, and there have been
widespread predictions, especially among smaller truckers, of
bankruptcies.   While this scenario may seem excessively gloomy, it
should be remembered that even a relatively robust carrier such as
Harbourt came close to financial collapse as a result of an earlier
enlargement of the Newark air terminal area.[2]   We have seen how the
Civil Aeronautics Board has used periodic carrier performance review
as a basis for some of its policy changes.   The Commission, too,
should have examined the impact of enhanced forwarder pickup and
delivery rights on motor carriers following the 1964 codification of
the Kenny doctrine.   In refusing to do so the agency has lost an
opportunity to collect and evaluate the kind of information needed
for the formulation of a new air terminal area policy.

The truckers clearly have cause to worry about the monetary
value of their operator's certificates.[3]   Issued by the ICC, these
certificates have in the past shielded their owners from most

---

[1] Commissioner of Internal Revenue v. Estate of Noel, 380 U.S. 678, 682
(1965).   See also Brewster v. Gage, 280 U.S. 327, 337 (1930) and United States v.
Dakota-Montana Oil Co., 288 U.S. 459, 466 (1933).

[2] See above, pp. 232-233.

[3] See above, p. 303.

nonregulated competitors, and it seems certain that, in some instances at least, their value will fall significantly following the implementation of the 100-mile proposal. Another concern is that competition from new entrants will lower rates to unprofitable levels. This too cannot be rejected out of hand since some form of rate-cutting will almost certainly take place (at least in the short run) as newcomers seek to establish themselves in the enlarged zones. The truckers also believe that their most lucrative markets will be captured by the newcomers. This fear seems to be borne out by the initial statements of their competitors, who make no secret of the fact that, while they expect to go on interlining traffic with the certificated motor carriers, they intend to use their own vehicles in selected markets, i.e., large-volume markets. Federal Express, for instance, identifies several points which it would serve with its own equipment within an expanded New York-Newark zone,[1] and Associated Air Freight, a forwarder, notes that, although

> smaller volume shipments would continue to be tendered to [the air freight motor carrier specialists], . . . larger shipments, or a significant volume of shipments coming in, for example, in a single container and destined for a single point would be more advantageously transported by Associated Air Freight itself.[2]

Understandable though their apprehension may be, the truckers cannot claim to have been ignorant of the Commission's inherent right to redefine its exemption criteria. That right, as was shown above, has been affirmed by the Supreme Court. In addition, a lower court has reminded the certificated operators that "freedom from competition is not constitutionally protected."[3] However, if the truckers, as is now evident, placed too much confidence in the preservation of the status quo, the fault lies partly with the Commission, which on several occasions has emphasized the need to safeguard their position. Thus, one of the conclusions reached in the pivotal Motor Transportation of Property Incidental to Transportation by Aircraft proceeding was that any substantial deviation from the 25-mile rule was unacceptable, since a larger zone would

> serve only to divert traffic from authorized motor carriers and thereby defeat various sections of the Interstate Commerce Act and the national transportation policy stated therein.[4]

---

[1] See above, p. 310.

[2] Verified Statement of Anthony v. Desimone on Behalf of Associated Air Freight, Inc., Docket MC-C-3437 (1977), p. 5.

[3] Law Motor Freight, Inc. v. Civil Aeronautics Board, p. 144.

[4] Motor Transportation of Property Incidental to Transportation by Aircraft (1964), p. 91.

In another instance it was found necessary to curtail the scope of forwarder activities for,

> otherwise, the regulated motor common carriers upon whom the public must depend for service would be subjected to unwarranted inroads by the air forwarders into the traffic and revenues they now enjoy.[1]

The Commission can obviously not accept blindly all the dire predictions made by the truckers. At the same time, a number of their misgivings are well-founded and raise questions about the agency's statutory responsibility for the economic well-being of those carriers which Congress has placed under its control. The ICC has acknowledged this responsibility in the past and has stated categorically that "greatly" enhanced nonregulated transportation at the expense of the certificated carriers is not compatible with the language of the Interstate Commerce Act unless preceded by an appropriate "legislative directive." The agency's apparent disregard for the possible effects of the 100-mile rule on the regulated air freight motor carrier specialists invites comparison with the Motor Carrier--Air Freight Forwarder Investigation, above. In the initial phase of that proceeding, it will be recalled, the CAB's grant of forwarder authority to several long-haul motor carriers was found unacceptable by an appellate court, which held the action was unsupported by "the careful investigation [and] the substantial evidence" required of an expert agency before it can

> lawfully embark on a new course apparently so fraught with danger to the industry Congress has confined to its regulation and seemingly so opposed to the general policy Congress has long decreed.[2]

Only after the Civil Aeronautics Board had given assurances that the independent forwarders would be protected through the imposition of a "monitored entry" policy was its action sustained by the court.

The ICC has long regarded the regulation of surface movements to and from airports as one of its duties under the Interstate Commerce Act. In performing this duty the agency has placed a narrow interpretation on the scope of the section 203(b)(7a) exemption and has repeatedly stated that a substantially broader construction violated its legislative mandate, a position the courts have upheld. The 100-mile rule will effectively deregulate the surface operators serving the nation's air terminals and represents a unilateral repudiation of a statutory responsibility. Moreover, the Commission's proposal was not accompanied by supporting

[1] Emery Air Freight Corporation Freight Forwarder Application, p. 37.

[2] See above, p. 101.

traffic/financial data and the agency gives no indication of having
examined adequately the proposal's economic implications for the
regulated air freight motor carrier specialists. For these reasons
it is suggested that implementation of the new distance rule be
attempted only with the concurrence of Congress. "In the absence of
a clear legislative directive," as the Commission once put it,[1]
a somewhat more cautious approach to the question of zonal enlargement would seem to be in order. (It is important to keep the
agency's responsibility vis-à-vis the certificated carriers in
perspective. After all, the Supreme Court itself has stated that
its rulings "have dispelled any notion that the Commission's primary
obligation is the protection of firms holding existing certificates."[2]
Criticism of the 100-mile proposal is not meant to imply that concern
for certificate holders should block all future air terminal area
modifications. Rather, the point being made here is that in view
of the ICC's mandate the proposed exemption is excessive, and less
extreme alternatives should have been formulated.)

Although the ICC has frequently emphasized that "compelling
reasons" and "convincing evidence" were required before large-scale
exemptions could be contemplated, it has not conducted an appropriate
investigation of truck movements to and from the nation's air
terminals. Earlier origin and destination studies have focused
primarily on air passengers, and our knowledge about the actual
size of airport freight tributary areas remains scanty at best.
A suitable starting point for an amended air terminal area policy
would be a nationwide air freight survey aimed at clarifying the
various points now at issue. Such a survey might best be undertaken
by the ICC in cooperation with the CAB (the latter has required air
freight forwarder affiliates of long-haul surface carriers to report
the amount of freight originated/terminated at given distances of
each airport served) and should yield information about the size of
airport tributary areas and the relative importance of the various
carrier groups involved (e.g., regulated air freight motor carrier
specialists, other certificated truckers, air freight forwarders,
Air Cargo, Inc. agents, independent short-haul truckers, etc.).
The investigators should also ascertain how terminal area enlargements are viewed by shippers, especially by small-volume shippers
located at various mileage intervals outside the 25-mile zones. An

---

[1] See above, p. 319.

[2] Bowman Transportation, Inc. v. Arkansas-Best Freight System, Inc., 419
U.S. 281, 298 (1974).

investigation of this type must, of course, be recognized as a
lengthy and difficult undertaking. The data generated, however,
would remove a number of uncertainties and should provide the
framework within which the Commission, in the words of the Supreme
Court, could "adapt [its] rules and practices to the Nation's needs
in a volatile, changing economy."[1]

In the case of some airport cities the aforementioned data may
well reveal a genuine need for a limited departure from existing
zonal boundaries (e.g., 10-15 miles), and here such changes might
be possible without violating the Commission's regulatory responsibility. In New York-Newark, however, where the air terminal area
already extends substantially beyond the conventional 25-mile limit,
freight flow patterns (table 17) argue against major new
enlargements, and blanket boundary changes should be confined to the
addition of those section 203(b)(8) commercial zones which are
intersected by the terminal area's perimeter.[2] (The proposed
inclusion of entire commercial zones within air terminal areas is
to be welcomed because "all motor carrier operations in a single
metropolitan area should be regulated on the same basis."[3]) With
the exception of the Trenton-Philadelphia region, boundary adjustments would thus be relatively minor, and much of the New
York-Newark air terminal area would essentially retain its current
contours. In the past the growth of this area has been made
possible through the approval, on an ad hoc basis, of pickup/delivery
requests initiated largely by the major forwarders. Pickup/delivery
rights should be extended to any carrier wishing to operate within
the terminal area, with applications for new off-line points being
examined on an individual basis as before. For the forwarders this
situation would signify relatively little change. Air Cargo, Inc.,
which has not sought New Jersey pickup and delivery points outside
the 25-mile zone, could, if it wished, continue to use its air/truck

---

[1]See above, p. 316. An initial contribution along these lines has been
made by the ICC's Bureau of Economics. The Bureau's air shipper survey, released
in July of 1978, focuses on six airport cities (Boston, Chicago, Houston, Kansas
City, San Francisco-Oakland, and Tampa-St. Petersburg) and recommends adoption
by the Commission of a new 35-mile exempt zone. The Bureau has not examined
the air service needs of shippers beyond a 50-mile airport zone (firms having
fewer than 25 employees are not included in the survey) and is not concerned
with the possible effects a 100-mile zone might have on any particular carrier
group. Interstate Commerce Commission, Bureau of Economics, Air Terminal Exempt
Zones and the Intermodal Movement of Air Cargo (Washington D.C.: Interstate
Commerce Commission, July, 1978).

[2]See above, p. 302, note 1.

[3]Comments of the United States Department of Transportation, p. 7.

service in this area (as opposed to broadening its pickup/delivery work), and Federal Express would automatically receive pickup and delivery rights for Long Branch-Asbury Park (New Jersey) and Poughkeepsie (New York) but not for New London-Norwich (Connecticut) and Scranton (Pennsylvania). The independent short-haul truckers would now be free to expand their pickup and delivery operations considerably, and it is this carrier group which would exert most of the new competitive pressure against the certificated air freight motor carrier specialists.[1] Some of the latter might well be adversely affected, but the terminal area's impact on this group as a whole would lack the severity of the 100-mile rule. Clearly, a compromise along these lines cannot be expected to satisfy all of the parties involved. Rather, it should be seen as an attempt to "weigh the competing interests and arrive at a balance that is deemed 'the public convenience and necessity.'"[2]

Section 101(24) of the Federal Aviation Act empowered the Civil Aeronautics Board to regulate air commerce "whether such commerce moves wholly by aircraft or partly by aircraft and partly by other forms of transportation." This, together with the Interstate Commerce Act's section 203(b)(7a) exemption, led early industry observers to suppose that the regulatory responsibility for combined air-surface traffic was vested solely in the CAB. That notion was dispelled as the ICC, with the support of the courts, assumed a role which in a sense gave it a veto over the pickup and delivery points accepted by the CAB. Prior to 1964 this kind of dual authority presented no major problem. In that year, however, the ICC adopted new regulations allowing for a review of exempt transportation independently of the Board, and since then several situations have arisen in which the Commission has in effect overruled the Board because the latter's pickup and delivery points failed to meet the section 203(b)(7a) exemption criteria. While it is true that a U.S. district court has found "no real dissonance, in theory or in practice, between the voices of the Commission and the [Civil] Aeronautics Board in this area, taking into consideration their respective objectives and functions,"[3] it must

---

[1] If the experience of the forwarders is anything to go by, regulatory freedom will prove to be no panacea for the new entrants. Financial statistics collected by the CAB indicate that only fifty percent of the forwarders originating freight in New York-Newark (1972) reported an overall profit.

[2] Bowman Transportation, Inc. v. Arkansas-Best Freight System, Inc., p. 293.

[3] Wycoff Company, Inc. v. United States, 240 F. Supp. 304, 309 (D. Utah 1965).

be borne in mind that the court's words were spoken barely one year after the ICC adopted its new rules, a time when differences between the two agencies were not as apparent as was later to be the case (table 16). In recent years it could not be said that "no real dissonance" marked the two agencies' approach to air freight regulation. Indeed, their overlapping responsibilities produced a regulatory situation which was burdened by internal contradictions and which has not always served the best interests of the air freight industry.

The CAB has traditionally been charged with the promotion and regulation of air transportation, while the ICC has had to regulate and "preserve the inherent advantages" of those surface carriers under its control. The conflicting interests of the two agencies have made it impossible for them to view air freight from the same perspective. The CAB regards pickup and delivery operations as an integral part of air freight service, whereas for the ICC these operations are only an adjunct to air transportation.[1] The Board has always recognized that shipper acceptance of air transportation rests largely on the efficiency of the related ground services and, unlike the Commission, would like to have achieved closer air-surface integration by giving air carriers greater control over surface movements.[2] The Commission has often been accused of having held back the development of the air freight industry. The agency, of course, rejects this position and notes that a number of its actions were specifically designed to aid the industry.[3] It remains a fact, however, that the overlapping responsibilities of the two agencies have led to what the U.S. Department of Transportation rightly calls a "conflicting, duplicative and inconsistent" regulatory situation,[4] and, as an alternative to the 100-mile rule or some other ICC-sponsored air terminal area, Congress should long ago have stripped the ICC of its role in this field and given the Board exclusive jurisdiction over air freight pickup and delivery service.[5] The placing of all air freight specialists under the sole

---

[1] See above, p. 104.

[2] See above, p. 117.

[3] These include: (1) making air terminal areas larger than commercial zones, and (2) the creation of "intermodal freight forwarders."

[4] Comments of the United States Department of Transportation, p. 10.

[5] See above, pp. 120-121. Obviously, a recommendation along these lines would have little meaning today, given the Board's uncertain future (p. 168).

control of the Board would have brought greater cohesion to the regulatory process and would have simplified the cumbersome procedure which some carriers have used in seeking redress of their grievances. [1]

In putting forward its 100-mile proposal, the Commission has rekindled the controversy over the nature of bona fide pickup and delivery service. The certificated combination airlines have always supported the CAB's 25-mile limit but now regard a 10-mile extension as acceptable. The 100-mile radius, on the other hand, produces an exempt zone of about 31,400 square miles,[2] an area so large that the "essential characteristics" of ACI's pickup and delivery service would be destroyed.[3] In several airport cities, however, ACI provides pickup and delivery service at points considerably beyond its suggested 35-mile limit (Poughkeepsie, one such point, lies about 80 miles north of Kennedy Airport; Bethel, Bridgeport, and Danbury are located between 60 and 70 miles northeast of Kennedy). Obviously, the volume of business generated by these points is such as to offset the economic and administrative difficulties ACI associates with a major enlargement of air terminal areas[4] and suggests that if the airlines were persuaded that profitable operations are possible within a greatly expanded area ACI would be prepared to redefine its pickup and delivery work in terms of the 100-mile radius.

It should be noted that the 25-mile exempt zone was accepted as "reasonable" by the ICC because it provided an apparently realistic delineation between pickup and delivery and line-haul (i.e., nonexempt) transportation. The mileage rule reflected the belief that the former was basically an intracity operation while the latter was largely a movement between cities. This was formally stated in Commercial Zones and Terminal Areas as follows:

> line-haul service is essentially intercommunity in character. In contrast, collection and delivery service which supplements and combines with line-haul service to constitute a complete door-to-door transportation service is essentially intracommunity in character.[5]

The ICC's definition was upheld in National Bus Traffic Association

---

[1]See above, pp. 113-115.

[2]Area = πr^2, where r is the radius.

[3]Representations of Air Cargo, Inc., on Behalf of the Scheduled Certificated Airlines of the United States, p. 17.

[4]See above, p. 308.

[5]54 MCC 21, 63 (1952).

v. United States, above, at page 872, the court declaring that "the intercity trip . . . is not generally 'incidental' to the air transportation." Obviously, in many areas urban expansion has blurred the once clear distinction between inter- and intracity activities. Nevertheless, the 100-mile rule makes possible numerous nonregulated surface movements which cannot but be described as intercity in nature (some examples for New York City are: Kennedy Airport to [1] Allentown, Pennsylvania; [2] Atlantic City, New Jersey; [3] Hartford, Connecticut; [4] Monticello, New York; and [5] New London, Connecticut). It would thus be advisable that, irrespective of the size of future air terminal areas, no such terms as "intercity," "intercommunity," "intracity," etc., be used to distinguish between exempt and nonexempt transportation.

The certificated truckers have never recognized forwarder activities beyond the 25-mile limit as bona fide pickup and delivery service. They contend, inter alia, that the extensive terminalling (consolidation and break-down) which lies at the center of forwarder operations interrupts traffic flows between shippers/receivers and airline terminals to such an extent that the flows must be viewed as independent line-haul movements. If the forwarders win greatly enhanced operating rights terminalling delays may well increase, reinforcing the truckers' complaints. Ideally, of course, a truck haul should be coordinated with a predetermined flight. As the court stated in Wycoff,

> to constitute a movement incidental to air transportation, we believe that such movement must be incidental to some particular air transportation, not merely to the broad system of air traffic as a whole.[1]

Again, it would seem that a 100-mile air terminal area will further lessen the likelihood that surface movements can be coordinated with predetermined flights, and that in fact future shipments will increasingly leave on the next available flight following the operator's arrival at an airline's receiving station.

Although proponents of the 100-mile rule justify their position in terms of various benefits larger air terminal areas will bring the shipping public, it should be noted that the Commission's notice of proposed rule-making is not a response to widespread shipper criticism of existing air terminal areas. Indeed, one of the striking features of the air terminal area proceeding is that most of the air shippers outside the 25-mile zones tend to oppose the deregulatory measures favored by the Commission. Being mostly

---

[1] Wycoff Company, Inc. v. United States, p. 311.

small-volume shippers (for instance, Harbourt identifies roughly 1,500 air freight shippers in its operating territory [figure 6], of whom about 15 are large-volume shippers; Bayshore, another trucking concern, states that of its approximately 400 customers only 10 are considered "bread and butter" accounts), these parties believe that removal of regulatory controls will leave them with poorer and, in some cases, no motor service at all. Shipper support for the 100-mile zone has been expressed by several national trade groups,[1] whose members are, relatively speaking, large-volume operators.[2] The latter, knowing that truckers will continue to vie for their business, can be confident the proposed regulatory scheme presents no threat to the transportation service levels they now enjoy. Also, of course, many large-volume shippers operate their own trucks and are thus less dependent on common carrier service than their small-volume counterparts.

It is interesting to note that the Port Authority of New York and New Jersey and such organizations as the Connecticut Business and Industry Association (3,100 members), the New Jersey Business and Industry Association (13,000 members), and the New York Chamber of Commerce and Industry have not formally supported the Commission's proposal. On the other hand, the agency has received numerous letters from small businessmen throughout the tri-state area urging that the 100-mile zone not be put into effect. Some of the specific fears of these shippers are that nonregulated motor carriers will: (1) refuse to serve unprofitable points, (2) carry inadequate liability insurance coverage, (3) introduce inordinately high rates, and (4) use unqualified drivers and unsafe vehicles.[3]

Most of the certificated air freight motor carrier specialists serving the New York-Newark airports believe that if the Commission's

---

[1] Comments of the National Industrial Traffic League on the Proposed Regulations, Docket MC-C-3437, September 19, 1977; Comments of the National Small Shipment Traffic Conference and Drug and Toilet Preparation Traffic Conference.

[2] The Drug and Toilet Preparation Traffic Conference's 110 members, for instance, account for most of the pharmaceutical tonnage shipped in the United States.

[3] Examining the attitude of 64 shippers in five airport cities towards pickup and delivery zones, the Systems Analysis and Research Corporation found (1975) that "practically [no shipper] felt that the use of air freight would immediately increase" if zones were enlarged. Shippers opposing expanded zones believed "the market is not sufficiently large to support an influx of competitive facilities, that as a result the present satisfactory service would be jeopardized and costs probably would rise." Systems Analysis and Research Corporation, p. 118.

proposal is adopted the major competitive threat will come not from the forwarders (many of whom already have pickup and delivery rights in areas that would form part of the new exempt zone) but from new unregulated motor carriers. In order to remain competitive, say the certificated operators, they will have to eliminate service at relatively unprofitable points now included in their tariffs. Released from their common carrier obligation (within the redefined zone), they will be able to concentrate on their more lucrative accounts. Factors which will lead to the possible loss of service (or increased rates) at particular points include:[1] (1) an unsatisfactory volume of business, (2) the shipper's (or receiver's) poor location, (3) the need to work overtime, and (4) the absence of loading/unloading facilities. Some truckers also say that they intend to automatically eliminate all household accounts. The outlook, then, is one of improved service for favored customers and a deterioration or loss of service at many less attractive points. The likelihood of such a development suggests that, if introduced, major air terminal area changes should be reviewed at the end of an experimental period so that their impact on all sectors of the shipping public can be fully evaluated.

Concluding Remarks

The reader has now looked at the New York-Newark air terminal area from various perspectives and traced its growth and development through several stages. Chapter II examined the statutory framework for pickup/delivery service and showed how, during the 1960s, certain operators moved decisively to enhance the scope of nonregulated truck services to/from Newark Airport (figure 2). In chapter VI, which presented the terminal area in terms of the mid-1970s (figure 5), the subject was treated largely from the standpoint of Air Cargo, Inc. agents and forwarders. Commodity flows were shown in chapter VII (figures 7a-12b), which also probed the conflicting interests surrounding the question of terminal area boundary changes during the late-1970s. The terminal area appears again in chapter VIII, where reference is made to its significance as a generator of freight for the airlines.

While independent of Public Law 95-163, the Interstate Commerce Commission's proposal introducing a 100-mile pickup/delivery limit can be viewed within the context of air freight transportation

---

[1]Told the author by various certificated truckers operating to and from the New York-Newark airports.

deregulation, for, if implemented, the new mileage rule would signify, in effect, the deregulation of surface movements to and from air terminals. The proposal has shocked and angered many truckers but delighted the forwarders and all-cargo air carriers. The certificated air freight motor carrier specialists see the new rule as a betrayal by the Commission, which had long protected the truckers from uncontrolled competition and had stated throughout the 1960s and early-1970s that any major, blanket air terminal area enlargement would have to rest on "compelling reasons" and "convincing evidence." Furthermore, the agency had repeatedly acknowledged its statutory duty to interpret narrowly the scope of the section 203(b)(7a) exemption and had insisted legislative action was needed to legitimate an expansionist air terminal area policy.

It is surely no coincidence that the Commission's proposal was released at a time when the Congress was already deeply committed to air transportation deregulation. After rejecting, over a period of many years, appeals for a broader exemption policy, the Commission suddenly argued that a major zonal enlargement would enhance intermodalism and give the carriers increased flexibility. Its own greater flexibility may well be due to the fact that the agency, now fully exposed to Washington's proreform currents, feared that, after stripping the CAB of most of its discretionary authority, the Carter Administration and the Congress would turn their attention to surface transportation and make the Commission the target of a new deregulation drive. (Both the Carter Administration and the Congress have indicated their support for the partial deregulation of interstate trucking. If enacted into law, future reform legislation will presumably reduce the Commission's present powers. The legislation could also lead to the enlargement or elimination of the air terminal pickup and delivery zones.)

The Commission should seek Congressional approval for what is essentially a deregulation measure. If the 100-mile zone fails to win such approval, the ICC, possibly in conjunction with other governmental bodies, should launch a nationwide airport tributary area study with a view to establishing the relative importance of the several surface carrier classes providing service to/from air terminals, the service levels they offer the shipping public (particularly small-volume shippers), and the trucking needs of shippers/receivers located beyond the conventional 25-mile pickup/delivery zone. Such information could form the basis for a new air terminal area standard, replacing an essentially arbitrary mileage factor. We have seen that, in the case of New York-Newark, many shippers feel a greatly enlarged exempt zone will not be in their interests. This indicates future shipper surveys may be helpful in clarifying the nature of any zone-related difficulties and in suggesting further regulatory policy changes.

CHAPTER VIII

THE NEW YORK-NEWARK AIRPORTS AS PART OF THE

NATIONAL AIR FREIGHT SYSTEM

This chapter examines the freight activities of the U.S. airlines with respect to New York-Newark. Airlines provide the critical link between airport cities and, in a sense, are the most visible components of an air freight system; indeed, the tendency on the part of most people is probably to equate them with the system itself. Despite their central role, the direct air carriers, as we have had occasion to see, do not function as truly independent entities but, rather, depend in large measure on various ground services. This dependence is reemphasized in this chapter, which considers further the question of cooperation and competition within the system. Additional topics include the types of aircraft used, the nature of the commodities carried, the traffic patterns which have evolved under the entry/exit regulations discussed in chapter I, and the initial reactions to Public Law 95-163. The major airlines are examined individually and are grouped according to carrier classification. With the exception of Pan American and Seaboard, the information given refers to interstate, i.e., domestic traffic, only. The statistical data for the chapter cover the period mid-1976 to mid-1977 and thus describe the situation as it existed on the eve of deregulation.

Trunk Carriers

American Airlines. American Airlines enplanes more domestic freight in New York-Newark than any other airline. It derives about ten percent of its revenues from freight transportation and, in the sense that it was the first carrier to issue a freight tariff,[1] can be considered the "senior" airline in the scheduled air freight transportation field. The company was issued a section 401 certificate of public convenience and necessity in 1938,[2] and, since then, the length of its domestic route network has grown from 6,826

---

[1] See above, p. 3.

[2] See above, p. 4, note 4.

miles to 42,884 miles (1977).[1] New York-Newark, which is American'
leading freight originating station, is one of 49 domestic points
for which the company held operating rights immediately prior to th
deregulation of air freight transportation.

About ninety percent of the domestic load American enplanes
in New York-Newark is surface-to-air traffic. The remainder is
air-to-air traffic, which includes intraline shipments as well as
shipments the company receives from other airlines for onward
transportation. About five percent of the outbound load is later
interlined with carriers flying to destination points not served
by American Airlines. The surface-to-air tonnage, approximately
ninety percent of which originates within the New York-Newark air
terminal area (figure 5), is received by the company as follows:
(1) about 65 percent is tendered by the forwarders, (2) 15 percent
comes from local cartage agents, (3) 10 percent is obtained from
long-haul truckers,[2] and (4) the remainder is brought to American's
terminals by the shipping public.

Generally speaking, the company's outbound traffic volume is
in balance with the inbound flow. The major commodities carried
include apparel and other textile products, electrical and
nonelectrical machinery and parts, perishable items (especially cut
flowers, strawberries, and vegetables), printed material (including
newspapers, magazines, display equipment, etc.), rubber goods, and
transportation equipment and parts. About 45 percent of the two-wa
load is containerized, the major containers used being types A, LD-
and M (table 7). The forwarders contribute roughly three-quarters
of the containerized load.

Figure 13 gives an overview of American's freight flows
between New York-Newark and some twenty-five of the company's other
domestic service points.[3] The ten leading freight exchange points

---

[1]These figures appear in the Board's annual reports to the Congress.

[2]The ICC-regulated truckers, it was shown earlier, operate both in- and
outside the air terminal area.

[3]Figures 13 and 22-30 give, for the carriers indicated, scheduled
origin-destination freight movements during the twelve-month period July, 1976 -
June, 1977. Only shipments appearing on domestic airbills and carried under
domestic tariff rates are included. The traffic flows, shown here in generalize
form, represent a 10 percent freight sample and are based on (1) data generated
for the Domestic Air Freight Rate Investigation, above, and (2) information the
author obtained through company interviews. (A detailed review of the reporting
requirements, sampling procedure, etc., used in [1] forms part of Docket 22859
and can be found in the Board's Washington offices.) Although not all airport
cities appear in the figures, those shown account (in the case of each carrier
and [figure 30] carrier class) for over 95 percent of the interstate freight
flown to/from New York-Newark. The Board's Form 298-C data provided the basis f
figures 31-32.

335

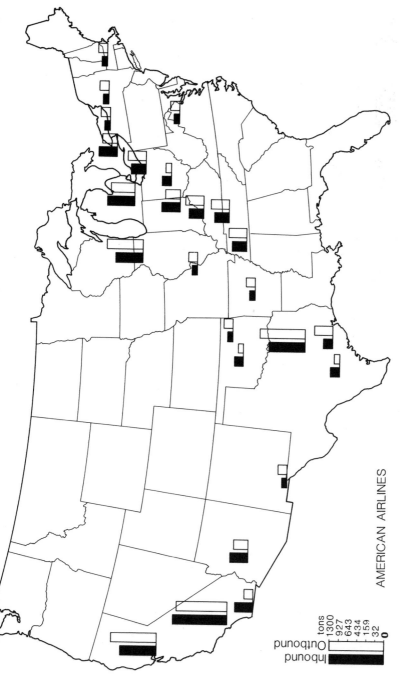

AMERICAN AIRLINES

Fig. 13. American Airlines: freight carried to and from New York–Newark
(Ten percent airbill sample, July 1976 – June 1977)

TABLE 18

ALL-CARGO AIRCRAFT: SELECTED INDICES

	\multicolumn{6}{c}{Aircraft}					
	DC-8-50F	DC-8-63F	B-727-100QC	B-747F	Electra L-188F	Skyvan SH-7
Main Dimensions						
Length (ft.)	150.7	187.4	133.2	231.3	104.5	40.1
Height (ft.)	43.0	43.0	34.0	63.4	32.8	15.0
Wing span (ft.)	142.4	148.4	108.0	195.8	99.0	64.8
Freight Compartment						
Fixed floor length (usable) (ft.)	101.5	138.3	66.4	178.0	76.0	18.6
Main freight door size						
Height (ft.)	7.1	7.1	7.2	8.2[a]	6.7	5.7
Width (ft.)	11.7	11.7	11.2	12.0	11.7	6.5
Type loading	side	side	side	front	side	rear
Main compt. bulk volume (cu. ft.)	7,476	10,330	4,560	30,647	4,950	780
Unitized volume (cu. ft.)	5,720	8,274	3,240	22,850[b]	3,131	444
Number and type of containers[c]	13A	18A	8A	30B;15C	8D;1E	2F
Secondary freight volume (cu. ft.)	1,415	2,525	890	7,353	528	–
Weights and Performance						
Operating weight[d] (lbs.)	130,000	151,574	85,270	315,871	54,842	7,620
Maximum freight[e] (lbs.)	91,000	103,000	43,753	274,129	34,147	3,880
Range with maximum freight[f] (nm)	3,200	2,300	1,125	2,450	1,415	–
Freight with full fuel[e] (lbs.)	38,700	40,837	32,634	166,000	24,174	2,560
Maximum cruise speed at mlw[g] (knots)	490	515	522	530	344	170

[a] Main compartment. Belly side doors: height--68 in., width--104 in.

[b] Includes main and auxiliary compartments.

[c] A: length--125 in., width--88 in.; B: length--117.7 in., width--96 in.; C: height--64 in., length--186 in., width--60.5 in.; D: length--108 in., width--88 in.; E: length--54 in., width--88 in.; F: length--88 in., width--65 in.

[d] Includes installed loading system, except in the Skyvan.

[e] Includes weight of pallets, nets, etc. May be limited by the fuel reserve required at maximum landing weight.

[f]

for New York-Newark are Chicago, Cincinnati, Cleveland, Dallas, Detroit, Los Angeles, Memphis, Phoenix, San Diego, and San Francisco, and together they account for about four-fifths (by weight) of the total two-way traffic. In regional terms, three principal markets may be identified, these being New York-California, New York-Midwest, and New York-Texas. The California points (Los Angeles, San Diego, and San Francisco) account for roughly fifty percent of the company's two-way tonnage. For the Middle West (Chicago, Cincinnati, Cleveland, Dayton, Detroit, and St. Louis) and Texas (Dallas, El Paso, Houston, and San Antonio) the figure is about twenty percent in both cases.

The company faces competition from other trunklines as well as all-cargo carriers. Turning again to the high-density traffic routes, its principal competitors are: (1) California--Flying Tiger Line, Trans World Airlines, United Airlines; (2) Middle West--Trans World and United, also Flying Tiger (especially in Chicago and Detroit) and Northwest Airlines (especially in Cleveland and Detroit); (3) Texas--Airlift International and Braniff, also Delta and Eastern (especially in Houston). American's approximate traffic share in these three markets is 30, 20, and 40 percent, respectively.

American Airlines currently uses the following combination-service equipment: B-707, B-727, B-747, and DC-10. Direct, wide-body passenger-freight flights link New York-Newark (June, 1977) with Boston, Chicago, Cleveland, Dallas, Los Angeles, Philadelphia, Phoenix, and San Diego. In addition, the company's fleet includes two types of freighter (B-707, B-747), which are used between New York-Newark and Chicago, Dallas, Detroit, Los Angeles, and San Francisco. Table 18 lists various operational parameters and related indices for the B-747F and several other all-cargo aircraft forming part of the New York-Newark air freight system. A few of the system's aircraft and container types are shown in figures 14-21.

Discounts applied to transportation rates for individual commodities have long been an integral part of the U.S. airlines' rate structure. In recent years the promotional role of discount-rated tariffs has been viewed with considerable skepticism, and a number of carriers have more or less abandoned the use of specific commodity rates. Its approach to "reduced rates in the form of specific commodity rates," American Airlines told the Civil Aeronautics Board during the 1973-1974 hearings forming part of the Domestic Air Freight Rate Investigation, above, was that they

338

(Pan American World Airways)

Fig. 14. Type LD-3 containers being loaded into the lower-lobe compartments of a passenger-freight B-747 aircraft

Fig. 15. Bulk freight entering a B-747 freighter via the aircraft's main-deck side cargo door

(Flying Tiger Line)

(Air Transport Association of America)

Fig. 16. A DC-8 freighter being loaded; note how the containers (type A) are contoured to the aircraft's interior

(Seaboard World Airlines)

Fig. 17. Nose door loading: An M-2 container entering the main-deck section of a B-747 freighter

Fig. 18. Five M-2 containers shown end to end in a B-747 freighter

(Boeing Company)

343

Fig. 19. A livestock shipment being intermingled with various containers (the aircraft is the B-747 freighter)

(Air Transport Association of America)

(Boeing Company)

Fig. 20.   Part of the passenger deck of a B-747 converted to hold freight

(Seaboard World Airlines)

Fig. 21.   A "stretched" DC-8 passenger aircraft converted to carry livestock

should be permitted only when it can be demonstrated that they are essential to divert significant volumes of traffic from surface to air transportation and/or to develop new markets for the favored products. Using these premises, American proposes to retain reduced rates for fruits/vegetables, cut flowers, florists/nursery stock, fish and seafood, newspapers, magazines and periodicals.[1]

Within the context of the New York-Newark air freight system American today offers only a few bulk specific commodity rates, and these only for a small number of airport cities, namely Chicago, Honolulu, Los Angeles, and San Francisco.[2] A considerably larger number of specific commodity rates are applied to container traffic, and here too they are found mainly in the company's leading East-West markets.

Another form of discount rate, the directional general commodity rate, has fallen into disfavor with practically all carriers, and, with respect to bulk shipments, has been virtually abolished. Directional general commodity rates were formerly widely applied to major East-West and North-South routes in the hope that they would correct the air freight industry's directional imbalances.[3] Like most trunklines, American Airlines believes two-way transcontinental traffic flows have been equalized to the point where these rates have lost their justification, and, as can be seen in table 19, the company has essentially removed directional rate differentials from bulk freight moving in its New York-California markets. Container rates, on the other hand, continue to show directional disparities, which, however, are to be eliminated in the future.[4]

Since American Airlines "provided scheduled all-cargo air service . . . during the period from January 1, 1977 through the

---

[1]Statement of Position (American Airlines), Docket 22859, December 21, 1973, pp. 6-7. The application (by American and its competitors) of specific commodity rates to the large volume of eastbound perishables has tended to depress the yield (cents per revenue ton-mile) on the California to New York routes below that for the reverse direction. The yield differential has been reinforced by directional general commodity rates for bulk and container traffic.

[2]The special case of human remains is disregarded here.

[3]See above, p. 14.

[4]Table 19 gives American Airlines' bulk and container rates for the New York-Los Angeles and New York-San Francisco markets. The bulk rates are shown in terms of the minimum charge, the rate per pound over the minimum charge, and the rate per 100 pounds for the standard weight breaks. (A number of forwarders are highly critical of this weight breaks structure, claiming it hinders their consolidation efforts. See above, p. 249). It will be noted that, in the case of bulk traffic, only for shipments in the 200-1,000 pound range moving from Los Angeles to New York-Newark does a rate reduction apply.

TABLE 19

AMERICAN AIRLINES: NEW YORK-CALIFORNIA RATES
(Airport to Airport, May 1977)

Bulk General Commodity Rates

	New York-Newark to Los Angeles	Los Angeles to New York-Newark	New York-Newark to San Francisco	San Francisco to New York-Newark
Minimum Charge	$19.70	$19.70	$19.80	$19.80
Rate/Pound	0.63	0.63	0.68	0.68
Weight Breaks	Rate/100 lbs.	Rate/100 lbs.	Rate/100 lbs.	Rate/100 lbs.
100 lbs.	$43.00	$43.00	$43.95	$43.95
200	43.00	40.00	43.95	43.95
1,000	37.80	37.80	38.75	38.75
2,000	37.30	37.30	38.35	38.35
3,000	37.25	37.25	38.25	38.25

Container Rates

	New York-Newark to Los Angeles		Los Angeles to New York-Newark		New York-Newark to San Francisco		San Francisco to New York-Newark	
Container Type[a]	Charge/Container	Rate/100 lbs.	Charge/Container	Rate/100 lbs.	Charge/Container	Rate/100 lbs.	Charge/Container	Rate/100 lbs.
A-2	$1,135	$21.20	$1,028	$19.30	$1,164	$21.95	$1,078	$20.00
D	193	24.25	193	21.65	198	26.15	199	22.95
LD-3	415	21.85	362	19.30	433	23.60	381	20.00

SOURCE: American Airlines.

NOTE: The charge per container is based on the net weight for the container shown. The rate per 100 pounds (container rates) is the rate for the net weight in excess of the pivot weight. The pivot weight is defined as the maximum net weight allowable at the charge per container shown. The pivot weights are: (1) A-2 (3,200 lbs.), (2) D (521 lbs.), (3) LD-3 (1,100 lbs.).

[a] See table 7.

date of enactment" of Public Law 95-163,[1] it was able to receive the new section 418 certificate during the first phase of deregulation. The company has inaugurated nonstop freighter flights between San Francisco and Philadelphia but states it has, as yet, no plans for new freighter services for New York routes.

American Airlines, as indeed most trunklines, strongly disapproves of the elimination of the section 403 tariff filing requirement. The Board's action, the company claims, is contrary to Congressional intent[2] and deprives shippers of the advance rate information needed "for rational decision making." The Board's contention that under deregulation rate sheets and other documents can serve in place of traditional rate/rules tariffs is rejected by American, which believes that only the retention of the section 403 filing provisions can guarantee the Board's ability to move against predatory pricing and other unlawful activities. Tariffs, the company adds,

> protect carriers against extortionate demands by large shippers. The carriers must abide by tariffs and cannot be forced to provide special rates in order to retain traffic, except upon notice to the public, with the opportunity for opposition by other carriers or shippers.[3]

American Airlines believes that Public Law 95-163 and the Cannon-Kennedy deregulation bill of 1978 (S.2493),[4] far from representing true deregulation, are "simply an exercise in reregulation." The company's vice president for freight marketing notes that under the new legislation American retains its status as a certificated common carrier and is unable to discriminate among shippers or engage in other "unfair" practices. Like virtually all the trunklines, American rejects the reformers' promise of reduced rates and fares under deregulation. It concedes the reform legislation will lead to additional airlift in some markets but insists this "could have been accomplished through the more traditional route case approach."[5]

Braniff International. Braniff International, which, with the exception of Pan American originates less domestic freight in New York-Newark than any other trunkline, derives about 7 percent of its

---

[1]See above, p. 153.

[2]See above, p. 159.

[3]Comments of American Airlines, Inc., Docket 33093, September 11, 1978, p. 9.

[4]See above, p. 166.

[5]McCusker, op. cit.

domestic transport revenues from freight. Its U.S. routes have
expanded from 2,543 miles (1938) to 23,269 miles (1977); its
certificated service points from 21 to 39. After Dallas and Chicago,
New York-Newark is the company's most important freight generating
point, accounting for about 10 percent of its tonnage enplaned
nationwide.

Forwarders contribute close to 80 percent (by weight) of
Braniff's surface-to-air traffic in New York-Newark, Air Cargo, Inc.
agents a further 10 percent, and long-haul truckers about 5 percent.
Another 5 percent is carried in trucks owned by shippers.
Approximately 85 percent of its surface-to-air tonnage originates
within the air terminal area. The company notes that less than a
third of its freight moving through the New York-Newark system
is containerized and that the indirect carriers account for some
four-fifths of the unitized load. The most common container used
is type A.

Braniff's freight activities are heavily slanted towards
Texas, Oklahoma, and Tennessee, with points in these states
accounting for about 90 percent of the two-way tonnage flowing
through the New York-Newark air terminals (figure 22). The most
important market by far is New York-Dallas, which produces a traffic
volume about seven times greater than the second most important city
pair, New York-Houston. Braniff's competitors in its principal
markets are Airlift International, American, Delta, and Eastern.
The company uses all-cargo equipment (B-727-100QC) on its Dallas and
Houston routes (as do Airlift and American) and controls about 25
percent of the total freight carried over these routes. Among the
major commodities handled are apparel, chemicals, electrical and
nonelectrical machinery, hardware and tools, plastic and rubber
material, and printed matter. The overall outbound:inbound traffic
ratio at New York-Newark is 3:2. In attempting to correct this
imbalance, the company has found discount rates "largely ineffectual"
and has essentially eliminated directional general commodity rates
and specific commodity rates. Braniff International received its
section 418 grandfather certificate in January of 1978. Its
director of cargo sales states that Public Law 95-163 has not
affected the company "in any great measure" and that "our operation
and policy [following deregulation] have remainded very much the
same.[1]

----

[1]Told the author by Stephen J. Facsko, Director, Cargo Sales, Braniff
International, 1978.

349

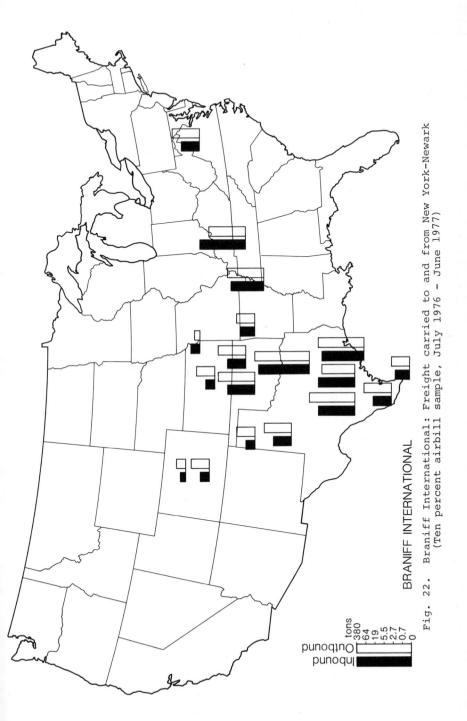

BRANIFF INTERNATIONAL

Fig. 22. Braniff International: Freight carried to and from New York-Newark
(Ten percent airbill sample, July 1976 - June 1977)

Delta Air Lines. About 7 percent of Delta's revenues can be traced to its freight operations. The carrier received its CAB permit in 1938 and, since that time, has expanded its services from 13 certificated points to almost 80 points. Its 1938 route mileage was 1,091; today it is roughly 46,500. At New York-Newark, which is its third largest freight originating station, the company enplanes just over 5 percent of the total domestic tonnage leaving the system's three airports on scheduled flights.

The overwhelming majority (about 90 percent) of Delta's surface-to-air traffic at the New York-Newark terminals originates within the air terminal area. Roughly 65 percent of the surface-to-air load is tendered by the forwarders, with certificated truckers and shippers carrying a further 5 percent each. The balance is contributed by local cartage agents. About 30 percent of the outbound traffic is containerized, and here the most common container employed is the LD-3. Delta discontinued all-cargo service in 1973. Its equipment includes the B-737, DC-8, DC-9, and the wide-body L-1011.

Delta is one of the major air carriers operating in the eastern part of the United States, with Atlanta serving as its major hub. I also has authority to fly to several West Coast and southwestern cities, which, in the absence of direct connections with New York-Newark, it has not, as yet, developed into major traffic points Its ten leading origin-destination points for New York-Newark are Atlanta, Boston, Charlotte, Fort Lauderdale, Houston, Jackson, Memphis, Miami, New Orleans, and Tampa (figure 23). Together these ten cities account for roughly 75 percent of the freight tonnage Delta handles in New York-Newark. Atlanta, its single most important market, contributes about one-third of the company's traffic at the New York-Newark air terminals, with Florida points in second place with about 25 percent. Delta's leading competitors over its major North-South routes are Airlift International, Eastern, and National. In other important markets it also faces competition from American and Braniff. In the New York-Atlanta market, where it operates considerably more wide-body flights than the competing trunk carrier (Eastern), it handles roughly 40 percent of the total air freight tonnage; in the Florida market its traffic share falls to 20 percent.

The major commodities flowing through the system (two-way) include electrical machinery, hardware and tools, household appliances, office equipment, plastic goods, and printed material (especially newspapers and magazines). Horticultural products,

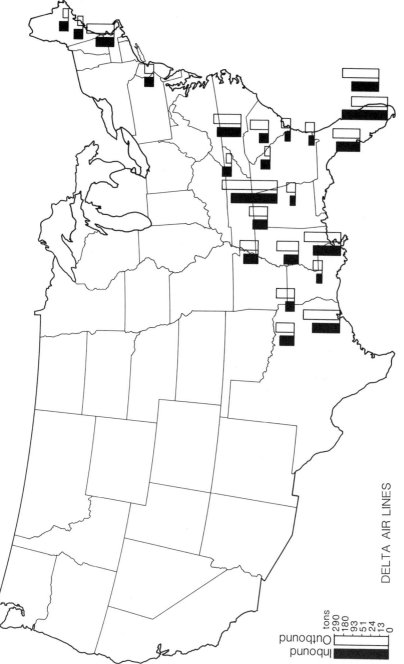

DELTA AIR LINES

Fig. 23. Delta Air Lines: Freight carried to and from New York-Newark
(Ten percent airbill sample, July 1976 – June 1977)

particularly cut flowers, constitute another important item and are carried mainly from Florida to New York-Newark. Horticultural products form as much as 35 percent of Delta's Florida to New York-Newark air freight tonnage and, since transportation rates for perishables are lower than for manufactured items, tend to depress the company's yield in this market. The average yield (mid-1976 to mid-1977; cents per revenue ton-mile) for the Miami to New York-Newark traffic is 34, for Tampa to New York-Newark, 37 (in the reverse direction the figures are, respectively, 46 and 53). Some other originating points produce the following average yields: Atlanta, 62.9; Dallas, 70.5; and Houston, 47.6.

About 70 percent of Delta's outbound traffic at New York-Newark is carried directly to destination airports. The remainder is routed to the Atlanta hub, where it is transferred to other aircraft for onward transportation. Almost the entire transfer load, however, remains intraline traffic. Generally speaking, Delta's outbound:inbound traffic ratio at the New York-Newark air terminals has stabilized at 3:2. During the aforementioned 1973-1974 freight rate hearings, the company noted that directional imbalace had ceased to be a major problem and that the industry had "matured" to the point where an extensive application of promotional rates was no longer justified. The company has supported the abolition of all directional general commodity rates and, following a recent reappraisal of its rate structure, also eliminated most of its specific commodity rates, retaining these only for cut flowers moving to New York-Newark and for southbound printed material.

Delta Air Lines has been one of the staunchest defenders of the Board's traditional regulatory powers (chapter III). More extravagant in its praise of the Federal Aviation Act than virtually any other carrier, Delta views the Act as "probably one of the most remarkable pieces of legislation ever passed by Congress." The Act is "flexible . . . [and] always forward-looking and, in this respect, is not unlike the U.S. Constitution itself."[1] The company questions the objectives of the reform movement and doubts whether recent reform legislation can produce bona fide deregulation. Delta (in common with other certificated airlines) must currently comply with the rules and regulations of about twenty Federal agencies and departments (these include, for instance, the Departments of Justice Labor, and Transportation, the Civil Aeronautics Board, the

---

[1] James W. Callison, The Airline Reform Movement--Is It Deregulation or Re-Regulation? remarks made before the American Society of Women Accountants, Atlanta, May 9, 1978, mimeographed, p. 5.

Environmental Protection Agency, the Equal Employment Opportunity
Commission, the Federal Communications Commission, and the Interstate
Commerce Commission) and believes any genuine reform effort should
give priority to the removal of the regulatory overlap and confusion
inevitably created by so large a number of regulators. President
Carter's assertion that airline deregulation will help combat
inflation is termed "ludicrous" by Delta officials, who, along with
representatives of various other airlines, feel recent reform
measures will contribute to higher air transportation costs.

Eastern Air Lines. Like its principal competitors, Eastern
Air Lines was certificated in 1938. The period 1938-1977 has seen
the company's authorized U.S. service points grow from 42 to 71,
while the length of its routes has expanded from 5,276 to 42,456
miles. About 6 percent of the total scheduled domestic air freight
tonnage enplaned at New York-Newark is carried by Eastern Air Lines.
New York-Newark is Eastern's third most important freight originating
point. The company derives only about 4 percent of its domestic
transportation revenues from freight, a figure lower than that of any
other trunkline.

Approximately 90 percent (by weight) of Eastern's surface-to-air
traffic in New York-Newark originates within the air terminal area.
Over half of the load is tendered to the company by the forwarders.
About 30 percent of the total outbound freight has been containerized,
the containers most commonly used being the LD-3, LD-11, and E.

Partly as a result of the fuel crisis, Eastern discontinued most
of its all-cargo flights in 1973-1974; all-cargo service (in the New
York-Newark system) was totally abandoned in mid-1975 with the
cancellation of a freight interchange program which the company had
operated jointly with Seaboard World Airlines. Eastern had been
providing direct all-cargo flights between New York-Newark and
Atlanta, Boston, Charlotte, Houston, Los Angeles, Miami, New Orleans,
and St. Louis. Termination of these and other freighter schedules
was severly criticized by the major forwarders, some of whom, as we
have seen, raised the matter during Congressional hearings on
deregulation and justified their use of charter flights in terms of
the trunklines' reduced nighttime freight capacity. Today Eastern's
aircraft fleet consists of the wide-body L-1011 and the narrower
DC-9 and B-727, with the DC-9 and B-727 accounting for about half of
the company's domestic departures from New York-Newark. Direct,
wide-body connections exist between New York-Newark and Boston,
Hartford, Houston, Miami, Orlando, and San Antonio.

As its name suggests, this carrier's activities are concentrated
in the eastern part of the United States; fully 85 percent of its

authorized points are located East of the Mississippi. Eastern's role as a freight carrier within the New York-Newark system is shown in figure 24. The ten major freight exchange points for New York-Newark are Atlanta, Boston, Charlotte, Fort Lauderdale, Houston, Miami, Orlando, Raleigh, San Antonio, and Washington, D.C., which collectively account for about 70 percent (by weight) of the freight flowing through the New York-Newark air terminals. Important secondary points include Greensboro, New Orleans, Tampa, and West Palm Beach. Eastern, it should be pointed out, also serves such leading air traffic centers as Chicago, Dallas-Fort Worth, Los Angeles, Portland, and Seattle, which, however, are not directly linked with New York-Newark (freight movements between these points and New York-Newark are relatively insignificant and do not appear in figure 24). The principal items carried by Eastern include apparel, chemicals and pharmaceuticals, household effects, horticultural products, and printed matter. Broadly speaking, the overall inbound freight tonnage at the New York-Newark airports is equal to the outbound flow.

The company's single most important freight axis is the New York-Florida market, which accounts for some 40 percent (by weight) of Eastern's two-way traffic in New York-Newark. Since about a quarter of the northbound traffic consists of perishable items such as horticultural products, seafood products, and vegetables (which are carried under lower rates than industrial commodities), this market's contribution to Eastern's New York-Newark revenues is lower than would otherwise be the case. The difference in yield between northbound perishables and manufactured items is pronounced. Thus, for Miami-enplaned cut flowers, frozen fish, and vegetables the average yields (mid-1976 to mid-1977) are, respectively, 28, 11, and 9 cents per revenue ton-mile; for electrical machinery, fabricated metal products, and printed material, on the other hand, the respective figures are 48, 53, and 54 cents per revenue ton-mile. For the total northbound commodity mix the average yield is, for example, 31 cents/rtm (Miami) and 42 cents/rtm (Tampa); in the reverse direction the figures rise to 45 and 60 cents/rtm, respectively. Eastern's chief competitors in the New York-Florida market are Delta and National; Airlift International is a relatively minor competitor. A comparison of their airport-to-airport bulk general commodity rates (New York-Newark to Miami) is given in table 20. As is the case with most of the freight system's markets, little difference exists between the rate levels set by the major competing carriers.

355

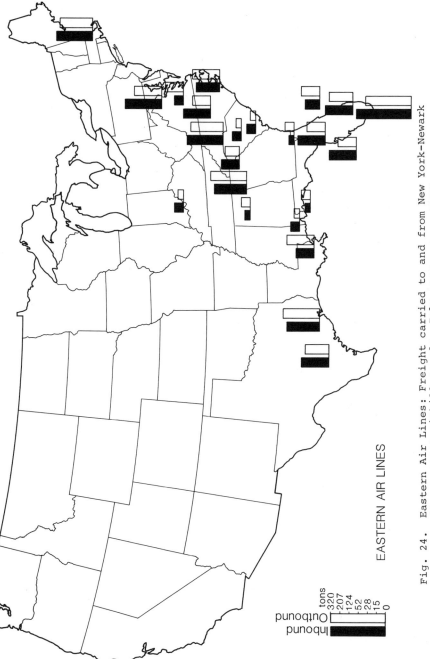

EASTERN AIR LINES

Fig. 24. Eastern Air Lines: Freight carried to and from New York-Newark
(Ten percent airbill sample, July 1976 – June 1977)

tons
320
207
124
52
28
15
0

Outbound
Inbound

TABLE 20

BULK GENERAL COMMODITY RATES: NEW YORK-NEWARK
TO MIAMI (May 1977)

	Airlift	Delta	Eastern	National
Minimum Charge	$18.00	$14.00	$14.00	–
Rate/Pound	0.45	0.31	0.31	$ 0.31
Weight Breaks		Rate per 100 Pounds		
100 lbs.	$22.60	$23.55	$23.55	$23.55
1,000	19.35	20.45	20.45	20.45
2,000	18.35	19.45	19.45	19.45
3,000	–	18.65	18.65	18.65

National Airlines. This carrier's interstate freight
activities generate about 5.5 percent of its transportation revenues.
National, which in 1938 operated over an 871-mile route network
linking 13 airport cities, today serves 36 cities distributed across
a network of 8,425 miles. Miami and New York-Newark are its first
and second freight originating points, respectively. Approximately
one-fifth of the company's total domestic freight load is enplaned
at the New York-Newark air terminals.

In New York-Newark National receives about 60 percent of its
surface-to-air traffic from the indirect carriers and another 25
percent from local cartage agents. Roughly 10 percent is brought
to its terminals by long-haul truckers and an additional 5 percent
by shippers using their own surface vehicles. Over three-quarters
of the entire load originates within the pickup and delivery zone.
National utilizes no all-cargo aircraft. Its schedules are wholly
passenger-oriented, its fleet consisting of the B-727 and the
wide-body DC-10. An estimated 60 percent of New York-Newark's
two-way traffic is carried in the DC-10, the remainder in the B-727.
About 30 percent of the load is containerized (the LD-3 is the
most common container employed), with virtually all container
traffic being tendered by the forwarders.

Figure 25 identifies New York-Newark's major freight exchange
points. It will be noted immediately that these are essentially
concentrated along the Eastern Seaboard and the Gulf Coast. National
also has authority to serve several Western cities such as Los
Angeles, San Diego, and San Francisco, but, since no direct flights
are offered between these hubs and New York-Newark, the freight
carried in East-West markets remains minimal. The Florida-New
York route is the company's dominant freight market; indeed, of
the ten leading origin-destination points, only four are found in
states other than Florida. The ten points are Charleston, Fort
Myers, Jacksonville, Miami, New Orleans, Norfolk, Orlando, Tampa,

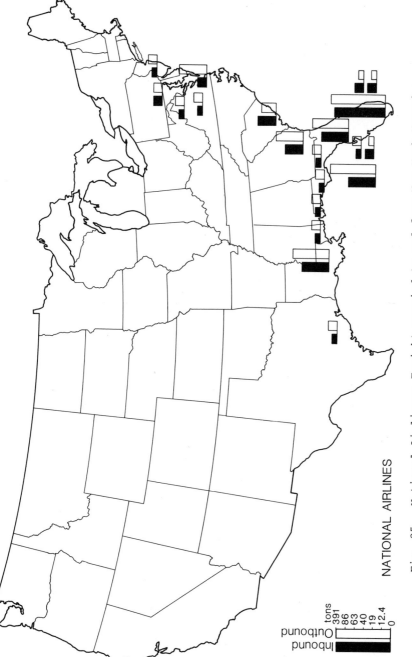

NATIONAL AIRLINES

Fig. 25. National Airlines: Freight carried to and from New York-Newark
(Ten percent airbill sample, July 1976 – June 1977)

Washington, D.C., and West Palm Beach, which together account for over 90 percent (by weight) of New York-Newark's two-way traffic flow.

Roughly four-fifths of the company's freight traffic at the New York-Newark terminals moves to/from points in Florida. The outbound:inbound weight ratio for this market is 3:2. Manufactured items (especially textile goods, printed material, audio components, and machine parts) dominate the outbound flow, while vegetables and horticultural products (cut flowers and nursery stock) constitute about 25 percent (by weight) of the traffic moving in the opposite direction. It was pointed out in the case of Delta and Eastern that the average yield for freight moving to Florida exceeds the figure for the reverse direction. This also holds for National Airlines, which has an average northbound yield (Miami to New York) that is about 30 percent below the average yield for freight flown to Miami. Florida traffic contributes (in terms of the New York-Newark system) about 70 percent of National's freight revenues.

National carries about 44 percent (by weight) of the entire freight exchanged between New York-Newark and Florida, more than any other airline. An important reason for this is that for several Florida points it offers later departures than those of its competitors, thus giving forwarders additional time to tender their consolidated loads. The company has discontinued its specific commodity rates for New York-bound perishables, concluding that these rates will no longer divert additional traffic from surface to air transportation. It also questions the promotional value of directional general commodity rates and has sharply curtailed their use in its freight operations.

Northwest Airlines. Northwest's route network today extends over 30,927 miles and connects 35 airport cities; in 1938, the year in which the carrier received its operating certificate, these figures were, respectively, 2,507 and 21. The company carries about 6 percent (by weight) of the scheduled domestic freight flown out of New York-Newark. New York-Newark is its fourth largest freight originating center. It derives about 11 percent of its domestic transportation revenues from freight operations.

An estimated 80 percent (by weight) of Northwest's surface-to-air freight tonnage leaving New York-Newark originates within the air terminal area. Roughly half of the outbound load is tendered by the forwarders. The shippers themselves carry another 25 percent, while long-haul motor operators deliver about 15 percent. The balance is received from local cartage agents.

The commodity flows between New York-Newark and a number of Northwest's other airport cities are shown in figure 26. The company's flights, it will be noted, are restricted largely to the northern part of the United States, direct service being offered between New York-Newark and cities in the northwestern, northcentral, and northeastern regions of the country. The carrier's operating authority encompasses several important air traffic centers in the South and on the West Coast (e.g., Atlanta, Miami, Los Angeles, San Francisco). No direct flights (via Northwest) link these cities with New York-Newark and, with the exception of Los Angeles, they do not exchange sufficient traffic with New York-Newark to merit inclusion in figure 26. New York-Newark's ten leading freight exchange points are: Chicago, Cleveland, Detroit, Los Angeles, Madison, Milwaukee, Minneapolis-St. Paul, Portland, Seattle, and Spokane. Together these cities account for roughly 95 percent of the freight moving through the New York-Newark air terminals. Northwest's equipment includes the B-747 freighter (which is used between New York-Newark and Chicago, Milwaukee, Minneapolis-St. Paul, and Seattle), two types of wide-body combination aircraft (B-747, DC-10), and the smaller B-727.

The single most important freight exchange point for New York-Newark is Minneapolis-St. Paul, accounting for about one-third of the former's two-way freight tonnage. Northwest is by far the most important carrier in the New York-Minneapolis market, transporting roughly 90 percent of the air freight moving between these two airport centers. The reasons for this dominance include: (1) Northwest is the only carrier providing nighttime freighter service in this market, (2) it is the only carrier using wide-body combination aircraft, (3) it provides the largest number of direct flights, and (4) several of its combination flights have later departure times than those of other airlines connecting New York-Newark with Minneapolis-St. Paul. The principal commodities carried to Minneapolis-St. Paul are chemicals and pharmaceuticals, electrical machinery and parts, food preparations, printed matter, and wearing apparel; in the reverse direction the traffic includes electronic components, fabricated textile products (exclusive of apparel) and fur pelts, office machinery (e.g., calculating equipment), plastic and rubber goods, and printed matter. In terms of weight, the westbound flow is approximately equal to the eastbound flow in this market; the average yield (mid-1976 to mid-1977; cents per revenue ton-mile) to Minneapolis-St. Paul is 48, from Minneapolis-St. Paul, 44. Of the total load leaving New York-Newark, about 5 percent moves to destination airports as interline traffic.

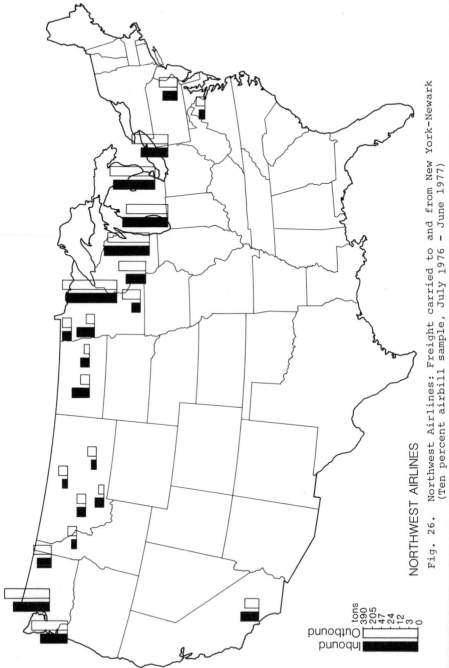

NORTHWEST AIRLINES

Fig. 26. Northwest Airlines: Freight carried to and from New York-Newark
(Ten percent airbill sample, July 1976 – June 1977)

Combination rather than joint rates are applied to interline movements.

Northwest Airlines, like several other trunk carriers, was issued a section 418 grandfather certificate in January, 1978. The company states that this has had "no impact" on its interstate operations and notes that it has no immediate plans to expand freighter service to new markets. Northwest discontinued specific commodity rates about ten years ago. Also, the company has eliminated or reduced the use of directional bulk general commodity rates in its major East-West markets. Thus, for example, in the New York-Portland market directional discounts (for traffic moving to New York-Newark) are offered only where shipments (1) are below 100 pounds and (2) weigh more than 3,000 pounds (table 21).

TABLE 21

NORTHWEST AIRLINES: DIRECTIONAL BULK GENERAL COMMODITY
RATES (New York-Portland, May 1977)

	New York-Newark to Portland	Portland to New York-Newark
Minimum Charge	$18.00	$18.00
Rate/Pound	0.64	0.60
Weight Breaks	Rate per 100 Pounds	
100 lbs.	$39.65	$39.65
1,000	35.00	35.00
2,000	34.50	34.50
3,000	34.45	34.05

SOURCE: Northwest Airlines.

Pan American World Airways. Pan American is the nation's leading international air carrier. The company, which has its corporate headquarters in New York City, today serves some 150 foreign points (as opposed to about 50 in 1938) and derives 18 percent of its transportation revenues from the carriage of freight. In New York-Newark, where it originates more freight than in any other U.S. city, it accounts for about 40 percent (by weight) of the international traffic enplaned by U.S. airlines.

Half of Pan American's freight load flown out of New York-Newark represents surface-to-air traffic. Another 30 percent is intraline traffic (i.e., shipments the company has enplaned at domestic points other than New York-Newark), while the remainder is freight which is received from other airlines. Roughly two-thirds of the surface-to-air tonnage originates within the air terminal area; the other third is trucked to New York from distances of up to about

800 miles and, for the greater part, represents surface-for-air substitutions. Substitute service is performed on a regular rather than sporadic basis and is legal since the truck hauls, of course, represent only a fraction of the total origin-destination movements involved (table 9). Substitute traffic moves under through air rates, which, for the points in question, are cheaper than combined air-truck rates.

The majority of Pan American's freight is tendered by the forwarders, with the latter acting as consolidators and IATA agents. Most of the company's two-way traffic at its New York-Newark terminals is containerized, the most common units being the LD-7 and the M-1. About two-thirds of the freight is exchanged with points in Western Europe.

Under the former regulatory regime Pan American was essential barred from engaging in interstate transportation. An exemption (which had to be applied for on a flight-by-flight basis) allowed it to carry race horses between New York and Miami, and a similar arrangement made possible some all-cargo service between New York-Newark, on the one hand, and Los Angeles, San Francisco, and several Midwest points, on the other. Limited though this all-cargo service was, it sufficed to qualify Pan American for a section 418 grandfather certificate, enabling the company to initiate regular domestic freighter flights between New York-Newark and Chicago, Houston, Los Angeles, Miami, and San Francisco (the equipment used is the B-707 and the B-747). Deregulation of the passenger sector will, of course, permit Pan American to offer additional domestic freight capacity. Company officials have stated, however, that, rather than developing their own interstate route network, they would prefer a merger with one of the domestic carriers. National Airlines is most frequently cited in this connection.

Trans World Airlines (TWA). Freight produces roughly 9 perce of TWA's domestic transportation revenues. The company's certificated U.S. service points have grown from 27 (1938) to 40 (1977); its interstate routes from 5,740 to 28,000 miles. After Lo Angeles, New York-Newark is the company's most important freight originating station, producing about one-fifth of its entire domes freight load. Trans World Airlines, one of the major freight carriers operating in the New York-Newark system, accounts for roughly 14 percent (by weight) of the interstate freight enplaned a the system's three airports.

Approximately 75 percent (by weight) of TWA's surface-to-air tonnage originating in New York-Newark is forwarder traffic, while

an additional 20 percent is brought to the air terminals by local
pickup/delivery agents. Long-haul trucking concerns account for
about 5 percent; only 1 percent of the total load is carried
directly by the shippers. About 85 percent of the domestic
surface-to-air traffic originates within the New York-Newark air
terminal area. According to a company spokesman, roughly 40 percent
of the two-way traffic moving through the system is containerized,
with forwarders producing about 75 percent of the containerized
load. The container types most frequently used are the A and LD-3.

Figure 27 depicts the freight flows between New York-Newark
and other important air traffic centers. The ten leading
origin-destination points for New York-Newark are Chicago, Cincinnati,
Columbus, Dayton, Indianapolis, Kansas City, Los Angeles, Phoenix,
St. Louis, and San Francisco, which together account for about 90
percent of the two-way tonnage handled by the company at the New
York-Newark airports. The aircraft used include the wide-body B-747
and L-1011 (direct, wide-body flights are offered between New
York-Newark and Boston, Chicago, Denver, Kansas City, Las Vegas, Los
Angeles, Phoenix, and San Francisco) and the DC-9, B-727, and B-707
(the latter is used both for passenger-cargo and all-cargo service).
All-cargo flights connect New York-Newark with Chicago, Indianapolis,
Kansas City, Los Angeles, Philadelphia, St. Louis, and San Francisco.
Largely as a result of rapidly rising fuel prices, the company's
freighter operations have become increasingly unprofitable and it
has reported that these operations caused it to lose over $8 million
in 1977 alone. The company believes deregulation will exacerbate
this problem (since additional competitors, using more economical
equipment such as the stretched DC-8, are now free to enter its
markets) and has indicated its all-cargo services will soon be
terminated. Freight service will, of course, be continued with
combination aircraft, and TWA states that through fleet enlargement
and greater use of wide-body equipment its freight capacity will,
within three to four years, exceed that which it provides under
present conditions.

Apparel, electrical and nonelectrical machinery and parts,
fruits and vegetables, printed matter, pharmaceuticals, and
transportation and communications equipment constitute about
four-fifths (by weight) of the two-way load moving through TWA's
New York-Newark terminal facilities. Generally speaking, the
outbound flow is in balance with the inbound flow. Roughly 95
percent of the outbound tonnage is carried to destination airports
by TWA, the remainder being interlined with other carriers. The

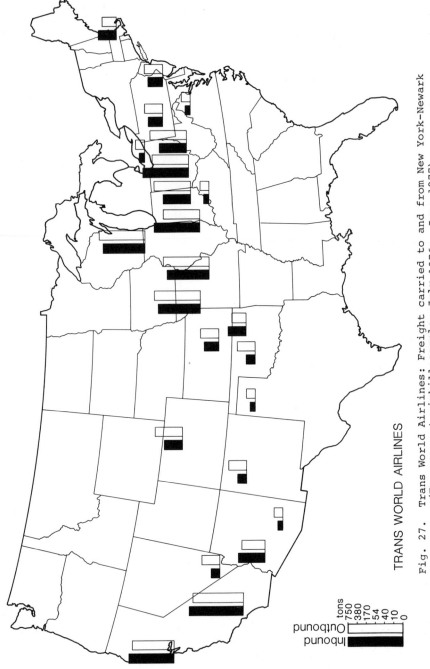

TRANS WORLD AIRLINES

Fig. 27. Trans World Airlines: Freight carried to and from New York-Newark
(Ten percent airbill sample, July 1976 – June 1977)

ompany, for example, has a joint-rate agreement with Frontier
irlines, under which shipments flown to Denver are received by
rontier for onward transportation to smaller regional air centers.

Trans World Airlines believes that directional imbalance, which
ormerly plagued the leading interstate carriers, has ceased to be
 major concern, and it has discarded virtually all of its
irectional bulk general commodity rates. Also, the company does
ot favor the widespread use of specific commodity rates, but feels
uch rates are justified in certain instances. About 90 specific
ommodity rates are offered for bulk traffic (a lesser number for
nitized shipments) moving to/from New York-Newark, one third of
hich are applied to animal products, horticultural products, and
ruits and vegetables flown from Los Angeles and San Francisco to
ew York-Newark. Table 22 lists the airport-to-airport rates for
hree commodities and indicates the cost savings (relative to the
eneral commodity rate) available to shippers of these items.

TABLE 22

TRANS WORLD AIRLINES: GENERAL COMMODITY V. SPECIFIC
COMMODITY RATES (San Francisco to
New York-Newark, May 1977)

eight Breaks	Gen. Com. Rate	Specific Commodity Rate		
		Nursery Stock	Straw-berries	Electrical Appliances
		Rate per 100 Pounds		
100 lbs.	$43.95	$34.85	-	-
200	40.95	-	-	-
500	-	-	$26.25	$30.00
,000	38.75	32.05	24.00	27.95
,000	38.35	30.10	17.50	27.10
,000	38.25	28.60	16.10	26.80

SOURCE: Trans World Airlines.

United Airlines. After American Airlines, United enplanes
ore freight in New York-Newark than any other interstate carrier.
he company, which receives about 9 percent of its transportation
evenues from freight traffic, has expanded its operational pattern
rom 38 certificated points and 5,320 route miles (1938) to 88
oints and 48,000 miles (1977). Its domestic enplanements in
hicago, Los Angeles, and San Francisco exceed those of New
ork-Newark. New York-Newark, where United handles roughly 16
ercent (by weight) of the total domestic outbound traffic, contributes
pproximately 10 percent of its combined load enplaned nationwide.

About 90 percent (by weight) of United's surface-to-air traffic leaving the three New York-Newark terminals originates within the air terminal area. The carrier receives roughly 55 percent of its outbound freight from forwarders and another 20 percent from local pickup and delivery agents. A further 20 percent is received from the shippers themselves, while over-the-road truckers contribute 5 percent. One third of United's two-way traffic is containerized, the most commonly used units being types A and LD-3. Eighty-five percent of the container traffic is tendered to United by the forwarders.

The major freight movements linking New York-Newark with other airport cities are shown in figure 28. The ten leading freight exchange points for New York-Newark are Chicago, Cleveland, Denver, Detroit, Los Angeles, Milwaukee, Portland, Salt Lake City, San Francisco, and Seattle, and together they account for about 90 percent of United's two-way freight flow in New York-Newark. The company's single most important city pair is New York/Newark-Chicago which generates about 25 percent of the tonnage handled at its New York-Newark terminals. United, which provides considerably more freight capacity (including late-afternoon and evening flights) in this market than do its competitors (American, Flying Tiger, Trans World), carries about half the total air freight tonnage moving between New York-Newark and Chicago. West Coast points (Los Angeles, San Diego, San Francisco, Seattle, Portland) constitute another critical market (here United's traffic share is roughly 30 percent) and account for about 50 percent of New York-Newark's inbound-outbound freight tonnage.

About 55 percent of the company's New York-Newark freight load is carried in pure freighters (DC-8-50F), which link New York-Newark directly with Chicago, Denver, Los Angeles, Portland, San Francisco, and Seattle. In addition, the company operates wide-body combination flights (B-747, DC-10) in these markets. United's aircraft fleet also includes the passenger-freight DC-8, B-727, and B-737.

Apparel, electrical equipment and components, nonelectrical machinery and parts, perishable items (cut flowers, food preparations, fruits, vegetables), and printed matter make up about 65 percent of the load carried by United. Other important commodities include fabricated metal products, plastic and rubber goods, and pharmaceuticals. The company does not believe that directional general commodity rates represent a useful developmental tool, and virtually none of these rates are offered today. Specific commodi-

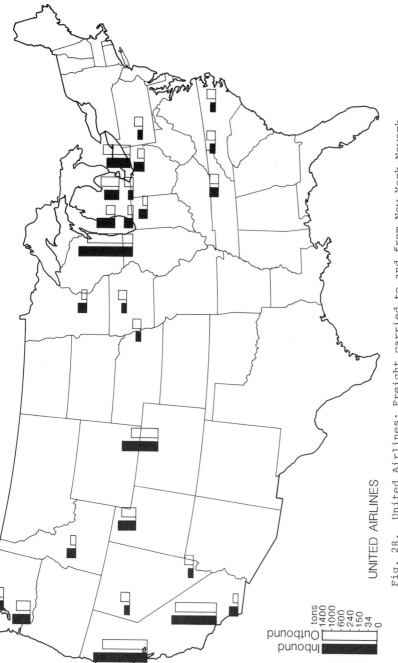

UNITED AIRLINES

Fig. 28.   United Airlines: Freight carried to and from New York-Newark
(Ten percent airbill sample, July 1976 – June 1977)

rates, on the other hand, have been retained for about 20 New York-Newark routes, most of the rates being applied to shipments originating in California and the Pacific Northwest. Specific commodity rates are credited with having attracted large quantities of eastbound freight (particularly fruits, horticultural products, and vegetables) to air transportation, and it is these perishables which explain (for the West Coast-New York market) why the New York-bound traffic volume exceeds freight flows in the reverse direction.

A section 418 grandfather certificate was issued to United at the beginning of 1978. The company does not expect the new free entry rules to affect its New York freighter operations in the foreseeable future.

All-Cargo Carriers

All three of the nation's section 401 certificated scheduled all-cargo airlines serve the New York-Newark area. The carriers in question are Airlift International, the Flying Tiger Line, and Seaboard World Airlines. The first two have long held interstate authority, which, in the case of the Flying Tiger Line, was augmented through a grant (1969) of scheduled international authority (Transpacific Route Investigation, above). Seaboard, on the other hand, has traditionally been an international carrier, and it was only in 1978 that it was able to operate in domestic markets on a regular basis.

Airlift International. Airlift was issued its section 401 certificate in 1956.[1] The company's fluctuating financial fortunes have caused it to restructure its operations on several occasions, and the number of authorized domestic points (originally 25) now stands (1977) at 21 (at several of which service has been suspended). The length of its interstate route network has grown from 3,820 miles to 10,650 miles. After Los Angeles, Airlift enplanes more scheduled domestic traffic in New York-Newark than in any other airport city. Its New York-Newark operations are unusual (for a certificated route carrier) in that a substantial proportion of the total outbound traffic moves on charter flights. These charter activities (which are not further considered here) were protested by one of its competitors, the Flying Tiger Line, and, the reader will recall, the Civil Aeronautics Board to institute the Air Freight Forwarder Charters Investigation, above.

---

[1] See above, p. 15.   [2] See above, p. 35.

Roughly three-quarters of Airlift's domestic surface-to-air·
traffic leaving the New York-Newark airports originates from within
the air terminal area. The forwarders, from whom the company
receives about 60 percent of its business, constitute its single
most important traffic source; the remaining tonnage comes directly
from large-volume shippers and over-the-road truckers. Surface-to-air
traffic comprises about 80 percent of the outbound load, air-to-air
transfers accounting for the remainder. Virtually all of the
shipments enplaned in New York-Newark reach destination airports as
intraline traffic. About three-quarters of the company's two-way
traffic passing through New York-Newark is containerized, the most
common containers being types A and B.

Airlift uses the DC-8. The major traffic exchange points for
New York-Newark are Atlanta, Dallas, Houston, Los Angeles, and Miami.
The leading commodities carried include electrical and nonelectrical
machinery, printed matter, and textile goods. A serious directional
imbalance problem exists in several markets (New York-California,
New York-Texas), which Airlift, a relatively small company, attributes
to its inability to provide prime-time departures at each of the
points served. Unlike the Flying Tiger Line, Airlift maintained a
somewhat "low profile" during the deregulation controversy and,
although awarded a section 418 certificate, states it has no
immediate expansion plans.

Flying Tiger Line. In 1949 the CAB approved Flying Tiger's
certificate of public convenience and necessity.[1] Since that time,
the carrier has expanded its interstate route network from 3,820 to
10,656 miles (1977). This network links 15 points, a relatively
small number when compared with, say, the operations of such major
trunklines as American and United. The company can point with
pride to its contributions to the development of the nation's air
freight industry. These include the first nonstop transcontinental
freight schedules (1957) and use of the first turbine-powered
freighters (1961). In 1968 Flying Tiger introduced the DC-8-63F
freighter (table 18) and in 1974 it became one of the first airlines
to use wide-body aircraft in the all-cargo field. Its current
equipment consists of 15 DC-8-63s and 6 B-747s, which a company
brochure describes as "the largest all-cargo fleet of any airline
in the world."

Four-fifths of Flying Tiger's outbound freight in New
York-Newark consists of surface-to-air traffic; air-to-air transfers

---

[1]See above, p. 12.

make up the remaining fifth. At least three-quarters of the
surface-to-air traffic originates within the New York-Newark air
terminal area. The surface-to-air traffic comes from various
sources, as follows: forwarders--about 60 percent, local cartage
agents--25 percent, shippers--10 percent, and long-haul truckers--
5 percent. About half of its two-way traffic is containerized,
the principal container types being the A and LD-7. Approximately
three-quarters of the containerized load is tendered to the company
by the forwarders.

The Flying Tiger Line is one of the leading originators of
freight at the New York-Newark air terminals, where it enplanes
more interstate traffic than at any other hub with the exception of
Chicago. About 10 percent of the outbound freight is interlined
with other carriers for transportation to destination airports.
Seventy percent of its outbound freight leaves New York-Newark
between 12:00 A.M. and 7:00 A.M.; the remainder is carried during
daylight hours (under so-called daylight rates), allowing the aircraft to be repositioned for nighttime departures. The principal
commodities moved to and/or from New York-Newark include apparel
and other textile goods, machinery and parts, motor vehicles, and
perishables (especially cut flowers, strawberries, and vegetables).

Figure 29 shows the company's major traffic flows with respect
to the New York-Newark air terminals. Three points, Chicago, Los
Angeles, and San Francisco, account for about 80 percent (by weight)
of the total two-way traffic. Flying Tiger faces formidable competition in these markets and carries only about 20 percent of the air
freight moving between the three hubs and New York-Newark. Its
leading competitors (in these markets) are American Airlines,
Trans World Airlines, and United Airlines, whose combined freight
capacity far exceeds its own. For instance, Flying Tiger offers
15 departures per week from Chicago to New York-Newark (second
half of June, 1977), as opposed to the 31 all-cargo and 56 wide-body
combination flights of the other three carriers. Looking at another
route, New York-Newark to San Francisco, Flying Tiger provides 10
westbound flights per week compared with the 33 all-cargo and over
90 wide-body combination flights of the three trunklines. The
inbound:outbound ratio of Flying Tiger's overall interstate traffic
in New York-Newark is 2:1, an imbalance largely due to the massive
flow of perishables originating in California. The company fears
that shippers associations will divert eastbound perishables to

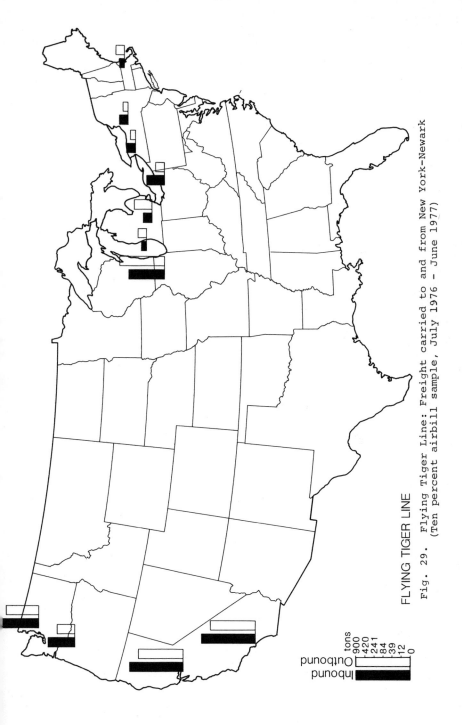

FLYING TIGER LINE

Fig. 29. Flying Tiger Line: Freight carried to and from New York-Newark (Ten percent airbill sample, July 1976 – June 1977)

charter operations and has sought to persuade the CAB to withhold charter rights from these organizations.[1]

Like the other two all-cargo route carriers, Flying Tiger received its section 418 certificate in January of 1978. An ambitious expansion program is contemplated, the first stage of which will see scheduled service at Atlanta, Charlotte, Cincinnati, Dallas-Fort Worth, Houston, Miami, Portland, San Juan, and Washington-Baltimore. The company has also announced that it will seek a merger with Seaboard World Airlines.

Seaboard World Airlines. Founded in 1946, Seaboard was certificated in 1955, enabling it to undertake scheduled operations between the United States and Western Europe. Since 1955 its route network has grown from 14,825 to 16,293 miles. The company claims to have performed the first commercial landing and takeoff at Kennedy Airport following that terminal's opening in 1948 and was the first U.S. carrier to use the B-747 freighter in the North Atlantic market. Barred (under the former regulatory regime) from engaging in regular interstate transportation, Seaboard has developed as an international carrier to the point where, after Pan American, it enplanes more international freight at Kennedy than any other U.S. airline and accounts (mid-1976 to mid-1977) for about a quarter of the scheduled international freight leaving the airport in American-owned aircraft.

Roughly 85 percent of the company's outbound traffic is tendered by the forwarders (who may act as consolidators and/or IATA agents). Surface-to-air and air-to-air shipments constitute 80 percent and 20 percent of the outbound traffic, respectively. Only about half of the surface-to-air load originates within the New York-Newark air terminal area, the remainder being trucked to New York from various parts of the United States, particularly from the Northeast and the Middle West. For these latter areas the through air rate is cheaper than the combined air-truck rate, and here motor hauls are treated as surface-for-air substitutions (chapter VI).

Approximately half of Seaboard's two-way traffic is containerized, the major units being the 88 in. x 125 in. igloo and the M-1 and M-2 containers. The latter (8' x 8' x 20') was introduced in 1974 and, the company concedes, encountered initial shipper resistance (one difficulty being the absence of appropriate IATA rates). Beginning with 50 M-2s in 1974, the company quickly

---

[1] See above, p. 277.

expanded this number and today is one of the largest owners of 20-foot air containers in the world. Built to Seaboard's specifications, these units weigh about 2,100 pounds, roughly half that of a comparable sea container. The M-2, to say nothing of larger versions, is carried in the B-747 freighter and can be transferred directly from truck to aircraft (figure 17) without first entering Seaboard's terminal building.

The M-2 containers are made of aluminium and contain various features designed to enhance their compatibility with road transportation. Unlike most other air containers, they are not contoured to an aircraft's interior and, in the view of many industry observers, constitute the first "truly" intermodal air-land containers. "They are," in the words of a Seaboard pamphlet, "equally at home on the road and in the air." Current expansion plans for Seaboard's Kennedy terminal include a stacker-storage and nose dock system capable of accommodating one hundred 20-foot containers. The company believes specific commodity rates act as a stumbling block to the development of containerization and has urged that they be abolished.

Seaboard World Airlines was granted a section 418 certificate at the beginning of 1978 and is now able to offer unrestricted interstate service. The company's commitment to large-volume containerization suggests it will focus its efforts on that portion of the traffic not readily carried in combination aircraft. Its small fleet and a move from the DC-8 to the B-747 (which is most profitably used in long-haul markets) mean that, in the immediate future at least, Seaboard will fly between only a small number of U.S. cities. The Board, as we have seen, had earlier refused to grant Seaboard domestic fill-up rights between New York and various other airport cities.[1] This made service at the latter points largely unprofitable, and in mid-1977 operations there were suspended. Deregulation allows Seaboard to return to its former coterminals and it intends as a first step to restore its air link between New York and Chicago, Los Angeles, and San Francisco.

Local Service Airlines

Six local service carriers serve the New York-Newark airports. With the exception of Air New England, which was certificated in 1975,[2] all received their certificates of public convenience and

---

[1] See above, p. 43.

[2] See above, p. 194-195.

necessity during the period 1947-1950. The group as a whole derives about 6 percent of its revenues from freight transportation and in 1977 operated over a route network of 33,700 miles, a three-fold increase since 1950. In terms of the number of airport cities served, Allegheny is the major carrier in the group (85 points in 1977) and Air New England the smallest (13 points). The local service carriers are involved with only a very small proportion of the system's traffic flow, accounting for about 3 percent (by weight) of the scheduled domestic freight tonnage enplaned at the New York-Newark airports. The group is important, however, in that it provides air transportation between New York-Newark and numerous communities not ordinarily served by the trunklines.[1]

Approximately 5 percent (by weight) of the local service airlines' total freight enplaned in New York-Newark consists of air-to-air transfers; the remainder is surface-to-air traffic, virtually all of which orginates within the air terminal area. There is little potential for freight consolidations in the low-density markets generally served by this carrier class, and, as one would expect, the forwarders are relatively less important here than in the case of the trunks and the all-cargo carriers. Roughly 30 percent of the locals' surface-to-air traffic in New York-Newark is tendered by the forwarders, the remainder by local cartage firms and shippers. About 5 percent of the total outbound traffic is interlined with other airlines for onward transportation to desti-nation airports.

The local service carriers do not provide all-cargo flights. Freight is carried in combination aircraft, which include the B-727, B-737, BAC-11, CV-580, and the DC-9. Use of this equipment, of course, imposes significant size/weight limitations on the shipments which can be transported. For instance, Piedmont Airlines, which, after Allegheny, enplanes more freight in New York-Newark than any other carrier in this group, will not accept units measuring in excess of 45 in. x 34 in. x 68 in. The weight limit per package is normally 200 pounds, which, with advance arrangements, Piedmont will raise to 400 pounds.

The local service carriers have traditionally had a well-defined regional orientation. Thus, Allegheny has long concentrated its efforts in the Northeast (especially Ohio, Pennsylvania, and New York), Air New England connects New York-Newark with various points in New England, while North Central Airlines and Ozark are primarily identified with the northcentral and midwestern areas of the nation,

[1]See above, p. 4, note 5.

respectively. The remaining local service airlines operating in New York-Newark are Piedmont and Southern, and these link the area with points in the Mid-Atlantic states, West Virginia, Kentucky, Tennessee, and the South and Southeast. These service patterns are not likely to be disturbed by the deregulation of air freight service. The local service airlines are almost wholly concerned with passenger transportation and have no interest in initiating all-cargo flights. Deregulation of the passenger sector (Public Law 95-504), on the other hand, has significant implications for this carrier class. It was noted earlier in this study that some of these airlines have in the past reduced or eliminated service in certain markets, a practice which can be expected to grow with the relaxation of (passenger) entry/exit controls. At the same time, of course, the locals will presumably add larger traffic centers to their route networks and expand their operating territories. Allegheny Airlines, for example, has already indicated that it wishes to change its status from a regional to that of a transcontinental carrier.

Some of the airlines in this group appear to have softened their earlier opposition to deregulation and in the latter part of 1978 felt Public Law 95-163 "will ultimately strengthen our industry." Particularly welcome is the new freedom to alter freight rates and service rules, enabling the carriers to operate "in a more businesslike fashion." At the same time, these companies insist "full" support for Public Law 95-163 is impossible. They believe the effect of free entry is not yet apparent and fear revenue losses "should our established markets be flooded by all-cargo carriers."[1]

Figure 30 provides an overview of the freight volumes carried to and from New York-Newark by the local service airlines. About two-thirds of the total load is transported by Allegheny Airlines, the only carrier in this class operating at a substantial number of hubs which are also served by trunklines. The ten leading freight exchange points for New York-Newark are Baltimore, Buffalo, Dayton, Indianapolis, Norfolk, Pittsburgh, Roanoke (Va.), Rochester, Syracuse, and Tri-City Airport (Tenn.), which together account for about 65 percent (by weight) of the total two-way traffic. Other relatively important traffic centers include Albany, Erie (Pa.), Fayetteville (N.C.), Hartford (Ct.), Lexington (Ky.), Louisville (Ky.), Memphis (Tenn.), Milwaukee, Providence, and Wilmington (N.C.). About four-fifths of the air freight tonnage exchanged with New York-Newark

---

[1] Comments made to the author by Charles A. Creech, Manager-Cargo Development, Piedmont Airlines, and John S. Minerich, Manager-Cargo Administration, North Central Airlines, 1978.

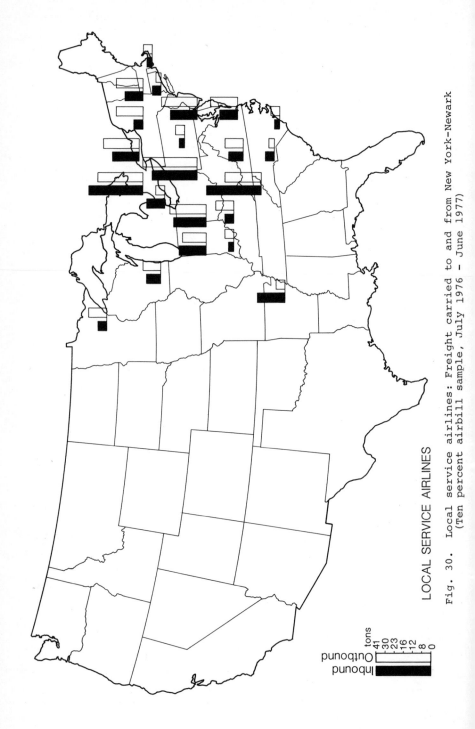

LOCAL SERVICE AIRLINES

Fig. 30. Local service airlines: Freight carried to and from New York–Newark
(Ten percent airbill sample, July 1976 – June 1977)

consists of electrical and nonelectrical machinery and parts,
printed matter, and textile products. Generally speaking, the
carriers do not have a directional imbalance problem vis-à-vis
New York-Newark. Virtually all of their traffic moves under bulk
general commodity rates. No directional incentives are offered.

Commuter Airlines

Although perhaps most widely known for their passenger
services, the commuter airlines are making increasingly important
contributions to freight transportation. About 20 members of this
carrier class provide regular flights to/from the New York-Newark
airports. For the most part these are passenger-oriented companies
(e.g., Monmouth Airlines, Newport Aero, Pilgrim Aviation, Pocono
Airlines, Ransome Air, and Suburban Airlines) with only a peripheral
interest in freight traffic. A few, however, are freight specialists,
and it is these (principally Federal Express, Pinehurst Airlines,
and Summit Airlines) which account for most of the freight carried
by the group as a whole.

The commuters have traditionally been exempt from the Federal
Aviation Act's entry/exit restrictions and tariff filing requirements.
The price paid for their freedom from economic regulation has been
a Board-imposed capacity limitation (part 298 of the Board's
Economic Regulations), under which the exempt carriers were enjoined
from operating aircraft having (1) a capacity of more than 30
passenger seats or (2) a payload capacity in excess of 7,500 pounds.[1]
This has produced a commuter fleet consisting of such aircraft as
the Beech-99, DC-3, Falcon DA-20, Nord 262A, Piper PA-31, and Skyvan
(table 18), and it comes as no surprise that several Part 298
operators, anxious to overturn the CAB's capacity rule, strongly
supported Congress' deregulation efforts. The first section 418
all-cargo certificates were issued to commuter airlines in January
of 1978, and, in what has been the most decisive response to the
new legislation by one of these carriers, Federal Express immediately
acquired the B-727 (all-cargo configuration), placing it into service
between Memphis and Los Angeles (February), Memphis and New
York-Newark (April), and Memphis and San Francisco (June). Several
other commuters serving New York-Newark are also adding new aircraft
to their fleets, but here smaller equipment than the B-727 is
involved. (For example, Monmouth and Summit intend to purchase the
Convair 580 [the all-cargo version has a maximum payload of about

[1] See above, p. 23, note 4.

17,000 pounds] and Pinehurst the YS-11.) The majority of the part
298 carriers, it should be noted, lack Federal's financial resources
and are in no position to purchase aircraft such as the B-727.
Indeed, the willingness of many of these companies to exercise their
section 418 rights is open to question. One reason for this is that
the Board has raised (June, 1978) the part 298 capacity ceiling from
7,500 to 18,000 pounds, meaning that commuters are now able to acquire
substantially larger aircraft without holding section 418 certificates. The advantage of this, in the view of many airline officials
is that the revised part 298 capacity limit satisfies their
foreseeable expansion requirements without at the same time
subjecting their companies to the record retention regulations,
reporting obligations, and insurance rules attached to section
418 certification.

Federal Express accounts for about 60 percent (by weight) of
the commuters' freight traffic flowing through the New York-Newark
air terminals. The company differs from other commuters in that it
operates on a nationwide basis and uses a hub-and-spoke method,
channeling all traffic to a central sorting facility in Memphis
from where it is flown to destination cities. Packages weighing
more than 70 pounds are not accepted. Furthermore, the length of a
package may not exceed 54 inches.

An integral part of Federal's door-to-door operation is its
pickup and delivery service, which it performs with its own vans.
Virtually all of its freight originating in New York-Newark is
picked up by the company (in 1977 about 55 vehicles were used for
this purpose) and loaded into the B-727 (which has a maximum payload
of about 36,000 pounds) for the flight to Memphis. Use of the B-727
has led to the elimination of multiple small aircraft flights
(prior to deregulation the 6,500-pound Falcon DA-20 was used) and
their attendant diseconomies.[1] About 90 percent of the freight
picked up in New York reaches consignees by noon on the following
business day. Federal sees the forwarders, not the other commuters
as its chief competitors, and its chairman has vowed "to drive
[the former] out of business."

Figure 31 shows Federal's traffic flown to and from the New
York-Newark area. The area's ten leading freight exchange points
are Atlanta, Boston, Chicago, Dallas, Detroit, Los Angeles, Miami,
Minneapolis-St. Paul, San Francisco, and Washington, D.C. These

---

[1]See _Testimony of Frederick W. Smith_, Chairman, Federal Express
Corporation, remarks made before the House Aviation Subcommittee, June 9, 1976,
mimeographed, pp. 16-17. See also above, p. 140.

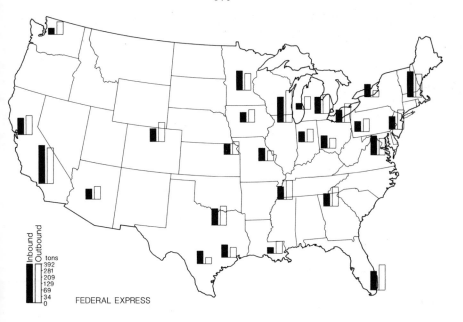

Fig. 31. Federal Express: Freight carried to and from
New York-Newark (July 1976 - June 1977)

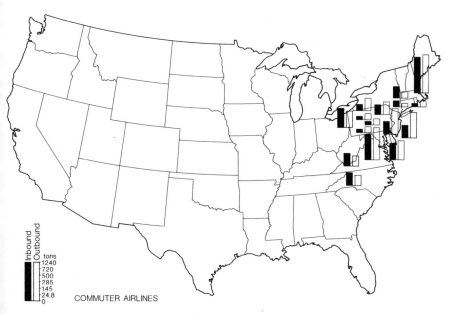

Fig. 32. Commuter Airlines: Freight carried to and from
New York-Newark (exclusive of Federal Express,
July 1976 - June 1977)

cities account for 50 percent of this carrier's two-way New York-Newark traffic volume.

Unlike the trunklines and local service airlines, Federal views Public Law 95-163 as an "unmixed blessing for carriers and shippers alike." The company has always been exempt from the section 403 tariff filing provisions and, again unlike the other carriers, has raised no objections to the elimination of domestic freight tariffs. It believes that rate sheets, used in lieu of tariffs, will permit the Board to carry out its "remaining monitoring functions."

We have already identified several differences separating Federal Express from the other commuters. In addition to these it should be noted that, whereas Federal Express operates almost exclusively on a scheduled basis, charter service is important to many commuter airlines. Also, unlike Federal Express, the commuters as a whole do not offer pickup/delivery service and receive their freight (1) "over-the-counter" from shippers and (2) from forwarders. In come instances the dependence on the forwarders is extreme (Summit Airlines, for instance, obtains 90 percent of its business from this source), and here nighttime departures reflect the forwarders' need for next-day delivery. In contrast to Federal Express, several commuter operators state that a substantial proportion (20 to 30 percent) of their total domestic traffic leaving New York-Newark represents interline traffic, in other words, freight which has been received from other airlines.

The equipment used by this carrier class as a whole dictates short- and medium-haul flights, which, in the case of all-cargo service, are mostly performed overnight, with emphasis on markets from which the trunklines have withdrawn their own freighter operations. Also, many commuter airlines, of course, connect New York-Newark with communities not receiving any trunkline service, and thus do not compete with the larger carriers. The commuters' scheduled traffic flows between New York-Newark and other airport cities are depicted in figure 32, the major origin-destination points (accounting for some 85 percent of the tonnage) being Baltimore, Boston, Philadelphia, Pittsburgh, Richmond, and Washington D.C. Secondary freight exchange points for New York-Newark include Charlotte (N.C.), Harrisburg (Pa.), Hartford (Ct.), Lancaster (Pa.), New Haven (Ct.), New London (Ct.), Reading (Pa.), Roanoke (Va.), Wilkes-Barre-Scranton (Pa.), and Williamsport (Pa.).

Supplemental Airlines

Five supplemental carriers are currently active in the New York-Newark area and account for about 10 percent (by weight) of the freight leaving the area on domestic charter flights. The attraction of these charter specialists, of course, is that their rates are based on a 100 percent load factor and thus tend to be less than those of scheduled operators whose charges reflect considerably lower load factors. The supplementals have in the past come forward with various new rate/fare proposals and were the first to use the convertible DC-10. These and other innovations have brought them much applause and have frequently been cited by those who believe the CAB's controls over the certificated route carriers have stifled creativity in the scheduled air transportation field.

The supplemental carriers operating at the New York-Newark airports are Capitol International, Evergreen International, Trans International, World Airways, and Zantop International. They have a diversified revenue base, which includes passenger transportation, freight transportation, and equipment leasing. Thus, for instance, in the case of Trans International, the largest airline in the group, revenues are generated as follows (1976): (1) civilian traffic-- (a) passengers--46.2 percent; (b) freight--17.7 percent, (2) military traffic--32.6 percent; (3) leases--3.5 percent. Passengers are the dominant revenue source for these carriers generally. An important exception is Zantop International, an all-cargo airline, which, until recently, was a private carrier serving the automotive industry, while also recognized by the Board (August, 1977) as a supplemental carrier operating under contracts with the U.S. Defense Department.

As one might expect, the major forwarders, with their large-volume traffic, are this carrier class' leading purchasers of freight transportation. Emery Air Freight, for example, has concluded an agreement (August, 1976) with Evergreen International, under which the latter, using the DC-8-33 freighter, furnishes two-way overnight charter service linking New York with Atlanta, Charlotte (N.C.), Cleveland, Miami, and Ypsilanti. The agreement calls for flights "on a five consecutive days per week basis" and stipulates a price of $24,858 per two-way flight. Under a similar arrangement with Trans International, Emery has secured charter service between New York and Houston via Dayton, Memphis, and Dallas, the aircraft used being the Electra L-188 (table 18).

Regular charter services of this type have, as we have seen, been denounced by several scheduled carriers. The Board, however, has upheld their lawfulness, stating that "forwarder charters have not had sufficient impact on scheduled services" to justify punitive measures.[1]

Despite this carrier group's support for the deregulation of air transportation (both with respect to freight and passengers), its ability to significantly affect the future development of the New York-Newark air freight system is clearly limited. As previously emphasized, the supplementals' orientation is basically towards the passenger market. A related factor, of course, is the number of available aircraft (for new services), which, relative to the size of the established scheduled carriers' fleets, must be considered small. While welcoming Public Law 95-245,[2] the supplementals' response to the new regulatory situation has been mixed. Evergreen International indicates it will offer scheduled nighttime freighter service between New York and Atlanta (and possibly Boston), and Capitol International is interested in providing scheduled combination flights between New York-Newark and California. World Airways, its earlier attempts to offer scheduled transcontinental service frustrated by the Board,[3] can also be expected to inaugurate scheduled passenger-freight flights between New York and major West Coast cities. Trans International maintains that its plans for scheduled operations do not include New York-Newark, which is also the position of several supplemental carriers (e.g., Overseas National) currently not flying to/from the New York-Newark airports. A spokesman for Zantop International, on the other hand, states his company foresees substantial scheduled service in New York-Newark. The section 418 certificate will enable this Detroit-based operator to become a common carrier, and it expects to offer direct, scheduled nighttime flights linking Newark Airport with various cities including Boston, Cleveland, Detroit, Indianapolis, and St. Louis.

Overview

This chapter has described the operations of the U.S. air carriers in New York-Newark and the freight exchanges between the

---

[1] See above, p. 269.

[2] See above, p. 156.

[3] See above, p. 28; p. 73, note 5.

area's three airports and a nationwide network of air traffic hubs. The carriers' activities and flow patterns have been presented for mid-1976 to mid-1977, in other words, for the period immediately preceding the deregulation of domestic air freight service. Reference has also been made to the initial steps taken by the carriers (1978) as they begin to grapple with the problems and opportunities inherent in the deregulation of their industry.

The trunks have always been, and continue to be, the most important carrier class operating at the New York-Newark air terminals. They enplane approximately 75 percent of the scheduled domestic freight tonnage leaving the system's three airports. The all-cargo carriers are in second place with about 15 percent of the tonnage. The commuters and local service airlines account for a further 7 percent and 3 percent, respectively. The trunklines and all-cargo carriers also enplane most of the charter tonnage, which, however, represents less than 5 percent of the total domestic freight transported by these two carrier classes. Only about 10 percent of the outbound charter traffic is carried by the supplemental companies.

About 90 percent of the scheduled, outbound domestic freight at New York-Newark's airports is surface-to-air traffic; air-to-air transfers make up the remaining 10 percent. Roughly 5 percent of the enplaned load must be interlined with other carriers in order to reach destination airports. The cooperating airlines use both combination and joint rates for these interline movements, the latter rate being the more common of the two. Approximately 85 percent of the domestic surface-to-air traffic originates within the New York-Newark air terminal area, a percentage which has remained relatively stable throughout the early and mid-1970s. Airline deregulation,[1] to say nothing of the Interstate Commerce Commission's interest in a redefinition of pickup and delivery zones, can clearly be expected to lead to changes in this figure. (In the event that deregulation of surface transportation becomes a reality,[2] the pickup and delivery zones, of course, may cease to exist.)

The airlines transport a virtually unlimited range of commodities. The bulk of the domestic traffic, however, consists of apparel and other textile items, chemicals and pharmaceuticals, electrical and nonelectrical machinery and equipment, perishables

---

[1]See above, p. 235.

[2]See above, p. 331.

(especially fruits, horticultural products, and vegetables), printed matter, and transportation equipment and parts.

Approximately 65 percent of the trunks' and all-cargo carriers surface-to-air traffic is tendered directly by the forwarders (for the local service airlines the figure is considerably lower); the remainder is brought to the air terminals by local cartage agents, long-haul truckers, and the shipping public. If we consider only the containerized load, the forwarders assume an even larger role, for fully four-fifths of the containerized tonnage handled at the system's three airports has been received from the forwarders. Containerized freight constitutes roughly 35 percent of the trunks' domestic tonnage, a somewhat higher proportion in the case of the all-cargo operators.

Contrary to the popular view, only a very small proportion of unitized traffic moves in true intermodal containers. The reason for this is that until recently the design criteria for air containers were entirely subservient to an aircraft's fuselage characteristics and thus could not necessarily exploit the advantages peculiar to land/sea transportation. The shape of most air containers, for instance, reflects an aircraft's contours and may present loading problems for the trucker. Certainly this is the case with the LD-3, one of the most widely used containers in the New York-Newark air freight system. Its shape is such that truckers must use special restraining devices and loading configurations to prevent toppling and sliding. Another barrier to true intermodality is the structural weakness of various air containers; if improperly stacked, these units may be crushed during the course of surface transportation. With the advent of the 747 freighter, new units have come into use (M-1, M-2), and it is these which provide the best examples of true intermodal containers. These new containers are carried on conventional truck trailer chassis and can withstand the stress associated with travel by land and sea. Their capacity, of course, restricts their use to major forwarders and large-volume shippers.

A carrier entering new markets under section 418 authority has the right (with respect to the new routes) not to carry mail. If, however, the company decides to carry mail, it must adhere to the general rules and regulations governing mail transportation. Under the terms of the airlines' certificates of public convenience and necessity, mail has been given precedence over freight. This practice remains unaffected by deregulation and, according to most of the system's route carriers, leads to difficulties in that freight moving over various high-density routes must frequently be held back (for later flights) in order that mail shipments may be accommodated. As might be expected, this problem is most acute during the Christmas holiday season.

We have seen that the Board, in what was to be one of its last formal actions (prior to deregulation) regarding the domestic freight rate structure, authorized the retention of various discount rates.[1] Its endorsement of specific commodity rates, daylight container rates, etc., reflected the agency's view that discount rates have increased the utilization of belly space in wide-body aircraft and have helped to correct the industry's directional imbalance problem. The carriers themselves are divided over the value of promotional rates. For instance, some companies (Braniff, Delta, Eastern, National, and Northwest) believe specific commodity rates are no longer effective traffic generators and have either discontinued these rates or apply them only to a very small number of commodities in one or two markets. Others (American, Flying Tiger, TWA, and United), on the other hand, view specific commodity rates as a useful developmental tool and continue to use them, particularly over the major West Coast-New York routes. Controversy similarly surrounds daylight container rates. These rates, which apply to containers tendered between 4:00 A.M. and 4:00 P.M. for carriage in the lower deck of wide-body combination aircraft, are favored by several of the largest trunk carriers. Unlike the price-inelastic, time-sensitive shipments which require nighttime air transportation (i.e., pickup at the end of the business day and delivery during the early part of the next business day), daylight time-of-tender traffic consists largely of shipments which would normally be hauled by a surface carrier but where, because of a promotional rate, the shipper concludes air service with second- or even third-day delivery is preferable to surface transportation. Lower-deck container discounts, the use of which has been protested by the Flying Tiger Line on the ground that they diverted traffic not from surface carriers but from prime-time air service, represent a partial answer to the problem of underutilized freight space in wide-body combination aircraft. "Moreover," as the CAB has noted approvingly, the discounts, where expressed as a flat charge per container, "encourage dense traffic because they are entirely space-related with no weight penalty. This is a desirable feature for combination carriers whose bellies can tolerate densities greater than the

---

[1]See above, p. 61.

overall design density of the plane to compensate for the relative
lack of density in the passenger compartment."[1]

Directional general commodity rates, once frequently applied
to bulk traffic moving over major East-West and North-South routes,
have all but disappeared from the New York-Newark air freight
system. More freight was originally being carried from East to West
and Southwest, and from North to South, than in the reverse directions, and the Board, seeking to increase load factors on eastbound
and northbound flights, sanctioned the use of directional rate
differentials.[2] By the early 1970s directional freight imbalances
had largely ceased to be a major problem for various carriers, and,
indeed, in some markets (table 23) more freight now moves eastward

TABLE 23

THE NEW YORK-NEWARK AIR FREIGHT SYSTEM'S
PRINCIPAL TRAFFIC ROUTES (1977)

Route	Freight (tons)	Route	Freight (tons)
To New York-Newark from:		From New York-Newark to:	
Chicago	103,148	Chicago	80,639
Los Angeles	60,449	Los Angeles	49,059
San Francisco	35,153	Boston	24,965
Dallas	28,411	Atlanta	21,849
Atlanta	18,034	Detroit	21,123
Detroit	16,085	Dallas	18,788
Washington	12,546	Miami	15,883
Miami	11,668	San Francisco	13,735
Boston	10,525	Washington	11,892
Milwaukee	9,890	Philadelphia	10,526

SOURCE: Civil Aeronautics Board, ER-586 Service Segment Data.

The figures include mail shipments.

than in the opposite direction. There is some question as to the
factors behind this partial correction of the traditional traffic
imbalance problem. Asked "did the directional [general commodity]
rates that have been in existence some 15 years cure the [East-West]
imbalance or did it take specific commodity rates to do that?" an
American Airlines executive replied: "I imagine it was a combination of both but I don't know that."[3] The Board, too, has been

---

[1] Domestic Air Freight Rate Investigation, p. 16.

[2] See above, pp. 14-15.

[3] Domestic Air Freight Rate Investigation, transcript of the
hearings, February 8, 1974, p. 519.

somewhat noncommittal on the subject, noting that today's greater directional equilibrium "may . . . only [be due to] the various kinds of discount rates used to generate traffic in the weak direction."[1] More significant than rates, perhaps, has been the role of regional shifts in the nation's industrial development. Thus, whereas initially low-value perishables dominated major north- and eastbound traffic flows, subsequent industrial growth in the West and Sun Belt states has added manufactured goods (e.g., electronics equipment and textile products), to say nothing of substantial volume, to eastbound and northbound freight movements. In any event, whatever the promotional value of directional general commodity rates may have been, the transcontinental carriers concluded in the 1970s that they had outlived their usefulness. Specific reasons given for the elimination of these rates include: (1) they unnecessarily diluted the carriers' eastbound and northbound yields; (2) they were discriminatory, giving shippers in the West and South an unjust advantage over their eastern counterparts; (3) they failed to divert additional traffic from surface to air transportation; and (4) in individual instances they could be replaced by specific commodity rates.

All domestic trunk carriers satisfying the section 17 operating requirements of Public Law 95-163[2] received their section 418 grandfather certificates in January of 1978. None of these airlines (American, Braniff, Northwest, Trans World Airlines, and United), however, has indicated an interest in instituting new all-cargo flights over any New York routes. Indeed, with TWA's move to abandon freighter operations the trend towards increased combination service by this carrier class is more firmly established than ever. In recent years the trunks' wide-body combination equipment has achieved an average load factor of only 35 percent for bulk freight, which, other considerations aside, makes any major expansion of all-cargo service by these carriers highly unlikely. The restructuring of the trunklines' routes will accelerate under deregulation, but, as in the case of the local service airlines, most route changes will reflect management's interest in the passenger market and the new entry/exit rights available through the deregulation of air passenger transportation.

In contrast to the trunks, the Flying Tiger Line has added a number of new airport cities to its interstate freighter operations,

---

[1] Ibid., Order 77-8-62, p. 11.

[2] See above, p. 153.

and Seaboard World and Pan American, two international carriers, are providing additional domestic service between New York and the West Coast. Several supplementals are also initiating scheduled domestic freighter service, which, at the outset at least, is to be restricted to the New York-California market. Also, under deregulation a number of air taxi operators have purchased, or intend to purchase, larger aircraft and are providing new freight capacity in many short- and medium-haul markets. Several of these air taxi services are geared entirely to the needs of the major forwarders.

In early 1978 United Airlines announced that it would eliminate its daylight time-of-tender discounts and replace these with new promotional rates. New rate reductions for shipments carried in wide-body combination aircraft were similarly announced by several other companies. The significance of the new rates is not so much that they are being introduced following deregulation--carriers could, of course, lower rates within the framework of the former regulatory regime--but that management now has the flexibility to respond to rapidly changing market conditions without first submitting rate proposals to the Board for review and analysis. Despite the aforementioned rate reductions, the overall trend in the industry is unmistakably towards higher freight rates. Escalating fuel prices and labor costs, as well as rising maintenance costs, landing fees, etc., simply rule out industry-wide rate reductions of the type promised by many of the deregulation advocates.

Few, if any, of the Board's recent actions have aroused as much airline opposition as its decision to eliminate the filing of freight rate and rules tariffs. The continued filing of these traditional tariffs (as we saw in chapter III) was deemed incompatible with the objectives of Public Law 95-163 and in 1978 was abolished for both section 401 and section 418 domestic air freight service. The agency believed that tariff filing encouraged pricing inefficiency on the part of the carriers and that its termination lessened the likelihood of collusion. Furthermore, the action was seen to provide a guide to the potential results of passenger tariff elimination in 1983.

Many shippers contend that the discontinuance of the statutory tariff filing obligation will harm the air freight industry, a view the airlines have also urgently pressed upon the Board. Trans World Airlines, for instance, has told the agency that its

customers need to know what rates are in effect and to know about planned rate changes so that they can calculate their costs, price their product to the customer, determine whether air transport is usable for a particular shipment, and maintain an orderly market for their product. If public tariffs are not required and if the Board does not require advance notice, not only will this disrupt shippers and the marketplace, but could well lead to a decline in air freight volumes. Since potential air customers will not be able to determine present and proposed rate changes readily, it is likely that some shippers will discontinue the use of air, and opt for surface transportation instead, since public tariffs will be available to them in a convenient form, and will give them the advance notice they need and prefer. Since air freight represents a minor portion of traffic for most shippers, the loss of assured prices through tariff filings could become a crucial factor in their routing decisions.[1]

A similar case is made by most of the freight carriers. One further example will suffice here:

> United [Airlines] fully understands the shippers' desires to retain the stability provided by the . . . filing requirements. Approximately 50 percent of United's cargo revenue is received from shippers who subscribe to industry cargo tariffs. The reason that so many entities would subscribe to this relatively expensive service is simple. Transportation costs are an essential factor in the pricing of most consumer products. Manufacturers and distributors need accurate and early knowledge of what their shipping costs will be in order to price their products. The . . . tariff filing requirements provide the shippers with stability and predictability, elements that the shippers are unanimously agreed are of more value than any price reductions potentially obtainable from a free price market.[2]

The airlines as a whole believe that rate sheets are no adequate substitute for traditional tariffs. They feel that the loss of tariffs may disrupt interline freight transfer agreements and will complicate the detection of discriminatory or otherwise unlawful behavior on the part of competitors. Their attitude towards the Board's action may be summarized in the words of a Delta spokesman, who finds the elimination of tariffs "incomprehensible, unjustified, illogical and illegal."[3]

Chapter VIII has focused almost entirely on interstate traffic. This orientation must not be allowed to obscure the importance of New York as the nation's principal gateway for international air shipments. Table 24 gives the relative position of the New York Customs District (which includes Newark Airport) within the context of U.S. airborne exports and imports and shows, for example, that in terms of value about half the total U.S. foreign air traffic passes through New York. Roughly one-third of New York's international air traffic ($ value) is handled by U.S.-flag carriers. Air shipments account for about one-third ($ value) of the New York Customs District's foreign trade.

---

[1] Comments of Trans World Airlines, Inc., Docket 33093, September 11, 1978, pp. 5-6.

[2] Comments of United Airlines, Inc., Docket 33093, September 11, 1978, p. 7.

[3] Comments of Delta Air Lines, Inc., Docket 33093, September 11, 1978, p. 7.

390

TABLE 24

U.S. AIRBORNE FOREIGN TRADE: LEADING CUSTOMS DISTRICTS (1977)

Exports

Customs District	Shipping Weight (million pounds)		Value (million $)	
	All Air Carriers	U.S.-Flag Air Carriers	All Air Carriers	U.S.-Flag Air Carriers
Boston	52	18	745	277
Chicago	173	76	1,853	850
Los Angeles	121	29	2,196	460
Miami	341	114	1,386	458
New York	691	209	9,452	2,597
San Francisco	61	26	1,493	541
United States	1,796	585	20,253	6,532

Imports

Customs District	Shipping Weight (million pounds)		Value (million $)	
	All Air Carriers	U.S.-Flag Air Carriers	All Air Carriers	U.S.-Flag Air Carriers
Boston	33	10	381	112
Chicago	84	42	862	385
Los Angeles	134	38	1,546	376
Miami	153	34	436	120
New York	612	285	6,445	2,657
San Francisco	93	49	1,358	597
United States	1,311	532	12,573	4,955

	Value of Air Exports as a % of the Value of Total U.S. Air Exports	Value of Air Exports as a % of the Value of All Exports	Value of Air Imports as a % of the Value of Total U.S. Air Imports	Value of Air Imports as a % of the Value of All Imports
Boston	4	67	3	11
Chicago	9	80	7	27
Los Angeles	11	35	12	12
Miami	7	37	3	31
New York	46	47	51	25
San Francisco	7	28	11	23
United States	100	16	100	9

SOURCE: U.S. Department of Commerce.

CHAPTER IX

SUMMARY AND CONCLUSIONS

Consisting of two subsystems (a regulatory subsystem and a
physical subsystem), the New York-Newark air freight system has been
examined in terms of the relationships linking its principal
elements, defined here as (1) for the regulatory subsystem: the
Congress, the Civil Aeronautics Board, the Interstate Commerce
Commission, the White House, the courts, and the Port Authority of
New York and New Jersey and (2) for the physical subsystem: the
three New York-Newark airports, the airlines, the forwarders, and
the motor carriers. The study has shown how the interaction among
these elements has delineated the scope and nature of various
freight-related services and has described the system's freight
flows (1) within the New York-Newark air terminal area and (2)
between New York-Newark and other U.S. airport cities.

The present volume encompasses a forty-year time span,
beginning with the enactment of the Civil Aeronautics Act of 1938
(amended as the Federal Aviation Act of 1958) and ending with the
passage of the Airline Deregulation Act of 1978. During this period,
public utility-type controls, imposed on the air transportation
industry in the form of the 1938 Act and administered by the Civil
Aeronautics Board, regulated the economic behavior of the air
carriers. Towards the end of 1977 the Congress essentially
deregulated interstate air freight transportation (Public Law
95-163) and a year later passed corresponding legislation for air
passenger service (Public Law 95-504). The reform bills of 1977
and 1978 constitute, in effect, a rejection of a regulatory
philosophy and course, which, until recently, were widely perceived
as permanent fixtures on the nation's socio-economic landscape.

Public Law 95-163, which came fully into force in the latter
part of 1978, represents by far the most significant air
freight-related legislation since the passage of the Civil
Aeronautics Act. This, however, should not be taken to mean that
the administrative and regulatory controls of the pre-deregulation
era were static and impervious to all change. These earlier years,
for instance, saw the creation, by the Board, of various classes
of direct and indirect air carriers, Congressional action vis-à-vis

nonscheduled air service, and the ad hoc enlargement of
pickup/delivery rights through joint action of the Board and the
Interstate Commerce Commission. Many of the CAB's and ICC's rulings
were challenged by the carriers and, in some instances, were reverse
or otherwise modified by order of the courts. These and other
regulatory developments were analyzed in the foregoing pages and
provided the necessary background for a discussion of the freight
services available to shippers utilizing the New York-Newark air
terminals. The regulatory framework presented here and its
significance for the development of the air freight industry are, of
course, not restricted to New York-Newark, and it is the author's
hope that this book may be of value to students of transportation
interested in examining this industry in other airport cities of
the nation.

The New York-Newark air freight system's three airports,
Kennedy, La Guardia, and Newark, have been under the jurisdiction of
the Port Authority of New York and New Jersey since the late 1940s.
Linked to the United States Government through a series of agreement
under which it receives Federal airport-related funds and technical
assistance while managing the terminals along Federally-approved
guidelines, the Port Authority has from the beginning viewed the
terminals as complementary rather than competitive units and has
sought "so far as practicable" to unify its airport operations.
This objective was endorsed by the Civil Aeronautics Board, which
long ago approved (and recently upheld) a common-rating formula for
the three terminals and which, rather than restricting an airlines'
flights to a particular facility, designated the three airports (in
several route proceedings) as a single service point. Integration
within the system has been further aided by various arrangements
among carriers of the same mode (cooperation) and among carriers
belonging to different modes (coordination), and is a prerequisite
for the freight services ultimately available to the shipping
public. Shown below is a summary of the major examples of
cooperation and coordination discussed in this study. No rigid
compartmentalization is implied; indeed, the system's existence
demands the overlapping of various cooperative and coordinative
measures and of the administrative, financial, regulatory, and
technological principles on which they rest.

I. Cooperation

1. Airline-airline: freight exchange, joint and combined rates,
   joint pickup/delivery program

2. Forwarder-forwarder: freight exchange (authorized by the Board
   only in 1978), joint loading

   3. Shipper-shipper: freight pooling (shippers associations, recognized as indirect carriers)

II. Coordination

   1. Air-truck operations: joint and combined services

   2. Surface-for-air substitutions

   3. Door-to-door forwarder service

   4. Air-sea service

Despite various levels of cooperation and coordination, the fundamental relationship between the carriers, of course, remains a competitive one, and competition within the system has been examined from the following perspectives: (1) airline v. airline, (2) forwarder v. airline, (3) trucker v. airline, (4) trucker v. trucker, (5) trucker v. forwarder, (6) forwarder v. forwarder, and (7) forwarder v. shippers association.

The New York-Newark airports lead the nation's air traffic hubs in terms of scheduled aircraft departures, enplaned freight, and enplaned priority mail. The trunklines constitute the system's most important air carrier class, accounting for about 75 percent of the scheduled domestic freight tonnage leaving the system's three airports by air. The next most important air carrier class consists of what, under the former regulatory scheme, were referred to as the certificated all-cargo route carriers.

The forwarders represent the airlines' single most important traffic source, contributing roughly two-thirds of the overall and four-fifths of the containerized domestic traffic handled by the airlines.

Convinced that the Board's anticompetitive actions were needlessly lowering the air carriers' efficiency and innovativeness, the Congress acted in 1977 and 1978 to deregulate the airline industry. The Board's time-consuming and cumbersome regulatory procedures, critics of regulation believed, prevented carriers from adjusting prices and services to rapidly changing market conditions, penalizing both travelers and shippers. The airline industry, it was contended, was now "mature" and no longer in need of the protection afforded by the Federal Aviation Act (Civil Aeronautics Act). Referring specifically to freight service, reform advocates correctly noted that the architects of the Civil Aeronautics Act had been concerned almost exclusively with the airlines' passenger business and had not considered the special needs and problems of shippers and receivers. The trunks exercised their all-cargo rights on a permissive basis, and, when freighter flights were withdrawn by several of these companies in the early 1970s, some of the larger forwarders were compelled to reach beyond

the certificated carriers in order to ensure the continuation of
their overnight freight service. At the same time, Board-imposed
restrictions had excluded such established interstate carriers as
the Flying Tiger Line from numerous airport cities and had barred
other airlines from entering the domestic market. Reform-minded
legislators also noted that the success of Federal Express, a
small-package specialist, was due in large measure to the company
having developed its operations outside the traditional regulatory
framework.

The carriers' attitude towards deregulation placed them into
one of two groups. Generally speaking, supporters of the measure
included the certificated all-cargo airlines (especially Flying
Tiger), the commuters/air taxis, the supplementals, and the major
forwarders. The reasons for their support varied, and reflected
the self-interests of the companies concerned. Thus, for example,
Public Law 95-163 freed the Flying Tiger Line from its former route
restrictions and enabled Seaboard World Airlines to institute regular
domestic service. Commuters and air taxi operators were now able to
acquire substantially larger equipment, and supplementals were
authorized to provide scheduled flights. For the forwarders,
deregulation meant additional freight capacity in some markets
(due to new entry), as well as the opportunity to initiate their
own direct air services. Ranged against these carriers were
opponents of major statutory reform, these including the trunklines
(with the exception of Pan American World Airways and United
Airlines), the local service airlines, many smaller forwarders,
and the certificated air freight motor carrier specialists. The
trunks and local service carriers viewed open entry as a threat
to profitable operations in their major (passenger) markets and
foresaw (following deregulation) a loss of air service at numerous
small communities, increasing difficulties in attracting investment
capital, and deteriorating aviation safety standards. The
objections of some forwarders focused on the possibility of
destructive rate wars and on the loss of freight capacity due to the
collapse of the weaker airlines. The latter point was also made by
various truckers, who, in addition, feared deregulation would tempt
some airlines to establish their own trucking services.

The deregulation controversy extended far beyond the carriers
themselves. The U.S. Department of Justice, for instance, had long
called for comprehensive reform legislation on the ground that the
Board's traditional powers were incompatible with Federal antitrust
laws. Support for deregulation also came from the U.S. Department

of Transportation. The AFL-CIO and other labor groups, on the other hand, rejected deregulation, believing it undermined the job security of aviation industry workers. Airport operators such as the Port Authority of New York and New Jersey were similarly hostile towards deregulation, which would, they declared, weaken their financial position and encourage route abandonment in many low-density traffic markets.

Public Law 95-163 is unique in that it represents the first successful effort by the Federal Government to deregulate a sector of the nation's transportation industry. While the law is clearly the single most important deregulation measure adopted with respect to air freight service, we should not lose sight of various other recent legislative and administrative actions whose objective also has been the removal of regulatory constraints surrounding air freight transportation. Examples of such actions discussed in this study include: (1) the Interstate Commerce Commission's decision to substantially enlarge pickup/delivery zones (announced May, 1977); (2) abolition by the Civil Aeronautics Board of the "monitored entry" policy formerly applied to long-haul surface carriers and their affiliates wishing to become air freight forwarders (June, 1977); (3) passage of Public Law 95-245 (March, 1978), which shortened the supplemental carriers' waiting period for Section 418 certificates; (4) the elimination of various regulatory distinctions between forwarders and shippers associations, and authorization of freight exchanges among forwarders (March, 1978); (5) the introduction by the Interstate Commerce Commission of a new definition of a "through air bill of lading" (April, 1978); (6) the raising of the Part 298 capacity limit (June, 1978); (7) passage of Public Law 95-504 (October, 1978; here the legislators were concerned primarily with the deregulation of air passenger service); and (8) the Board's discontinuance of the freight tariff filing requirement (November, 1978). These and related developments made 1977 and 1978 tumultuous years for the air freight industry, and a lengthy transition period will have to elapse before we can fully assess the cumulative effect of these changes on the New York-Newark air freight system and on the industry as a whole. Some tentative conclusions are given below and are based in part on the carriers' initial reactions to the deregulation process.

Deregulation, in an overall sense, provides the carriers with greater operational flexibility, allows management to experiment with new marketing programs, and enlarges price and service options for the shipping public. At the same time, however, external

constraints acting on the system and on the nation's air freight
industry in general (these include rapidly rising fuel prices,
possible fuel shortages, and equipment shortages) can be expected
to rule out the lower rates and large-scale establishment of new
carriers so enthusiastically predicted by some deregulation advocates.
Air freight's "breakthrough," foreseen in numerous Board proceedings
of the 1950s and 1960s, and which some proponents of deregulation
felt would follow on the heels of reform legislation, appears as
elusive as ever. Air freight activity, as air transportation as a
whole, is heavily influenced by the general economic health of the
nation, and a number of recently revised national and regional
economic forecasts suggest that earlier hopes for air freight
expansion have been unrealistic. In the case of the New York
metropolitan region, studies conducted by the Tri-State Regional
Planning Commission now indicate that the region's ongoing population
losses, combined with higher economic growth rates for other areas of
the nation, will see the region's share of total U.S. domestic air
traffic fall from about 8 percent (1975) to roughly 6.3 percent
in 1995.

In the first half of 1978 the Flying Tiger Line and several
trunks introduced rate increases averaging about 10 percent, and, in
view of escalating fuel prices, labor costs, landing fees, etc., it
seems clear that shippers will shortly face new rate increases rather
than the industry-wide rate reductions expected by a few of the more
optimistic proponents of deregulation. Higher rates, airline spokesmen noted, had become necessary in part because of the low rates
formerly imposed by the Board and would help their companies to
improve the quality of freight service. At the same time a variety
of rate discounts have been announced, some of which would have been
disallowed under the former regulatory scheme. The Airline
Deregulation Act of 1978 can be expected to raise significantly the
number of carriers operating in the major passenger markets (e.g.,
New York-Chicago, New York-Miami, New York-West Coast) and, given
the attendant growth in belly capacity, could have a moderating
effect on freight rate increases in these markets.

Deregulation has essentially removed the Civil Aeronautics
Board's traditional antitrust powers. The agency no longer opposes
various types of air-truck mergers/acquisitions, making possible new
forms of air-surface integration. An example here would be a
vertically integrated firm engaged in air transportation, surface
transportation, and forwarding. The efficiency gains of such a firm
should, theoretically at least, lead to cost savings for the

shipping public. In addition, forwarders are now able to become direct air carriers. The costs involved, however, make this an unlikely prospect for all but the very largest of these companies.

The deregulation legislation has not as yet persuaded any of the domestic trunks serving the system's airports to initiate new freighter service to/from New York-Newark. On the contrary, one carrier, Trans World Airlines, has announced its freighter operations will be terminated, attributing this, in part, to the competitive impact of deregulation. The all-cargo flights of the other trunks face, at best, an uncertain future, and a number of factors (excess belly capacity in their passenger equipment, rising fuel prices, the cost of retrofitting all-cargo aircraft to satisfy Federal antinoise rules, and the threat of curfews on nighttime service at some airports) could well lead these carriers to phase out their remaining all-cargo flights during the 1980s. Such a development would presumably prompt the freight specialists (including the leading forwarders) to enlarge their own all-cargo operations in order to meet the overnight and seasonal transportation requirements of certain air shippers. Fuel prices and availability have become perhaps the most urgent concerns of the entire transportation industry. These concerns should spur the development of more fuel-efficient aircraft and may also lead to greater use of charter service in order to take advantage of higher load factors.

New scheduled freight capacity is being added to several of the system's domestic routes (particularly in transcontinental markets) by Pan American World Airways and Seaboard World Airlines. In addition, Flying Tiger and several of the supplementals (now known as charter airlines) have initiated new scheduled all-cargo services as a result of deregulation, linking New York-Newark with various Sun Belt, West Coast, and Midwestern cities. The commuters/air taxis are also expanding their freight activities (this includes, in a few cases, the purchase of larger aircraft) and can be expected to show considerable growth, especially in short- and medium-haul markets. The commuters are currently (1978) facing an equipment shortage and fear that a future fuel allocation program will favor the largest airlines at the expense of the small companies.

The air freight industry has entered a transition period, and a primary objective of future research should be an evaluation both of the quality of freight service under deregulation and of the contribution the reforms of 1977-1978 are making to the carriers' ability to help meet the changing needs of shippers and receivers in the years ahead. Thus, for example, we shall want to look at

the impact on shippers (especially small-volume shippers) of greatly
enlarged pickup/delivery zones and of the elimination of the tariff
filing requirement. A significant route realignment is taking
place, and it will be interesting to see how this affects shippers
in particular markets. Airline deregulation is being viewed by
some as a precursor to similar legislative action in other sectors
of the transportation industry. Public Law 95-163 affords
researchers an opportunity to examine the responses of air shippers
and carriers to statutory reform and to assess the implications
similar legislation may have for the nation's other transportation
modes.

APPENDIX

Shown below are various recent (1977-1978) amendments to the
Federal Aviation Act.   Only those amendments particularly germane to
this study are given here.

DECLARATION OF POLICY: THE BOARD
FACTORS FOR INTERSTATE AND OVERSEAS AIR TRANSPORTATION

SEC. 102. [72 Stat. 740, as amended by 91 Stat. 1283, 1284, 92 Stat. 1706, 49
U.S.C. 1302] (a) In the exercise and performance of its powers and duties under
this Act with respect to interstate and overseas air transportation, the Board
shall consider the following, among other things, as being in the public interest,
and in accordance with the public convenience and necessity:
    (1) The assignment and maintenance of safety as the highest priority in air
commerce, and prior to the authorization of new air transportation services,
full evaluation of the recommendations of the Secretary of Transportation on
the safety implications of such new services and full evaluation of any
report or recommendation submitted under section 107 of this Act.
    (2) The prevention of any deterioration in established safety procedures,
recognizing the clear intent, encouragement, and dedication of the Congress to
the furtherance of the highest degree of safety in air transportation and
air commerce, and the maintenance of the safety vigilance that has evolved
within air transportation and air commerce and has come to be expected by the
traveling and shipping public.
    (3) The availability of a variety of adequate, economic, efficient, and
low-price services by air carriers without unjust discriminations, undue
preferences or advantages, or unfair or deceptive practices, the need to
improve relations among, and coordinate transportation by, air carriers, and
the need to encourage fair wages and equitable working conditions.
    (4) The placement of maximum reliance on competitive market forces and on
actual and potential competition (A) to provide the needed air transportation
system, and (B) to encourage efficient and well-managed carriers to earn
adequate profits and to attract capital.
    (5) The development and maintenance of a sound regulatory environment which
is responsive to the needs of the public and in which decisions are reached
promptly in order to facilitate adaption of the air transportation system to
the present and future needs of the domestic and foreign commerce of the
United States, the Postal Service, and the national defense.
    (6) The encouragement of air service at major urban areas through secondary
or satellite airports, where consistent with regional airport plans of regional
and local authorities, and when such encouragement is endorsed by appropriate
State entities encouraging such service by air carriers whose sole responsibility in any specific market is to provide service exclusively at the
secondary or satellite airport, and fostering an environment which reasonably
enables such carriers to establish themselves and to develop their secondary
or satellite airport services.
    (7) The prevention of unfair, deceptive, predatory, or anticompetitive
practices in air transportation, and the avoidance of--
        (A) unreasonable industry concentration, excessive market domination,
        and monopoly power; and
        (B) other conditions;
that would tend to allow one or more air carriers unreasonably to increase
prices, reduce services, or exclude competition in air transportation.
    (8) The maintenance of a comprehensive and convenient system of continuous
scheduled airline service for small communities and for isolated areas, with
direct Federal assistance where appropriate.

(9) The encouragement, development, and maintenance of an air transportation system relying on actual and potential competition to provide efficiency, innovation, and low prices, and to determine the variety, quality, and price of air transportation services.

(10) The encouragement of entry into air transportation markets by new air carriers, the encouragement of entry into additional air transportation markets by existing air carriers, and the continued strengthening of small air carriers so as to assure a more effective, competitive airline industry.

FACTORS FOR ALL-CARGO AIR SERVICE

(b) In addition to the declaration of policy set forth in subsection (a) of this section, the Board, in the exercise and performance of its powers and duties under this Act with respect to all-cargo air service shall consider the following, among other things, as being in the public interest:

(1) The encouragement and development of an expedited all-cargo air service system, provided by private enterprise, responsive to (A) the present and future needs of shippers, (B) the commerce of the United States, and (C) the national defense.

(2) The encouragement and development of an integrated transportation system relying upon competitive market forces to determine the extent, variety, quality, and price of such services.

(3) The provision of services without unjust discriminations, undue preferences or advantages, unfair or deceptive practices, or predatory pricing.

FACTORS FOR FOREIGN AIR TRANSPORTATION

(c) In the exercise and performance of its powers and duties under this Act with respect to foreign air transportation, the Board shall consider the following, among other things, as being in the public interest, and in accordance with the public convenience and necessity:

(1) The encouragement and development of an air transportation system properly adapted to the present and future needs of the foreign and domestic commerce of the United States, of the Postal Service, and of the national defense.

(2) The regulation of air transportation in such manner as to recognize and preserve the inherent advantages of, assure the highest degree of safety in, and foster sound economic conditions in, such transportation, and to improve the relations between and coordinate transportation by air carriers.

(3) The promotion of adequate, economical, and efficient service by air carriers at reasonable charges, without unjust discriminations, undue preferences or advantages, or unfair or destructive competitive practices.

(4) Competition to the extent necessary to assure the sound development of an air transportation system properly adapted to the needs of the foreign and domestic commerce of the United States, of the Postal Service, and of the national defense.

(5) The promotion of safety in air commerce.

(6) The promotion, encouragement, and development of civil aeronautics.

SEC. 401. [72 Stat. 754, as amended by 76 Stat. 143, 82 Stat. 867, 90 Stat. 883, 91 Stat. 1281, 92 Stat. 1710, 49 U.S.C. 1371.]

ISSUANCE OF CERTIFICATE

(d)(1) The Board shall issue a certificate authorizing the whole or any part of the transportation covered by the application, if it finds that the applicant is fit, willing, and able to perform such transportation properly and to conform to the provisions of this Act and the rules, regulations, and requirements of the Board hereunder, and that such transportation--

(A) in the case of interstate or overseas air transportation, is consistent with the public convenience and necessity; and

(B) in the case of foreign air transportation, is required by the public convenience and necessity;
otherwise such application shall be denied.

(2) In the case of an application for a certificate to engage in temporary air transportation, the Board may issue a certificate authorizing the whole or any part thereof for such limited periods--

(A) in the case of an application for interstate or overseas air transportation, as is consistent with the public convenience and necessity; and

(B) in the case of an application for foreign air transportation, as may be required by the public convenience and necessity;
if it finds that the applicant is fit, willing, and able properly to perform such transportation and to conform to the provisions of this Act and the rules, regulations, and requirements of the Board hereunder.

(3) In the case of an application for a certificate to engage in charter air transportation, the Board may issue a certificate to any applicant, not holding a certificate under paragraph (1) or (2) of this subsection on January 1, 1977, authorizing interstate air transportation of persons, which authorizes the whole or any part thereof--

(A) in the case of an application for interstate or overseas air transportation, for such periods, as is consistent with the public convenience and necessity; and

(B) in the case of an application for foreign air transportation, for such periods, as may be required by the public convenience and necessity;
if it finds that the applicant is fit, willing, and able properly to perform the transportation covered by the application and to conform to the provisions of this Act and the rules, regulations, and requirements of the Board hereunder.

TERMINATIONS, REDUCTIONS, AND SUSPENSIONS OF SERVICE

(j)(1) No air carrier holding a certificate issued under [section 401] shall--

(A) terminate or suspend all air transportation which it is providing to a point under such certificate; or

(B) reduce any such air transportation below that which the Board has determined to be essential air transportation for such point;
unless such air carrier has first given the Board, any community affected, and the State agency of the State in which such community is located, at least 90 days notice of its intent to so terminate, suspend, or reduce such air transportation. The Board may, by regulation or otherwise, authorize such temporary suspension of service as may be in the public interest.

(2) If an air carrier holding a certificate issued pursuant to section 401 of this Act proposes to terminate or suspend nonstop or single-plane air transportation between two points being provided by such air carrier under such certificate, and such air carrier is the only air carrier certificated pursuant to such section 401 providing nonstop or single-plane air transportation between such points, at least sixty days before such proposed termination or suspension, such air carrier shall file with the Board and serve upon each community to be directly affected notice of such termination or suspension.

CERTIFICATE FOR ALL-CARGO AIR SERVICE APPLICATION

SEC. 418. [Added by 91 Stats. 1284, 1285, 1286, as amended by 92 Stat. 156, 49 U.S.C. 1388] (a)(1) Any citizen of the United States who has a valid certificate issued under section 401(d)(1) of this title and who provided scheduled all-cargo air service at any time during the period from January 1, 1977, through the date of enactment of this section may, during the forty-five-day period which begins on the date of enactment of this section, submit an application to the Board for a certificate under this section to provide all-cargo air service. Such application shall contain such information and be in such form as the Board shall by regulation require.

(2) Any citizen of the United States who (A) operates pursuant to an exemption granted by the Board under section 416 of this title, and (B) provided scheduled all-cargo air service continuously (other than for interruptions caused by labor disputes) during the 12-month period ending on the date of enactment of this

section, or whose predecessor in interest provided such service during such period, may, during the forty-five-day period which begins on the date of enactment of this section, submit an application to the Board for a certificate under this section to provide all-cargo air service. Such application shall contain such information and be in such form as the Board shall by regulation require.

(3) Any citizen of the United States who has a valid certificate issued under section 401(d)(3) of this title and who provided supplemental air transportation carrying only cargo at any time during the period from January 1, 1977, through the date of enactment of this section may, during the forty-five day period beginning on April 1, 1978, submit an application to the Board for a certificate under this section to provide all-cargo air service. Such application shall contain such information and be in such form as the Board shall by regulation require.

(4) After the three hundred and sixty-fifth day which begins after the date of enactment of this section, any citizen of the United States may submit an application to the Board for a certificate under this section to provide all-cargo air service. Such application shall contain such information and be in such form as the Board shall by regulation require.

ISSUANCE AND REVOCATION OF CERTIFICATE

(b)(1)(A) Not later than sixty days after any application is submitted pursuant to paragraph (1), (2) or (3) of subsection (a) of this section, the Board shall issue a certificate under this section authorizing the all-cargo air service covered by the application.

(B) No later than one hundred and eighty days after any application is submitted pursuant to paragraph (4) of subsection (a) of this section, the Board shall issue a certificate under this section authorizing the whole or any part of the all-cargo air service covered by the application unless it finds that the applicant is not fit, willing, and able to provide such service and to comply with any rules and regulations promulgated by the Board.

(2) Any certificate issued by the Board under this section may contain such reasonable conditions and limitations as the Board deems necessary, except that such terms and conditions shall not restrict the points which may be served, or the rates which may be charged, by the holder of such certificate.

(3) Not withstanding any other provision of this section, no certificate issued by the Board under this section shall authorize all-cargo air service between any pair of points both of which are within the State of Alaska or the State of Hawaii.

(4) If any all-cargo air service authorized by a certificate issued under this subsection is not performed to the minimum extent prescribed by the Board, it may by order, entered after notice and opportunity for a hearing, direct that such certificate shall, thereafter, cease to be effective to the extent of such service.

EXEMPTIONS

(c) Any applicant who is issued a certificate under this section shall, with respect to any all-cargo air service provided in accordance with such certificate, be exempt from the requirements of section 401(a) of this Act, and any other section of this Act which the Board by rule determines appropriate, and any rule, regulation, or procedure issued pursuant to any such section.

AIR CARRIER STATUS

(d) Any applicant who is issued a certificate under this section shall be an air carrier for the purposes of this Act, except to the extent such carrier is exempt from any requirement of the Act pursuant to this section.

THE PRESIDENT OF THE UNITED STATES

SEC. 801. [72 Stat. 782, as amended by 86 Stat. 96, 92 Stat. 1740, 49 U.S.C. 1461] (a) The issuance, denial, transfer, amendment, cancellation, suspension, or revocation of, and the terms, conditions, and limitations contained in, any

certificate authorizing an air carrier to engage in foreign air transportation, or
any permit issuable to any foreign air carrier under section 402 of this Act,
shall be presented to the President for review.   The President shall have the
right to disapprove any such Board action concerning such certificates or permits
solely upon the basis of foreign relations or national defense considerations
which are within the President's jurisdiction, but not upon the basis of economic
or carrier selection considerations.   Any such disapproval shall be issued in a
public document, setting forth the reasons for the disapproval to the extent
national security permits, within sixty days after submission of the Board's
action to the President.   Any such Board action so disapproved shall be null and
void.   Any such Board action not disapproved within the foregoing time limits
shall take effect as action of the Board, not the President, and as such shall be
subject to judicial review as provided in section 1006 of this Act.

   SEC. 1002. [72 Stat. 788, as amended by 86 Stat. 96, 91 Stats. 1282, 1286, 1287,
1288, 1289, 92 Stat. 1741, 1742, 49 U.S.C. 1482.]

                          RULE OF RATEMAKING

   (e) In exercising and performing its power and duties with respect to determining
rates, fares, and charges described in paragraph (1) of subsection (d) of this
section, the Board shall take into consideration, among other factors--
        (1) the criteria set forth in section 102 of this Act;
        (2) the need for adequate and efficient transportation of persons and pro-
    perty at the lowest cost consistent with the furnishing of such service;
        (3) the effect of prices upon the movement of traffic;
        (4) the desirability of a variety of price and service options such as peak
    and off-peak pricing or other pricing mechanisms to improve economic
    efficiency and provide low-cost air service; and
        (5) the desirability of allowing an air carrier to determine prices in
    response to particular competitive market conditions on the basis of such air
    carrier's individual costs.

BIBLIOGRAPHY

Civil Aeronautics Board Proceedings

AAXICO, Suspension of Service. 29 CAB 1329 (1959).

AFFA Code of Fair Trade Practices. Agreement 17003, Order E-19984.

Agreement Adopted by IATA Relating to North Atlantic Cargo Rates.
    Order 73-2-24.

Agreement Establishing Air Cargo, Inc., Petitions of Eastern Air
    Lines, Inc., and United Air Lines, Inc., for Reconsideration.
    9 CAB 468 (1948).

Air Freight Case. 10 CAB 572 (1949).

Air Freight Certificate Renewal Case. 23 CAB 186 (1956).

Air Freight Forwarder Authority Case. 40 CAB 673 (1964).

Air Freight Forwarder Case. 9 CAB 473 (1948).

Air Freight Forwarder Case. (International.) 11 CAB 182 (1949).

Air Freight Forwarder Investigation. 21 CAB 536 (1955).

Air Freight Forwarder Investigation. (Supplemental Opinion.) 23 CAB
    376 (1956).

Air Freight Forwarder Investigation. (Second Supplemental Opinion.)
    24 CAB 755 (1957).

Air Freight Forwarders' Charters Investigation. Docket 23287, Order
    77-7-25.

Air Freight Rate Case. 18 CAB 22 (1953).

Air Freight Rate Case, Minimum Rates for Air Freight Forwarders.
    26 CAB 339 (1958).

Air Freight Rate Investigation. 9 CAB 340 (1948).

Air Freight Rate Investigation--Directional Rates. 11 CAB 228 (1950).

Air Freight Rate Investigation--Directional Rates. 16 CAB 254 (1952).

Airlift International, Inc.--Renewal and Amendment of Certificates.
    Order 73-3-59.

Airlift-Slick Route Transfer. Order E-26810.

Application of Burlington Northern Air Freight, Inc. for Domestic
    and International Air Freight Forwarder Authority. Order
    72-3-3.

Application of Evergreen International Airlines, Inc. for an Exemption Pursuant to Section 416(b) of the Federal Aviation Act. Order 78-2-49.

Application of the Flying Tiger Line, Inc. Order E-25910.

Application of World Airways for a Certificate of Public Convenience and Necessity. Order 76-1-88.

Blocked Space Air Freight Tariffs. Order 68-12-118.

Brief of Emery Air Freight Corporation to the Civil Aeronautics Board. Docket 26907 (1975).

Brief of The Port Authority of New York and New Jersey to Administrative Law Judge Greer M. Murphy. Docket 22973, January 15, 1973.

Brief of The Port Authority of New York and New Jersey to Associate Chief Administrative Law Judge Ross I. Newmann. Docket 25908, September 9, 1974.

Brief of The Port of New York Authority to Examiner Richard A. Walsh. Docket 18401, February 7, 1969.

Brief to the Civil Aeronautics Board of Burlington Northern Applicants. Docket 26907 (1975).

Comments of Air Express International to Petition of Novo Airfreight. Docket 30783, June 13, 1977.

Comments of American Airlines, Inc. Docket 33093, September 11, 1978

Comments of Delta Air Lines, Inc. Docket 33093, September 11, 1978.

Comments of Eight Local Service Airlines on the Proposed Aviation Act of 1975. Docket 28490, January 20, 1976.

Comments of Federal Express Corporation. Docket 33093, September 11, 1978.

Comments of Member Carriers of the National Air Carrier Association. Docket 28256, June 10, 1976.

Comments of Trans World Airlines, Inc. Docket 33093, September 11, 1978.

Comments of United Airlines, Inc. Docket 33093, September 11, 1978.

Comments of the Flying Tiger Line, Inc. Docket 28256, June 10, 1976.

Comments of the Flying Tiger Line, Inc. Docket 31272, December 7, 1977.

Deferred Air Freight Renewal Case. 27 CAB 627 (1958).

Detroit-California Nonstop Service Investigation. 43 CAB 557 (1966).

Domestic Air Freight Rate Investigation. Order 77-8-62.

Domestic Cargo-Mail Service Case. 36 CAB 344 (1962).

Domestic Coterminal Points--Europe All-Cargo Service Investigation.
      Orders E-25122 and 69-4-140.

Domestic Minimum Air Freight Rates. 43 CAB 800 (1965).

Domestic Service Mail Rate Investigation of Priority and Nonpriority
      Mail. Docket 23080.

Exceptions of the Nine Independent Air Freight Forwarders. Docket
      26907 (1975).

Express Service Investigation. Order 73-12-36.

Household Goods Air Freight Forwarder Investigation. Orders 72-7-33
      and 72-10-59.

International Air Freight Forwarder Investigation. 27 CAB 658 (1958).

International Air Freight Forwarder Investigation. (Supplemental
      Opinion.) 30 CAB 13 (1959).

Intra-Area Cargo Case. 28 CAB 200 (1959).

Investigation of Local, Feeder, and Pickup Air Service. 6 CAB 1
      (1944).

Investigation of Nonscheduled Air Services. 6 CAB 1049 (1946).

Joint Petition of the Flying Tiger Line, Inc. and Pan American World
      Airways, Inc. for Reconsideration of Order 77-7-25. Docket
      23287, August 2, 1977.

Large Irregular Air Carrier Investigation. 22 CAB 838 (1955).

Large Irregular Air Carrier Investigation. 28 CAB 224 (1959).

Liberalized Regulation of Indirect Cargo Carriers. Docket 32318,
      EDR-350.

Long-Haul Motor/Railroad Carrier Air Freight Forwarder Authority Case.
      Docket 26907, initial decision (served: October 22, 1975), and
      Order 77-6-126.

Los Angeles Airways Renewal Case. 27 CAB 36 (1958).

Minimum Charges per Shipment of Air Freight. Orders 72-4-105 and
      72-6-68.

Minimum Rates Applicable to Air Freight. 34 CAB 263 (1961).

Motor Carrier--Air Freight Forwarder Investigation. Orders E-25725
      and 69-4-100.

Multicharter Cargo Rates Investigation. 47 CAB 626 (1967).

New England Service Investigation. Order 74-7-70.

New York City Area Helicopter Service Case. 15 CAB 259 (1952).

New York-San Francisco Nonstop Service Case. 29 CAB 811 (1959).

New York-San Juan Cargo Rates Investigation. 44 CAB 599 (1966).

North-South Air Freight Renewal Case. 22 CAB 253 (1955).

Pacific Islands Local Service Investigation. Order 71-7-174.

Petition for Investigation. Docket 29525, July 16, 1976.

Petition for Rule Change to Allow Hawaii Air Cargo Shippers Association to Charter. Docket 28256 (1975).

Petition of Novo Airfreight. Docket 30783, April 25, 1977.

Railway Express Agency, Inc.--Air Freight Forwarder Application. 27 CAB 500 (1958).

Railway Express Agency, Inc.--Certificate of Public Convenience and Necessity. 2 CAB 531 (1941).

Reopened Detroit-California Nonstop Service Investigation. 47 CAB 201 (1967).

Revised Air Freight Rate Structure Proposed by the Flying Tiger Line Order 68-10-111.

Saturn-AAXICO Merger Case. 43 CAB 150 (1965).

Service to Omaha and Des Moines Case. Docket 18401.

Service to Puerto Rico Case. 26 CAB 72 (1957).

Slick Corporation, Suspension of Service. 43 CAB 742 (1965).

Southern Pacific--Santa Fe Air Freight Forwarder Case. Order 70-10-1

Southern Transcontinental Service Case. 33 CAB 701 (1961).

Statement of Position (American Airlines). Docket 22859, December 21, 1973.

Substitution of Other Services for Air Transportation Rule Proceedin Order 75-3-37.

Supplemental Air Service Proceeding. 45 CAB 231 (1966).

Supplemental Renewal Proceeding. Order 77-1-98.

The Flying Tiger Line, Inc. Additional Points Case. Order 71-11-33.

The Flying Tiger Line, Inc., Air-Truck Service. 30 CAB 242 (1959).

Transatlantic Cargo Case. 21 CAB 671 (1954).

Transatlantic Route Proceeding. Order 78-1-118.

Transatlantic, Transpacific, and Latin American Mail Rates Case. Docket 26487.

Transcontinental and Western Air, Inc. et al., Additional North-Sout California Services. 4 CAB 373 (1943).

Transpacific Route Case. 32 CAB 928 (1961).

Transpacific Route Investigation. Order 68-12-105.

United States-Europe-Middle East Cargo Service Case. 15 CAB 565
     (1952).

Universal Air Freight Corporation--Investigation of Forwarding
     Activities. 3 CAB 698 (1942).

                Interstate Commerce Commission Proceedings

Acme Fast Freight, Inc., Common Carrier Application. 8 MCC 211 (1938).

California Commercial Association v. Wells, Fargo and Co. 14 ICC
     422 (1908).

Chicago and Wisconsin Points Proportional Rates. 10 MCC 556 (1938).

Civil Aeronautics Board. Comments of the Civil Aeronautics Board on
     the Proposal of the Interstate Commerce Commission to Modify
     Its Rules Governing the Motor Transportation of Property and
     Passengers Incidental to Transportation by Aircraft.
     Mimeographed, n.d.

Colorado Cartage Co., Inc. v. Murphy. 100 MCC 745 (1966).

Comment of Federal Express Corporation. Docket MC-C-3437 (1977).

Comments of American Trucking Associations, Inc. Docket MC-C-3437,
     September 19, 1977.

Comments of American Trucking Associations, Inc. (Supplemental
     Comments.) Docket MC-C-3437, October 14, 1977.

Comments of Members of the Air Freight Forwarders Association of
     America. Docket MC-C-3437, August 8, 1977.

Comments of Members of the Air Freight Forwarders Association of
     America. (Supplemental Comments.) Docket MC-C-3437, September
     19, 1977.

Comments of Ozark Air Lines, Inc. Docket MC-C-3437, August 5, 1977.

Comments of Teamsters Union. Docket MC-C-3437 (1977).

Comments of the Flying Tiger Line, Inc. Docket MC-C-3437 (1977).

Comments of the National Industrial Traffic League on the Proposed
     Regulations. Docket MC-C-3437, September 19, 1977.

Comments of the National Small Shipment Traffic Conference and Drug
     and Toilet Preparation Traffic Conference. Docket MC-C-3437,
     September 19, 1977.

Comments of the United States Department of Justice. Docket
     MC-C-3437, September 23, 1977.

Comments of the United States Department of Transportation. Docket
     MC-C-3437, September 19, 1977 and September 15, 1978.

Comments on Behalf of Kerek Air Freight Corporation, Airport
     Transportation Service, Inc. and R and G Airfreight, Inc.
     Docket MC-C-3437, August 31, 1977.

Commercial Zones and Terminal Areas. 53 MCC 451 (1951).

Commercial Zones and Terminal Areas. 54 MCC 21 (1952).

Commercial Zones and Terminal Areas. Ex Parte No. MC-37, Sub-No. 26 (1976).

Commodity Haulage Corp. Common Carrier Application. 69 MCC 527 (1957)

Commodity Haulage Corp. Common Carrier Application. 106 MCC 135 (1967).

Complainants' Reply to Defendant's Motion to Dismiss. Docket MC-C-6746 (1970).

Emery Air Freight Corporation Freight Forwarder Application. 339 ICC 17 (1971).

Exempt Zone--La Guardia and Kennedy International Airports. 111 MCC 284 (1970).

Exempt Zone (Passengers)--Chicago, Ill., O'Hare Airport. 126 MCC 332 (1977).

Exempt Zone (Passengers)--Savannah, Ga., Airport. 114 MCC 804 (1971)

Exempt Zone--Philadelphia International Airport. 113 MCC 189 (1971).

Export Shipping Co. v. Wabash R. R. Co. 14 ICC 437 (1908).

Formal Complaint for Violations of the Interstate Commerce Act. Docket MC-C-6746 (1970).

Freight Forwarding Investigation. 229 ICC 201 (1938).

Graff Common Carrier Application. 48 MCC 310 (1948).

Interpretation of Operating Rights Authorizing Service at Designated Airports. 110 MCC 597 (1969).

Interstate Commerce Commission. Internal Staff Study Recommendations Announced in Commission's Review of Regulatory Modernization. No. 187-75, July 7, 1975.

In the Matter of Express Rates, Practices, Accounts, and Revenues. 24 ICC 380 (1912).

Kenny Extension--Air Freight. 49 MCC 182 (1949).

Kenny Extension--Air Freight. 61 MCC 587 (1953).

Letter sent to the Commission by Francis P. O'Brien, President, Direct Airport Service, Inc., June 22, 1977 (Docket MC-C-3437).

Letter sent to the Commission by Jerry Schorr, Director of Cargo Sales, Eastern Air Lines, August 12, 1977 (Docket MC-C-3437).

Marotta Air Service, Inc., Petition for a Declaratory Order. 129 MCC 100 (1978).

Miami and Fort Lauderdale, Fla.--Air Terminal Areas. 125 MCC 519 (1976).

Motor Transportation of Property Incidental to Transportation by Aircraft. 95 MCC 71 (1964).

Motor Transportation of Property Incidental to Transportation by Aircraft. 112 MCC 1 (1970).

New York, N.Y. Commercial Zone. 1 MCC 665 (1937).

Panther Cartage Co. Extension--Air Freight. 88 MCC 37 (1961).

Philadelphia International Airport, Philadelphia, Pa.--Exempt Zone. 123 MCC 228 (1975).

Practices of Motor Common Carriers of Household Goods. 17 MCC 467 (1939).

Re. Express Companies. 1 ICC 677 (1887).

Representations of Air Cargo, Inc., on Behalf of the Scheduled Certificated Airlines of the United States. Docket MC-C-3437 (1977).

Representations of the Air Terminal Zone-Special Project Group, Air Freight Motor Carriers Conference, Irregular Route Common Carrier Conference. I, Docket MC-C-3437 (1977).

Savage Contract Carrier Application. 108 MCC 205 (1968).

Statement on Behalf of the Port of New York Authority in Support of Proposed Amendment of Section 1041.23, 49 CFR. Docket MC-C-3437 (Sub-No. 4), August 8, 1969.

Statement Pursuant to Proposed Rule-Making on Behalf of the Port of New York Authority. Docket MC-C-3437, November 15, 1961.

Thurber v. N.Y.C. and H. R.R. Co. 2 ICC 742 (1890).

Verified Statement of Anthony V. Desimone on Behalf of Associated Air Freight, Inc. Docket MC-C-3437 (1977).

Verified Statement of Robert M. Van Why, Sr. for R. and G. Airfreight, Inc. Docket MC-C-3437, August 31, 1977.

Verified Statement of Roger Doll for Dyoll Delivery Service, Inc. Docket MC-C-3437 (1977).

Wallkill Air Freight Corporation Common Carrier Application. 125 MCC 639 (1975).

William R. Fisher and Montford R. Fisher Common Carrier Application. 83 MCC 229 (1960).

Legal Proceedings

ABC Air Freight Co., Inc. v. Civil Aeronautics Board. 391 F. 2d 295 (2d Cir. 1968).

ABC Air Freight Co., Inc. v. Civil Aeronautics Board. 419 F. 2d 154 (2d Cir. 1969); certiorari denied, 397 U.S. 1006 (1970).

Aircraft Owners and Pilots Association v. Port Authority of New York. 305 F. Supp. 93 (E.D. N.Y. 1969).

Air Dispatch, Inc. v. United States. 237 F. Supp. 450 (E.D. Pa. 1964); affirmed per curiam, 381 U.S. 412 (1965).

Air Line Pilots Association v. Civil Aeronautics Board. 458 F. 2d
     846 (D.C. Cir. 1972).

Air Line Pilots Association v. Civil Aeronautics Board. 515 F.
     2d 1010 (D.C. Cir. 1975).

All American Airways, Inc. v. United Air Lines, Inc. 364 U.S. 297
     (1960).

American Airlines, Inc. v. Civil Aeronautics Board. 178 F. 2d 903
     (7th Cir. 1949).

American Airlines, Inc. v. Civil Aeronautics Board. 348 F. 2d 349
     (D.C. Cir. 1965).

American Airlines, Inc. v. Civil Aeronautics Board. 359 F. 2d 624
     (D.C. Cir. 1966).

American Airlines, Inc. v. Civil Aeronautics Board. 365 F. 2d 939
     (D.C. Cir. 1966).

American Trucking Associations, Inc. v. Atchison, Topeka and Santa
     Fe Railway Co. 387 U.S. 397 (1967).

Associated Press v. United States. 326 U.S. 1 (1945).

Big Bear Cartage, Inc. v. Air Cargo, Inc. 419 F. Supp. 982
     (N.D. Ill. 1976).

Bowman Transportation, Inc. v. Arkansas-Best Freight System, Inc.
     419 U.S. 281 (1974).

Breen Air Freight, Ltd. v. Air Cargo, Inc. 470 F. 2d 767 (2d Cir.
     1972).

Brewster v. Gage. 280 U.S. 327 (1930).

British Airways Board v. The Port Authority of New York and New
     Jersey. 431 F. Supp. 1216 (S.D. N.Y. 1977).

British Airways Board v. The Port Authority of New York and New
     Jersey. 558 F. 2d 75 (2d Cir. 1977).

British Airways Board v. The Port Authority of New York and New
     Jersey. 437 F. Supp. 804 (S.D. N.Y. 1977).

British Airways Board v. The Port Authority of New York and New
     Jersey. 564 F. 2d 1002 (2d Cir. 1977).

Burlington Truck Lines v. United States. 371 U.S. 156 (1962).

Chicago and Southern Air Lines, Inc. v. Waterman Steamship Corp.
     333 U.S. 103 (1948).

City of Philadelphia v. Civil Aeronautics Board. 289 F. 2d 770
     (D.C. Cir. 1961).

Civil Aeronautics Board v. Delta Air Lines, Inc. 367 U.S. 316 (1961)

Commissioner of Internal Revenue v. Estate of Noel. 380 U.S. 678
     (1965).

Commonwealth of Virginia v. Civil Aeronautics Board. 498 F. 2d 129
   (4th Cir. 1974).

Delta Air Lines, Inc. v. Civil Aeronautics Board. 247 F. 2d 327 (5th
   Cir. 1957).

Delta Air Lines, Inc. v. Civil Aeronautics Board. 543 F. 2d 247
   (D.C. Cir. 1976).

Diggs v. Civil Aeronautics Board. 516 F. 2d 1248 (D.C. Cir. 1975);
   certiorari denied, 424 U.S. 910 (1976).

Douglas v. Seacoast Products. 431 U.S. 265 (1977).

Federal Communications Commission v. Schreiber. 381 U.S. 279 (1965).

Frank W. Scroggins v. Air Cargo, Inc. 534 F. 2d 1124 (5th Cir. 1976).

Interstate Commerce Commission v. Delaware, L. and W. R.R. 220 U.S.
   235 (1911).

Law Motor Freight, Inc. v. Civil Aeronautics Board. 364 F. 2d 139
   (1st Cir. 1966); certiorari denied, 387 U.S. 905 (1967).

National Air Carrier Association v. Civil Aeronautics Board. 442 F.
   2d 862 (D.C. Cir. 1971).

National Bus Traffic Association v. United States. 249 F. Supp. 869
   (N.D. Ill. 1965); affirmed per curiam, 382 U.S. 369 (1966).

National Labor Relations Board v. Brown. 380 U.S. 278 (1965).

National Motor Freight Traffic Association, Inc. v. Civil Aeronautics
   Board. 374 F. 2d 266 (D.C. Cir. 1966); certiorari denied, 387
   U.S. 905 (1967).

Pan American World Airways, Inc. v. Civil Aeronautics Board. 517 F.
   2d 734 (2d Cir. 1975).

People of the State of California v. Civil Aeronautics Board. 567 F.
   2d 1 (D.C. Cir. 1977).

Pillai v. Civil Aeronautics Board. 485 F. 2d 1018 (D.C. Cir. 1973).

Saturn Airways, Inc. v. Civil Aeronautics Board. 483 F. 2d 1284
   (D.C. Cir. 1973).

Short Haul Survival Committee v. United States. Brief of Petitioner,
   American Trucking Associations, Inc., in Civil Action nos.
   77-1070, 77-1774, and 77-2083; 9th Cir.

Transcontinental Bus System, Inc. v. Civil Aeronautics Board. 383 F.
   2d 466 (5th Cir. 1967).

Trans World Airlines, Inc. v. Civil Aeronautics Board. 545 F. 2d 771
   (2d Cir. 1976).

United Air Lines, Inc. v. Civil Aeronautics Board. 198 F. 2d 100
   (7th Cir. 1952).

United Air Lines, Inc. v. Civil Aeronautics Board. 278 F. 2d 446
   (D.C. Cir. 1960).

United States v. Chicago Heights Trucking Co. 310 U.S. 344 (1940).

United States v. Civil Aeronautics Board. 511 F. 2d 1315 (D.C. Cir. 1975).

United States v. Dakota-Montana Oil Co. 288 U.S. 459 (1933).

Utah Agencies v. Civil Aeronautics Board. 504 F. 2d 1232 (10th Cir. 1974).

World Airways, Inc. v. Civil Aeronautics Board. 547 F. 2d 695 (D.C. Cir. 1976).

Wycoff Company, Inc. v. United States. 240 F. Supp. 304 (D. Utah 1965).

Periodical Articles

"A Rate Fracas Bubbles Up." Cargo Airlift 58, no. 1 (1971):16-20.

"AFFA on Blocked Space." Air Transportation 45, no. 4 (1964):39-41.

"AFL-CIO Still Opposed to Airline Deregulation." Journal of Commerce 2 March 1977, p. 3.

"Adams Urges Changes in Aviation Regulation." Journal of Commerce, 4 April 1977, p. 23.

"Air Cargo for the Far Corners of the Earth." Air Transport 2, no. 5 (1944):37-39.

"Air Forwarder Case to Be Heard in January by U.S. Court of Appeals." Traffic World 83, no. 1 (1949):42.

"Air Freighter Options for the '80s." Traffic World 170, no. 12 (1977):66-68.

"Airline Maneuvering Intensifies in Wake of Cargo Deregulation." Air Transport World 15, no. 1 (1978):53-56.

"Airline Rules Shift Snagged by Lobbying." New York Times, 15 August 1977, p. 30.

"Airlines' Experts Back North Beach." New York Times, 13 September 1939, p. 27.

"Air Mail Rejects Bennett Field Site." New York Times, 25 August 1935, II, p. 1.

"Airport Control Assailed by Airlines." New York Times, 20 January 1947, p. 26.

"Airport Fight Widens." Newark Star Eagle, 26 November 1934, pp. 1-2.

"All-Cargo Air Carriers Ask CAB to Ease Competition from Trunks." Aviation Week and Space Technology 79, no. 12 (1963):51.

"All-Cargo Airlines Feuding Over Small Shipment Role in 'Blocked-Space' Service." Traffic World 120, no. 7 (1964):64-65.

"American Air Cargo Development." Air Affairs 2, no. 1 (1947):93.

"American Airlines Freight Tariff." Traffic World 74, no. 12 (1944): 699-700.

"American Cargo Jet Starts Daily Flights." Aviation Week and Space Technology 80, no. 2 (1964):36.

"Automation of Cargo Flow Data Sought." Aviation Week and Space Technology 102, no. 2 (1975):34-35.

"Baltimore Interests Urge Airport Rate Equalization on Trans-Atlantic Cargo." Traffic World 136, no. 10 (1968):70.

"Bargain Day for Airport." Newark Evening News, 20 April 1940, p. 1.

Bertalanffy, L. von. "An Outline of General System Theory." British Journal for the Philosophy of Science 1, no. 2 (1950):134-165.

Blalock, H. M., and Blalock, Ann B. "Toward a Clarification of System Analysis in the Social Sciences." Philosophy of Science 26, no. 2 (1959):84-92.

"Blocked-Space Rates Denied Despite Likelihood that CAL Will Lose Shipper's Traffic." Traffic World 125, no. 4 (1966):80.

"Brady's Statement." Newark Evening News, 8 August 1946, p. 2.

Braunagel, Herbert. "Die gegenwärtige Lage der Luftfracht vom Luftfracht-Spediteur aus generell betrachtet." Wirtschaft und Technik im Transport 40, no. 192 (1972):142-143.

"Breaking the Data Dam." Cargo Airlift 60, no. 3 (1972):10-12.

"Byrne Is Vetoing Routine Actions by Port Authority." New York Times, 26 May 1977, p. B2.

"CAA Absolved of Bias." New York Times, 20 March 1940, p. 20.

"CAA Decision on North Beach Pleases Mayor." Brooklyn Eagle, 8 November 1939, p. 28.

"CAB Acts to Ease Rules on Blocked-Space Service and Off-Route Charters." Traffic World 132, no. 5 (1967):20.

"CAB Experiment in Deregulation Not Possible, Staff Study Finds." Aviation Week and Space Technology 104, no. 3 (1976):26.

"CAB Is Accused of Ignoring Its Rules on Fiscal Disclosure." New York Times 17 September 1975, p. 29.

"CAB Is Likely to Withdraw International Route Awards Made in Trans-Pacific Case." Traffic World 137, no. 7 (1969):83-84.

"CAB Member Is in Midst of Controversy Involving Stock Ownership by His Wife." Wall Street Journal, 19 May 1975, p. 10.

"CAB Power Faces Crucial Test." Aviation Week and Space Technology 103, no. 16 (1975):12-13.

"CAB Seeks Broader Discretion." Aviation Week and Space Technology 104, no. 24 (1976):25.

Callison, James W. "Airline Deregulation--A Hoax?" Journal of Air Law and Commerce 41, no. 4 (1975):747-791.

"Carey Doubts the Supreme Court Can Overrule Governor on SST."
New York Times, 13 October 1977, p. B2.

"Carter Renews Call to Free Airline Rein; Bill Faces Fight." New
York Times, 21 June 1977, p. 41.

"Carter Signs Airline-Deregulation Law; CAB Will Grant Routes More
Generously." Wall Street Journal, 25 October 1978, p. 2.

"Carter Signs Bill; Deregulates Airfreight." Tigereview 31, no. 7
(1977):1.

"City Delay Seen on Port Decision." Newark Star-Ledger, 14 August
1946, p. 1.

"City Delays Action on Airport Plans." New York Times, 16 January
1947, p. 2.

"City Takes Lease on Queens Airport." New York Times, 5 December
1934, p. 25.

"Containerization: Present and Future." Traffic World 170, no. 12
(1977):26-28.

Cook, John C. "Air Freight Breakthrough Lags Behind Predictions."
Air Transport World 14, no. 3 (1977):32-35.

"Court Delays CAB Exemption Order." Aviation Week and Space
Technology 49, no. 22 (1948):36.

"Decision on Port by Sept. 15 Seen." Newark Star-Ledger, 19
August 1946, p. 1.

"Decontrol May Bring an Air Freight War." New York Times, 3 December
1977, p. 29.

"Delay Is Hit in Port Deal." Newark Evening News, 19 June 1947, p. 1.

"Demoted Chief of CAB Quits Agency at White House Request." New
York Times, 11 December 1975, p. 36.

De Vany, Arthur S. "The Effect of Price and Entry Regulation on
Airline Output, Capacity and Efficiency." Bell Journal of
Economics 6, no. 1 (1975):327-345.

Dupré, Steven C. "A Thinking Person's Guide to Entry/Exit
Deregulation in the Airline Industry." Transportation Law
Journal 9, no. 2 (1977):273-307.

Eads, George. "The Effect of Regulation on the Cost Performance and
Growth Strategies of the Local Service Airlines." Journal of
Air Law and Commerce 38, no. 1 (1972):1-34.

"Editorial." Air Cargo 13, no. 7 (1969):42.

"Editorial." Aviation Week and Space Technology 102, no. 17 (1975):
11.

"Editorial." New York Times, 23 May 1977, p. 26.

"Editorial." New York Times, 14 October 1977, p. A26.

"Editorial." Wall Street Journal, 17 July 1975, p. 18.

"Emcon's Electronic Bead on Consignments Gives Shippers Instant Whereabouts." Skytrader 9 (July 1970):9-12.

"Emery Lays Out Welcome Mat." Journal of Commerce, 10 November 1977, p. 1.

"Farley Again Bars City Airport Plea." New York Times, 22 March 1936, sec. 2, p. 1.

"Few Approve, Many Criticize CAB's Experimental Reforms." Aviation Week and Space Technology 103, no. 12 (1975):25-26.

"Flying Tiger Is Logical Choice to Operate Pacific All-Cargo Runs, Says CAB Examiner." Traffic World 134, no. 3 (1968):76-77.

"Flying Tiger Line Enters Subsidy Fray." Air Cargo 2, no. 6 (1958): 26.

"Ford Proposes Cut in Controls Over Airline Service and Fares." New York Times, 9 October 1975, p. 37.

"For Tube Purchase by Port Authority." New York Times, 19 June 1946, p. 24.

Frederick, John H., and Lewis, Arthur D. "History of Air Express." Journal of Air Law and Commerce 12, no. 3 (1941):203-231.

"Freight Division Will Operate Independent of American Airlines." American Aviation 10, no. 2 (1946):24.

Gifford, Gilbert L. "The Evolution of Air Mail Rate Making." Journal of Air Law and Commerce 22, no. 3 (1955): 298-342.

Hale, G. E., and Hale, Rosemary D. "Competition or Control IV: Air Carriers." University of Pennsylvania Law Review 109, no. 3 (1961):311-360.

Hall, A. D., and Fagen, R. E. "Definition of System." General Systems 1 (1956):18-28.

Hilton, George W. "The Basic Behavior of Regulatory Commissions." American Economic Review 62, no. 2 (1972):47-54.

"How the Air/Truck Program Grew--and Grew." Air Transportation 51, no. 4 (1967):46-49.

"Industry's Lowest Freight Rates Offered by Slick Airways Tariff." Aviation Week and Space Technology 47, no. 2 (1947):52.

"Inquiry Refused on Airport Shift." Newark Evening News, 15 March 1940, p. 1.

"Intermodal Questions Widely Discussed at International Air Freight Forum." Traffic World 160, no. 2 (1974):35-39.

Jones, Harold A. "The Anomaly of the Civil Aeronautics Board in American Government." Journal of Air Law and Commerce 20, no. 2 (1953):140-157.

Keeler, Theodore E. "Airline Regulation and Market Performance." Bell Journal of Economics 3, no. 2 (1972):399-424.

"La Guardia Balks at Air Landing Here, Ends Flight in New York." Newark Sunday Call, 25 November 1934, p. 1.

Maclay, Hardy K., and Burt, William C. "Entry of New Carriers into Domestic Trunkline Air Transportation." Journal of Air Law and Commerce 22, no. 2 (1955):131-156.

"Mayor Is Honored for New Airport." New York Times, 4 October 1939, p. 30.

"Mayor Urges Need for Airport Here." New York Times, 10 May 1935, p. 10.

Miller, James C. "The Optimal Pricing of Freight in Combination Aircraft." Journal of Transport Economics and Policy 7, no. 3 (1973):258-268.

"New Airport Data Due Next Week." New York Times, 29 November 1941, p. 33.

"Newark Groups Back Port Authority Plan." New York Times, 11 August 1946, p. 47.

"Nixon Rescinds Transpacific Airline Routes Awarded by Johnson: Move Likely Will Affect Domestic Runs." Wall Street Journal, 27 January 1969, p. 3.

"O'Dwyer Fights Plan for Airport Control." New York Times, 9 February 1946, p. 28.

"Overseas Routes for 11 New Cities Get Approval from the President." New York Times, 22 December 1977, p. D11.

"Pilots Find Field Safest in the U.S." New York Times, 16 October 1939, p. 21.

Pilson, Neal. "The Exemption Provision of the Civil Aeronautics Act: The Problems Inherent in the Exercise of 'Pure' Administrative Power." Journal of Air Law and Commerce 29, no. 4 (1963): 255-298.

"Planning Board Group Favors Airport Offer." Newark Evening News, 6 August 1946, pp. 1-2.

"Port Authority May Shop Elsewhere for Air Field." Newark Evening News, 6 June 1947, p. 5.

"Port Board Asked for Airfield Plan." New York Times, 3 August 1946, p. 27.

"Port Body Action to Bar Concorde for Noise Level in 1985 Vetoed by Byrne." New York Times, 28 December 1977, p. B2.

"President Carter Supports Airline Deregulation Bill; Plans One Energy Agency." Traffic World 169, no. 9 (1977):15.

"President Nixon and CAB Finally Resolve Issues in Trans-Pacific Route Case." Traffic World 139, no. 4 (1969):70.

"Promises Airport Inquiry." Newark Evening News, 9 February 1940, p. 2.

"Prospects of Easing Regulations Over Airlines Worrying Lenders." New York Times, 26 March 1977, p. 25.

"Quarantine Center for Animals to Move to State." New York Times, 9 August 1975, p. 21.

"Quick Port Action: Control by Authority Spurred by Chamber." Newark Star-Ledger, 17 August 1946, p. 1.

"Review Planned for Rulings in New York-San Juan Case." Traffic World 123, no. 2 (1965):59-60.

"San Juan Prelude." Air Transportation 50, no. 3 (1967):13-25.

"Scheduled Airlines See Irregular-Forwarder Air Freight Threat." Traffic World 83, no. 7 (1949):45-46.

"Senate Passes Aviation Package." Commuter Airline Digest 3, no. 9 (1977): 1.

"747F Will Test Air Cargo Market Potential." Aviation Week and Space Technology 95, no. 22 (1971):25-26.

"Slick Airways Asks Over-All Investigation of Profitless Growth Pattern in Air Cargo." Traffic World 123, no. 5 (1965):61-62.

"Slick Airways Would Extend Suspension of Services." Traffic World 124, no. 10 (1965):68.

"Slick, Losing $10,000 Daily, Asks that CAB Expedite Service Discontinuance Plea." Traffic World 123, no. 7 (1965):62.

"Slick Quits Air Freight Service; Rentzel Blames CAB, Pentagon." American Aviation 21, no. 21 (1958):14.

Stigler, George J. "The Theory of Economic Regulation." Bell Journal of Economics 2, no. 1 (1971):3-21.

Streit, Kurt W. "Luftfracht: IATA-Stiefkind auch in 1973?" Wehr und Wirtschaft 17, no. 1 (1973):29.

"Stress Study of Port Plan." Newark Evening News, 14 August 1946, p. 1.

"Suspension of FTL Tariff on 'Blocked Space' Sought by United, American, TWA." Traffic World 120, no. 8 (1964):77.

"Text of City's Port Proposal." Newark Evening News, 18 September 1946, p. 21.

"The Airlines' Shaky Cartel." Wall Street Journal, 15 October 1975, p. 24.

"The Reform Movement--Is It Running Out of Gas?" Traffic World 164, no. 2 (1975):31-32.

"The Route to Lower Air Fares." Boston Globe, 20 June 1975, p. 25.

"The Spectre of Deregulation: To Think It Will Work Is Nonsense!" Air Transport World 14, no. 5 (1977):33-34.

"3 All-Cargo Carriers Aim at Major Market in Pacific Case." Aviation Week and Space Technology 86, no. 24 (1967):59.

Torgerson, Harold W. "History of Air Freight Tariffs." Journal of Air Law and Commerce 15, no. 1 (1948):47-63.

"Total Regulatory Reform Urged by Ford." Aviation Week and Space Technology 104, no. 20 (1976):34.

"Transfer of Slick Airways' Cargo Route to Airlift Is Approved by CAB Examiner." Traffic World 132, no. 7 (1967):154-155.

"Transpacific Routes and the Transpacific Shipper." Air Transportation 52, no. 5 (1968):14-22.

"U.S. Brief Opposes Port Authority Ban on Concorde Flights." New York Times, 7 June 1977, p. 1.

"U.S. Court of Appeals Hears Oral Argument in Air Forwarder Case." Traffic World 83, no. 6 (1949):51-52.

"What's New in Cargo Equipment." Air Transport World 14, no. 7 (1977):37-43.

"Where Do We Go from Here?" Air Transportation 44, no. 3 (1964): 38-42.

Williamson, Oliver E. "Predatory Pricing: A Strategic and Welfare Analysis." Yale Law Journal 87, no. 2 (1977):284-340.

"World Air Forwarders' Presidential Seminar." Freight Management 5 no. 54 (1971):50-63.

"Worries Over Recovery Limit Gains for Investors." U.S. News and World Report 79, no. 24 (1975):28-30.

Public Documents

Act of July 14, 1960. Pub. L. no. 86-661, 74 Stat. 527.

Act of July 10, 1962. Pub. L. no. 87-528, 76 Stat. 143.

Act of November 9, 1977. Pub. L. no. 95-163, 91 Stat. 1278.

Act of March 14, 1978. Pub. L. no. 95-245, 92 Stat. 156.

Act of October 24, 1978. Pub. L. no. 95-504, 92 Stat. 1705.

"Airline Deregulation Act of 1978 (S. 2493)." Weekly Compilation of Presidential Documents 14, no. 43 (1978):1837-1839.

Civil Aeronautics Administration. Statistical Handbook of Civil Aviation. Washington, D.C.: U.S. Government Printing Office, 1949.

Civil Aeronautics Board. Air Freight Loss and Damage Claims. Washington, D.C.: Civil Aeronautics Board, November, 1977.

_____. Annual Report. Washington, D.C.: U.S. Government Printing Office, 1977.

_____. Report of the CAB Special Staff on Regulatory Reform. Washington, D.C.: Civil Aeronautics Board, 1975.

Comptroller General of the United States. Comments on the Study: "Consequences of Deregulation of the Scheduled Air Transportation Industry." Washington, D.C.: General Accounting Office, 1977.

Congressional Record 83, part 6 (1938):6401-6413, 6626-6637, 6724-
    6732; 86, appendix, part 15 (1940):2688; 108, part 5 (1962):
    5985; 121, part 25 (1975):32177; 122, no. 117 (1976):S12983;
    (October 20, 1977):S17530-S17535; (November 2, 1977):H12044-
    H12051; (November 3, 1977):H12138-H12139; (October 14, 1978):
    S18796-S18800; (November 9, 1978):S19559-S19560.

Economic Report of the President. Washington, D.C.: U.S. Government
    Printing Office, 1965.

Economic Report of the President. Washington, D.C.: U.S. Government
    Printing Office, 1967.

Economic Report of the President. Washington, D.C.: U.S. Government
    Printing Office, 1971.

Economic Report of the President. Washington, D.C.: U.S. Government
    Printing Office, 1975.

Economic Report of the President. Washington, D.C.: U.S. Government
    Printing Office, 1977.

Executive Order 11920 (June 10, 1976).

Federal Aviation Act. Act of August 23, 1958, Pub. L. no. 85-726,
    72 Stat. 731.

14 CFR, section 296.

40 FR 28722-28783 (July 8, 1975).

49 CFR, sections 1047.40 and 1082.1.

42 FR 26667-26669 (May 25, 1977).

"International Air Transportation Policy." Weekly Compilation of
    Presidential Documents 6, no. 26 (1970):804-805.

Interstate Commerce Act, part II (Motor Carrier Act). Act of August
    9, 1935, Pub. L. no. 255, Stat. 543.

Interstate Commerce Act, part IV. Act of May 16, 1942, Pub. L. no.
    558, 56 Stat. 284.

Interstate Commerce Commission. Annual Report. Washington, D.C.: U.S.
    Government Printing Office, 1930.

_____. Bureau of Economics. Air Terminal Exempt Zones and the
    Intermodal Movement of Air Cargo. Washington, D.C.:
    Interstate Commerce Commission, July, 1978.

National Resources Planning Board. Transportation and National Policy.
    Washington, D.C.: U.S. Government Printing Office, 1942.

Newark, N.J. Board of Commissioners. Minutes of Meetings, October,
    1947.

New Jersey. Laws. 145th Leg., Ch. 151 (1921); 171st Leg., Ch. 43
    (1947).

New York. Laws. 144th Sess., Ch. 154 (1921); 170th Sess.,
    Ch. 802 (1947).

_____. Public Papers of Governor Nelson A. Rockefeller, 1971.

_____. Select Legislative Committee on Transportation. Transportation Progress in New York State. Legislative Document no. 25 (1974).

New York City Airport Authority. Airport Program for New York City. New York: New York City Airport Authority, January 13, 1947.

New York, N.Y. Board of Estimate. "Board of Estimate; Port of New York Authority--Approval of Agreement Relative to Municipal Air Terminals." Journal of Proceedings 3 (1947):3183-3218.

New York, New Jersey Port and Harbor Development Commission. Joint Report with Comprehensive Plan and Recommendations. Albany: J. B. Lyon Co., 1920.

Port Authority of New York and New Jersey. Kennedy International Airport--Concorde Operations. Resolution of March 11, 1976.

Port of New York Authority. A New Major Airport for the New Jersey-New York Metropolitan Area. New York: Port of New York Authority, 1959.

_____. Considerations Submitted to the Mayor of the City of New York by the Port of New York Authority, in Answer to the Attacks Made by the City Airport Authority upon the Port Authority's Report Entitled: "Summary of Proposal for the Development of New York City Airports." January 15, 1947.

_____. Development of Newark Airport and Seaport. New York: Port of New York Authority, 1946.

_____. Statements by Honorable John F. Sly, Austin J. Tobin, Fred M. Glass for the Port of New York Authority before the Joint Legislative Committee of Senate and House Assembly of the State of New Jersey. New York: Port of New York Authority, 1952.

_____. Summary of Proposal for the Development of New York City Airports. New York: Port of New York Authority, December 18, 1946.

_____. Tentative Report of Deputy Manager on an Airport for the New York Metropolitan District. New York: Port of New York Authority, 1927.

_____. The City of New York and the Port of New York Authority: Agreement with Respect to the Newark Marine and Air Terminals. New York: Port of New York Authority, October 22, 1947.

Presidential Advisory Committee on Transport Policy and Organization. Revision of Federal Transportation Policy. Washington, D.C.: U.S. Government Printing Office, 1955.

Secretary of Commerce. Issues Involved in a Unified and Coordinated Federal Program for Transportation. Washington, D.C., 1949. (Mimeographed.)

Secretary of Transportation. A Study of National Transportation Policy. Washington, D.C.: U.S. Government Printing Office, 1975.

Tri-State Regional Planning Commission. Public Policy Toward Aviation. New York: Tri-State Regional Planning Commission, May, 1978.

U.S. Congress. House. H. R. 14330, 94th Cong., 2d sess., 1976.

_____. H. R. 6010, 95th Cong., 1st sess., 1977.

_____. H. R. 8813, 95th Cong., 1st sess., 1977.

_____. House Document no. 45, 95th Cong., 1st sess., 1977.

_____. House Document no. 92, 95th Cong., 1st sess., 1977.

_____. House Report no. 2254, 75th Cong., 3d sess., 1938.

_____. House Report no. 1177, 87th Cong., 1st sess., 1961.

_____. House Report no. 1950, 87th Cong., 2d sess., 1962.

_____. House Report no. 842, 92d Cong., 2d sess., 1972.

_____. House Report no. 773, 95th Cong., 1st sess., 1977.

_____. House Report no. 1211, 95th Cong., 2d sess., 1978.

U.S. Congress. House. Committee on Armed Services. Military Airlift.
    Hearings before the Subcommittee on Military Airlift, House of
    Representatives, 91st Cong., 2d sess., 1970.

U.S. Congress. House. Committee on Public Works and Transportation.
    Aviation Economics. Joint Hearings before the Subcommittee on
    Investigations and Review and the Subcommittee on Aviation,
    House of Representatives, 94th Cong., 2d sess., 1976.

_____. Aviation Regulatory Reform. Hearings before the
    Subcommittee on Aviation, House of Representatives, on H. R.
    8813, 95th Cong., 1st sess., 1977, part 1.

_____. Reform of the Economic Regulation of Air Carriers.
    Hearings before the Subcommittee on Aviation, House of
    Representatives, 94th Cong., 2d sess., 1976.

U.S. Congress. House. Committee on the Judiciary. New Jersey-New
    York Airport Commission Compact. Hearings before Subcommittee
    no. 3, House of Representatives, on H. J. Res. 375, et al.,
    1970-1972.

U.S. Congress. Senate. S. 2551, 94th Cong., 1st sess., 1975.

_____. S. 3536, 94th Cong., 2d sess., 1976.

_____. S. 3684, 94th Cong., 2d sess., 1976.

_____. S. 292, 95th Cong., 1st sess., 1977.

_____. S. 689, 95th Cong., 1st sess., 1977.

_____. S. 2493, 95th Cong., 2d sess., 1978.

_____. Senate Document no. 15, 74th Cong., 1st sess., 1935.

_____. Senate Report no. 1661, 75th Cong., 3d sess., 1938.

_____. Senate Report no. 445, 87th Cong., 1st sess., 1961.

_____. Senate Report no. 688, 87th Cong., 1st sess., 1961.

_____. Senate Report no. 1353, 90th Cong., 2d sess., 1968.

_____. Senate Report no. 1160, 92d Cong., 2d sess., 1972.

_____. Senate Report no. 631, 95th Cong., 2d sess., 1978.

_____. Senate Report no. 638, 95th Cong., 2d sess., 1978.

U.S. Congress. Senate. Committee on Commerce. Regulatory Reform in Air Transportation. Hearings before the Subcommittee on Aviation, Senate, on S. 2551, S. 3364, and S. 3536, 94th Cong. 2d sess., 1976.

U.S. Congress. Senate. Committee on Commerce, Science, and Transportation. Regulatory Reform in Air Transportation. Hearings before the Subcommittee on Aviation, Senate, on S. 292 and S. 689, 95th Cong., 1st sess., 1977. (Four Parts.)

U.S. Congress. Senate. Committee on the Judiciary. Civil Aeronautics Board Practices and Procedures. Subcommittee on Administrative Practice and Procedure, Committee Print, 94th Cong., 1st sess. 1975.

_____. Oversight of Civil Aeronautics Board Practices and Procedures. Hearings before the Subcommittee on Administrative Practice and Procedure, Committee Print, 94th Cong., 1st sess. 1975. (Three Volumes.)

U.S. Department of Commerce. Federal Transportation Policy and Program. Washington, D.C.: U.S. Government Printing Office, 1960.

United States Code (1976 ed.). Title 49.

Waterfront Commission of New York Harbor. Report on True Extent of Cargo Thefts at the New York-New Jersey Airports. March 7, 1975.

Reports and Books

Air Freight Forwarders Association. Petition to the Civil Aeronautic Board for a Moratorium on the Admission of New Forwarders and for Certification of the Air Forwarding Industry. Washington, D.C.: Air Freight Forwarders Association, 1973.

Association of Local Transport Airlines. Position on Legislative Proposals for Regulatory Reform. Washington, D.C.: Association of Local Transport Airlines, 1977.

Bard, Erwin W. The Port of New York Authority. New York: Columbia University Press, 1942.

Bey, Ingward. Simulationstechnische Analyse der Luftfrachtabfertigun Schriftenreihe des Instituts für Verkehrswesen der Universität Karlsruhe, no. 7, 1972.

Bird, Frederick L. A Study of the Port of New York Authority. New York: Dun and Bradstreet, 1949.

Brancker, J. W. S. IATA and What It Does. Leiden: A. W. Sijthoff, 1977.

Brewer, Stanley H., and Rosenzweig, James E. Military Airlift and Its Relationship to the Commercial Air Cargo Industry. Seattle: Graduate School of Business Administration, University of Washington, 1967.

California Lettuce--A Brief Total Cost of Distribution Analysis. Marietta: Lockheed-Georgia Co., Commercial Operations Analysis Department, Advanced Studies Division, ER-10518, June, 1969.

Calkins, P. F. The Density Story. Marietta: Lockheed-Georgia Co., 1968.

Capron, William M., ed. Technological Change in Regulated Industries. Washington, D.C.: The Brookings Institution, 1971.

Caves, Richard E. Air Transport and Its Regulators. Cambridge, Mass.: Harvard University Press, 1962.

Chuang, Richard Y. The International Air Transport Association. Leiden: A. W. Sijthoff, 1972.

Clarke, David J., and Tyrchniewicz, Edward W. Air Shipment of Perishable Fruits and Vegetables into Canada: Potentials and Problems. Center for Transportation Studies, University of Manitoba, Research Report no. 13, July, 1973.

Douglas, George W., and Miller, James C. Economic Regulation of Domestic Air Transport: Theory and Practice. Washington, D.C.: The Brookings Institution, 1974.

Electronic Equipment--A Brief Total Cost of Distribution Analysis. Marietta: Lockheed-Georgia Co., Commercial Operations Analysis Department, Advanced Studies Division, ER-10517, June, 1969.

Haanappel, Peter P. C. Ratemaking in International Air Transport. Deventer: Kluwer, 1978.

Hammel, Alfred L. Wm. Frederick Harnden, 1813-1845. New York and Montreal: The Newcomen Society of North America, 1954.

Harlow, Alvin F. Old Waybills. New York and London: D. Appleton-Century Co., 1934.

IATA Financial and Economic Studies Subcommittee. Economics of Air Cargo Carriage and Service. Montreal: International Air Transport Association, October, 1969.

Jackson, Richard M. The Second Generation Speaks Out. New York: Seaboard World Airlines, 1978.

Jordan, William A. Airline Regulation in America: Effects and Imperfections. Baltimore: The Johns Hopkins Press, 1970.

Kahn, Alfred E. The Economics of Regulation. 2 vols. New York: John Wiley and Sons, Inc., 1970-1971.

Keyes, Lucile. Federal Control of Entry into Air Transportation. Cambridge, Mass.: Harvard University Press, 1951.

McIntosh, Colin Hugh. The Economics of Air Cargo: An Analysis of Profits Unnecessarily Diminished. Washington, D.C.: ATW Marketing Services, 1977.

Mahoney, John H. Intermodal Action--The Challenge of Today. Speech given at the National Conference and Shipper's Dialogue, 1974.

Manalytics, Inc. Cargo Flows and Facility Requirements at the New Montreal International Airport. San Francisco: Manalytics, Inc. 1973.

Maurer, R. Pallets and Containers in Air Transport. Paris: Institut du Transport Aérien, 1970.

_____. Role of Air Transport in International Shipments of Flowers in Europe. Paris: Institut du Transport Aérien, 1967.

Meyer, C. E., Jr. Business and the Regulatory Environment. New York: Trans World Airlines, 1978.

Miller, James C., ed. Perspectives on Federal Transportation Policy. Washington, D.C.: American Enterprise Institute for Public Policy Research, 1975.

Norton, Hugh S. Modern Transportation Economics. 2d ed. Columbus: Charles E. Merrill, 1971.

Pegrum, Dudley F. Public Regulation of Business. rev. ed. Homewood: Richard D. Irwin, Inc., 1965.

_____. Transportation: Economics and Public Policy. 3d ed. Homewood: Richard D. Irwin, Inc., 1973.

Phillips, Charles F. The Economics of Regulation: Theory and Practice in the Transportation and Public Utility Industries. Homewood: Richard D. Irwin, Inc., 1965.

Sletmo, Gunnar K. Demand for Air Cargo: An Econometric Approach. Bergen: Norwegian School of Economics and Business Administration, 1972.

Snoek, Gerd. Wettbewerbs- und Wachstumsprobleme im internationalen Luftfrachtverkehr. Forschungsberichte des Instituts für Weltwirtschaft an der Universität Kiel, no. 79, 1967.

Specht, Wolfgang. Die IATA: Eine Organisation des grenzüberschreitenden Luftlinienverkehrs und ihre Allgemeinen Beförderungsbedingungen. Bern and Frankfurt/M.: Lang, 1973.

Stein, Harold, ed. Public Administration and Policy Development. New York: Harcourt, Brace and Company, 1952.

Straszheim, Mahlon R. The International Airline Industry. Washington, D.C.: The Brookings Institution, 1969.

Systems Analysis and Research Corporation. Intermodal Movement of Air Cargo. 2 vols. Washington, D.C.: Systems Analysis and Research Corporation, 1975.

TransPlan, Inc. and Seelye Stevenson Value & Knecht, Inc. A Study for the Development of Stewart Airport. Summary Report. New York: TransPlan, Inc. and Seelye Stevenson Value & Knecht, Inc., 1973.

Wells, H. Sketch of the Rise, Progress, and Present Condition of the Express System. Paper presented before the American Geographic and Statistical Society, February 4, 1864.

Wood, Frank E. Air Cargo Container Study. Reynolds Metals Co., 1968.

Unpublished Material

Callison, James W. "The Airline Reform Movement--Is It Deregulation
or Re-Regulation?" Remarks made before the American Society of
Women Accountants, Atlanta, May 9, 1978. (Mimeographed.)

"Comments of Edward E. Carlson, Chairman, United Airlines." Remarks
made during a Cleveland civic luncheon, October 30, 1975.
(Mimeographed.)

Corry, Francis E. "An Analysis of the Domestic Air Freight Rate and
Cost Structures." M.A. thesis, Northwestern University, 1973.

Demakopoulos, Steve A. "Methods and Efficacy of Long-Range Industry
Forecasts: A Case Study of the Domestic Air Cargo Industry."
Ph.D. dissertation, New York University, 1970.

Emery, John C. "A Good Place to Start--Deregulate Air Freight First!"
n.d. (Mimeographed.)

Igoe, Robert. "An Administrative Review of the Individual Functions
and Overall Performance of the Port of New York Authority."
Ph.D. dissertation, New York University, 1962.

McCusker, Fred H. "Airline Deregulation." Remarks made to the Western
Traffic Conference, San Diego, May 16, 1978. (Mimeographed.)

Orion, Henry. "Domestic Air Cargo, 1945-1965: A Study of Competition
in a Regulated Industry." Ph.D. dissertation, Columbia
University, 1967.

"Remarks by Deputy Secretary of Transportation John W. Barnum."
Airline Industry Seminar, Financial Analysts Federation, New
York, July 28, 1976. (Mimeographed.)

"Remarks by Richard J. Ferris, President, United Airlines." The
Wings Club, New York, March 16, 1977. (Mimeographed.)

"Remarks of Frederick W. Bradley, Jr., Vice President, Citibank."
Airline Industry Seminar, Financial Analysts Federation, New
York, July 28, 1976. (Mimeographed.)

"Remarks of Senator Howard W. Cannon." Aero Club, Washington, D.C.,
April 26, 1977. (Mimeographed.)

Schad, Thomas W. "An Econometric Study of the Demand for Air Freight
in the Domestic United States." Ph.D. dissertation, Wayne State
University, 1970.

"Statement of Edward J. Driscoll, President, National Air Carrier
Association." Remarks made before the House Aviation
Subcommittee, June 8, 1976. (Mimeographed.)

"Statement of Edward J. Driscoll." Remarks made before the House
Aviation Subcommittee, October 5, 1977. (Mimeographed.)

"Statement of Joseph J. Healy, Executive Vice President, Flying Tiger
Line." Remarks made before the House Aviation Subcommittee,
August 23, 1977. (Mimeographed.)

"Statement of Richard J. Ferris, President, United Airlines."
   Remarks made before the House Aviation Subcommittee, March 24,
   1977. (Mimeographed.)

"Statement of William T. Seawell, Chairman, Pan American World
   Airways." Remarks made before the Senate Aviation Subcommittee
   March 24, 1977. (Mimeographed.)

"Statement of William T. Seawell." Remarks made before the House
   Aviation Subcommittee, October 12, 1977. (Mimeographed.)

Stephenson, Russel V. "The Need for Regulatory Reform." Remarks made
   before the National Association of State Aviation Officials,
   Seattle, August 31, 1977. (Mimeographed.)

"Testimony of C. E. Meyer, Jr., President, Trans World Airlines."
   Remarks made before the Senate Aviation Subcommittee, March
   24, 1977. (Mimeographed.)

"Testimony of Francisco A. Lorenzo, Chairman, Association of Local
   Transport Airlines." Remarks made before the House Aviation
   Subcommittee, October 11, 1977. (Mimeographed.)

"Testimony of Frederick W. Smith, Chairman, Federal Express
   Corporation." Remarks made before the House Aviation
   Subcommittee, June 9, 1976. (Mimeographed.)

"Testimony of L. C. Burwell, Chairman, Pinehurst Airlines." Remarks
   made before the House Aviation Subcommittee, October 6, 1977.
   (Mimeographed.)

"Testimony of L. Edwin Smart, Chairman, Trans World Airlines."
   Remarks made before the House Aviation Subcommittee, October
   12, 1977. (Mimeographed.)

THE UNIVERSITY OF CHICAGO
DEPARTMENT OF GEOGRAPHY
RESEARCH PAPERS (Lithographed, 6×9 inches)

Available from Department of Geography, The University of Chicago, 5828 S. University Avenue, Chicago, Illinois 60637, U.S.A. Price: $8.00 each; by series subscription, $6.00 each.

LIST OF TITLES IN PRINT

134. PYLE, GERALD F. *Heart Disease, Cancer and Stroke in Chicago: A Geographical Analysis with Facilities, Plans for 1980*. 1971. 292 p.

135. JOHNSON, JAMES F. *Renovated Waste Water: An Alternative Source of Municipal Water Supply in the United States*. 1971. 155 p.

136. BUTZER, KARL W. *Recent History of an Ethiopian Delta: The Omo River and the Level of Lake Rudolf*. 1971. 184 p.

139. McMANIS, DOUGLAS R. *European Impressions of the New England Coast, 1497–1620*. 1972. 147 p.

140. COHEN, YEHOSHUA S. *Diffusion of an Innovation in an Urban System: The Spread of Planned Regional Shopping Centers in the United States, 1949–1968*, 1972. 136 p.

141. MITCHELL, NORA. *The Indian Hill-Station: Kodaikanal*. 1972. 199 p.

142. PLATT, RUTHERFORD H. *The Open Space Decision Process: Spatial Allocation of Costs and Benefits*. 1972. 189 p.

143. GOLANT, STEPHEN M. *The Residential Location and Spatial Behavior of the Elderly: A Canadian Example*. 1972. 226 p.

144. PANNELL, CLIFTON W. *T'ai-chung, T'ai-wan: Structure and Function*. 1973. 200 p.

145. LANKFORD, PHILIP M. *Regional Incomes in the United States, 1929–1967: Level, Distribution, Stability, and Growth*. 1972. 137 p.

146. FREEMAN, DONALD B. *International Trade, Migration, and Capital Flows: A Quantitative Analysis of Spatial Economic Interaction*. 1973. 201 p.

147. MYERS, SARAH K. *Language Shift Among Migrants to Lima, Peru*. 1973. 203 p.

148. JOHNSON, DOUGLAS L. *Jabal al-Akhdar, Cyrenaica: An Historical Geography of Settlement and Livelihood*. 1973. 240 p.

149. YEUNG, YUE-MAN. *National Development Policy and Urban Transformation in Singapore: A Study of Public Housing and the Marketing System*. 1973. 204 p.

150. HALL, FRED L. *Location Criteria for High Schools: Student Transportation and Racial Integration*. 1973. 156 p.

151. ROSENBERG, TERRY J. *Residence, Employment, and Mobility of Puerto Ricans in New York City*. 1974. 230 p.

152. MIKESELL, MARVIN W., editor. *Geographers Abroad: Essays on the Problems and Prospects of Research in Foreign Areas*. 1973. 296 p.

153. OSBORN, JAMES F. *Area, Development Policy, and the Middle City in Malaysia*. 1974. 291 p.

154. WACHT, WALTER F. *The Domestic Air Transportation Network of the United States*. 1974. 98 p.

155. BERRY, BRIAN J. L., et al. *Land Use, Urban Form and Environmental Quality*. 1974. 440 p.

156. MITCHELL, JAMES K. *Community Response to Coastal Erosion: Individual and Collective Adjustments to Hazard on the Atlantic Shore*. 1974. 209 p.

157. COOK, GILLIAN P. *Spatial Dynamics of Business Growth in the Witwatersrand*. 1975. 144 p.

159. PYLE, GERALD F. et al. *The Spatial Dynamics of Crime*. 1974. 221 p.

160. MEYER, JUDITH W. *Diffusion of an American Montessori Education*. 1975. 97 p.

161. SCHMID, JAMES A. *Urban Vegetation: A Review and Chicago Case Study*. 1975. 266 p.

162. LAMB, RICHARD F. *Metropolitan Impacts on Rural America*. 1975. 196 p.

163. FEDOR, THOMAS STANLEY. *Patterns of Urban Growth in the Russian Empire during the Nineteenth Century*. 1975. 245 p.

164. HARRIS, CHAUNCY D. *Guide to Geographical Bibliographies and Reference Works in Russian or on the Soviet Union*. 1975. 478 p.

165. JONES, DONALD W. *Migration and Urban Unemployment in Dualistic Economic Development*. 1975. 174 p.

166. BEDNARZ, ROBERT S. *The Effect of Air Pollution on Property Value in Chicago*. 1975. 111 p.

167. HANNEMANN, MANFRED. *The Diffusion of the Reformation in Southwestern Germany, 1518–1534*. 1975. 248 p.

168. SUBLETT, MICHAEL D. *Farmers on the Road. Interfarm Migration and the Farming of Noncontiguous Lands in Three Midwestern Townships, 1939-1969*. 1975. 228 pp.

169. STETZER, DONALD FOSTER. *Special Districts in Cook County: Toward a Geography of Local Government*. 1975. 189 pp.

170. EARLE, CARVILLE V. *The Evolution of a Tidewater Settlement System: All Hallow's Parish, Maryland, 1650–1783*. 1975. 249 pp.

171. SPODEK, HOWARD. *Urban-Rural Integration in Regional Development: A Case Study of Saurashtra, India—1800–1960* . 1976. 156 pp.

172. COHEN, YEHOSHUA S. and BERRY, BRIAN J. L. *Spatial Components of Manufacturing Change.* 1975. 272 pp.

173. HAYES, CHARLES R. *The Dispersed City: The Case of Piedmont, North Carolina.* 1976. 169 pp.

174. CARGO, DOUGLAS B. *Solid Wastes: Factors Influencing Generation Rates.* 1977. 112 pp.

175. GILLARD, QUENTIN. *Incomes and Accessibility. Metropolitan Labor Force Participation, Commuting, and Income Differentials in the United States, 1960–1970.* 1977. 140 pp.

176. MORGAN, DAVID J. *Patterns of Population Distribution: A Residential Preference Model and Its Dynamic.* 1978. 216 pp.

177. STOKES, HOUSTON H.; JONES, DONALD W. and NEUBURGER, HUGH M. *Unemployment and Adjustment in the Labor Market: A Comparison between the Regional and National Responses.* 1975. 135 pp.

179. HARRIS, CHAUNCY D. *Bibliography of Geography. Part I. Introduction to General Aids.* 1976. 288 pp.

180. CARR, CLAUDIA J. *Pastoralism in Crisis. The Dasanetch and their Ethiopian Lands.* 1977. 339 pp.

181. GOODWIN, GARY C. *Cherokees in Transition: A Study of Changing Culture and Environment Prior to 1775.* 1977. 221 pp.

182. KNIGHT, DAVID B. *A Capital for Canada: Conflict and Compromise in the Nineteenth Century.* 1977. 359 pp.

183. HAIGH, MARTIN J. *The Evolution of Slopes on Artificial Landforms: Blaenavon, Gwent.* 1978. 311 pp.

184. FINK, L. DEE. *Listening to the Learner. An Exploratory Study of Personal Meaning in College Geography Courses.* 1977. 200 pp.

185. HELGREN, DAVID M. *Rivers of Diamonds: An Alluvial History of the Lower Vaal Basin.* 1979. 399 pp.

186. BUTZER, KARL W., editor. *Dimensions of Human Geography: Essays on Some Familiar and Neglected Themes.* 1978. 201 pp.

187. MITSUHASHI, SETSUKO. *Japanese Commodity Flows.* 1978. 185 pp.

188. CARIS, SUSAN L. *Community Attitudes toward Pollution.* 1978. 226 pp.

189. REES, PHILIP M. *Residential Patterns in American Cities, 1960.* 1979. 424 pp.

190. KANNE, EDWARD A. *Fresh Food for Nicosia.* 1979. 116 pp.

191. WIXMAN, RONALD. *Language Aspects of Ethnic Patterns and Processes in the North Caucasus.* 1980. 224 pp.

192. KIRCHNER, JOHN A. *Sugar and Seasonal Labor Migration: The Case of Tucumán, Argentina.* 1980. 158 pp.

193. HARRIS, CHAUNCY D. and FELLMANN, JEROME D. *International List of Geographical Serials, Third Edition, 1980.* 1980. 457 p.

194. HARRIS, CHAUNCY D. *Annotated World List of Selected Current Geographical Serials, Fourth Edition, 1980.* 1980. 165 p.

195. LEUNG, CHI-KEUNG. *China: Railway Patterns and National Goals.* 1980. 235 p.

196. LEUNG, CHI-KEUNG and NORTON S. GINSBURG, eds. *China: Urbanization and National Development.* 1980. 280 p.

197. DAICHES, SOL. *People in Distress: A Geographical Perspective on Psychological Well-being.* 1981. 199 p.

198. JOHNSON, JOSEPH T. *Location and Trade Theory: Industrial Location, Comparative Advantage, and the Geographic Pattern of Production in the United States.* 1981. 107 p.

199-200. STEVENSON, ARTHUR J. *The New York-Newark Air Freight System.* 1982. 440 p. (Double number, price: $16.00)

201. LICATE, JACK A. *Creation of a Mexican Landscape: Territorial Organization and Settlement in the Eastern Puebla Basin, 1520-1605.* 1981. 143 p.

202. RUDZITIS, GUNDARS. *Residential Location Determinants of the Older Population.* 1982. 117 p.

203. LIANG, ERNEST P. *China: Railways and Agricultural Development, 1875-1935.* 1982. 186 p.

204. DAHMANN, DONALD C. *Locals and Cosmopolitans: Patterns of Spatial Mobility during the Transition from Youth to Early Adulthood.* 1982. 146 p.